ROUTLEDGE LIBRARY EDITIONS: SOCIAL THEORY

Volume 2

AGENCY AND STRUCTURE

AGENCY AND STRUCTURE
Reorienting Social Theory

Edited by
PIOTR SZTOMPKA

LONDON AND NEW YORK

First published 1994 by Routledge

2 Park Square, Milton Park, Abingdon, Oxfordshire OX14 4RN
711 Third Avenue, New York, NY 10017

Routledge is an imprint of the Taylor & Francis Group, an informa business

First issued in paperback 2017

Copyright © 1994 Taylor & Francis

All rights reserved. No part of this book may be reprinted or reproduced or utilised in any form or by any electronic, mechanical, or other means, now known or hereafter invented, including photocopying and recording, or in any information storage or retrieval system, without permission in writing from the publishers.

Notice:
Product or corporate names may be trademarks or registered trademarks, and are used only for identification and explanation without intent to infringe.

British Library Cataloguing in Publication Data
A catalogue record for this book is available from the British Library

ISBN: 978-0-415-72731-0 (Set)
ISBN: 978-1-138-78200-6 (Volume 2) (hbk)
ISBN: 978-1-138-91297-7 (Volume 2) (pbk)

Publisher's Note
The publisher has gone to great lengths to ensure the quality of this reprint but points out that some imperfections in the original copies may be apparent.

Disclaimer
The publisher has made every effort to trace copyright holders and would welcome correspondence from those they have been unable to trace.

AGENCY AND STRUCTURE

Reorienting Social Theory

Edited by

Piotr Sztompka

GORDON AND BREACH
Switzerland Australia Belgium France Germany
Great Britain India Japan Malaysia Netherlands
Russia Singapore USA

Copyright © 1994 by OPA (Amsterdam) B.V. All rights reserved. Published under license by Gordon and Breach Science Publishers S.A.

Gordon and Breach Science Publishers

Y-Parc
Chemin de la Sallaz
1400 Yverdon, Switzerland

Post Office Box 90
Reading, Berkshire RG1 8JL
Great Britain

Private Bag 8
Camberwell, Victoria 3124
Australia

3-14-9, Okubo
Shinjuku-ku, Tokyo 169
Japan

12 Cour Saint-Eloi
75012 Paris
France

Emmaplein 5
1075 AW Amsterdam
Netherlands

Christburger Str. 11
10405 Berlin
Germany

820 Town Center Drive
Langhorne, Pennsylvania 19047
United States of America

Library of Congress Cataloging-in-Publication Data

Agency and structure : reorienting social theory / edited by Piotr Sztompka.
   p. cm. -- (International studies in global change, ISSN 1055-7180 ; v. 4)
   Revised versions of papers presented at the World Congress of Sociology held in 1990 in Madrid.
   Includes bibliographical references and index.
   ISBN 2-88124-592-7 (hardcover) 2-88124-597-8 (softcover)
   1. Sociology.   2. Sociology--Philosophy.   3. Social action.
4. Social structure.   I. Sztompka, Piotr.   II. Series.
HM24.A35 1993
301--dc20   93-19945
                                                                      CIP

No part of this book may be reproduced or utilized in any form or by any means, electronic or mechanical, including photocopying and recording, or by any information storage or retrieval system, without permission in writing from the publisher. Printed in the United States of America.

CONTENTS

Introduction to the Series vii

Introduction ix

PART I   **BETWEEN AGENCY AND STRUCTURE: AN OVERVIEW OF THE DEBATE**

    ONE   Agency-Structure, Micro-Macro, Individualism-Holism-Relationism: A Metatheoretical Explanation of Theoretical Convergence between the United States and Europe
George Ritzer and Pamela Gindoff 3

    TWO   Evolving Focus on Human Agency in Contemporary Social Theory
Piotr Sztompka 25

PART II   **DIVERGENT PERSPECTIVES ON HUMAN AGENCY IN CLASSICAL AND CONTEMPORARY SOCIAL THEORY**

    THREE   The Double Representation of the Actor in Theoretical Tradition: Durkheim and Weber
Elisa P. Reis 63

    FOUR   Marxism, Post-Marxism and the Actionalist Turn in Social Theory
Miguel A. Cainzos 83

    FIVE   Hermeneutics and the Theory of Social Action
Franco Crespi 125

| SIX | Away from Structuralism and the Return of the Actor: Paradigmatic and Theoretical Orientations in Contemporary French Sociology
Francois Chazel | 143 |

PART III DIMENSIONS OF AGENCY AND STRUCTURE: TOWARD A THEORETICAL CONVERGENCE

SEVEN	Postmodernism as Pseudohistory: Continuities in the Complexities of Social Action *Craig Calhoun*	167
EIGHT	Two Conceptions of Human Agency: Rational Choice Theory and the Social Theory of Action *Tom R. Burns*	197
NINE	Society as Social Becoming: Beyond Individualism and Collectivism *Piotr Sztompka*	251
TEN	Sociology as a Discipline of Disagreements and as a Paradigm of Competing Explanations: Culture, Structure and the Variability of Actors and Situations *Göran Therborn*	283

Index 307

INTRODUCTION TO THE SERIES

This book series brings together under one banner works by scholars of many disciplines. All of these researchers have distinguished themselves in their specialties. But here they have ventured beyond the frontiers of traditional disciplines and have developed new, innovative approaches to the study of social systems and social change.

Why? What has prompted this foray into uncharted territory? What is the reason for broadening theoretical perspectives and developing new methodologies? The impetus comes from the world we seek to understand. Scholars have traditionally made "boundary" assumptions that limited their scope of inquiry to the concerns of a discipline. Such limitations facilitate concentration, though they have always been artificial. The interpenetration of social, economic and environmental phenomena, and the precipitous pace of change in the late twentieth century make it clear that such convenient intellectual boundaries are not only unrealistic, they are untenable.

In the last quarter of the twentieth century, social theory is radically transforming as we develop insights into the rapidly changing human condition. This volume is a key contribution to that emergence of new social theory. By drawing on contributors from a broad diversity of nations and intellectual traditions, it reflects the globalization of social theory, too long an Anglo-European province. And it wrestles with an issue at the heart of contemporary theory: the problem of human agency. Human agency is central in the dynamics of the contemporary world, and the concept of agency is producing equally important innovations in social theory. This volume offers a global perspective on agency, bringing together the contributions of the finest scholars wrestling with this difficult but critical theoretical issue. We are proud to offer it as the fourth volume in this series.

How complex waves of change sweep through the contemporary world, altering the natural environment, technology, the economy and social systems; the interaction of these forces, their impact on nations, communities, families and individuals; and the response to them by individuals and collectivities — this is the focus of the research to be presented in this series. The scholars writing in the series are themselves engaged in social change — the restructuring of our way of thinking about the world.

Tom R. Burns
Thomas Dietz

INTRODUCTION

The Return of Grand Theory

Nine years have passed since Quentin Skinner heralded the return of grand theory in the social sciences (Skinner 1985). Today it seems even more obvious. We are witnessing the true renaissance of theoretical thinking.

In this century, the attitudes toward general theory have gone through various phases. We had the Poverty of Theory period dominated by narrow-empiricism and the absurd accusation of theory for being "metaphysical." We had the Crisis of Theory period marked by disenchantment with proliferating, polarized, mutually exclusive theories (Eisenstadt and Curelaru 1976; Sztompka 1979). Hopefully, we have left both of these phases behind. At the end of this century we find ourselves in the Return to Theory period, and facing the fundamental Reorientation of Sociological Theory.

It is good to remind oneself that the founding fathers of our discipline — Comte and Spencer, Marx and Weber, Simmel and Durkheim — have been primarily and preeminently the grand theorists. Thus, we are returning to the very roots of sociology; not like mythical Sisyphus in the helpless and hopeless mood of starting the enterprise anew, rather we are much wiser with the cumulative experience of more than a century — both historical experience of societies and intellectual experience of sociologists (not the least of which consists of the critical reevaluation of the masters themselves). We return critically, self-consciously and selectively. The time was not lost; we are richer in conceptual sophistication, reliable empirical foundations, elaborate strategies of theory construction; we are liberated from various biases, one-sided dogmatisms, logical fallacies, spurious dilemmas. We are ready for true reorientation.

There are two senses in which sociology may be seen as returning to theory. First, theorizing as such, as a valid and principally indispensable mode of sociological discourse, is winning ground, and second, a particular style of theorizing is becoming dominant, focusing on synthesis and overcoming extreme one-sided positions in favor of their creative reconciliation.

More concretely, there are two traits of recent theory which seem unique. There is the renewed link with philosophy, and particularly with ontology. Also, there is the substantive focus on the relationship between actions and institutions, actors and organizations, or in a most general formulation, agency and structure.

Revival of Ontological Preoccupations

The relationship between sociology and philosophy has always been ambivalent: sociological inquiry sooner or later led to philosophical questions, and yet for a long time sociologists tried to distance themselves from philosophy; they needed philosophy, and yet hesitated to enter philosophical domain. This strain began at sociology's inception. Born as a sort of illegitimate offspring to philosophy and history, it inherited the whole load of philosophical assumptions and riddles but at the same time, like all illegitimate children, frantically attempted to find its identity by cutting off the roots. Struggling to become a "true science," sociology landed in the embrace of naturalism and positivism. For positivists of all shades, the questions of substance, essence, mode of being and ultimate nature of social reality were metaphysical (read: irrelevant) and had to be purged from the realm of science.

But the return to philosophy was inevitable. With the anti-naturalist and anti-positivist revolution initiated in the nineteenth century and evolving into a powerful trend of humanistic sociology — the whole range of objects unknown to the world of nature (symbols, signs, meanings, values, norms, actions) suddenly appeared in the focus of sociological attention. Their constitution, forms of existence and modes of operation were by no means self-evident. It was even more problematic how this soft, subjective reality could be grasped at all from the inside, by the sociologists inevitably immersed in their very subject matter. This suggested the issues of objectivity, rationality, relativism and reflexiveness of social knowledge. In effect the fundamental ontological and epistemological queries had to be faced.

Epistemology seemed to gain the upper hand, at least for the time being. Perhaps because of its kinship with methodology, it was more digestible to sociologists bred in positivist climate than the seemingly far-fetched, ontological inquiries of "first philosophy." Thus philosophical reflection entered back through epistemological doors. The tendency to replace the question, What exists? by the question, How can it be known? or to substitute the problem, What is the knowledge about? by the problem, How can knowledge be reached? started to reign in sociology and led to epistemic fallacy (Bhaskar 1986:6). But once inside sociology's castle, philosophy proved to be contagious. It pushed the sociological imagination toward the most fundamental questions of existence and constitution of the social being.

Recently, sociologists of various schools are finally returning to the old, but hardly solved, riddle: *What is society?* Anthony Giddens is quite emphatic:

> Concentration upon epistemological issues draws attention away from the more ontological concerns of social theory... Rather than becoming preoccupied with epistemological disputes and with the question of whether or not anything like "epistemology" in its time-honoured sense can be formulated at all, those working in social theory, I suggest, should be concerned first and foremost with reworking conceptions of human being and human doing, social reproduction and social transformation. (Giddens 1984)

As a side-effect of the new wave of grand theories spreading in sociology in the eighties, the relations between sociology and philosophy have not only been tightened but in fact reversed. Sociology has fallen under stronger influence of philosophy, but at the same time philosophy has become much more sociological (Giddens 1987:53). Instead of merely learning or borrowing from philosophy, sociology seems to have reached some theoretical insights which turn out to be helpful and useful for philosophy. Randall Collins calls for sociological philosophy as a new focus on those philosophical problems which are suggested by the empirical and theoretical practice of sociology. And this refers also to the "ontological questions of realism and anti-realism, materialism and idealism. Having been invoked at first in epistemology, sociology now seems to point even deeper into philosophy's core, into metaphysics" (Collins 1988:691). In this way sociology is starting to repay its original debt to philosophy.

But is there any reason to return to the ontological fundamentals of sociology instead of simply *doing* sociology? The principal reason is there is no escape, one cannot really do without ontological options. They may be critically accepted, or swept under the rug, but no sociological research can dispense with them. They make up the very bedrock of presuppositions, even more basic than epistemological or methodological ones, controlling the direction and course of sociological research and the meaning of sociological results. I share the post-positivist creed of Jeffrey Alexander:

> Science can be viewed as an intellectual process that occurs within the context of two distinctive environments, the empirical observational world and the non-empirical metaphysical one. (Alexander 1982:2)

Both shape inquiry, which must therefore be seen as a two-tiered process, propelled as much by theoretical as by empirical argument (Alexander 1982:30). If they are inescapable anyway, it is certainly better to be aware of ontological premises than ignore them.

The Attempt at Theoretical Synthesis: Agency and Structure

Now if we turn to the content of theories, to the substantive focus of sociological theory during the last decade, we observe what Jeffrey Alexander labels as the new theoretical movement (Alexander 1988). In the seventies the field became split between macro-theories emphasizing hard organizational, institutional and structural aspects of society (e.g., conflict theory, structuralist Marxism, neo-Weberian institutional orientation), and micro-theories emphasizing individual actions, meanings, symbols, awareness and subjective construction of reality (e.g., exchange and rational choice, symbolic interactionism, dramaturgical theory, ethnomethodology, phenomenology). Mutual debates imply dogmatic, extreme formulations of theoretical positions. "One-sided theories are provocative, and at certain junctures they can be highly fruitful. Once the dust of theoretical battle has settled, however, the cognitive content of their theorizing is not easy to maintain. Revisionism is the surest sign of theoretical discontent" (Alexander 1988:89). What began as partial openings toward competing theories (Eisenstadt and Curelaru 1976:245–295), led to the attempts at reconciliation and syntheses.

The present intellectual climate clearly seems to favor synthetic efforts at the level of grand theories of highest generality. The search for syntheses, reconciliations, mutual openings, multidimensional positions and many-sided standpoints is clearly in the air. Of course the winds of the new integrative doctrine were felt much earlier. Occasionally, we hear the calls for integration, synthesis, golden mean or via *media* (in the sixties and seventies). For example, in 1979 I outlined the program of such a synthesis at the metatheoretical level, indicating the ways to overcome six basic sociological dilemmas haunting sociological theory since the early nineteenth century (Sztompka 1979). In 1982-83 the monumental effort to reread the sociological classics undertaken by Jeffrey Alexander was subordinated to the search for multidimensional theory (Alexander 1982-83). But only recently has it come to the fore of theoretical sociology to become the leading preoccupation.

Contemporary observers give unanimous testimony: "Throughout the centers of Western sociology — in Britain and France, in Germany and the United States — synthetic rather than polemical theorizing now is the order of the day" (Alexander 1988:77). "A wide range of synthetic efforts are under way in contemporary sociological theory... The consensus in sociological theory is ... on the need to create new theories through a variety of synthetic efforts" (Ritzer 1989:36-37).

The focus of such synthesizing efforts has come to be defined as the problem of agency versus structure. Starting from different theoretical and philosophical backgrounds, several grand theorists try to grasp the analytical complexity of society in a unified picture. Just by way of selected examples: Jeffrey Alexander follows in the footsteps of Parsons with his account of multidimensionality (Alexander 1982-83, 1988b); Pierre Bourdieu puts forward an idea of habitus (1980); Anthony Giddens, starting from more microsociological and phenomenological inspirations, suggests the powerful concepts of structuration and duality of structure as fundamental for the constitution of society (Giddens 1984); Margaret Archer rephrases and articulates earlier hunches appearing in the action-versus-structure debate, and develops the idea of morphogenesis (Archer 1988); Piotr Sztompka attempts to elaborate the notion of social becoming as an integrating concept (Sztompka 1991).

Thus, as one contemporary observer puts it, "In the present decade a strikingly different phase of theoretical argument has begun to take shape. Stimulated by the premature theoretical closure of the micro and macro traditions, this phase is marked by an effort to link theorizing about action and structure once again" (Alexander 1988:89). Four years later the same author takes stock of ongoing theoretical developments under the telling title "Recent Sociological Theory between Agency and Social Structure" (Alexander 1992). This warrants the label of a true theoretical reorientation.

Recognizing the importance of this trend one must also be aware of its limitations. What such grand theoretical syntheses say is most general, and therefore by definition cannot be very specific. They draw a map of social terrain in extremely large relief. They allow us to see the overall picture from a distance. Other theories must take up some fragments, aspects or dimensions and render them in fine-grained details. The vogue for synthetic theories does not diminish the importance of analytic theories. Synthetic theories try to account for the links, interconnections and bridges, but there must be more specific theories about what is being linked, connected or bridged: theories of structures and actions, personality and social organization, culture and personality, social roles and institutions, groups and movements, etc. The old program of middle range theories put forward more than four decades ago by Robert K. Merton (Merton 1949) is equally valid today. Most theories must stay within this middle range of generality, and not because sociology is unripe, unprepared or underdeveloped — as Merton seemed to believe. It is precisely here, at this level, that the more specific, linear, explanatory and predictive hypotheses linked to empirical data and research results are to be found. And these are indispensable to answer more mundane, immediate, practical human concerns. The grand theories alone will not do.

Some Words about the Present Volume

This book originated at the World Congress of Sociology in Madrid in 1990, at the sessions of the recently established Research Committee on Theory of the ISA (Research Committee 16), chaired by Jeffrey Alexander and Piotr Sztompka. The papers presented there by an international group of theorists have been thoroughly reworked by their authors and brought up-to-date, in view of later exchanges and discussions. The contributors to this volume approach the issue of agency and structure from various points of view, dictated by their own diverse backgrounds, theoretical predilections, and even national traditions. In effect, a vast panorama of positions and perspectives is presented; by no means exhaustive of the debate, but certainly representative of some of its major themes.

The contributions have been arranged in three sections. The first section is metatheoretical. It gives an overview and appraisal of the debate about agency and structure, micro and macro focus, as well as the philosophical opposition of individualism and collectivism. George Ritzer and Pamela Gindoff analyze various attempts to reconcile agency and structure, and identify the main incentive toward synthesis in the gradual emergence of a new philosophical position: methodological relationism to replace the traditional opposition of individualism and holism. Piotr Sztompka traces the movement away from structural determinism toward incorporation of creative human agency at the level of sociological theory proper, and attributes this shift to the gradual ascendance of two powerful schools: theories of agency and historical sociology.

The second section provides examples of various theoretical perspectives — classical and contemporary — from which the problem of agency and structure can be approached. Elisa Reis traces back the two prevalent images of the actor — *homo sociologicus* and *homo aeconomicus*, a peculiar variety of the collectivism-individualism theme — to the work of Emile Durkheim and Max Weber, reconstructing a sort of imaginary dialogue between two classical authors and showing their lasting validity for contemporary debates. Miguel Cainzos turns toward Karl Marx, analyzing the way in which neo-Marxism and what he calls "post-Marxism" liberate the theory from orthodox structural bias, conceptualizing free, creative action within Marxist tradition. Franco Crespi roots his analysis in the phenomenological and hermeneutic tradition, and takes a critical stand against rationalistic, positivistic and teleological accounts of action, drawing an alternative image of action as primary human experience, full of affective and irrational components and preceding cognition. Francois Chazel characterizes some theoretical turns in contemporary French sociology — and in particular, the return of the actor — clearly influenced by the wider, worldwide trends, but at the same time strongly flavored by indigenous, French traditions.

The third part of the volume consists of three different and highly controversial substantive proposals, attempting to push the debate forward toward comprehensive, synthetic formulations. Craig Calhoun relates the analysis of action and agency with another leading theoretical focus of contemporary sociology — the problem of modernity and postmodernity — presenting a strong case against some fashionable postmodernist claims. Tom Burns departs from exchange theory and the theory of rational choice to construct a perspective which he calls the social theory of games (SGT), considered as most suitable for interpreting the link between agency and structure. Piotr Sztompka returns to the debate between individualism and collectivism and outlines the theory of social becoming (TSB) and the idea of socio-individual field as foundations of an alternative ontology of society, overcoming the traditional dichotomy of individuals and societal wholes.

Finally, the contribution of Göran Therborn is fit as a closing reminder that sociological theory is, and will remain, pluralistic and multi-paradigmatic, and that the linkage of agency and structure is only one of its many focal topics.

The gratitude of the editor goes to all contributors, without whom, obviously, this volume could not take shape. But there is one who has made the extra effort to convince me that the project was worthwhile, and who helped tremendously during its execution: without friendly encouragement and editorial help from Tom R. Burns, this book would not have been possible.

Piotr Sztompka

Bibliography

Alexander, J. C. (1982–83). *Theoretical Logic in Sociology*. Vols. 1–4. Berkeley: California University Press.

——— (1988). "The New Theoretical Movement." In: *Handbook of Sociology*, ed. Neil J. Smelser, pp. 77–102. Newbury Park: Sage.

——— (1992). "Recent Sociological Theory between Agency and Social Structure." *Revue suisse de sociologie* 18(1):7–11.

Archer, M. (1988). *Culture and Agency*. Cambridge: Cambridge University Press.

Bhaskar, R. (1986). *Scientific Realism & Human Emancipation*. London: Verso.

Bourdieu, P. (1980). *The Logic of Practice*. Paris: Les Editions Minuit (Cambridge: Polity Press, 1990).

Collins, R. (1988). "For a Sociological Philosophy." *Theory and Society* 17: 669–702.

Eisenstadt, S. N., and M. Curelaru (1976). *The Form of Sociology: Paradigms and Crises*. New York: John Wiley.

Giddens, A. (1984). *The Constitution of Society*. Cambridge: Polity Press.

——— (1987). *Social Theory and Modern Sociology*. Cambridge: Cambridge University Press.

Merton, R. K. (1949). *Social Theory and Social Structure*. Glencoe: Free Press.

Ritzer, G. (1989). "Agency-Structure and Micro-Macro Syntheses: Consensus in Contemporary Theorizing." Uppsala: SCASSS (mimeographed).

Skinner, Q. (1985). *The Return of Grand Theory in the Human Sciences*. Cambridge: Cambridge University Press.

Sztompka P. (1979). *Sociological Dilemmas: Toward a Dialectic Paradigm*. New York: Academic Press.

——— (1991). *Society in Action: The Theory of Social Becoming*. Chicago: The University of Chicago Press; Cambridge: Polity Press.

I.

Between Agency and Structure:
An Overview of the Debate

I.

Between Myself and the
Question of the Future.

Chapter ONE

Agency-Structure, Micro-Macro, Individualism-Holism-Relationism: A Metatheoretical Explanation of Theoretical Convergence between the United States and Europe

George Ritzer and Pamela Gindoff

PARALLEL THEORETICAL TRENDS: THE US AND EUROPE

A great deal of attention has been devoted recently in American sociological theory to the issue of micro-macro linkage, while in Europe this has been paralleled by a similar level of interest in the relationship between agency and structure. There has been considerable movement on both sides of the Atlantic away from theoretical extremism and toward more integrative orientations. Europeans have moved away from feeling the need to choose between, for example, structural and existentialist theories. Similarly, American theorists have been rejecting the necessity of choosing between macro-theories like structural functionalism and micro-theories like symbolic interactionism.

This paper seeks to offer a metatheoretical explanation for the convergence on the issue of integration in theoretical work in the United States and Europe in the 1980s and early 1990s. There are undoubtedly many explanations for this convergence. For example, it could be hypothesized that the tendency to think integratively is related to sociopolitical changes in the world as a whole. At the peak of the Cold War in the 1950s and 1960s, with the schism between communism and capitalism, sociological theory on both continents was similarly split into warring, extremist factions. However, with the decline and virtual disappearance of the global division between capitalism and communism in the 1980s, sociological theory began to pull away from extremist dichotomies and to move toward more integrative conceptualizations. While causality cannot be proven here, there is at least a parallel between the end of a worldwide dichotomy and the movement away from dichotomous thinking in the social sciences. There is certainly a relationship between the social world and social theory and it is not unreasonable to hypothesize that changes in the former will lead to transformations in the latter.

At a very different level, it seems clear that theorists on both sides of the Atlantic were growing tired of traditional theoretical differences. Thus, in addition to being related to changes on the world scene, the movement toward integration is also tied to internal developments within social theory. For example, on the continent, Pierre Bourdieu (1989) was fed up with the split between objectivism (structure) and subjectivism (agency) and sought to develop an integrative (agency-structure) alternative he labelled "constructivist structuralism." Here is the way Bourdieu puts his integrative position:

> On the one hand, the objective structures ... form the basis for ... representations and constitute the structural constraints that bear upon interactions: but, on the other hand, these representations must also be taken into consideration particularly if one wants to account for the daily struggles, individual and collective, which purport to transform or to preserve these structures. (Bourdieu 1989:15).

Taking Ritzer's (1981) work as an example of a similar orientation in the United States, he argued that theorists were wearying of the need to choose between macro-oriented ("social facts") and micro-oriented ("social definition" and "social behavior") paradigms. Instead, he perceived a need for, and a movement toward, the development of an "integrated" sociological paradigm. Such a paradigm deals not only with the integration of micro and macro, but also subjectivity and objectivity. Thus, a series of developments *within* social theory in both the United States and Europe also help to account for the move toward theoretical integration.

The above are but two of many explanations that can be offered for the dramatic changes that have taken place in social theory. The objective in this paper is to offer a very different kind of explanation for the international movement toward theoretical integration. Our thesis is that theorists on both sides of the Atlantic had increasingly found, at least implicitly, the choice offered to them by philosophers of science between methodological individualism and methodological holism to be too confining and largely irrelevant to their work. The work of these social theorists involves the tacit development of methodological relationism as an alternative to individualism and holism. It was this implicit development of relationism that provided the base for social theories of the relationship between agency-structure and micro-macro.

The fact is that the offerings of philosophers have grown increasingly extraneous to work at the cutting edge of social theory. Few social theorists today can be described as either individualists or holists. Yet, these are the only two options offered to them by philosophers. Philosophers have clearly grown increasingly out of touch with contemporary work in social theory. They have continued to debate individualism-holism among themselves while ignoring recent work in social theory. In the past philosophers developed their conceptions of individualism and holism, at least in part, from a study of the work of social theorists. For example, Weber's work on social action was seen as paradigmatic of individualism, while Durkheim's ideas on social facts were a model for holism. However, philosophers have failed to revise their positions and develop new orientations in light of recent work in social theory. Thus, social theorists have had to create, albeit unknowingly, a philosophy of science adequate to their theoretical needs. Philosophers of social science need to immerse themselves in this body of theoretical work, just as their predecessors based their conceptualizations of holism and individualism on the work of social theorists like Durkheim and Weber. They need to create a fully formed methodological relationism to parallel their conceptualizations of individualism and holism.

The second objective of this paper is to reflect on the nature of metatheorizing and metatheory based on the analysis described above. In analyzing the relationship between micro-macro, agency-structure, and individualism-holism-relationism, we are clearly in the realm of metatheorizing (Ritzer 1988, 1990b, 1991a, 1991b, 1992). The term *metatheorizing* may be used in at least three different ways — the process of studying theories in order to produce better understanding of those theories, to produce new theories, and to produce metatheories (for a possible fourth alternative, see Colomy 1991). This paper involves the latter type of metatheorizing; more specifically, we are concerned with various *metatheories*, in the sense of overarching perspectives, produced by the process of metatheorizing. Thus, we are distinguishing between metatheorizing as a process of study and metatheory as one outcome of that study.

The three sets of ideas to be discussed in this paper (micro-macro, agency-structure, individualism-holism-relationism) are clearly metatheories in the sense of being perspectives that overarch sociological theories. However, it seems clear that they are *not* all metatheories of the same order. That is, micro-macro and agency-structure are of a different order of abstraction than individualism-holism-relationism. Thus, in the final section of this paper we will reflect on the implications of this difference and demonstrate the need to refine our sense of metatheory.

This paper is divided into five sections. We begin by offering brief overviews of the sociological literatures on micro-macro and agency-structure integration. These are followed by a section devoted to methodological individualism-holism as well as one dealing with the limitations of this dichotomy and the need for, and outlines of, methodological relationism. In the final section, we return to the issue of the implications of all of this in terms of the two objectives detailed above.

MICRO-MACRO RELATIONSHIP

The micro-macro linkage issue emerged as the central problematic in (largely) American sociological theory in the 1980s (Ritzer 1990a). However, efforts in the United States to analyze the micro-macro relationship predate the 1980s (Wagner 1964; Wallace 1969). Nevertheless, in the mid-1970s Kemeny (1976:731) concluded at that time that so "little attention is given to this distinction that the terms 'micro' and 'macro' are not commonly even indexed in sociological works." Kemeny called for greater attention to the micro-macro distinction as well as to the ways in which micro and macro relate to one another.

As if heeding Kemeny's call, in the 1980s there was substantial growth in metatheoretical work on the micro-macro linkage issue. Collins (1986:1350) argued that work on this topic "promises to be a significant area of theoretical advance for some time to come."[1] In their introduction to a two-volume set of books, one devoted to macro theory (Eisenstadt and Helle 1985a) and the other to micro theory (Helle and Eisenstadt 1985), Eisenstadt and Helle (1985b:3) conclude that "the confrontation between micro- and macro-theory belong[s] to the past."[2] Similarly, Munch and Smelser (1987:385), in their conclusion to the anthology, *The Micro-Macro Link* (Alexander et al. 1987) assert that "those who have argued polemically that one level is more fundamental than the other ... must be regarded as in error. Virtually every contributor to this volume has correctly insisted on the mutual interrelations between micro and macro levels."[3]

Some Americans focusing on micro-macro integration are concerned with synthesizing micro and macro *theories*,[4] while others see it as a problem of developing a theory that deals with the linkage between micro and macro *levels* (Edel 1959; Alford and Friedland 1985; Wiley 1988; Ritzer 1989) of social analysis. For example, in the previous paragraph we quoted Eisenstadt and Helle (1985b:3) who concluded that the confrontation between micro and macro *theories* was behind us, while in contrast Munch and Smelser (1987:385) came to a similar conclusion about the need to choose between emphasizing either micro or macro *levels*. There are important differences between trying to integrate macro (e.g., structural functionalism) and micro (e.g., symbolic interactionism) theories and attempting to develop a theory that can deal with the relationship between macro (e.g., social structure) and micro (e.g., personality) levels of social analysis. In spite of these differences, the key point from our point of view is that both bodies of literature deal with micro-macro relationships.

Among those who define it, at least in part, as a problem of integrating theories are Burt (1982), Fararo and Skvoretz (1986), Hechter (1983) and Smelser (1987). On the other side are those who define the task primarily in terms of developing a theory that focuses on integrating micro and macro levels of social analysis including Alexander (1982), Coleman (1986), Collins (1981), Munch (1987), Ritzer (1981) and Wiley (1988). Gerstein (1987:86) offers a good example of the latter approach when he distinguishes between the two basic levels of analysis and then argues for the need "to create theoretical concepts that translate or map variables at the individual level into variables characterizing social systems, and vice versa."

In addition, there are substantial differences within the groups working toward theoretical integration and integration of levels of social analysis. Among those seeking to integrate micro and macro theories, there are important differences depending on which specific theories are being integrated. For example, Hechter (1983) analyzed the relationship between rational choice theory and normative and structural theories, Burt (1982) tried to bridge the schism between atomistic and normative orientations, Fararo and Skvoretz (1986) endeavored to integrate structural theory and expectation states theory, and Smelser (1987) sought to synthesize psychoanalytic and sociological perspectives.

There are similar differences among the theorists seeking to deal with the relationship between micro and macro levels of social analysis. For example, they may seek to integrate micro and macro structures, micro and macro processes, or more specific aspects of the micro and macro levels of social reality. More specifically, differences in levels are reflected in Alexander's (1982:65) multidimensional sociology involving an "alternation of freedom and constraint" in both action and order, Ritzer's (1981) integrated paradigm focusing on the dialectical interrelationship of macro objectivity and subjectivity and micro objectivity and subjectivity, Collins (1981) focus on "interaction ritual chains," Coleman's (1986) interest in the relationship between action and system, Wiley's (1988) concern with the integration of self, interaction, social structure and culture, and Munch's (1987: 320) work on the "interrelation between microinteraction and macrostructures."

It is clear that there is a large and variegated literature on micro-macro linkage. However, whatever the differences, there is an overarching concern for the *relationships* between micro and macro.

AGENCY-STRUCTURE

Similar to Ritzer's contention about the micro-macro issue in the United States, in Europe, Margaret Archer (1988:ix) has asserted that: "The problem of structure and agency has rightly come to be seen as the basic issue in modern social theory." In fact, she argues that dealing with this linkage (as well as a series of other linkages implied by it) has become the "acid test" of a general social theory and the "central problem" in theory (Archer 1988:x). Earlier, Dawe (1978:379) went even further than Archer: "Here, then, is the problematic around which the entire history of sociological analysis could be written: the problematic of human agency." Implied in Dawe's concern with agency is also an interest in social structure as well as the constant tension between them.[5]

A concern for the agency-structure linkage lies at the core of the work of a number of theorists who write in the European tradition[6] such as Giddens' (1979, 1982, 1984) structuration theory, Archer's (1982) interest in morphogenesis, as well her (Archer 1988) later concern for the linkage between culture and agency, Burns' (1986; Burns and Flam 1986) social rule-system theory, Lukes' (1977; see also Layder 1985) power and structure. Abrams' (1982) historical structuring, Bourdieu's (1977, 1989) habitus and field, Touraine's (1977) self-production of society, and Crozier and Friedberg's (1980) game-theory approach.

However, as is the case with work on micro-macro integration in the United States, there are substantial differences among Europeans working on the agency-structure issue. For example, there are considerable dissimilarities in this literature on the nature of the agent. Most of those working within this realm tend to treat the agent as an individual actor (e.g., Giddens, Bourdieu), but Touraine's "actionalist sociology" deals with collectivities such as social classes as agents. In fact, Touraine (1971:459) defines agency as "an organization directly implementing one or more elements of the system of historical action and therefore intervening directly in the relations of social domination." A third, middle-ground position on this issue is taken by Burns and Flam (see also Crozier and Friedberg 1980) who regard either individuals or collectivities as agents. This lack of agreement on the nature of the agent is a source of substantial differences in the agency-structure literature.

There is considerable disagreement even among those who focus on the individual actor as agent. For example, Bourdieu's agent dominated by habitus seems far more mechanical than Giddens' agent. Bourdieu's (1977:72) habitus involves "systems of durable, transposable *dispositions*, structuring structures, that is, as principles of the generation and structuring of practices and representations." The habitus is a source of strategies "without being the product of a genuine strategic intention" (Bourdieu 1977:73). It is neither subjectivistic nor objectivistic, but combines elements of both. It clearly rejects the idea of an actor with "the free and wilful power to constitute" (Bourdieu 1977:73). Giddens's agents may not have intentionality and free will either, but they have much more wilful power than Bourdieu's. Where Bourdieu's agents seem to be dominated by their habitus, by internal ("structuring") structures, the agents in Giddens' work are the perpetrators of action. They have at least some choice; at least the possibility of acting differently than they do. They have power and they make a difference in their worlds (see also Lukes 1977). Most importantly they constitute (and are constituted by) structures. In contrast, in Bourdieu's (1977:72) work, a sometimes seemingly disembodied habitus is involved in the "dialectic of the internalization of externality and the externalization of internality."[7]

Similarly, there are marked differences among agency-structure theorists on precisely what they mean by structure.[8,9] Some adopt a specific structure as central such as the organization in the work of Crozier and Friedberg and Touraine's relations of social domination as found in political institutions and organizations, while others (e.g., Burns 1986:13) focus on an array of social structures such as bureaucracy, the polity, the economy and religion. Giddens (1984:25) offers a very idiosyncratic definition of structure ("recursively organized sets of rules and resources") that is at odds with virtually every other definition of structure in the literature (Layder 1985). However, his definition of systems as "reproduced relations between actors or collectivities, organized as regular social practices" (Giddens 1984:25) is very close to what many sociologists mean by structure. In addition to the differences among those working with structure, Archer excoriates Giddens (and implicitly all of the others) for focusing on structure to the exclusion of culture.

The attempts at agency-structure linkage flow from a variety of very different theoretical directions. For example, within social theory Giddens seems to be animated by functionalism and structuralism versus phenomenology, existentialism and ethnomethodology, and more generally by new linguistic structuralism, semiotics and hermeneutics (Archer 1982), while Archer is mainly influenced by systems theory, especially that of Walter Buckley. One result of this is that Giddens's agents tend to be active and creative people ("corporeal beings" with selves) involved in a continual flow of conduct, while Archer's are often reduced to systems, particularly the sociocultural system. In France, Crozier develops his orientation primarily on the basis of organizational and game theory, while Bourdieu seeks to find a satisfactory alternative to subjectivism and objectivism within anthropological theory. One of the reasons for the substantial differences in work on agency-structure is basic differences in theoretical roots.

While we have focused on a variety of differences within this body of work, the overriding fact is that, as is true of the micro-macro literature within its domain, it is unified in its concern for linkage and integration.

METHODOLOGICAL INDIVIDUALISM-METHODOLOGICAL HOLISM[10]

The irony of the preceding discussion of the micro-macro and agency-structure relationship literatures is that such foci emerged in spite of the fact that theorists on both continents were confronted by two *non*-relational philosophies of social science — individualism and holism. Let us look briefly at them.

The problem with defining individualism and, to an even greater degree, holism is that there is no consensus on a definition among those who have worked with these concepts. If one traces the way in which individualism has been used from one of its earliest sources in Mill, through the works of Dilthey, Weber, Mises, Hayek, Schumpeter, Popper and Watkins, to name just a few of the major figures in this tradition, one finds substantial disagreement and much internal debate. In spite of these differences, we need to attempt to characterize individualism-holism.

First, and most importantly, individualism involves the idea that *explanations* of *all* social phenomena must be rendered in terms of individuals and their actions. Within individualism there are the subjectivist and objectivist branches. The subjectivists seek to explain all social phenomena in terms of the mental processes of individuals. Weber is usually seen as the paradigmatic subjectivist among methodological individualists (Mises and Hayek are also important here) because of his view that "for the subjective interpretation of action in sociological work these collectivities must be treated as *solely* the resultants and modes of organization of the particular acts of individual persons, since these alone can be treated as agents in a course of subjectively understandable action" (Weber [1921] 1968:13). Action, as Weber defines it, is the subjective meaning which an individual attaches to his/her behavior, and social action exists when its "subjective meaning takes account of the behavior of others and is thereby oriented in its course" (Weber [1921] 1968:4). The main representatives of a more objectivistic individualism are Popper and Watkins who accept the explanatory importance of such subjective motives, but argue that to such phenomena must be added a concern for more objective actions, social relationships and the situations in which they occur.

Second, individualists do not deny the existence of macro-level social concepts or phenomena. What they almost invariably contend, however, is that all social concepts and/or phenomena must be *defined* in terms of individuals. In other words, definitions must refer to some or all of the following characteristics — individuals, their psychic state, physical state, action and interaction (Udehn 1987:43).[11] Third, individualists do not deny the utility of macro social concepts in the *understanding* of social phenomena or action. They begin to have difficulty with the utilization of social concepts in *explanations* of social phenomena or action. They argue that explanations must be rendered in terms of individuals, and the aforementioned characteristics *only*. Therefore, individualists see a place for macro social concepts (in the realm of understanding social phenomena), however, such concepts do not belong in the realm of explanation.

Turning to holism, one of the main distinctions between it and individualism is the position taken on the issue of reducibility and irreducibility. Individualists believe that social phenomena are reducible to statements about individuals, whereas holists feel that there are societal concepts which are not reducible to psychological facts without remainder (Mandelbaum 1955). Holism is based on the premise that the properties of wholes or systems cannot be *explained* in terms of the properties of their parts (Phillips 1976:34). According to Phillips, this is the type of holism which is directly opposed to the doctrine of individualism (1976:41). In order to properly analyze and explain complex social phenomena, or systems, it is necessary to study the whole, for the parts do not explain such phenomena.

There are several basic premises of holism that parallel the basic ideas of individualism. First, explanations of macro-level social phenomena must be rendered largely in terms of other macro-level phenomena. To put it another way, macro-level phenomena cannot be fully explained by micro-level (individual) phenomena. Thus, philosophers of science who adopted a holistic perspective tended to acknowledge the importance of micro-level phenomena arguing that the whole cannot be properly understood without comprehending the parts and their interrelationships. However, many sociologists and structuralists have ignored this holistic concern for the parts and the internal structure of the whole.

Within holism, as was the case with individualism, there are subjectivists and objectivists. The subjectivists seek to explain social phenomena in terms of macro-level subjective phenomena like ideas, culture,[12] norms and values, social institutions, nonmaterial social facts, and so on. The objectivists seek to explain social phenomena in terms of material social facts, social structures, social positions, and the like. Second, holists do not deny the existence of micro-level social phenomena. However, they insist that all macro-level phenomena be defined in terms of other macro-level phenomena. Finally, no holist denies the utility of using micro-level social phenomena to understand social phenomena, but they have difficulty with the idea that explanations can be rendered in terms of such individual phenomena. There is a place for micro-level concepts in holism, but it does not lie in the realm of explanation.

LIMITATIONS IN INDIVIDUALISM-HOLISM AND THE NEED FOR RELATIONISM

While theorists interested in micro-macro or agency-structure linkage can gain insights from an exposure to the individualism-holism literature, there are limitations to what they can acquire. For one thing, neither micro nor agency is always equated with individualism, and macro and structure are not always equivalent to holism. Micro and agency can refer to collectivities, while macro and structure can relate to parts of the social whole. This less than perfect correspondence among the literatures limits what can be derived from the work on individualism-holism. It also points to the need for some effort to address the relationship between the micro-macro and agency-structure literatures since micro is often not the same as agency and macro is frequently not identical to structure.

Another limitation in the effort to derive insights from work on individualism-holism stems from the fact that individualism focuses on what is usually the micro/agency side while holism is concerned with what is ordinarily considered the macro/structural pole. However, what interests theorists in both the micro-macro and agency-structure literatures is the *relationship* between them. Individualism and holism are oriented to reducing the issue of the relationship to either an individual or a holistic matter. The fact is that *both* holism and individualism are inadequate orientations from the point of view of those social theorists who are interested in micro-macro and agency-structure *integration*.

The work in social theory on micro-macro and agency-structure linkage demonstrates the need for another broad metatheoretical orientation, to parallel individualism and holism, that can be termed *relationism*. While individualism tends to focus on the micro-agency pole and holism the macro-structural pole, relationism points in the direction of the linkages between micro and macro and agency and structure. And, after all, it is the relationships that matter most to both micro-macro and agency-structure theorists. This points to the fact that developments in sociological theory required a new metatheoretical orientation. It is our contention that social theorists have, at least tacitly, created the outlines of such a metatheory. Thus, in addition to learning from the largely philosophical individualism-holism literature, sociological theorists have implicitly contributed to the development of an orientation that should prove of interest to philosophers who have been so taken with individualism-holism.

In previous papers we have gone into some detail on the development of relationism as an alternative to individualism and holism (Ritzer and Gindoff 1990, 1992). In this paper we will merely offer an overview of this new metatheory based, at least in part, on our reading of micro-macro and agency-structure theories.

Methodological relationism contends, first, that explanations of the social world must involve the relationships among individuals and society.[13] The view here is that neither social individuals nor social wholes can be explained without analyzing the social relationships between them. Furthermore, neither individuals nor wholes can be adequate explanations of relational phenomena. Relationists can be concerned with subjective (e.g., mind and culture) and objective (e.g., behavior and structure) relationships, or some combination of the two. Second, relationists do not deny the existence of either individuals or wholes. Concepts can be developed to deal with both individuals and wholes, but those concepts must be defined to include the relations between them. Third, individualistic and holistic concepts may be useful for gaining an understanding of social phenomena, but relational concepts must be employed if our goal is explanation.

It is our contention that this more general philosophical position of relationism has been suggested, and its outlines delineated by, the work of sociologists on the micro-macro and agency-structure linkage.

It should be mentioned that at least some philosophers of science within the individualism-holism tradition can be seen as having anticipated relationism, at least in part. This work, along with the sociological work on micro-macro and agency-structure linkage, will provide the base for the fuller delineation of relationism.

We can begin with Karl Popper's (1961) effort to include institutions within his individualist perspective. Based on Popper's ideas, Agassi (1960) developed the even more clearly relational notion of "institutionalistic individualism." While both Popper and Agassi suggest a relational viewpoint, they see themselves as remaining within the individualistic orientation. More clearly relational is Jarvie's (1964) idea of "situational logic," but even Jarvie remains locked in the individualism-holism orientation. While Popper, Agassi and Jarvie approach relationism from the individualistic point of view, Mandelbaum (1955, 1957) suggests a relational orientation from a holistic perspective. While these are all suggestive and promising, they are limited by their roots in individualism and holism. More promising are Goldstein's (1956) ideas on methodological collectivism. Thus, there are leads in the philosophical literature on relationism, but they certainly have not as yet coalesced into the kind of distinctive, relational perspective being articulated here.

It should also be pointed out that some sociologists and social scientists have also suggested perspectives that have some affinity to the idea of relationism being explicated, at least provisionally, here. Most notable is Udehn's (1987:202) work, but also relevant are Piaget's (1970:8–9) relational alternative, "operational structuralism," to individualism and holism, Ollman's (1971) discussion of the importance of relations in Marx's work, and Szmatka's (1989) recent case for "multilevel explanations."

It should also be noted that the idea of relationism is likely to be met with coolness, if not hostility, from both individualists' and holists. Since it accepts the idea of emergent social realities, relationism is apt to be rejected by individualists. Holists are less liable to be hostile to relationism, but they will be uncomfortable with the emphasis on individuals.

Even some of those who can be seen as forerunners to relationism will be discomfited by it. For example, the focus in the relationism being espoused here is connections between individuals and wholes. However, it is possible to focus only on relations at the level of individuals or of wholes. Thus, there is need to sort out the various possible meanings of relationism. For this, and other reasons discussed above, there is much work to be done in terms of the development of relationism.

IMPLICATIONS

There are two major sets of implications to be derived from this paper. First, sociological theorists engaged in micro-macro and agency-structure integration have clearly, albeit implicitly, developed a new philosophy of science — methodological relationism — to complement methodological individualism and methodological holism. The simple fact is that if they had worked with either individualism or holism, they could not have created their relational theories. Clearly, none of these theorists explicitly outlined the problems with extant philosophies, nor did any of them attempt to specifically describe a relational alternative. Yet simultaneously, theorists on both sides of the Atlantic came to operate with a relational philosophy of science. Thus, we have sought to argue that the movement toward micro-macro and agency-structure integration is explained, at least in part, by an underlying dissatisfaction among social theories with extant philosophies of social science and the creation, at least implicitly, of a relational alternative. Such a philosophy is clear, albeit to varying degrees, when one looks back on their work. However, it is now time for a systematic elaboration of methodological relationism. It is the responsibility of philosophers of social science to develop this approach and outline its relationship to individualism and holism. In so doing, they should study the recent literatures on micro-macro and agency-structure integration. These literatures will provide them the base they need to create relationism.

The second set of implications of this paper relates to metatheorizing in sociology. Two different kinds of metatheories, in the sense of overarching perspectives, are discussed in this paper. The first type encompasses micro-macro and agency-structure integration. These are metatheories in the sense that they overarch a wide set of specific theories (for example, in the case of agency-structure, Giddens's structuration theory and Bourdieu's theory of the relationship between habitus and field) about micro-macro and agency-structure relations in the social world. It is these theories, and not the social world, that were the subject of the first two sections of this paper devoted to micro-macro and agency-structure integration. If theories are one step removed from the social world, then these two metatheories are two steps removed with the theories themselves standing between the metatheories and the social world. Theories (for example, those of Giddens and Bourdieu) are about the social world and metatheories are about sets of theories.

This all seems clear enough, but where does this leave individualism, holism and relationism? Surely they are metatheories, but are they metatheories in the same sense that agency-structure and micro-macro are metatheories? The answer is clearly no! These philosophical positions are broader and more abstract. They can be said to overarch agency-structure and micro-macro integration as metatheories. Weinstein and Weinstein (1992) have made a similar, although not identical, distinction between metatheory and philosophical sociology. In his previous work, the senior author of this paper has tended to treat all metatheories as the same; to not differentiate among different types of overarching perspectives. What this paper makes clear is that not all metatheories are the same and that we need to carefully differentiate among different types and levels of metatheories. Furthermore, we need to begin to explicate the nature of the relationship between the different types of metatheories.

Finally, the above leads to some additional reflection on the nature of metatheorizing in sociology. Metatheorizing is a process involving the study of theory. As a process, metatheorizing is clearly different from a metatheory. In fact, the creation of a metatheory may be seen as one end-product of the process of metatheorizing. Thus, a reflection on specific theoretical works, say on the work of Giddens and Bourdieu, would involve metatheorizing in the sense described above. But in much of this paper we have not reflected on theories, but rather on metatheories — agency-structure and micro-macro as metatheories, as well as individualism, holism and relationism. This implies that much of this paper is best described *not* as metatheoretical, but rather as *meta-metatheoretical* since the subject of study has been these metatheories. On several occasions the senior author of this paper has been criticized for the use of the term "meta-metatheoretical." In fact, one reviewer of an earlier version of this paper described that idea as "ludicrous." I hope the preceding discussion has made it clear that there *is* a clear and useful distinction to be made between metatheorizing and meta-metatheorizing. Just as it can be fruitful to study theories, the study of metatheories can also provide useful insights for social scientists. Indeed the main thrust of this paper has involved a study of various types and levels of metatheories in order to explain the emergence of a new philosophy of science which, in turn, helps to explain major theoretical developments in the United States and Europe.

Metatheorizing as a type of study, as well as an area of sociological inquiry, is in its infancy. This essay indicates that specific metatheoretical studies are not only useful in terms of what they tell us about theory, but also because they help us to clarify the nature of metatheorizing in sociology. It is hoped that future studies of this type will continue to provide this kind of double-edged reward.

Notes

1. However, Collins devotes only a few lines to the issue in the context of a broader discussion of current trends in sociology.
2. However, by creating separate macro- and micro-volumes, Eisenstadt and Helle have done more to heighten the split than to develop an integrated approach.
3. The citation of people like Munch, Eisenstadt and Helle in this discussion of the micro-macro linkage clearly indicates that some Europeans are involved in that debate just as some Americans work on the agency-structure issue.
4. Yet to be dealt with adequately is the issue of whether at least some of these theories are incommensurable and therefore impossible to integrate. On the latter, there are some (Gergen and Gergen 1982; Bhaskar 1982:285) who argue against the possibility of theoretical integration and their position needs to be considered by those who are working on such integration. (For an argument for theoretical integration, see Giddens 1984:xxii.)
5. In fact, agency is often used in such a way as to include a concern for structure (Abrams 1982:xiii).
6. We are dealing here with work than can clearly and unequivocally be placed in the agency-structure context. I am *not* endeavoring to survey all of European theory (or, for that matter, all of American theory). This leads to a number of omissions, most notably Jurgen Habermas. Habermas's work, especially in his recent turn to a concern for the relationship between the life world and the social system, *could* be seen as related to the agency-structure (or micro-macro) literatures. However, Habermas's work is so complex that it cannot be easily encompassed by the agency-structure rubric and, in any case, his work is not ordinarily thought of as part of that literature. Further complicating our ability to think about Habermas in these terms is the fact that his ideas have recently been heavily influenced by American theorists (e.g., Parsons, Mead and Schutz [who spent much of his adult life in the US]). Also not dealt with is the postmodernist, poststructuralist literature which can be seen as attempting to do away with agency and structure and thereby the issue of their linkage.

7. While we are emphasizing the differences between Giddens and Bourdieu on agency, Giddens (1979:217) sees at least some similarities between the two perspectives.
8. In a useful paper, Porpora (1989) distinguishes among four concepts of social structure: patterns of aggregate behavior stable over time (e.g., Homans, Collins), lawlike regularities governing the behavior of social facts (e.g., Blau, Mayhew), systems of human relationships among social positions (Marxian and network theory), and collective rules and resources structuring behavior (e.g., Giddens).
9. We are focusing here mainly on Europeans who deal with social structure and not those who see structure as hidden, underlying elements of culture.
10. We will deal only with methodological issues in this paper. For a discussion of ontological and epistemological issues, see Ritzer and Gindoff (1990, 1992).
11. Udehn, drawing on Watkins, also includes social situation and physical environment in this list, but they are excluded here because they clearly move us away from individualism and toward holism.
12. To us holists conceive of culture as macro-objective, but they are focusing on the objective products of culture such as books, works of art, and the like. While culture does have objective components, it is mainly a macro-subjective phenomenon involving collective ideas of various kinds.
13. For the sake of simplicity, we are treating agency and micro as coterminous and equivalent to the individual and structure and macro as identical and the same as society. As we have seen, however, the situation is far more complex than that.

Bibliography

Abrams, P. (1982). *Historical Sociology*. Ithaca: Cornell University Press.

Agassi, J. (1960). "Methodological Individualism." *The British Journal of Sociology* 11:244–270.

Alexander, J. C. (1982). *Theoretical Logic in Sociology, Volume I, Positivism, Presuppositions, and Current Controversies*. Berkeley: University of California Press.

Alexander, J. C., et al. (Eds.) (1987). *The Macro-Micro Link*. Berkeley: University of California Press.

Alford, R. R., and R. Friedland (1985). *Powers of Theory: Capitalism, the State, and Democracy*. Cambridge: Cambridge University Press.

Archer, M. S. (1982). "Morphogenesis versus Structuration: On Combining Structure and Action." *British Journal of Sociology* 33:455–483.

_____ (1988). *Culture and Agency: The Place of Culture in Social Theory*. Cambridge: Cambridge University Press.

Bhaskar, R. (1982). "Emergence, Explanation, and Emancipation." In: *Explaining Human Behavior*, ed. Paul F. Secord, pp. 275–310. Beverly Hills: Sage.

Bourdieu, P. (1977). *Outline of a Theory of Practice*. Cambridge: Cambridge University Press.

_____ (1989). "Social Space and Symbolic Power." *Sociological Theory* 7:14–25.

Burns, T. R. (1986). "Actors, Transactions, and Social Structure: An Introduction to Social Rule System Theory." In: *Sociology: The Aftermath of Crisis*, ed. U. Himmelstrand, pp. 8–37. London: Sage.

Burns, T. R., and H. Flam (1986). *The Shaping of Social Organization: Social Rule System Theory with Applications*. Beverly Hills: Sage.

Burt, R. (1982). *Toward a Structural Theory of Action: Network Models of Social Structure*. New York: Academic Press.

Coleman, J. (1986). "Social Theory, Social Research, and a Theory of Action." *American Journal of Sociology* 91:1309–1335.

Collins, R. (1981). "On the Microfoundations of Macrosociology." *American Journal of Sociology* 86:925–942.

_____ (1986). "Is 1980s Sociology in the Doldrums?" *American Journal of Sociology* 91:1336–1355.

Colomy, P. (1991). "Metatheorizing in a Postpositivist Frame." *Sociological Perspectives* 34:269–286.

Crozier, M., and E. Friedberg (1980). *Actors and Systems: The Politics of Collective Action*. Chicago: University of Chicago Press.

Dawe, A. (1978). "Theories of Social Action." In: *A History of Sociological Analysis*, eds. Tom Bottomore and Robert Nisbet, pp. 362–417. New York: Basic Books.

Edel, A. (1959). "The Concept of Levels in Sociological Theory." In: *Symposium on Sociological Theory*, ed. L. Gross, pp. 167–195. Evanston, IL: Row Peterson.

Eisenstadt, S. N., and H. J. Helle (Eds.) (1985a). *Macro-Sociological Theory: Perspectives on Sociological Theory*, Vol. 1. London: Sage.

_____ (1985b). "General Introduction to Perspectives on Sociological Theory." In: *Macro-Sociological Theory*, eds. S. N. Eisenstadt and H. J. Helle, Vol. 1, pp. 1–3. London: Sage.

Fararo, T. J., and J. Skvoretz (1986). "E-State Structuralism: A Theoretical Method." *American Sociological Review* 51:591–602.

Gergen, K. J., and M. M. Gergen (1982). "Explaining Human Conduct: Form and Function." In: *Explaining Human Behavior*, ed. Paul F. Secord, pp. 127–154. Beverly Hills: Sage.

Gerstein, D. (1987). "To Unpack Micro and Macro: Link Small with Large and Part with Whole." In: *The Micro-Macro Link*, eds. J. C. Alexander et al., pp. 86–111. Berkeley: University of California Press.

Giddens, A. (1979). *Central Problems in Social Theory: Action, Structure and Contradiction in Social Analysis*. Berkeley: University of California Press.

_____ (1982). *Profiles and Critiques in Social Theory*. Berkeley: University of California Press.

_____ (1984). *The Constitution of Society: Outline of the Theory of Structuration*. Berkeley: University of California Press.

Goldstein, L. J. (1956). "The Inadequacy of the Principle of Methodological Individualism." *The Journal of Philosophy* 53:801–813.

Hechter, M. (1983). "A Theory of Group Solidarity." In: *The Microfoundations of Macrosociology*, ed. M. Hechter, pp. 16–57. Philadelphia: Temple University Press.

Helle, H.J. and Eisenstadt, S.N. (Eds.) (1985). *Micro-Sociological Theory: Perspectives on Sociological Theory*, Vol. 2. London: Sage.

Jarvie, I. C. (1964). *The Revolution in Anthropology*. New York: The Humanities Press.

Kemeny, J. 1976. "Perspectives on the Micro-Macro Distinction." *Sociological Review* 24:731–752.

Layder, D. (1985). "Power, Structure and Agency." *Journal for the Theory of Social Behaviour* 15:131–149.

Lukes, S. (1977). "Power and Structure." In: *Essays in Social Theory*, ed. Steven Lukes, pp. 3–29. London: MacMillan.

Mandelbaum, M. (1955). "Societal Facts." *The British Journal of Sociology* 6:305–316.

_____ 1957. "Societal Laws." *The British Journal for the Philosophy of Science* 8:211–224.

Munch, R. (1987). "The Interpenetration of Microinteraction and Macrostructures in a Complex and Contingent Institutional Order." In: *The Micro-Macro Link*, eds. J. C. Alexander et al., pp. 319–336. Berkeley: University of California Press.

Munch, R., and N. J. Smelser. (1987). "Relating the Micro and Macro." In: *The Micro-Macro Link*, eds. J. C. Alexander et al., pp. 356–387. Berkeley: University of California Press.

Ollman, B. (1971). *Alienation: Marx's Conception of Man in Capitalist Society*. Cambridge: University Press.

Phillips, D. C. (1976). *Holistic Thought in Social Science*. Stanford: Stanford University Press.

Piaget, J. (1970). *Structuralism*. New York: Harper Colophon.

Popper, K. (1961). *The Poverty of Historicism*. London: Routledge and Kegan Paul.

Porpora, D. (1989). "Four Concepts of Social Structure." *Journal for the Theory of Social Behaviour* 19:195–211.

Ritzer, G. (1981). *Toward an Integrated Paradigm: The Search for an Exemplar and an Image of the Subject Matter*. Boston: Allyn and Bacon.

_____ (1988). "Sociological Metatheory: Defending a Subfield by Delineating Its Parameters." *Sociological Theory* 6:187–200.

_____ (1989). "Of Levels and 'Intellectual Amnesia.'" *Sociological Theory*.

_____ (1990a). "The Micro-Macro Linkage: Threats to an Emerging Consensus." In: *Frontiers of Social Theory: The New Syntheses*, ed. G. Ritzer.

_____ (1990b). "Metatheorizing in Sociology." *Sociological Forum* 5:3–15.

_____ (1991a). *Metatheorizing in Sociology*. Lexington, MA: Lexington Books.

_____ (Ed.) (1991b). "Recent Explorations in Sociological Metatheorizing." *Sociological Perspectives* 34(3).

_____ (Ed.) (1992). *Metatheorizing*. Newbury Park, CA: Sage Publications.

_____ "Agency-Structure and Micro-Macro Linkages: Crossroads in Contemporary Theorizing." In: *Social Theory and Human Agency*, ed. Bjorn Wittrock. London: Sage (forthcoming).

Ritzer, G., and Gindoff, P. (1990). "Methodological Individualism, Methodological Holism, and the Case for Methodological Relationism." Paper presented at the International Sociological Association Meetings, Madrid, Spain.

_____ (1992). "Methodological Relationism: Lessons for and from Social Psychology." *Social Psychology Quarterly*.

Smelser, N. J. (1987). "Depth Psychology and the Social Order." In: *The Micro-Macro Link*, eds. J. C. Alexander et al., pp. 267–286. Berkeley: University of California Press.

_____ (1988). "Sociological Theory: Looking Forward." *Perspectives: The Theory Section Newsletter* 11:1–3.

Szmatka, J. (1989). "Holism, Individualism, Reductionism." *International Sociology* 4:169–186.

Touraine, A. (1971). *The Self-Production of Society*. Chicago: University of Chicago Press.

Udehn, L. (1987). *Methodological Individualism: A Critical Appraisal*. Uppsala, Sweden: Uppsala Universitet.

Wagner, H. (1964). "Displacement of Scope: A Problem of the Relationship Between Small-Scale and Large-Scale Sociological Theories." *American Journal of Sociology* 69:571–584.

Wallace, W. (1969). "Overview of Contemporary Sociological Theory." In: *Sociological Theory*, ed. Walter Wallace, pp. 1–59. Chicago: University of Chicago Press.

Weber, M. [1921] (1968). *Economy and Society*, Vol. 1. New York: Bedminster Press.

Weinstein, D., and M. A. Weinstein. (1992). "The Postmodern Discourse of Metatheory." In: *Metatheorizing*, ed. George Ritzer, pp. 135–150. Newbury Park, CA: Sage.

Wiley, N. (1988). "The Micro-Macro Problem in Social Theory." *Sociological Theory* 6:254–261.

Chapter TWO

Evolving Focus on Human Agency in Contemporary Social Theory

Piotr Sztompka

IN SEARCH FOR AGENCY

Probably since the dawn of human self-reflection people have been seeking the ultimate causes of events, driving motors of phenomena and processes, and forces responsible for their fate. Inevitably, it became one of the perennial, leading themes of social thought, and much later of sociological science. Here it was defined as the quest for the underlying forces of social dynamics; the operation and transformation of society. In this long evolution of human thought the agency has been gradually secularized, humanized and socialized.

In the beginning it was placed outside of the human and social world, in the domain of the supernatural. Whether in the guise of animistic forces, personified deities, singular gods, or metaphysical providence, the agency was always operating from the outside, shaping and controlling individual and collective life, human biographies and social histories.

In the next stage the agency was brought down to earth, located in the slowly unraveled natural forces of various sorts. Human society, its functioning and change were believed to be direct products of natural determination: physical, chemical, biological, climatic, geographic, even astronomical. The agency became secularized. It was still outside of humanity and society, but somehow closer.

It took some more time before agential powers were ascribed to human beings. The agency, however, was exclusively located in Great Men: prophets, heroes, leaders, commanders, discoverers, inventors, geniuses. They were the movers *of* society, but their charismatic capacities were not *from* society; rather they were inborn, genetically inherited and individually developed. The agency became humanized, but not yet socialized.[1]

With the birth of sociology, a surprising twist occurred; the agency became socialized, but dehumanized again. It was located squarely within society, but society itself was conceived in organismic terms, as the self-regulating and self-transforming whole. The metaphor of an organism used to describe the functioning of society, and the metaphor of growth applied to its development, had the same implication: the agency was treated as inherent power of the social organism, its specific, but unanalyzed, taken-for-granted élan vital, manifesting itself in social life and in directional, irreversible social change. This sociological fallacy (Nisbet 1970:203), an original sin of our discipline, haunted sociology for a long time. It was underlying all varieties of evolutionism and developmentalism, with their visions of history as occurring somewhere above human agents; it became one of the most obvious weaknesses of orthodox functionalism, or mechanistic system theory, presenting us with strange models of society without people. The critics were demanding: "Let us get men back in, and let us put some blood in them" (Homans 1971:113). In due time those calls were heeded and the agency finally found its proper place: in the actions of social agents. It became humanized and socialized.

Great Men (and, as the times changed, Great Women) returned as agents, but their exceptional powers were treated as the emanation of society rather than inborn quality. They were seen as embodiments, crystallizers of structural tensions, social moods and historical traditions. They were the leaders but, paradoxically, only because they knew how to follow those they led. Their conduct took the form of representative activities: carried out on behalf of people, in order to keep futures open for them (Dahrendorf 1980:18), or the exercise of "meta-power," that is the "power to structure social relationships, to alter the 'type of game' the actors play, or to manipulate or change the distribution of resources or the conditions governing interaction or exchanges among the actors involved" (Baumgartner et al. 1976:225).

Then, a process parallel to what Weber called "the routinization of charisma" occurred in sociological thinking about agency. The focus moved from personal endowment to social roles, and particularly those roles which have inherent agential prerogatives to introduce and even enforce changes. The problem of legitimacy of offices and their incumbents came to the fore.

But perhaps the most crucial step was taken when the idea of agency was extended downward, to all people and not only the elect few, to all social roles and not only powerful offices. It was recognized that, obviously, *each* individual has only a minuscule say in social change, but at the same time social change must be treated as a composite result of what *all* individuals do. Distributively, each has a minor, practically invisible agential power, but collectively they are all-powerful. Two neighboring disciplines lend a hand to sociology at this theoretical junction. The metaphor of the market, borrowed from economics, helped to understand how the "invisible hand" emerges out of multiple and dispersed decisions taken by innumerable producers, consumers, buyers and sellers. And the metaphor borrowed from linguistics helped to understand how in everyday practices people create, recreate and change their own society, just as in daily conversations they produce, reproduce and modify their language. The notion of unintended, latent effects of human action (Merton [1936] 1976) became crucial, as social change was seen as the aggregated and historically accumulated result of what all societal members do for their own private reasons and egoistic purposes.

But, at least in modern society it has to be recognized that not all social change is unintended, and not all people act in isolation. The notion of intended, planned change, and the concept of collective, group action supplements the image of spontaneous change brought about by individuals. With this the agency finds its final embodiment: collective, or corporate, agents. Some of them are seen as enacting changes from above. They are governments, legislatures, corporations, administrative bodies, etc. Others are acting from below, crescively inducing change. They are associations, pressure groups, lobbies and social movements. Their complex interplay makes up the political stage of contemporary societies, and their intended outcomes intersect with the dispersed daily activities of individual actors, performed on the stage of common life. Thus, individuals and collectivities together shape the twisting course of human history.

We have retraced the odyssey of the idea of agency through the labyrinth of social and sociological thought. In the beginning it was entirely superhuman and extrasocial; in the end it appeared as fully human and fully social in two guises — one of individual actors and one of collective agents. Recent sociological theory focuses on both, attempting to unravel the secrets of their operation and the mechanisms through which they produce and reproduce social reality. Let us follow this route in more detail.

PARADOXES OF HUMAN EXPERIENCE

To understand the functioning of agency one must start from some fundamental ontological traits of human, i.e., social, existence. The striking feature of the human condition is its dual, contradictory, inherently split character. We are torn between opposite pressures. This is witnessed by common experience as well as all discursive forms of human consciousness (philosophy, literature, art, etc.) which constantly reflect two basic oppositions.

One is the opposition of autonomy and constraint (in other words, freedom and dependence, individuality and participation, uniqueness and membership, subjectivity and reification). All our life we feel the oppressive presence of what Ralf Dahrendorf calls the "vexatious fact of society"; we feel bound by norms, rules, traditions, expectations and requirements, and occasionally bounce our heads against the hard wall of social sanctions:

> We obey laws, go to the polls, marry, attend schools and universities, have an occupation, and are members of a church; we look after our children, lift our hats to our superiors, defer to our elders, speak to different people in different tongues, feel that we belong here and are strangers there. We cannot walk a step or speak a sentence without there intervening between us and the world a third element, one that ties us to the world and at the same time mediates between these two concrete abstractions: society. (Dahrendorf 1968:22–23)

But at the same time we perceive ourselves as persons, unique individuals with some identity, integrity, independence and freedom. We profess some level of control over our actions, feel responsible for our decisions, experience pride, guilt and shame. The facticity of the outside world, the way in which society is experienced by individuals — external, given and constraining — clashes with the individual capacity of "making and remaking it through their own imagination, communication and action" (Abrams 1982:2). This is a "two-sided world": "a world of which we are both the creators and the creatures, both makers and prisoners; a world which our actions construct and a world that powerfully constrains us" (p. 2). This leads to ambivalent and constantly alternating self-definitions as "puppet-masters" or "marionettes": "It is part and parcel of daily experience to feel both free and enchained, capable of shaping our own future and yet confronted by towering, seemingly impersonal, constraints" (Archer 1988:x).

In modern sociological idiom this is referred to as the dilemma of structure and action. The emphasis on one or the other aspect of this experiential bivalence produces two alternative models of society, to be found in various social theories. Those who focus on social constraints, and individual dependence opt for the structural model. To invoke classical archetype, one may speak of the Durkheimian approach. Those who focus on individual freedom and treat structures as loose and flexible opt for the action-model. This would be close to the Weberian approach.

The second universal human experience has to do with the opposition of persistence and change (in other words, stability and movement, repetition and novelty). On the one hand we perceive continuity and sameness of our world, even for long stretches of time. We live in the same houses, walk through the same neighborhoods, work in the same factories, curse the same governments, and watch the same programs on TV. But on the other hand we also face — to paraphrase Dahrendorf — the ever-present vexatious fact of history. We follow customs that originated long ago, live in towns planned and built by our ancestors, imagine the future post-industrial civilization, listen to Bach and read Shakespeare, feel a pang of nostalgia remembering our own youth, and experience an undefined fright in anticipation of our death. And from time to time, in those rare moments when history or biography suddenly accelerate, whether due to a social revolution or a personal crisis, we clearly see the movement and transition. Sociologists refer to this duality as the opposition of continuity and transformation. The emphasis on one or the other pole produces alternative models of society, to be found in social theories. Those who treat society as stable, permanent and continuous opt for the static model, and those who focus on change, discontinuity and novelty opt for the dynamic model.[2]

Those two oppositions — of structure and action, and of continuity and transformation — founded in ontological dualities of the human world, define the problematic field of sociological theory. They may be treated as two cross-cutting Cartesian axes organizing the area of theoretical work. Before sociological theory was able to raise itself above this maze and recognize both dualities as irreducible, as basic and indispensable traits of society requiring a multidimensional, synthetic approach, it was vainly pursuing one-sided solutions, splitting the ontological unity of opposites at the conceptual level and producing distorted, inadequate models. Vacillating between the poles of theoretical space, modern sociological theory was in fact replicating in a shorter time-span the whole story of classical sociological theory from the middle of the nineteenth century.

THE SWING OF THE THEORETICAL PENDULUM

For many years after World War II, the focus was clearly on the structural side. Carrying to the logical limit the "Durkheim Problem," society was seen as a self-regulating system, with individuals as its emanations, representatives and epiphenomena. Structural constraints (system requirements, needs, prerequisites) were treated as determining human conduct. And fully internalized structural imperatives (values, norms) were seen as main human motivations, making people behave in ways functional for the system. In other words, there was a perfect fit between the structure of the social system and the personality of its components (human actors). The imperialism of the object (Giddens 1984:2) of the reified social wholes was matched with the oversocialized conception of man (Wrong 1961), treated as a perfect, obedient replica of the system. With some important variations, this model was typical for the whole structural-functional school, dominating Western sociology until the end of the sixties.

In the wake of the critique of structural-functionalism, the pendulum swings to the opposite extreme. Taking up the "Weber Problem" and pushing it to the limit, sociologists move the focus to the individual. Human action instead of social structure becomes the main object of research. The dissection of its subtle, meaningful, symbolic components; the analysis of intimate, everyday interactions; the reconstruction of the processes through which individuals construct their subjective "life-worlds" — these replace almost entirely any interest in structures. Sociologists attempt to expose the endemic fragility and brittleness of social reality, its "merely" conversational groundings, its negotiability, perpetual and irreparable underdetermination (Bauman 1989:129). With the ascent of new humanism, new subjectivism, hermeneutics and interpretation, we enter the era of the imperialism of the subject (Giddens 1984:2). In spite of important differences, this is the common emphasis of such schools as symbolic interactionism, ethnomethodology, phenomenological sociology, dramaturgical sociology, radical microsociology, etc. The rightful call to bring people back into sociological theory (Homans 1971) ended, paradoxically, in sociological theory without society, concerned exclusively with individual people and their actions.

> Previous emphasis on structurally determined constraints to interaction gives way to a new concern with the process in which ostensibly 'solid' realities are construed and re-construed in the course of interaction... The overall outcome of such revisions is a vision of fluid, changeable social setting, kept in motion by interaction of plurality of autonomous and uncoordinated agents. (Bauman 1989:142)

A parallel swing of the pendulum may be observed along the second axis of theoretical space, from static to dynamic models. Both narrow-empiricism and grand theory of the functionalist sort, dominating in the fifties and sixties, entailed a neglect of change, except perhaps for the internal compensatory reactions producing the restoration of the status quo. The utopian quality of a social system, as pointed out by numerous critics, was its strange timelessness: "The system is the same however often we look at it. Children are born and socialized and allocated until they die; new children are born, and the same happens all over again. What a peaceful, what an idyllic world the system is!" (Dahrendorf 1968:117). This static bias of structural-functional models was not accidental; it was a logical implication of its fundamental idea of consensus, harmony and or equilibrium. As long as society was conceived in such terms, there was no way to accommodate the immanent, internally generated change.

No wonder that the correction of the static bias was started by the conflict theory of society, with its emphasis on dissension, disequilibrium, strains and tensions. Attacking structural functionalism, one of the earliest critics was proclaiming:

> A Galilean reformulation is required; we must realize that all units of social organization are continuously changing unless some force intervenes to arrest this change... Moreover, change is ubiquitous not only in time but also in space; that is to say, every part of every society is constantly changing, and it is impossible to distinguish between

"change within" and "change of," between "microscopic" and "macroscopic" change.³ (Dahrendorf 1968:126)

The focus on incessant change was also quite congenial for various theories of the new subjectivist school. The area of individual action, everyday conduct, communication and discourse was obviously full of contingency, fragility, fluidity, movement. And most of the symbolic father-figures of this orientation (Mead, Husserl, Wittgenstein, Gadamer) were strongly advocating processual, dynamic perspective. Sociologists embrace "the image of society in the state of a constant Brownian movement, a society construed ever anew out of the flexible stuff of personal interaction, a society without tough structure or firm developmental tendency" (Bauman 1989:133). Unfortunately, from the valid recognition of change, there was only a step toward an invalid absolutization of change. This step was taken by the fad of the eighties, the theory of postmodernism, or postmodernist sociology.

> The urge for change became the glorification of change. Change was seen as a value in itself... In all cultural forms, change, far from being the tool of modernity for achieving the goal of progress, has become an end in itself... There begins a period of no progress and no history, a period of "postculture." (Mongardini 1990).

The simultaneous shift of focus along two axes of problematic space, away from structure toward action and away from continuity toward change, has produced the domination of individualistic and dynamic sociology. What were the reasons for such complete reorienfation? As usual, they are to be sought in two developments. On the one hand, in purely intellectual terms, where internal developments of the structural-functional school, or more generally, one-sided structural determinism has led to the paradigm-crisis (Kuhn 1970): the exhaustion of further potential for elaboration, multiplying unresolvable puzzles, and growing perception of empirical inadequacy. Critical reaction led to the study of individual conduct and social change. But on the other hand, perhaps more importantly, the social and political transformations of the world in the late sixties and seventies have dramatically modified the very subject matter of sociological science. The diagnosis of the new, emerging shape of human society at the end of the twentieth century would lead us far beyond the scope of this book, and certainly exceed my competence. Thus, let me just venture some general observations.

The oppressive, rigid facticity of structures — political, economic, stratificational — was undermined by the growing activism of the masses, partly as the expression of accumulated grievances and deprivations, partly as the defense against by-products of expanding modernity (ecological destruction, nuclear threat, moral decay, etc.). The mobilization from below took the form of extensive social movements (both old, class based, and new, cutting across traditional alliances), the growing aspirations for participation, autonomy, self-management or freedom were strongly articulated in the political process. Even in totalitarian societies, people were raising their heads and asserting independence, often successfully initiating the transition to democracy. Sociological theory had to recognize that individuals and their actions *did* count, and sometimes quite decisively, even against the most repressive structures. At the same time the changes in social consciousness, prevailing *Weltanschauung*, led to the growing affirmation of a much more loose, open, flexible social structure. Even though the recent revelations about the end of history (Fukuyama 1989) are clearly the case of a perverse, counter-utopian utopia,[4] one point is certainly true: there is a worldwide ideological and political trend toward liberal democracy, with its ideas of pluralism, participation, representation and legitimacy growing in salience and acceptance. Hence, social (economic, political, cultural) structures are seen more and more as liberating rather than repressive, enabling rather than constraining, and opening rather than restricting the pool of human options and life chances (Dahrendorf 1979). Sociological theory could not respond to this spreading climate without affirming individual autonomy and releasing structural grip.

The turn away from the idea of an immutable, stable, persistent social system was brought about by the breakdown of postwar prosperity and harmony in the West in the sixties. The economic recession, international conflicts, eruption of ethnic, racial, intergenerational and class antagonisms galvanizes the imagination of the masses. The uncertainties of today encourage idealizations of yesterday, as well as dreams about tomorrow, both optimistic and catastrophic. The salience given by mass media to newsworthy social and political turmoil occurring even in the most remote regions of the world, adds to the feeling that nothing is eternal. People start to perceive their world as changing, sometimes even shaking and collapsing. The new mode of social consciousness, which A. Giddens describes as historicity spreads out:

> Consciousness of history as a progression of change, rather than as the constant re-enactment of tradition, and the availability of 'exemplars' located differentially in time or space for current processes of transfor-

mation, basically alter the overall conditions of social reproduction in the contemporary societies. (Giddens 1979:222)

At the same time, the breakdown of modernizing efforts and acute crises in the underdeveloped countries of the Third World, as well as the ever more obvious failure of planned social transformations in the countries of "real socialism," put into doubt the developmental schemes typical for neo-evolutionism, theory of modernization or theory of socioeconomic formations. Real societies refuse to be squeezed into Procrustean beds; they do not fit the postulated stages of growth, or phases of modernization, or sequences of formations. The unilinear accounts have to crumble in the face of multidirectional, multidimensional, cross-cutting, overlapping, often haphazard and chaotic episodes of change.[5]

> The theory of change embodied in both the classical theory of social evolution and the contemporary theories of neo-evolutionism and functionalism are singularly without merit when it comes to our understanding of the nature of change, the conditions under which change takes place, and the effects of change upon social behavior. (Nisbet 1969:270)

Under the pressure of changing realities and the growing awareness of change in popular consciousness, sociological theory could not but turn to the study of change. But the momentum of this theoretical reorientation easily carried it beyond reasonable balance, toward the one-sided absolutization of change, and complete neglect of persistence and continuation.

TOWARD A SYNTHETIC FRAMEWORK

Which brings us to the last decade and the new theoretical movement (Alexander 1988a) marked most clearly by the attempt at theoretical synthesis. More and more sociologists focus on the linkage, rather than one-sided opposite traditions. Some try to link and reconcile earlier theories, their assumptions, concepts and hypotheses. They work at the meta-theoretical level, since their subject matter is existing theory. Others look straight at the social world and try to grasp its ontological duality, multidimensionality and inherent dialectics. They work at the theoretical level proper, since their subject matter is existing society. Sometimes, both kinds of work are carried out by the same persons. Both attempts are complementary; the reinterpretation and revision of theories adds to the reconceptualization of society, and vice versa.

Both ontological dichotomies outlined earlier — structure-action and continuity-change — inspire theoretical syntheses. One important line of theoretical development is the theory of agency, taking up the first opposition (of structure and action) as its main preoccupation; another line is historical sociology, focusing on the second opposition (of continuity and change). From different points of departure they gradually converge on the common image of society as a dynamic process in which people, by their own actions, persistently produce and reproduce the context of their existence, social structures which later become the initial conditions — constraining or facilitating — for further actions. Social life as a process of structural emergence via actions, and the tension between actions and structures as the ultimate moving force of the process are the ideas that form the core of recent theories of agency, as well as of historical sociology.

MODERN THEORIES OF AGENCY

The genealogy of the modern theory of agency can be traced back to 1967 when Walter Buckley introduced the concept of morphogenesis (Buckley 1967). Coming from the traditions of structural-functionalism and general systems theory, he wanted to revise them by incorporating the insights of other theoretical orientations: exchange theory, symbolic interactionism, theory of games, and models of collective behavior. The basis for this integration was still the system model. He believed that the system model had the potential to synthesize the interaction models into a coherent conceptual scheme — a basic theory — of the sociocultural process (Buckley 1967:81). To the structural-functional model of a self-regulating, homeostatic (or as he called it, morphostatic) system pervaded with negative, compensatory feedbacks, he counterpoised the model of a morphogenetic system with positive, amplifying feedbacks, in which the structures were constantly being built and transformed.

> The model assumes an ongoing system of interacting components with an internal source of tension, the whole engaged in continuous transaction with its varying external and internal environment, such that the latter tend to become selectively 'mapped' into its structure in some way. (Buckley 1967:128)

And he defined the central, strategic notion: "Morphogenesis will refer to those processes which tend to elaborate or change a system's given form, structure or state" (Buckley 1967:58). The emphasis on the active, constructive side of social functioning was a significant breakthrough in theoretical perspective, even though Buckley still remained trapped in some premises of the framework he purportedly rejected — organismic and mechanistic models. His morphogenetic system emerges, comes to be built up, generates, elaborates and restructures itself. There is some automatism in all this, as well as some reified, hard quality of the system itself. Agency is not yet liberated from its systemic cage.

A year later Amitai Etzioni comes out with his seminal account of active society (Etzioni 1968), labelled later as the theory of self-guidance (Breed 1971). At the heart of this, there is the notion of mobilization, or societal activation:

> The theory of societal guidance differs most from other theories in contemporary social science in that it sees the mobilization drives of collectivities and societies as a major source of their own transformations and of the transformations of their relations to other societal units. As a societal unit mobilizes ... it tends to change its own structure and boundaries and the structure of the supra-unit of which it is a member. (Breed 1971:393)

Human society is seen as a macroscopic and permanent social movement engaged in an intensive and perpetual self-transformation (Etzioni 1968:viii). The driving force of this is found in the self-triggered transformability (p. 121) and creative responsiveness (p. 504) of the people; the locus of such capacities are the collectivities, groups and social organizations, and the mechanism is identified as the collective action, mostly in the framework of a political process.

> A theory of guidance asks how a given actor [understood as a collectivity — P.S.] guides a process and how he changes a unit's structure or boundaries... The theory of societal guidance asks, in addition, how a given structure was modelled, how it is maintained, how it can be altered, where are the seats of power, who commands knowledge, and who has the capacity to commit. (p. 78)

Even though Etzioni was also deriving his ideas from system theory, or cybernetics, he was able to avoid reification or automatism by finding true agents of social self-transformation in various kinds of collectivities. The hunt for elusive agency was made much more concrete.

In the second part of the seventies, some French contributions to the theory of agency were noticed. Since that time the rapid breakup of a reifying vision of society so typical for a particular French version of structuralism began (Chazel 1988:197). Perhaps the most important representative of this trend is Alain Touraine. From the time he outlined the image of the self-producing society (Touraine 1977), his prolific work has had strong critical edge. It was directed both against developmentalism and structuralism, and the main charge was that they subordinate the sense of collective action to immutable laws or requirements of historical reality (Touraine 1985:81), and in consequence eliminate the actor (the subject) from sociological perspective, treating him as an epiphenomenon:

> The evolutionist or historist conception appeals to comparative history or even to philosophy of history. It tries to show that societies are ordered in a march towards progress, rationality and the reinforcement of the nation-state. It is irrelevant to the study of social actors themselves: it is sufficient to analyze their acts as the expression either of positive tendencies or of the internal contradictions of a given system. (Touraine 1985:91)

The return of the actor is necessary (Touraine 1984): we must reaffirm the need to return to the idea that men make their own history (Touraine 1985:88). And this is possible only within an image of society as a contingent, fluid product of human efforts: society is nothing but the unstable and rather incoherent result of social relations and social conflicts (p. 85).

Making of society and history is carried out by collective action, and its principal agents for Touraine are social movements (Touraine 1985). This crucial embodiment of the agency is understood, rather idiosyncratically, as such forms of collective mobilization which directly attack the cultural foundations of society, its specific mode of historicity. "The social movement ... is first of all an actor, since historical reality is built through the conflicts and negotiations of social movements that give a specific social form to cultural orientations" (p. 87). The rejection of evolutionism and the ascent of social movements to the role of core actors is linked by Touraine with the emergence of postindustrial society, where the capacity for self-action is dramatically increased, and the scope of options and possibilities enlarged; therefore "these societies see themselves as the products of their own actions, rather than as part of a process of historical evolution" (p. 84). In the work of Touraine, that vague capacity of society to mobilize, transform itself and engender structures — perceived already by earlier authors — was pinned down much more concretely and relativized to the specific historical phase.

Another French contribution comes from Michel Crozier and Erhard Friedberg, sociologists of organizations who come to grips with the interdependence of actors and systems (Crozier and Friedberg 1977). They realize that actors do not exist outside of a system which determines their scope of freedom; at the same time, the system does not exist without the actors who had produced it, supported it and are solely empowered to change it. Like Touraine, they start from the rejection of the laws of history (with their automatism, finalism and inevitability), and also of strong determinism, particularly of the materialist or technological sort (which conceives of the forms of human organization as fully shaped by the material environment of the social system).

In its place they propose the image of social change as the continuous structuralization and restructuralization of the arena on which people conduct actions in response to problems and challenges they face. Social change is crescive; it emerges from their social games, negotiations, bargaining, conflicts and cooperation. Collective activities of this sort are inherently creative, due to the mechanism of collective learning, in which individual discoveries and innovations turn into shared social practices and become embedded in the system. In effect, the traits of the system are changed, and even the transformation of the very mechanisms of transformation may ensue (Crozier and Friedberg 1977:364). There is no necessary, inevitable or natural change; the social world is fundamentally undetermined or at least underdetermined. All change is the result of human inventiveness, creation and search. The recognition of such human, contingent genealogy of all systems — even those which are apparently most rigid and immutable — allows for a critical perspective, the realistic appraisal of organizational freedom and the potentiality to oppose and break with existing structural conditions. And such attitudes are among the prerequisites of what the authors call "the learning society." The discovery that collective learning is one of the fundamental mechanisms of social self-transformation is perhaps their crucial contribution to the ongoing search for the agency.

The British enter the debate most vigorously with the work of Anthony Giddens, elaborating for the last decade his theory of structuration (Giddens 1979, 1981, 1984). He distances himself from all theories typical for orthodox consensus which assume reification of social wholes, and social determination of actors (treating them as "structural or cultural dopes"). Combining such critique of functionalisms and structuralisms, with positive inspiration drawn from various brands of interpretative sociology, he goes so far as to deny the adequacy of the notion of structure itself. Putting the emphasis on the fluid, permanently changeable, fully contingent nature of social reality, whose only true ontological substratum is the actions and interactions of human subjects, he proposes to turn the static notion of structure into the dynamic category of structuration, as the description of human collective conduct. Our life passes in transformation (Giddens 1979:3) and its core content is the constant production and reproduction of society. Therefore, "to study the structuration of a social system is to study the ways in which that system, via the application of generative rules and resources, and in the context of unintended outcomes, is produced and reproduced in interaction" (p. 66). The rules and resources that actors use are reshaped by using them: "The structural properties of social systems are both the medium and the outcome of the practices that constitute those systems" (p. 69). This is called the theorem of the duality of structure.

The ultimate motor of "structuration" is human actors (or agents); pluralities of individuals in their everyday behavior. One of their core properties is knowledgeability, or reflectiveness: "all social actors know a great deal about the conditions and consequences of what they do in their day-to-day lives" (Giddens 1984:281). The fine-grained analysis of the practical consciousness and "discursive consciousness" of human actors goes far beyond earlier "interpretative sociologies," but does not lead to one-sided absolutization. Some conditions are admitted as unacknowledged and some consequences of action as unintended. Hence, even though history is seen as a contingent product of human agency, as made of "events of which an individual is the perpetrator, in the sense that the individual could, at any phase in a given sequence of conduct, have acted differently" (Giddens 1984:9), it does not mean that the product coincides with intentions: "Human history is created by intentional activities but is not an intended project; it persistently eludes efforts to bring it under conscious direction" (Giddens 1984:27). Another face of human agents is their material (corporeal, bodily, biological) constitution and consequently, their inescapable embeddedness in time and space. "Corporeality imposes strict limitations upon the capabilities of movement and perception of the human agent" (p. 111). The implications of this seemingly simple constatation are shown to be enormously complex, and rarely faced by sociologists.

With Giddens, the agency is finally embodied in individual human beings. It is no longer the vague tendency of the system, nor the undefined drive of change-oriented collectivities, classes or movements, but the everyday conduct of common people, often quite far from any reformist intentions that are found to shape and reshape human societies. Undoubtedly, in the richness and depth of his detailed analyses of individual actors, Giddens goes further than any of the earlier authors in unravelling the mystery of the agency.

The opposite side of the agency-structure equation is taken up by Tom R. Burns and Helena Flam in their theory of rule systems (Burns and Flam 1987). Even though they declare the intent of bridging of actor and structure levels (p. 9), their focus is not on the actors who shape, but rather on the structures being shaped, which are conceived in normative terms as complex networks of rules.[6] This is openly acknowledged:

> The theory is not concerned with individuals as such, in particular the psychological and social psychological processes whereby individuals learn, interpret and implement social rules. The theory does not provide a language and analytical tools to describe and analyze the formation and reformation of personal rule systems, that is "personalities," and individual performances of social or personal rule systems. (p. 31)

Hence, the main thrust of the theory is the sophisticated analysis of social rules, which make the "deep structures of human history" (p. ix). They are seen as clustering into three kinds of modules: rule systems, rule regimes and grammars. Rule systems consist of "sets of context-dependent and time specific rules organized for structuring and regulating social transactions, for carrying out certain activities, performing specific tasks, or interacting in socially defined forms with others" (p. 13). Rule regimes are authoritative, backed by social sanctions and networks of power and control, and hence acquire the objective, external quality in human perception. They are close to what are normally called institutions (in the normative sense of this ambiguous category). At the individual level, rule systems turn into "generative grammars for social action" used by the actors "to structure and regulate their transactions with one another in defined situations or spheres of activity."

This complex and multidimensional normative network is not treated as given — in traditional Durkheimian fashion — but rather as a product of human action: "Social rule systems are human constructions" (p. 30), "human agents continually form and reform social rule systems" (p. 26). They do it in three ways: creating them, interpreting them and applying them. All of these activities involve large margins of freedom and are underdetermined; they are also the area of social conflicts and struggles, the specific politics of rule-formation. Emerging from human actions, rule systems also impinge upon human actions. In full unison with Giddens the authors speak of a dual relation:

> [Social rule systems] organize and regulate social transactions, such as exchange or political competition, in terms of who is permitted to participate, what transactions are appropriate or legitimate, where and when may transactions be carried on, how are they to be carried out, and so forth. At the same time, transactional processes are essential to the formation and reformation of rule systems, as well as to their interpretation and implementation. (p. 10–11)

And thus, "human agents through their actions transform the very conditions of their actions" (p. 3). There is a hint, not developed further, that the key to this duality may be found in the historical dimension of human reality: "The systems which people follow currently have been produced and developed over long stretches of time. Through their transactions social groups and communities maintain and extend rule systems into the future" (p. 29). Burns and Flam add to the theory of agency a rich analysis of the normative structure, backed with detailed scrutiny of selected empirical cases, most relevant for contemporary society, such as economic markets, bureaucracy and technological complexes.

Margaret S. Archer, another British participant, enters the debate about agency in 1982, in a sort of destructive mood, with a strong criticism of Giddens's structuration theory (Archer 1982). But almost immediately, she proceeds to the constructive phase, raising her own version of the theory of morphogenesis, culminating with the important volume *Culture and Agency* (1988), and apparently continuing the project beyond this point (Archer 1989). The main virtue of morphogenetic perspective is found in the recognition that "the unique feature distinguishing social systems from organic or mechanical ones is their capacity to undergo radical restructuring" (Archer 1988:xxii). And such restructuring is ultimately due to human agency: "structural patterning is inextricably grounded in practical interaction" (Archer 1985:59). The central notion of morphogenesis "refers to the complex interchanges [between structures and actions] that produce change in a system's given form, structure or state" (p. xxii). To study such interchanges one must adopt the principle of analytical dualism, rather than conceptual duality. The former means that action and structure are conceived as analytically separable, because "the emergent properties which characterize sociocultural systems imply discontinuity between initial interactions and their product, the complex system" (Archer 1985:61). Contrary to that, the principle of dualism commits the fallacy of central conflation, "the elision of the two elements which withdraws any autonomy or independence from one of them, if not from both" (Archer 1988:xiii).

There are two arguments — one in favor of analytic duality, and the other against dualism. One is methodological. Presenting action and structure as constitutive of one another does not lead to propositions about their dependence and precludes any examination of their interplay, and hence their influences upon one another cannot be unravelled (pp. 13–14). Another, and more telling argument is ontological: it is the case that action and structure are actually distinct because structural conditioning, social interaction, and consequent structural elaboration occur at different moments in time. "Subsequent interaction will be different from earlier action because conditioned by the structural consequences of that prior action" (Archer 1985:61). More precisely, it means that "structure logically predates the action(s) which transform it; and ... structural elaboration logically post-dates those actions" (Archer 1985:72). With respect to culture, "cultural elaboration is the future which is forged in the present, hammered out of past inheritance by current innovation" (Archer 1988:xxiv). Thus the principle of dualism engenders the second assumption typical for the theory of morphogenesis, namely the sequential, cyclical nature of action-structure interchanges.

In her latest contribution, Archer adds a new insight, namely that "the self-same sequence by which agency brings about social transformation is simultaneously responsible for the systematic transforming of social agency itself... Agency leads to structural and cultural elaboration, but is itself elaborated in the process" (Archer 1989:2). This opens up a new field of interest: the morphogenesis of agency. In this context, the traits of agency are spelled out — reflectiveness, purposiveness, promotiveness and innovativeness — with strong reservations about its exaggerated knowledgeability, or omniscience (Archer 1989:5). Two types of agency, corporate agents and primary agents, are also distinguished, and different empirical sequences of their own morphogenesis (as well as their participation in morphogenesis) described. Thus, the third principle is added to the theory of morphogenesis. Crediting the concept to myself (Sztompka 1987), Archer names it "double morphogenesis," and describes it as a process "in which the elaboration of both structure and agency are conjoint products of interaction. Structure is the conditioning medium and elaborated outcome of interaction: agency is shaped and reshapes structure whilst reshaping itself in the process" (Archer 1989:33). Perhaps the most important message of Archer's theory is the grounding of action-structure dialectics in historical time. This brings her closest to the second theoretical lineage: historical sociology.

From Buckley to Archer, the debate on agency has come full circle. In the meantime, the theory of agency, focusing on the opposition of action and structure, and attempting to bridge it, has been elaborated and significantly enriched. In effect, social reality started to be perceived with a sort of agential coefficient. I propose to define this concept, summarizing the legacy of the theories of agency, as the set of six ontological assumptions: first, that society is a process and undergoes constant change; second, that change is mostly endogenous and takes the form of self-transformation; third, that the ultimate motor of change is agential power of human individuals or social collectivities; fourth, that the direction, goals and speed of change are contestable among multiple agents and become the area of conflicts and struggles; fifth, that action occurs in the context of encountered structures, which it shapes in turn, resulting in the dual quality of structures (as both shaping and shaped), and dual quality of actors (as both producers and products); and sixth, that the interchange of action and structure occurs in time, by means of alternating phases of agential creativeness and structural determination.

The evolving theory of agency became recognized as the central area of sociological theorizing. It is acknowledged not only by its cofounders who claim that "the problem of structure and agency has rightly come to be seen as the basic issue in modern social theory" (Archer 1988:ix), but also by more detached observers who are ready to admit that "the scope and intensity of this search for linkage is without precedent in the history of sociology" (Alexander 1988a: 287), and that it "promises to be a significant area of theoretical advance for some time to come" (Collins 1986:1350).

ASCENT OF HISTORICAL SOCIOLOGY

Already in the theories of agency, and particularly its more recent formulations, the recognition of time, the processual character and the historical dimension of social reality was clearly emerging.[7] But it was always a residual interest, a marginal consideration to the crucial relation of action and structure. This logic is reversed in historical sociology, which takes the opposition of continuity and change as its core problem, but solving it arrives sooner or later at the quite sophisticated notion of agency. In this sense, there is a fundamental convergence of both lines of theoretical development, but they approach from opposite starting points.

The story of gradual ascendance of historical sociology is both long and intricate (Sztompka 1986b). It is widely believed that sociology was born of history. Hence, the recent revival of historical interest among sociologists is sometimes considered as the return to the origins of the discipline. Nothing can be further from the truth. Historical sociology must be treated as a critical reaction to the traditional uses of history, typical for the founding fathers of sociological science. It is one thing to say that sociology was born of interest in historical events or processes, and quite another to say that sociology was born of the scientific study of history. The former is certainly true; European sociology of the nineteenth century was born as an attempt to comprehend and explain the great transition of traditional into modern society and all of the complex accompanying processes of industrialization, urbanization, accumulation of capital, pauperization, proletarianization, emergence of new states and nations, ascendance of new social classes, etc. In this sense, nineteenth-century European history provided the natural problematization for early sociological thought, and Comte's formula, *Savoir, pour prevoir, pour prevenir*, set its goals and rationale.

But the historical subject-matter was not approached by means of a truly historical method or by reconstructing concrete events and carefully generalizing them, reaching at the most strictly delimited laws concerning history (Mandelbaum 1948). Just the reverse — the universal, all-embracing and supposedly all-explaining laws of history, were stipulated *a priori*, and at most illustrated with random historical evidence gathered by means of what Comte labelled "comparative method." Evolutionist or developmental schemes of Comte, Spencer, Tonnies or early Durkheim were not derived from history, nor rooted in history, but rather imposed upon history (Nisbet 1969:164–165). They also shared certain characteristic assumptions: they treated history mechanistically as a autonomous domain, reality *sui generis*, from which human actors were strangely absent, and treated the direction of history as predetermined, fatalistic and independent of human efforts. Such abstract formulae were the offspring of historiosophy rather than historiography. The evolutionism and developmentalism did not in the least contribute to the emergence of a truly historical perspective. Just the opposite. Instead of bringing sociology closer to history, it represented the early form of ahistorism. We may call it, little paradoxically, a historiosophical ahistorism.

Even though dominant, this tendency was by no means exclusive. The nineteenth century may also pride itself on producing some models of truly historical sociology, firmly rooted in rich historical materials, historically limited in validity and recognizing the role of human actors — individual and collective — as the ultimate creators of the changing social world. Such theories reject mechanistic, fatalistic assumptions and reification of social processes, and restore man as a real historical subject. Three names among the early masters of sociology seem to represent this early, authentic historism: Karl Marx (at least in the earlier, historically focused period of his work),[8] Alexis de Tocqueville (to the extent that he may be considered a sociologist), and most fully and unambiguously — Max Weber. It is with the latter that historical sociology had come of age. All of his immense scholarship is firmly rooted in vast historical knowledge, reaching from the ancient civilizations to the birth of industrial capitalism. The application of historical perspective led Weber to reject ahistorical, mechanistic laws of history or developmental schemes, and to focus instead on concrete historical transitions, thresholds between epochs, eras, periods and especially on the birth of capitalism in Western Europe. It also implied the rejection of mechanistic or fatalistic interpretations of the historical process and gave human agents — their motivations, intentions and actions — the crucial role in producing social, economic and political structures, even of the largest macroscale. A contemporary commentator has good reason to describe Weber as "the most historically minded of the great sociologists" (Burke 1980:20). The recent rebirth of historical sociology must be linked with the heritage of Marx, Tocqueville and Weber, and their authentic historical work, rather than with the philosophical, *a priori* developmental schemes of Comte, Spencer, Tonnies or Durkheim.

But before such a rebirth was to occur, sociology witnessed a long eclipse of the historical perspective. It was partly due to the second generation of sociological thought beginning in the United States at the turn of the century. American sociology had radically different origins from European sociology. First of all, it was born in a different society: poor in historical traditions, existing from its very beginning within a single socioeconomic system of industrial capitalism, and thus unaware of the birth pangs of transition from traditional to modern society. At the same time, it was exceptionally complex in its racial, ethnic and class composition, ridden with multiple cleavages, contradictions and conflicts, and permeated with all brands of deviance and social pathology. The most pressing issue, therefore, was to ameliorate the present, existing order rather than to establish a new social formation. American sociologists focused on the safeguarding of the smooth operation of the social system, eradicating crime and social disorganization, integrating local communities, improving the effectiveness of institutions and raising the productivity of labor and efficiency of management. And the solutions to such problems were sought in concrete, empirical diagnoses, mainly at the microsociological level (Antonio and Piran 1978:1–2).

The melioristic, presentist, empirical and micro-sociological concerns led American sociologists to different intellectual sources: to the tradition of psychology rather than the philosophy of history. Typical indigenous theoretical orientations of American sociology — social behaviorism, symbolic interactionism, and later, exchange theory — were clearly inspired by a psychological orientation. And if the questions relating to the operation of the whole society in the macroscale had to be faced, Americans were ready to adopt the tradition of British functional anthropology of B. Malinowski and A. R. Radcliffe-Brown, which viewed society as a self-regulating, equilibratory, internally harmonious system (Sztompka 1974). As early as the forties, the school of structural functionalism was born and soon acquired dominance in American sociology which it held for the next thirty years. Both micro- and macrotheoretical traditions typical for American sociology were thus abstracting from the historical dimension of social reality. Together with the narrow empiricism and pragmatic attitude of uncritical research workers, they were responsible for the ahistorical bias of American sociology. I shall refer to this brand of ahistorism, born and bred in the United States but spreading all over the world, as presentist ahistorism.

Thus, as an effect of the double genealogy of sociological science — European and American — an ahistorical orientation is to reign in the discipline for the major part of the twentieth century. The heritage of the European origins of sociology is to be found in historiosophical ahistorism — sociology above history, well represented by various brands of evolutionism, neo-evolutionism, theories of economic growth, models of modernization, or fatalistic and deterministic versions of neo-Marxism. The heritage of the American origins of sociology is to be found in presentist ahistorism — sociology without history, well represented by narrow empiricism as well as by theories unabashedly ignoring the dimension of historical time.

In the epoch of reigning ahistorism, the historical perspective, though pushed to the margin, does not disappear completely. There are two bridges linking the tradition of Marx, Tocqueville and Weber with modern sociology. One is the rich stream of activist Marxism:

the works of A. Gramsci, G. Lukacs, the Frankfurt School, the New Left, etc. But this trend is mainly influential in philosophy and does not immediately affect the practice of sociology, at that time still programmatically anti-philosophical. Thus, another intellectual phenomenon seems of greater importance. It is the case of those "odd, if honored, grand older men of the discipline" (Skockpol 1984:357), who occasionally take up the roles of historians, studying some limited, concrete fragment of the past, but, being trained as sociologists, are ready to apply to such studies their sociological, conceptual and theoretical frameworks.[9] Even if exceptional, such works reach a wide audience and lay the groundwork for the full renaissance of a truly historical perspective in sociology that comes about only in the seventies and eighties.

Even at the end of the fifties, strong criticism is directed against narrow empiricism and presentism. It may be called the first crisis of postwar sociology. Arguing for the necessity of theory, some authors formulate a straightforward demand for the restoration of the historical perspective. For C. W. Mills, for example, it is a prerequisite for the true sociological imagination: "Every social science — or better, every well considered social study — requires a historical scope of conception and a full use of historical material" (Mills 1959:145). In the sixties and seventies, the next challenge is directed against the functional grand theory, mainly on the grounds that it implies a utopian, basically inadequate image of society. Thus, the second crisis of sociology ensues. The model of integration, consensus and stability is reshaped in the hands of conflict theorists into the model of conflict, coercion and change (Dahrendorf 1958, 1968; Rex 1969). The emphasis moves from the mechanistic self-regulation of the system toward the purposeful actions of individuals, groups, collectivities and social movements; social masses are treated as the causal agencies or at least carriers of social change. The formula of sociology without history, or presentist ahistorism, is slowly undermined. Criticism extends as well to the formula of sociology above history, or historiosophical ahistorism. The fatalistic, mechanistic, prophetic interpretation of Marxism is challenged by K. R. Popper (1945, 1957). The metaphor of growth, underlying all evolutionist and neo-evolutionist theories and understood as the progressive structural differentiation, is subjected to a devastating critique by R. Nisbet (1969, 1970). In a recent book C. Tilly unravels several typical and fallacious assumptions — as he calls them "eight pernicious postulates" — accepted by the developmental theories of big structures and large processes, and deriving straight from the nineteenth century (Tilly 1984a).

In the background of these deep changes in contemporary sociology, the "new historism" or "historical sociology" emerges as a separate theoretical and methodological orientation. Even though in its revived form it is still pretty young, it has already generated significant contributions, both concrete and general. On the substantive, concrete side, one may point to those works which, following the path of Marx, Tocqueville and Weber, or later of Merton, Smelser, Eisenstadt and others, take up concrete time-bound and localized historical problems and subject them to generalizing, sociological analysis.[10] But for our purposes we have to focus on another legacy of historical sociology: general philosophical, meta-theoretical and theoretical considerations throwing a new light on the very nature of social reality.[11]

The birth of modern historical sociology as more than historically rooted research but also a distinct theoretical perspective on the social world may be linked with the discovery and astonishing career of the long ignored work of Norbert Elias.[12] He is one of the first historical sociologists to raise a persistent attack against "the retreat of sociologists into the present" (Elias 1987:223), so typical for the orthodox consensus at the level of theory, as well as uncritical fact-finding at the level of empirical research. The antidote to that fallacy of abstracting from the diachronic and dynamic constitution of human society is found in the processual perspective, the recognition that "the immediate present into which sociologists are retreating ... constitutes just one small momentary phase within the vast stream of humanity's development, which, coming from the past, debouches into the present and thrusts ahead toward possible futures" (p. 224). The society is placed squarely in historical time: "every present society has grown out of earlier societies and points beyond itself to a diversity of possible futures" (p. 226). This process is mostly unplanned, even though it houses the shorter or longer episodes of planned, intentional social change. But there is no automatism or inevitable quality of change; the process is fully contingent, activated by human beings in their various complex interrelationships — interdependencies to which Elias gives the name "figurations." Their nodal points may be individual actors, but also groups, and even states. Figurations form a "flexible lattice-work of tensions ... a fluctuating tensile equilibrium, a balance of power moving to and from, inclining first to one side and then to the other" (Elias 1978:130–131). Such webs, or networks, of interhuman relations with power as the main bond (linking people but also opposing them, generating their cooperation but also conflicts), are inherently fluid and unstable, undergoing all kinds of permutations. They are moving patterns or, if you will, patterns of movement, of longer or shorter duration. People in their figurations make up the sole agency of historical change:

> Plans and actions, the emotional and rational impulses of individual people, constantly interweave in a friendly or hostile way. This basic tissue resulting from many single plans and actions of men can give rise to changes and patterns that no individual person has planned or created. From this interdependence of people arises an order *sui generis*, an order more compelling and stronger than the will and reason of the individual people composing it. It is this order of interweaving human impulses and strivings, this social order, which determines the course of historical change. (Elias 1982:230-231)

On the other hand, once the figurations are established they feedback on the actions: "individuals constitute historical figurations and are historically constituted by them" (Abrams 1982:250). Thus, the dilemma of continuity and transformation is resolved in this immanent order of change (Arnason 1987:193), and, as a by-product the notion of figurations, bridges the action-structure gap. As noticed by a contemporary commentator: "Throughout his work runs a strong tendency to get beyond the customary polarities in thought, and to avoid any position identified with these polarities" (Goudsblom 1987:332). In this sense Elias's project of historical sociology is synthetic *par excellence*.

The most radical case for historical sociology is put forward in 1982 by Philip Abrams. He argues for the complete integration of sociology and history, and claims that the only serious way in which sociology can be done is historical. That is so for ontological reasons, because both sociologists and historians deal with the same "maddeningly non-mechanical machine" (Abrams 1982:xiii) — human society. To grasp it both static, and traditional developmental approaches (proposing "laws and stages of evolution and development with a necessity of their own" (p. 8)) are totally inadequate.

> In my understanding of history and sociology ... there can be no relationship between them because, in terms of their fundamental preoccupations, history and sociology are the same thing. Both seek to understand the puzzle of human agency and both seek to do so in terms of the process of social structuring. (p. x)

The idea of a process helps to bridge both traditional oppositions, of statics and dynamics, as well as structure and action: "The diachrony-synchrony distinction is absurd. Sociology must be concerned with eventuation, because that is how structuring happens" (p. x), and sociology of process provides "an alternative to our tired and inadequate sociologies of action and system (p. xv), [because] process is the link between action and structure" (p. 3). Therefore, "society must be understood as a process constructed historically by individuals who are constructed historically by society" (p. 227). This process is incessant, sequential and cumulative; at each stage the actions are undertaken under given conditions (possibilities) produced in the past, and in turn reshape the circumstances for the future. This "continuous process of construction is the focal concern of social analysis" (p. 16). The process is made of historical events: "An event is a moment of becoming at which action and structure meet" (p. 192). The major turns of the process are effected by great events: "The great events make decisive conjunctions of action and structure; they are transparent moments of structuring at which human agency encounters social possibility and can be seen clearly as simultaneously determined and determining" (p. 199). The ultimate moving force of history is therefore the dialectics of human agency, and the course of history is set by the dialectics of structuring.

> The problem of agency is the problem of finding a way of accounting for human experience which requires simultaneously and in equal measure that history and society are made by constant and more or less purposeful individual action and that individual action, however purposeful is made by history and society. How do we, as active subjects make a world of objects which then, as it were, become subjects making us their objects? (p. xiii)

This is a core riddle setting the research program for both sociology and history, as well as their offspring — historical sociology.

The kind of personal synthesis of sociology and history is achieved by Charles Tilly, prolific social historian and historical sociologist. Apart from his rich substantive contributions, he makes some general programmatic statements about the historical nature of social reality and significance of historical angle in sociological studies. The emphasis on the cumulative process is clearly there: "As a phenomenon, history is the cumulative effect of past events on events of the present" (Tilly 1981:12). Any current situation is not a necessary phase in a predetermined developmental sequence, but rather "the outcome of a long, slow, historically specific process" (p. 39). And at the same time, it provides a set of possibilities for the continuation of the process: "Every structure or process constitutes a series of choice points. Outcomes at a given point in time constrain possible outcomes at later points in time" (Tilly 1984a:14). The actual historical process is pluralistic and differentiated, combines various overlapping, conflicting complementary and parallel processes: "There is no such thing as social change in general. Many large-scale processes of change exist; urbanization, industrialization, proletarianization, population growth, capitalization, bureaucratization all occur in definable, coherent ways. Social change does not" (p. 33). Of course some processes may acquire leading importance in concrete historical periods, overshadowing the impact of others: "Over the last few hundred years, the growth of national states and the development of capitalism in property and production have dominated the changes occurring in increasing parts of the world" (p. 49). But all this is contingent, and never inevitable. Similarly, his image of society departs from any reified facticity. Instead, he adopts a sort of field theory, perceiving social reality not as a system, but rather a fluid, changing network of "multiple social relationships, some quite localized, and some worldwide in scale" (p. 25). Thus, the constitution of society and the flow of history are ultimately dependent on concrete human actions. Among those, Tilly chose to focus on everyday behavior of common people (populist history rather than elitist history) and particularly their collective actions, "the ways that people act together in pursuit of shared interests" (Tilly 1978:5). They include, among others, the "contentious gatherings," collective violence, social movements and revolutions. The message of Tilly's substantive and programmatic work is straightforward: sociology should become "historically grounded" (Tilly 1981:12, 46), i.e., look at societies "comparatively over substantial blocks of space and time, in order to see whence we have come, where we are going, and what real alternatives to our present condition exist" (Tilly 1984:11). Such studies must be "assuming that the time and place in which a structure or process appears make a difference to its character, that the sequence in which similar events occur has a substantial impact on their outcomes" (p. 79).

Rich explication of a position labelled as "structurism" has recently been provided by Christopher Lloyd (1988 [1986]). The intention that guides his work is clearly synthetic:

> The problem ... is to bridge the subjective/objective and freedom/determinism gaps in order to show how people do indeed make their own history but also how particular circumstances, which are the result of people having made history in the past, condition their history-making. (Lloyd 1988:301)

The key to that puzzle is the processual nature of society: "drawing a line between past and present seems to be entirely arbitrary and pointless. The 'present' is always becoming the 'past' and processes continually exist in both directions" (p. 20). Hence, "social science must have as its basic aim the explanation of social transformation" (p. 10). And this implies the necessity of historical perspective: "Since structures are always changing they should always be studied in a historical mode" (p. 164). Within the process, there is the mutual, dialectic interplay of structures and actions: "Action is explainable by its structural and psychological imperatives and constraints, and structure and its history are explainable as the intended and unintended consequences of individual action and patterned mass behavior over time" (p. 10). The moving force of this dialectic and the ensuing historical process is human agency, located "within the conscious human agent, albeit an agent who always acts within a structural social, cultural, and geographical environment" (p. 192). Lloyd stresses: "Individual and collective human action is the fundamental agent of history" (p. 37). Agential persons are free within certain bounds of inherited choices, and they possess power to effect some limited changes in the world. They do it both intentionally, and, more often, unintentionally, producing unintended and even unrecognized structural results. Lloyd brings together these assumptions in the following account of his position:

> A structurist conception sees society as an ordered, independent but loosely integrated, constantly changing set of relations, rules, and roles that holds a collectivity of individual persons together. It transcends and has an existence independent of any individual but not all (or a significant proportion) of those individuals... In order to go on existing, it must be collectively reproduced by those individuals and it has a strong potential to be transformed into a different structure by their actions. (pp. 16–17)

As a result of the evolving emphasis on historical dimension, social reality is perceived ever more often with a sort of historical coefficient. I propose to use this name for a set of six ontological assumptions emerging as a common foundation of historical sociology. First, it is assumed that social reality is not a steady state, but rather a dynamic process. It is occurring rather than existing, it consists of events rather than objects. And time is an immanent, internal factor of social life. What happens, how it happens, why it happens, what results it brings about — all are taken to depend essentially on the time when it happens, the location in the processual sequence, and the place in the rhythm of events characteristic for a given process. Not only the properties or traits of phenomena, but their regularities (laws) are treated as time-dependent; in various phases of the process different causal forces of events are claimed to obtain. Second, it is claimed that social change is a confluence of multiple processes with various vectors, partly overlapping, partly convergent and partly divergent, and mutually supportive or destructive. The state of society is always a concrete crosspoint of those differentiated, heterogeneous and multidirectional processes. Third, society itself undergoing change is not perceived as an entity, object or system, but rather a fluid network of relations, pervaded with tension as well as harmony, conflict as well as cooperation. Fourth, the sequence of events within each of the social processes is treated as cumulative. Each phase of the process is seen as an accumulated outcome, effect, crystallization, point of arrival of all preceding phases, and at the same time the germ, embedded potentials, point of departure for the succeeding process. At each historical moment there opens up a determinate field of opportunities, possibilities and options for the future course of the process, significantly delimited by the whole past course of the process. Fifth, the social process is seen as constructed, created by human agents — individual or collective — through their actions. Behind every phase of the social process there are some people, collectivities, groups, social movements, associations, etc., whose actions have brought it about. And every phase of the social process provides a pool of opportunities, resources, facilities — one is tempted to say "raw materials" — for the people taking up the construction of social reality. Sixth, it is recognized that people do not construct society as they please, but construct only in given structural conditions inherited from the past, i.e., constructed for them by their predecessors, in their turn similarly structurally constrained. It follows that there is a dialectic of actions and structures, in which actions are partly determined by earlier structures, and later structures are produced by earlier actions.

Of course, any general acceptance of such a standpoint is still far away, and perhaps not easy to come by. But in the pluralist panorama of contemporary sociology, historical orientation is clearly on the ascendance. The scope and rapidity of this paradigmatic shift may be judged by comparing some opinions. In 1968, K. Erikson despaired: "Sociology in the US continues to lack historical focus... Most of what passes for sociological research in this country is not informed by much in the way of a historical perspective" (Erikson 1971:61). Twelve years later, K. Burke declared: "Historical sociology is now a stream" (Burke 1980:28). A year later, C. Tilly noted: "Some of America's best sociological talent is going into historical studies" (Tilly 1981:43). And in 1984, T. Skockpol proclaimed "a golden period of historical sociology" and concluded: "By now ... a stream of historical sociology has deepened into a river and spread out into eddies running through all parts of the sociological enterprise" (Skockpol 1984:xii or 356).

In the image of social reality as endowed with historical coefficient, the old dichotomies of continuity and change, statics and dynamics, and synchrony and diachrony are finally overcome. The historical process is seen as agential accomplishment, the accumulated effect of productive and reproductive efforts of human actors, undertaken in the structural conditions shaped by earlier generations. As we have seen, the notion of human agency as the ultimate motor of the process appears quite explicitly in the works of historical sociologists. And even though for them it is of residual interest, overshadowed with the riddle of stability and transformation, their work also contributes to bridging the gap of action and structure. The historical coefficient and the agential coefficient prove to be two complementary or even coextensive characterizations of social reality. The legacy of the theory of agency converges with the inheritance of historical sociology in outlining the contours of the new vision of the social world.

Notes

1. An interesting variant of this theme is to be found in modern structural-functionalism when the responsibility for the change of society (as opposed to changes in society) is ascribed to deviants. But deviance "occurs for sociologically — and that means structurally — unknown and unknowable reasons. It is the bacillus that attacks the system from the dark depths of individual psyche or the nebulous reaches of the outside world" (Dahrendorf 1968:116).
2. It is closely related to another opposition: consensus versus conflict. Society with reigning consensus, harmony, equilibrium has no conceivable, internal causes for change; whereas society permeated with

dissension, conflict and disequilibrium is naturally prone to transform itself. That is why some authors (e.g., Dahrendorf 1968; Rex 1961) link those dimensions and subsume what we call static and dynamic models under more comprehensive categories of consensus models versus conflict models.

3. From within the functionalist camp, the revisionist attempt to incorporate conflict and change was made by Robert Merton, resulting in his innovative dynamic functionalism (Sztompka 1986a).

4. Offering the utopian image par excellence (the vision of the homogeneous, unified, stable, harmonious social world based on liberal-democratic consensus) as the criticism of utopias as such (with their progressive and future-oriented message).

5. Less episodic and more fundamental diagnosis of the essence of postmodern society is suggested by Zygmunt Bauman, who draws a picture of a consumer society, replacing labor-oriented society. In the present phase of capitalism, he believes, "consumer conduct (consumer freedom geared to consumer market) moves steadily into the position of, simultaneously, the cognitive and moral focus of life, integrative bond of society, and the focus of systemic management" (Bauman 1989:137). This new social system must be grasped by means of new sociological theory and sociology of postmodernity.

6. The normative orientation is revealed in the first sentence of the volume: "Human activity — in all of its extraordinary variety and originality — is organized and governed largely by socially determined rules and rule systems" (Burns and Flam 1987:viii). One wonders (remembering that the authors work in Uppsala, Sweden) if there is some unwitting echo, or self-conscious continuity of an important indigenous development in Swedish sociology, sometimes known as the "Uppsala School," namely the normative ontology of the social world worked out by Torgny Segerstedt (1966): "Every kind of interaction and cooperation must presuppose common norms. It is because we have common norms and symbols with common meaning that we can make predictions" (p. 12).

7. This can be seen already in Giddens's emphasis on institutional time, the recursive nature of social life, and his explicit claim that "The theory of structuration ... rejects any differentiation of synchrony and diachrony or statics and dynamics" (Giddens 1979:69). We found some hints in this direction Burns and Flam's theory of rule systems. It is even more pronounced in Archer's notion of sequential morphogenetic cycles, operating at different time intervals (Archer 1986, 1988) and her recent account of the theory of morphogenesis as founded on two principles: the dualism of structures and actions, and sequentiality of their interaction: "the morphogenetic perspective is not only dualistic but sequential, dealing in endless cycles of structural conditioning/so-

cial interaction/structural elaboration — thus unravelling the dialectical interplay between structure and action" (Archer 1985:61).

8. The complex and ambivalent status of Marx's position requires more discussion. Here, let me just back my choice of Marx by the opinion of an informed commentator: "If you want to observe the coalescence of historical perception with theoretical penetration, you can do no better than the work of Karl Marx" (Tilly 1984b:642).

9. To give just a few examples: R. K. Merton traces the origins of experimental science in seventeenth-century England (1970 [1938]), N. J. Smelser describes the evolution of the cotton industry in Britain at the threshold of the modern era (1959); S. N. Eisenstadt analyzes political systems of ancient, centralized empires (1963); S. M. Lipset reconstructs the historical genealogy of the American nation (1967).

10. The most common procedure is the inductive and comparative study of selected historical cases, seeking for the common mechanism of social processes. For example B. Moore traces the mechanisms of peasant rebellions and bourgeois revolutions in France, the United States, China and Japan searching for the factors determining various scenarios of political development in the post-feudal area: democratic, fascist or communist (Moore 1966). C. Tilly studies the cases of social movements and collective protest in the "rebellious century" of 1830–1930, particularly in France, England and Italy, building on that basis an original theory of collective action (Tilly et al. 1975; Tilly 1978). T. Skockpol produces a comparative account of French, Russian and Chinese revolutions, suggesting a common political mechanism operating in all cases (Skockpol 1979). M. Mann produces a comprehensive account of the sources and origins of power in human societies, from Neolithic times, through ancient Near East civilizations, the classical Mediterranean age, and medieval Europe, to the Industrial Revolution in England (Mann 1986), and promises to carry this narrative on to the contemporary epoch, building a generalized model and theory of power on the basis of this extensive material.

11. I will discuss only those contributions which come from sociologists. The tendency toward reconciliation or integration of sociology and history has also originated in theoretical history, especially in the French school of "Annales" (e.g., Braudel 1980), and various branches of social history. Historians of this orientation often arrive at similar ontological images of society as historical sociologists. Emphasis on the processual, constructed, historical nature of society is also found in several contemporary philosophers (e.g., Bashkar 1986).

12. Contemporary commentators give a special name of "figurational sociology" to his contribution (see special issue of *Theory, Culture and Society* [4(2–3), 1987] devoted to his work), and he was awarded with two most prestigious academic prizes: the Adorno Prize in 1977 and the Premio Europeo Amalfi in 1988.

Bibliography

Abrams, P. (1982). *Historical Sociology*. Ithaca: Cornell University Press.

Alexander, J. C. (1988). *Action and Its Environments*. New York: Columbia University Press.

Antonio, R. J., and Piran P. (1978). Historicity and the poverty of empiricism. Uppsala IXth World Congress of Sociology (mimeographed).

Archer, M. S. (1985). "Structuration Versus Morphogenesis." In: *Macro-Sociological Theory*, eds. S. N. Eisenstadt and H. J. Helle, Vol. 1, pp. 55–88. London: Sage.

_____ (1988). *Culture and Agency*. Cambridge: Cambridge University Press.

_____ (1989). The morphogenesis of social agency. Uppsala: SCASSS (Swedish Collegium for Advanced Studies in the Social Sciences) (mimeographed).

Arnason, J. (1987). "Figurational Sociology as a Counter-Paradigm." In: *Theory, Culture & Society* 4(2–3):429–456.

Bauman, Z. (1989). "Sociological Responses to Postmodernity." In: *Moderno e Postmoderno*, eds. C. Mongardini and M. L. Maniscalco, pp. 127–152. Rome: Bulzoni.

Baumgartner, T., W. Buckley, T. R. Burns, and P. Schuster (1976). "Metapower and the Structuring of Social Hierarchies." In: *Power and Control*, eds. T. R. Burns and W. Buckley, pp. 215–288. Beverly Hills: Sage.

Breed, W. (1971). *The Self-Guiding Society*. New York: Free Press.

Buckley, W. (1967). *Sociology and Modern Systems Theory*. Englewood Cliffs: Prentice Hall.

Burke, P. (1980). *Sociology and History*. London: Allen and Unwin.

Burns, T. R., and Flam, H. (1987). *The Shaping of Social Organization*. Beverly Hills: Sage.

Chazel, F. (1988). "Sociology: From Structuralist Determinism to Methodological Individualism." In: *Contemporary France: A Review of Interdisciplinary Studies*, eds. J. Howorth, and G. Ross, Vol. 2, pp. 187–202. London: Pinter Publishers.

Collins, R. (1986). "Is 1980s Sociology in the Doldrums?" *American Journal of Sociology* 91:1336–1355.

Crozier, M., and Friedberg, E. (1982). *Czlowiek i system: ograniczenia dzialania zespolowego* (Man and System: The Limits of Collective Action). Warsaw: Państwowe Wydawnictwo Ekonomiczne.

Dahrendorf, R. (1959). *Class and Class Conflict in Industrial Society*. Stanford: Stanford University Press.

──────────── (1968). *Essays in the Theory of Society*. Stanford: Stanford University Press.

──────────── (1979). *Life Chances*. Chicago: University of Chicago Press.

──────────── (1980). "On Representative Activities." In: *Science and Social Structure: A Festschrift for Robert K. Merton*, ed. T. F. Gieryn, pp. 15–17. New York: New York Academy of Sciences.

Elias, N. (1978). *What is Sociology?* London: Hutchinson.

──────────── (1982). *The Civilizing Process*, Vols. 1 and 2. Oxford: Basil Blackwell.

──────────── (1987). "The Retreat of Sociologists into the Present." *Theory, Culture & Society* 4(2–3):223–248.

Erikson, K. T. (1971). "Sociology and the Historical Perspective." In: *The Sociology of the Future*, eds. W. Bell and J. A. Mau. New York: Russell Sage.

Etzioni, A. (1968). *Active Society*. New York: Free Press.

Fukuyama, F. (1989). "The End of History?" *The National Interest*, Summer 1989, pp. 3–18.

Giddens, A. (1979). *Central Problems in Social Theory*. London: Macmillan.

──────────── (1984). *The Constitution of Society*. Cambridge: Polity Press.

Goudsblom, J. (1987). "The Sociology of Norbert Elias: Its Resonance and Significance." *Theory Culture & Society* 4(2–3):323–338.

Homans, G. C. (1971). "Bringing Men Back." In: *Institutions and Social Exchange*, eds. H. Turk and R. L. Simpson, pp. 102–116. Indianapolis: Bobbs-Merrill.

Kuhn, T. S. (1970). *The Structure of Scientific Revolutions*. Chicago: University of Chicago Press.

Lloyd, C. [1986] (1988). *Explanation in Social History*. Oxford: Basil Blackwell.

Mandelbaum, M. (1948). "A Critique of Philosophies of History." *Journal of Philosophy* 45:365–378.

Merton, R. K. (1976). "The Unanticipated Consequences of Social Action." In: *Sociological Ambivalence*, R. K. Merton, pp. 145–155. New York: Free Press.

Mills, C. W. (1959). *Sociological Imagination.* New York: Oxford University Press.

Mongardini, Carlo (1990). "The Decadence of Modernity: The Delusions of Progress and the Search for Historical Consciousness." In: *Rethinking Progress*, eds. J. Alexander and P. Sztompka, pp. 53–66. London: Unwin & Hyman.

Nisbet, R. (1969). *Social Change and History.* New York: Oxford University Press.

_____ (1970). "Developmentalism: A Critical Analysis." In: *Theoretical Sociology*, eds. J. C. McKinney and E. A. Tiryakian, pp. 167–204. New York: Appleton-Century-Crofts.

Rex, J. (1969). *Key Issues in Sociological Theory.* London: Routledge & Kegan Paul.

Ritzer, G. (1989). Agency-Structure and Micro-Macro Syntheses: Consensus in Contemporary Theorizing? Uppsala: SCASSS (Swedish Collegium for Advanced Studies in the Social Sciences) (mimeographed).

Skockpol, T. (Ed.) (1984). *Vision and Method in Historical Sociology.* Cambridge: Cambridge University Press.

Sztompka, P. (1974). *System and Function.* New York: Academic Press.

_____ (1986). "The Renaissance of Historical Orientation in Sociology." *International Sociology* 1(3):321–337.

_____ (1987). "Social Movements: Structures in Statu Nascendi." *Polish Sociological Bulletin*, No. 2, pp. 5–26.

Tilly, C. (1978). *From Mobilization to Revolution.* Reading, MA: Addison-Wesley.

_____ (1981). *As Sociology Meets History.* New York: Academic Press.

_____ (1984). *Big Structures, Large Processes, Huge Comparisons.* New York: Russell Sage Foundation.

Touraine, A. (1977). *The Self-Production of Society.* Chicago: University of Chicago Press.

_____ (1981). *The Voice and the Eye.* Cambridge: Cambridge University Press.

_____ (1984). *Le retour de l'acteur.* Paris: Fayard.

_____ (1985). "Social Movements and Social Change." in: *The Challenge of Social Change*, ed. Orlando Fals Borda, pp. 77–92. London: Sage.

Wrong, Dennis (1961). "The Oversocialized Conception of Man in Modern Sociology." *American Sociological Review*, No. 2, pp. 183–193.

II.

Divergent Perspectives on Human Agency in Classical and Contemporary Social Theory

Chapter THREE

The Double Representation of the Actor in Theoretical Tradition: Durkheim and Weber

Elisa P. Reis

INTRODUCTION

This article discusses the images of a human being in Weberian and Durkheimian sociology as paradigmatic expressions of an inherent sociological duality. I have approached the topic from the understanding that unlike both economics, which postulates *homo oeconomicus* solely as a maximizer of utilities, and psychology, which postulates *homo psychologicus* as a bearer of volitions, sociology is characterized by its dual image of the prototypical actor.

Why have I selected Durkheim and Weber from among the classics? In my view, these two authors more than any other are prime exemplars within sociology. Their viewpoints, in many respects in opposition to each other, provide us with an opportunity to dramatize the constitutive duality of social theory insofar as their respective images of the sociological actor run parallel. Moreover, I must admit that I cannot resist the temptation of creating a hypothetical dialogue between Weber and Durkheim — something that fuels the imaginations of many of those interested in the classics of sociology.[1]

Durkheim's presupposition concerning the logical and moral precedence of the collective over the individual and Weber's individualistic analytical perspective serve as useful tools in highlighting the two constitutive imageries found in the universe of sociology — images that firmly resist any effort at a synthesis.

Section 1 deals with Durkheim's sociology and section 2, with Weber's. Given my limited objective of focusing on typical representations of the actor, I have deliberately simplified both authors' perspectives with the goal of sharpening the contrast between their two points of view. Section 3 comments on subsequent developments in both of these theoretical traditions and calls attention to the persistent duality found within this discipline.

Before delving into the discussion itself, a few preliminary remarks: To begin with, it is important to recall that, insofar as the preponderance of economic logic becomes incontestable as an ideology, as a socially widespread value or belief, the entire question of the artificially created "images of man" devised by the different social sciences also becomes problematic.[2] And insofar as economic logic becomes the "patroness of reason," it would seem as if the different *homines* typified by the different social sciences behaved analogically or in reflex to *homo oeconomicus*. Thus we find psychoanalysis, for example, speaking of the "economy of emotions."

The economism that permeates our whole way of thinking tends to impose the abstraction *homo oeconomicus* as a reference point for the most varied disciplines. All branches of social science are seen as dealing with maximizing individuals — only the nature of the maximized end varies. The archetypal man would be one and the same: the possessive, egoistical individual who, in his eagerness to satiate his passions, acts in a utilitarian manner. Even when the action appears disciplined and governed by contractual clauses, the contract appears solely as an instrument of the individual's self-interested, sovereign will.

Indeed, the sociology that was born in the nineteenth century was to a certain extent a reaction to the imperialism of economic thought then being consolidated. But it also emerged as a reaction to the major transformations taking place in the eighteenth and nineteenth centuries — as a critical reflection on the living conditions and environment of *homo oeconomicus*. In opposition to the ironclad logic of maximizing individualistic behavior, sociology affirms the existence of a collective reference point inseparable from the individual himself. The basic idea is that there exists something beyond our individual motivations, something that shapes and gives meaning to these motivations.

It would, however, be wrong to think of sociology as only a conservative reaction to the major transformations of the eighteenth and nineteenth centuries; it is also the fruit of these transformations, and as the offspring of Enlightenment places its reliance on progress. It is nevertheless important to bear in mind that as a discipline, sociology emerged as an alternative to the stylization of *homo oeconomicus*. Restoring the community (which is perceived as dichotomous to society) to a position of high esteem it accentuates solidaristic values and the collective motivations that transcend egoistical designs.[3]

In short, Durkheimian man and Weberian man — to be examined shortly — can be seen as twin brothers born of a difficult marriage between passion and compassion. These brothers affirm their identities through reciprocal oppositions, and their ancestors date back to Hobbes and Rousseau.[4] Living with a double representation of human agency, sociology seems to remain a captive of its original dilemma. That is to say, the idealization of a pervasive solidarism threatened by market individualization and the idealization of the emancipatory potentialities of individualization itself lie at the core of the genuine ambiguity that characterizes *homo sociologicus*.

DURKHEIM'S PERSPECTIVE

From Durkheim's point of view, society takes logical precedence over the individual. The self-perception of the individual as such is a historical result of the evolution of society. For Durkheim, individualism is the religion of modern society.[5] And religion in turn constitutes a "sanctified" representation of society itself. His analysis of the elementary forms of religion shows us that when primitive tribes represent themselves as plants or animals, they are creating a totemic identity that symbolizes the group, or collectivity.[6]

It would at first seem that Durkheim's sociological man is an entity propelled by reflexes, an actor who conforms entirely to the determinations of the social. This is indeed one of the recurrent interpretations of his works, one that considers Durkheim to be a strict determinist who sees social actors as being shaped exclusively by the whole of which they are part.[7] Durkheim's sharp, polemic style and his concern in rigidly defining the borders of sociology lend themselves easily to this type of interpretation.

While Durkheim may insist on distinguishing between individual and collective factors in order to preserve sociology's identity, he is nonetheless mindful of the tight relation between these factors — however much his sociological fervor might have led him into confusions and ambiguities in characterizing sociological man. As Lukes observes, in concentrating exclusively "on the impact of social conditions on individuals rather than the ways individuals perceive, interpret and respond to social conditions, [Durkheim was led] to leave inexplicit and unexamined the social-psychological assumptions on which his theories rested."[8]

More detailed, comprehensive interpretations of Durkheim's works, such as those offered by Lukes, allow us not only to map out the analytical assumptions that underlie his definition of the sociological actor but also to detect the impasses and possible contradictions contained in his theoretical construction. Although Durkheim vehemently refuses to accept individualistic premises of analysis, he does recognize an intrinsically collective dimension within the individual. His discussion of human nature stresses its constitutive dualism: human nature is at the same time sensual and moral, sensorial and conceptual, egoistical and solidaristic.[9] Faithful to his dichotomous model of reasoning, Durkheim identifies the second term of each pair with the society inscribed in individual conscience.

Not that Durkheim denies the egoistic, utilitarian dimension of the individual — but his purpose is rather to demonstrate the logical and moral precedence of the collective, solidaristic dimension. Society is a moral universe, a reality distinct from and superior to a mere summation of the individuals who comprise it. One of the basic questions that Durkheim poses is how we might resolve the problem of social order. Precisely put, his question is: How is a contract possible between egoistical, possessive actors? From his point of view, this contract — that is, the establishment of order — is only feasible because individuals have always shared a common repository of beliefs and sentiments that makes it possible to agree on the rules of the game.

It is quite clear that Durkheim-inspired sociology is part of the collectivist methodological tradition; his sociological actor is someone whose conscience is not only informed but also shaped by society. The theoretical and historical genesis of the individual as a maximizer of utilities is thus a product of the evolution of society. Looked at from this angle, we can see that men and women gained conscience of their individuality and their capacity for free will because society allowed them to do so as it became more and more complex and diversified, thereby stimulating functional specialization and, concomitantly, the development of new forms of solidarity.[10]

Once society elects the individual as its supreme value, the defense of individualism becomes a moral imperative. It is here that Durkheim finds justification for his endeavor to reconcile methodological collectivism and ethical individualism. While it may be true that his methodological rules exacerbate collective realism,[11] it is also true that in one of his few attempts to defend social realism from its critics, Durkheim, with his usual incisiveness, underscores the following:

> In general, we hold that sociology has not completely achieved its task so long as it has not penetrated into the mind (*le for intérieur*) of the individual in order to relate the institutions it seeks to explain to their psychological conditions. In truth — and this is doubtless what has given rise to the misunderstanding in question — man is for us less a point of departure than a point of arrival. We do not begin by postulating a certain conception of human nature so as to deduce from it a sociology: it is rather from sociology that we seek an increasing understanding of humanity.[12]

Durkheim's defense of the individualist morality that characterizes modern *conscience collective* is just as incisive as the following passage on organic solidarity illustrates:

> If, moreover, we remember that the collective conscience is becoming more and more a cult of the individual, we shall see that what characterizes the morality of organized societies, compared to that of segmental societies, is that there is something more human, therefore more rational, about them. It does not direct our activities to ends which do not immediately concern us; it does not make us servants of ideal powers of a nature other than our own, which follow their directions without occupying themselves with the interests of men. It only asks that we be thoughtful of our fellows and that we be just, that we fulfill our duty, that we work at the function we can best execute, and receive the just reward for our services.[13]

From Durkheim's point of view, the phenomenon of functional specialization is of interest to sociology not as an economic division of functions but as a social division of labor, as a socially generated phenomenon that promotes a specific form of sociability. It is also worth noting that while in classical economics the well-being of each guarantees the well-being of all, in Durkheim's sociology things are different: it is because society as a whole presupposes increasing specialization — due to the demographic and moral volume and density — that men move progressively toward specialization. It is through the social division of labor that men discover the advantages that specialization offers to all and consequently to each one. Thus, the very notion that the human personality can be developed through the creative activity of an individual performing a specialized vocation is a consequence of transformations in the basic forms of sociability.

Recapitulating: with Durkheim it is a question of proving that there exists a reality *sui generis* (the social) that cannot be reduced to social or individual psychological foundations. It is society that creates individuals — economic men who have not always existed but who are themselves the result of the development of life in society.

As far as psychology, Durkheim contends that in focusing on the identification of attributes common to all consciences this discipline cannot hope to explain social variations. Sociology's problem lies in identifying just how society acts on our consciences so as to attune them to the institutions that express them.[14] As far as economics, Durkheim's stance is often taken from his critique of utilitarianism undertaken in *The Division of Labor in Society*.

Durkheim would later be more specific in defining the nature of economic phenomena, during a discussion at a meeting of the Societe d'Economie Politique. At that time (1908), he emphasized that:

> The only primacy correctly attributable to economic factors resulted from those which "profoundly affect the way in which a population is distributed, its density, the form of human groups, and thereby often exercise a profound influence on the various states of opinion."[15]

Furthermore, Durkheim stated that the statute of political economy is no different from that of other social sciences: it is likewise a science of culture. Or, in his own words, economics also deals with "ideas" and "opinions." His argument was that "the value of things depends not only on their objective properties but also on opinions about these. For example, religious opinion or changes in taste could affect the exchange value of certain goods."[16] Just like social facts, economic facts can be considered a question of opinion, which is not to imply that they do not lend themselves to the formulation of generalities and laws.[17]

WEBER'S PERSPECTIVE

What horizons does Weberian sociology set before us? What image of man does it unfold? To begin with, what I find both curious and attractive about Weber is that he offers a critical reflection on the "imperialism" of economicism without renouncing to the atomized, individualized and egoistical view of social agents. Based on extremely rigorous logic and on creative reasoning, Weber generalizes the rudimentary psychology of *homo oeconomicus* while at the same time condemning economic motivation to limited territory, to the confines of just one of the many analytical dimensions into which we can categorize the action of individuals.[18]

The truth of the matter is that the Weberian *homo sociologicus* is analogous to *homo oeconomicus*. He is one of the possible analytical profiles of the atomized individual, produced by the same rationalization movement that gave birth to modern science, to capitalism and to the typification of the rational individual. What singularizes Weber's *homo sociologicus* is that the actions and decisions of this prototype are governed by the meaning he attaches to his actions and to the actions of others, as well as by his capacity to display empathy and by his very capacity to attach meaning. Social man is endowed with meaningful behavior. In the words of Weber:

> Sociology (in the sense in which this highly ambiguous word is used here) is a science concerning itself with the interpretive understanding of social action and thereby with a causal explanation of its course and consequences. We shall speak of "action" insofar as the acting individual attaches a subjective meaning to his behavior — be it overt or covert, omission or acquiescence. Action is "social" insofar as its subjective meaning takes account of the behavior of others and is thereby oriented in its course.[19]

Sociology aims at causal explanations, at the establishment of relations between concepts, and at the formulation of generalizations. But in historical-cultural sciences, the notion of causality is always partial and probabilistic; any explanations developed are always relative to a certain simplification, as informed by a given disciplinary angle and by the investigator's analytical assumptions. More importantly, the sociological explanation is grounded on the possibility of identifying the probabilities of individual actions based on the interpretive understanding.

The universe of *homo sociologicus* is divided into analytical slices: economic, political, or religious motivations or ideals in general are equally detectable in the behavior of individuals, while the disciplinary question is no more than a strategic tool useful to scientific activity and devoid of any claim to logical or ontological precedence.

> It is not the "actual" interconnections of "things" but the *conceptual* interconnections of *problems* which define the scope of the various sciences. A new "science" emerges where new problems are pursued with new methods and truths are thereby discovered which open up significant new points of view.[20]

Like Durkheim's *homo sociologicus*, the Weberian model is also to some extent a critical vision of *homo oeconomicus*. But while for Durkheim the individual is a creation of society — this entity that shapes individual conscience — for Weber it is the individual himself who is held responsible before history for his acts; individuals endowed with a conscience respond for the consequences of their passions, choices and actions.[21]

For Weber, the collectivity is not a reality in itself. Structures and institutions are realities fashioned by men, who attach meaning to them, and collective concepts only become intelligible through significant relations between individual behaviors.[22] In an incisive style reminiscent of Durkheim, Weber was to write:

> If I have become a sociologist (according to my letter of accreditation), it is mainly in order to exorcise the specter of collectivist conceptions which still lingers among us. In other words, sociology itself can only proceed from the actions of one or more separate individuals and must therefore adopt strictly individualistic methods.[23]

But Weber makes it clear that adopting a methodological approach centered on the individual does not entail any commitment to an individualistic value system. As he clarifies:

> Even a socialist economy would have to be understood sociologically in exactly the same kind of "individualistic" terms; that is, in terms of the action of individuals, the type of officials found in it, as would be the case with a system of free exchange analyzed in terms of the theory of marginal utility or a "better," but in this respect similar theory.[24]

Weber's fundamental assumption is always the individual endowed with volition, who chooses between alternative actions circumscribed by particular historical-structural conditions. In a certain sense, it does not matter that this individual — the bearer of a conscience, of volition, of freedom of choice, and of responsibility — is a historical-social product. Weber would say that science is likewise a historical-social product. If I need rationality to develop science and if the process of rationalization is what opens the way for the advent of scientific knowledge, it follows that I also need to presuppose the existence of a rational individual to exercise scientific thinking. Everything that I explain, including irrationality, I explain thanks to my reliance on the rational as a reference point. This is the basic assumption that allows us to elaborate ideal types — analytical instruments that can be viewed as utopian rationalizations of the phenomenon to be examined.[25]

Weber does not underestimate the affinity between the modern rational individual and the typological blueprint of *homo oeconomicus*. However, his critical step here is to destroy the illusion that rationality and rational economic behavior are one and the same thing. What we can deduce from his criticism of economicism (and, in fact, his criticism of any and all unicausal explanations) is that economic rationality is one of the possible logical modalities of rationality. In discussing the "economic point of view," he states:

> The justification of the one-sided analysis of cultural reality from specific "points of view" — in our case with respect to its economic conditioning — emerges purely as a technical expedient from the fact that training in the observation of the effects of qualitatively similar categories of causes and the repeated utilization of the same scheme of concepts and hypotheses (begrifflich-methodischen Apparates) offers all the advantages of the division of labor. It is free of the charge of arbitrariness to the extent that it is successful in producing insights into interconnections which have been shown to be valuable for the causal explanation of concrete historical events. However — the "one-sidedness" and the unreality of the purely economic interpretation of history is in general only a special case of a principle which is generally valid for the scientific knowledge of cultural reality.[26]

The maximization of political power, or of social prestige, likewise sheds light on individual motivations: "Interests, material as well as ideal, not ideas directly control action. But world images which are the product of ideas, have often served as the channels along which action is moved by the dynamics of interests."[27] Although it should be recognized that historically we are witnessing the primacy of economic interests in ordering social life, this primacy should be understood as a sociocultural product of the capitalism that emerged in the West and imposed itself on the rest of the world.[28]

Weber removes the rationalizing veil masking the world in which we live when he differentiates the notion of interest from the world of scarcity and material needs; in his approach, ideal interests are thoroughly valid.[29] His criticisms of unicausal explanations, his recognition of a constitutive tension between idealism and materialism, between action and structural determination[30] attest to an anti-totalizing perception of the historical-cultural sciences, at the same time that they preserve individualism as a fertile analytical tool for understanding individuals and collectivities.

CONFRONTATION AND CONCLUSION

Undeniably, both Durkheim's and Weber's points of view are of utmost usefulness. Albeit tense and problematic, a meeting of the two is at the same time rich and provocative, and does not necessarily require us to postulate the harmonization of their disagreements and contradictions. Both the Weberian social actor as well as Durkheim's sociological man have a long way to go before their analytical fecundity is exhausted, and it is easy to prove the continued relevance of these two sociological traditions.

It is interesting to note that the Durkheimian issue has found some common ground with Polanyi's thesis concerning the utopian character of the market society. According to Polanyi, the utopia of a sovereign market — the ideological construction of *homo oeconomicus* — constitutes a concrete threat to the preservation of the social fabric. The entire discussion presented in *The Great Transformation* defends the argument that society (the social whole) possesses self-protective mechanisms.[31] These mechanisms act as antidotes to the destructive impetus of market utopia, a utopia that denaturalizes the land (the epitome of nature) and labor (man's natural activity), turning these into commodities.

From Polanyi's point of view, it is as if there were an "invisible hand of society" that in the final analysis guarantees the continuity of an organic whole (the social fabric), which is a manifestation of an amalgam of interests. In short, it is a self-regulating society that is "natural," while a self-regulating market — the paradise of the egoistical individual — is a piece of fiction, a deleterious utopia that endangers the life of society.

Like Durkheim, Polanyi speaks of sociological individuals, in the plural and not in the singular, but this logical construction is just as orthodox as *homo oeconomicus*. In other words, in both Durkheim and Polanyi, the theoretical statute of a collective subject is as fundamental and irreducible as that of the individual motivated by the egoistical appetites of economics. While in the final analysis economic man guides himself by a set of quite simple, elementary psychological motivations, the sociological man of organicist inspiration does not guide himself, strictly speaking, but instead is guided by a collective reality that informs individual volitions and passions.

In opposition to the imperialism of economicism, or even of psychologism, this theoretical approach affirms the primacy of the social explanation. The very construction of the abstraction *economic man*, and its penetration into the modern collective imagery, can be explained as a social product.

As stated previously, logical primacy is awarded to the organic social whole, which evolves toward specializations of function, of knowledge, of human disciplinary models, as if it were possible to abstract out the subject, who is always a composite or, more precisely, an indivisible entity encompassing the economic, the social, the political and the psychological. Strictly speaking, it is sociability that lends unity and coherence to this whole and in fact dictates the abstract, artificial divisions that become ever more sharply accentuated with the march of history. Primitive men and women were not fragmented into analytical dimensions, nor were religion, philosophy and science separated from each other.[32]

To synthesize this line in sociological tradition: natural man is social man. In opposition to the imperialism of economicism, an imperialism of sociability is proposed. What we see here is an obvious idealization of society accompanied by a minimization of individual volition and free will, which historically even become predominant, as an unequivocal result of the evolution of sociability itself.

We must ask ourselves how seriously we should take a theoretical proposal that does not coincide with the way we perceive the organized life in which we take part. What is the value of this kind of viewpoint in a world organized according to the primacy of the market? In my opinion, this approach is extremely provocative insofar as it allows us to transcend the ironclad logic of the status quo and opens our minds to a critical perception of the economicist world engulfing us. This is the source of creativity and richness embedded in an organic, collectivist sociological perspective.

Back when sociology was first being constituted as a science, this approach displayed "conservative" tendencies — a reaction to the individualist-economicist ideology that guided the affirmation of the market as the main organizer of social life. It is thus curious to note that it has taken on critical-emancipatory connotations in today's world, where the "naturalness" of the market and the primacy of material interests seem uncontestable. To illustrate, we need only remember that the postulation of a social whole, of an amalgamated social fabric, still persists in socialist-type proposals as well as in neo-Marxist or progressive critiques of the modern welfare state.[33]

It is here that the time-honored defense of the primacy of the social over individual motivations can be revolutionary, as it calls our attention to the historical-cultural character of the generalizations established by social sciences and thereby returns us to a recognition of the specificity of these sciences, of their continuous self-questioning and their at once heroic and humble acceptance of perpetual renewal and inevitable caducity. The question of the provisionalness of knowledge transports us to the other theoretical perspective mentioned above — the Weberian perspective.

From Weber's point of view, it is not society that is a reality *sui generis* but rather the status of sociocultural sciences. Sociology concerns itself with the meanings that men and women attach to their actions, and this condemns social sciences to perpetual "immaturity," to the realm of "eternal youth," to use Weber's own terms.[34]

As mentioned earlier, in this second exemplary conception of sociology it is the agent who confers meaning to social facts. Even if we take into account that the objects to which he attaches meaning exercise a kind of "coercion" over this actor (to use Durkheim's expression), it is still valid to affirm that *homo sociologicus* obtains the raw material to be used in attaching meaning from the very parameters established by structural and supra-structural conditioning.

The Weberian conception of agency is, on the one hand, quite similar to the version of *homo oeconomicus* universalized and naturalized by the economicist ideology that pervades our modern world; on the other hand, in making the "naturalness" and "generality" of *homo oeconomicus* into sociocultural products, the Weberian tradition is sociologically relativizing economicism, in much the same way that Durkheim relativizes individualism. Nonetheless, rather than affirming the primacy of an organic whole responsible for sociability, *à la* Durkheim, the Weberian relativization simply postulates the ineludible perspectivism of all knowledge. The same human agency that holds a monopoly over the attachment of meaning is condemned to exercise this prerogative in a fragmentary form — since otherwise the complex, unending *real* is made indomitable to human understanding.

Weberian sociology is fully consonant with the experience of fragmentation typical of the contemporary world, something which partially explains the persistent attractiveness of this theoretical line. Equally in tune with modernity is Weberian sociology's recognition of the provisional, probabilistic nature of the scientific knowledge of sociocultural reality. Lastly, in calling attention to the fact that the agent is the sole instance capable of experiencing the impact of structural and institutional constraints, this analytical tradition awards subjectivity and intersubjectivity a central role — a role that has been preserved in a wide number of the most important approaches in contemporary sociology.

In order to illustrate this point, we should remember that the individualistic perspective, resting on the question of meaningful, intersubjective behavior, provides the foundation for what is most affirmative in current critical social thought.[35] At the same time, the sociological tradition based on individualism has inspired one of the most fertile orientations in contemporary social science, to wit, that which explores the analytical potential of rational choice models, and of game theory in particular.[36]

In conclusion, I hope these discussion notes will fulfill their intended role. I would like to believe that aside from presenting a somewhat idiosyncratic compilation of Durkheim's and Weber's nearly secular traditions, something new has been introduced in the dialogue proposed here. Not that I am claiming to have achieved any degree of inventiveness with my observations but simply because a here-and-now discussion of Weber's and Durkheim's formulations engages us in the adventure of contemporaneity. After all, who would dare to contend that the classics of sociology can be read in some kind of primitive purity, as if it were possible to restore, and restrict, their formulations to the universe of yesteryear, abstracting out our own temporality? Who can deny that it is historicity itself that testifies to the inconceivability of cleansing theory of history?

Theoretical and historical challenges walk hand in hand, and along this course sociology remains ever faithful to its duplicity. From Durkheim's lessons, it retains the idea that there is "an elementary manner" to frame the social issue, detectable in all forms of sociological knowledge; a return to past formulations will therefore always be elucidative. From the rich Weberian legacy, sociology reaps its understanding of the eternal youth of the sciences of culture, of their incessant "unfinished-ness." The dilemma between the conservation or renewal of sociological knowledge thus lays bare its purely analytical identity, preserving after all is said and done the richness and complexity of the sociological actor.

Notes

1. See, for example, Tiryakian (1966). Tiryakian failed to observe that Durkheim (1913) makes at least one reference to Weber, as pointed out by Steven Lukes (1975). But Lukes also makes it a point to underscore the curious lack of interest that Durkheim and Weber express in each other's work. Bendix's article (1971) defending the coexistence of two sociologies based on Durkheim and Weber, serves as another good illustration here. See also Monique Hirschhorn (1983).
2. In a suggestive article, Louis Dumont (1983) calls attention to the mutations of the word *valeur* (value) that have occurred in everyday language. This term, which comes from the Latin for vigor, strength, or health, was used to refer to the bravery of warriors (valor) during the Middle Ages; in today's world, *valeur* almost always refers to the capacity of money to measure all things, that is, it alludes to an exchange potential.
3. On the centrality of the dichotomous pair "community-society" in classical sociological thought, see Robert Nisbet (1966).
4. For a confrontation of Rousseau's and Durkheim's points of view, see Durkheim 1960. Focusing on the points of convergence between the two, Wolin (1960:372) affirms that "Durkheim has been the medium, so to speak, by which Rousseau has left his mark on modern social science." Dawe (1978), on the other hand, attempts to approximate Durkheim and Hobbes. It seems to me that Alan Dawe's perception is a consequence of his falling into the utilitarian trap and thus equating the problem of order (recognized as sociology's central problem) to the Hobbesian formulation. For a careful discussion of the convergences and divergences between Rousseau and Durkheim, see Lukes (1975, esp. pp. 283–284). Hobbesian dimensions are most evident both in the centrality of the concepts of "combat," "power" and "domination" in Weber's general sociology as well as in the crucial importance of the monopolization of violence in maintaining a legitimate political order (Weber 1978:3–62).
5. On the cult of individualism as a new form of religion and as the cement of social solidarity in the modern world, see Durkheim (1969: 14–30).
6. Durkheim (1968).
7. For an insightful discussion that logically differentiates the collectivist theoretical presupposition (which it approximates with determinism) from normative and nonrational presuppositions of action, see Alexander (1982a). For a specific discussion of presuppositions concerning (a) the nature of action and (b) the nature of the social order in Durkheim, see the same author (1982b). Alexander perceives a radical discontinuity between the metatheoretical suppositions of the works of

young Durkheim and his final works. While S. Lukes does not defend the idea of a "radical rupture," he does identify a clear shift in emphasis in Durkheim's work, which initially prefers explanations of a determinist-structural character but later moves progressively in the direction of an idealistic approach to explaining social phenomena. As Lukes points out (1975:34–35), Durkheim's sociological realism led him to "reify," or "deify," society — to treat it as a god *ex machina*.

8. Lukes (1975:35). This does not imply that Durkheim had no notion of "human agency." As Nisbet has emphasized, "Those who ascribe to Durkheim a purely passive view of the individual in relation to society have not read him carefully. Always he premises the notion of an active, acting person" (Nisbet 1966:119).
9. Durkheim (1973:149–166).
10. Durkheim (1973).
11. Durkheim (1956).
12. Durkheim (1909:733–758), as cited by Lukes (1975:498–499).
13. Durkheim (1964:407).
14. See Lukes (1975:499).
15. Lukes (1975:500).
16. Lukes (1975:499). Durkheim's affirmation that economic facts share common ground with the facts studied by sociology — for example, morality and religion, insofar as both of these disciplines deal with ideas and opinions — does not invalidate his defense of one sole model of science. Although the nature of their facts may differentiate forms of science, all sciences work with the same principles of causation and with the same notions of regularity and law.
17. Lukes (1975:499).
18. Although when Weber offers the possibility of typifying the motivational dimension of action, he is presupposing the operation of psychological mechanisms, this does not mean that the method of understanding advocated by Weber can be reduced to a psychologism. As Wrong has observed, what Weber's method of internal meaning presupposes is that the actor's goals and evaluations (the subjective meaning) are "efficient causes" of his behavior. There is no psychology of motivation in Weber, who in fact regarded with suspicion a certain tendency towards biological reductionism that marked the psychology of that era. See Wrong (1970:1–76, esp. pp. 22–23) and Weber (1978:18–19).
19. Weber (1978:4).
20. Weber (1949:68).
21. The idea of inalienable individual responsibility, of an ethical commitment, often appears in Weber (e.g., 1946:77–128). On Weber's "existen-

tialist" stance, see Aron, (1967:497–583). See also Wrong (1984:69–81, esp. pp. 77–78).
22. Weber (1978:13); see also Aron (1968, esp. pp. 500–511).
23. Letter from Weber to R. Liefmann, cited in Wrong (1968:92, n. 12).
24. Weber (1978:18).
25. As Aron points out: "Le concept de type idéal se situe au point d'aboutissement de plusieurs des tendances de la pensée wéberiénne. Le type idéal est lié à la notion de compréhension puisque tout type idéal est une organization de rapports intelligibles propres soit à un ensemble historique, soit à une consécution d'événements. D'autre part, le type idéal est lié à ce que est caractéristique de la société et de la science moderne, à savoir le procès de rationalisation. La construction de types idéaux est une expression de l'effort de toutes les disciplines scientifiques pour rendre intelligible la matière en dégageant la rationalité interne, éventuellement même en construisant cette rationalité à partir d'une matière à demi informe. Enfin, le type idéal se rattache aussi à la conception analytique et partielle de le causalité" (Aron (1968:519).
26. Weber (1949:71).
27. Max Weber, apud. Schluchter (1979:15).
28. See Weber 1958:13–31. This "Introduction" which Talcott Parsons included into the English edition of *The Protestant Ethic* was written in 1920 for volume 1 of *Gesammelte Aufsatze zur Religionssoziologie*.
29. See Bendix (1962, esp. chaps. 4 and 8).
30. The complex interaction of structural factors, on the one hand, and attitudes and values, on the other, stands out sharply in Weber's comparison of German and US society in "Capitalism and Rural Society in Germany" (Gerth and Mills 1946:363–385). In my opinion, this plural, complex perception of causality has contributed to the diversity of current interpretations of Weberian sociology. For a good synthesis of the main lines of interpretation on Weber's works, see Alexander (1983:129–130).
31. Polanyi (1957).
32. See Dumont (1970).
33. Offe (1983), for example, returns to Durkheim and Polanyi to discuss the "de-mercantilization" of labor within advanced capitalism.
34. For an incisive argument on the transitoriness and eternal renewal of knowledge within sciences of culture, see Weber (1949:49–112, esp. 104–105).
35. See, for example, Kellner (1985).
36. See, for example, Ordeshook (1986).

Bibliography

Alexander, J. C. (1982a). *Theoretical Logic in Sociology*, Vol. 1: *Positivism, Presuppositions and Current Controversies*. Berkeley: University of California Press.

_____ (1982b). *Theoretical Logic and Sociology*, Vol. 2: *The Antinomies of Classical Thought: Marx and Durkheim*. Berkeley: University of California Press.

_____ (1983). *Theoretical Logic in Sociology*, Vol. 3: *The Classical Attempt at Theoretical Synthesis: Max Weber*. London: Routledge and Kegan Paul.

Aron, R. (1967). *Les Étapes de la Penéee Sociologique*, Paris: Gallimard.

Bendix, R. (1962). *Max Weber, An Intellectual Portrait*, Garden City: Doubleday, Anchor Books.

_____ (1971). "Two Sociological Traditions." In: *Scholarship and Partisanship: Essays on Max Weber*, eds. R. Bendix and Roth, pp. 498–499. Berkeley: University of California Press.

Dawe, A. (1978). "Theories of Social Action." In: *A History of Sociological Analysis*, eds. Bottomore and Nisbet. New York: Basic Books.

Dumont, L. (1970). "Religion, Politics and Society in the Individualistic Universe." In: Proceedings of the Royal Anthropological Institute of Great Britain and Ireland.

_____ (1983). "La Valeur Chez le Moderne et Chez les Autres." *L'Esprit*, No. 7, pp. 3–29.

Durkheim, E. (1912). "Sociologie Religieuse et Théorie de la Connaissance." *Revue de Méthaphysique et de Morale* 17.

_____ (1909). *Les Règles de la Méthode Sociologique*. Paris: Presses Universitaires de France, 13th edition, pp. 733–758.

_____ (1960). *Montesquieu and Rousseau: Forerunners of Sociology*. Ann Arbor: University of Michigan Press.

_____ (1964). *The Division of Labor in Society*. New York: Free Press.

_____ (1968). *Les Formes Élémentaires de la Vie Religieuse*, 5th ed. Paris: Presses Universitaires de France.

_____ (1969). "Individualism and the Intellectuals." *Political Studies* 17:14–30 (translation and notes by S. Lukes).

_____ (1973). "The Dualism of Human Nature and its Social Conditions." In: *Emile Durkheim on Morality and Society*, ed. R. Bellah, pp. 149–166. Chicago: University of Chicago Press.

_____ (1973). *De la Division du Travail Social*, 9th ed. Paris: PUF.

Hirschhorn, M. (1983). "Max Weber et les Durkheimiens, brève histoire d'un rendez-vous manqué." *Revue de L'Institut de Sociologie*, Editions de l'Université de Bruxelles, No. 3–4, pp. 293–310.

Kellner, D. (1985). "Critical Theory, Max Weber, and the Dialectics of Domination." In: *A Weber-Marx Dialogue*, eds. R. Antonio and R. Glassman. Lawrence: University of Kansas Press,.

Lukes, S. (1975). *Emile Durkheim, His Life and Work*, Harmondsworth: Penguin Books.

Nisbet, R. (1966). *The Sociological Tradition*. New York: Basic Books.

_____ (1974). *The Sociology of Emile Durkheim*. New York: Oxford University Press.

Offe, C. (1983). *Contradictions of the Welfare State*. London: Hutchinson.

Ordeshook, P. (1986). *Game Theory and Political Theory*. Cambridge: Cambridge University Press.

Polanyi, K. (1957). *The Great Transformation*. Boston: Beacon Press.

Schluchter, W. (1979). "The Paradox of Rationalization: On the Relationship of Ethics and World." In: *Max Weber's Vision of History: Ethics and Method*, eds. G. Roth and W. Schluchter. Berkeley: University of California Press.

Tiryakian, E. (1966). "A Problem for the Sociology of Knowledge: The Mutual Unawareness of Émile Durkheim and Max Weber." *European Journal of Sociology* 7(2):330–336.

Weber, M. (1946). "Politics as a Vocation." In: *From Max Weber: Essays in Sociology*, eds. Gerth and Mills, pp. 77–128. New York: Oxford University Press.

_____ (1949). "'Objectivity' in Social Science and Social Policy." In: M. Weber, *The Methodology of the Social Sciences*, p. 68. New York: Free Press.

_____ (1958). "Author's Introduction." In: M. Weber, *The Protestant Ethic and the Spirit of Capitalism*, pp. 13–31. New York: Charles Scribner's and Sons

_____ (1978). "Basic Concepts of Sociology." In: *Economy and Society*, eds. G. Roth and C. Wittich, pp. 3–62. Berkeley: University of California Press.

Wolin, S. (1960). *Politics and Vision: Continuity and Innovation in Western Political Thought*. Boston: Little Brown.

Wrong, D. (Ed.) (1970). *Max Weber*. Englewood Cliffs: Prentice-Hall.
_____ (1984). "Marx, Weber, and Contemporary Sociology." In: *Max Weber's Political Sociology*, eds. R. M. Glassman and V. Murvar, pp. 69–81. Westport, CT: Greenwood Press.

Chapter FOUR

Marxism, Post-Marxism, and the Actionalist Turn in Social Theory

Miguel Cainzos

MARXISM, SOCIAL ACTION AND STRUCTURALIST REDUCTIONISM

It is a widespread opinion that one of the weak points of both classical Marxism and its diverse neo-Marxist variants has been their inability to construct a coherent theory of social action and agents, or even consciously to focus on this topic.[1] This failing is held to be reflected in the unstable coexistence of several different conceptions of social actor in Marxist theory. One is a utilitarian conception according to which social actors are rational agents acting strategically in pursuit of goals that are ultimately determined by the structure of their objective interests. Another is a structuralist conception according to which social agents are mere personifications of social relationships, bearers of social roles. A third is a peculiar rationalist conception of the proletariat that attributes to the latter a special capacity, a "higher order" rationality, in virtue of which it is able to rise above its intrasystemic interests and act in accordance with extra- or trans-systemic interests. Finally, a fourth conception is a normativist view of social agents as subject to a cognitive and evaluative universe imposed by the ideological domination of the ruling class; it is this framework of ideas and values that truly configures the agents' actions. The simultaneous presence of these four conceptions of social actor in Marxist social theory — and the absence of any systematic relationship integrating them in a single structure — leads to the application of large doses of pragmatism in the analysis carried out. This is reflected in opportunist resort to mutually contradictory categories that often (as in some instances of the use of "ideology" as "false consciousness") are of purely residual value.

"Classical Marxism" is not unique in suffering from an inability to construct a theory of social action that is both plausible and compatible with the explanatory principles of historical materialism. The problem is shared by the majority of what Anderson referred to as "Western Marxism" and by a large part of what, following Therborn, we may call "social-scientific Marxism" (Anderson 1976; Therborn 1985). This lack of a satisfactory theory of social action is directly linked with one of the recurrently criticized aspects of Marxist theory, its *determinism* and *structuralist reductionism*. According to many critics, Marxism inevitably tends to reduce the diversity of social arenas and dimensions to the sphere of economics, which for Marxism constitutes the essential, basic structure giving rise to other dimensions as effects, manifestations or epiphenomena devoid of their own independent substantivity. In particular, this structuralist reductionism denies autonomy to social practices, which are thought of as the mere execution or expression of the dynamics of the (ultimately economic) system. From this point of view, social agents are just the medium through which the structure exerts its causal efficacy.

If the above criticism is accepted, then the structuralist reductionism attributed to Marxism is perfectly in keeping with Marxism's lack of a systematic theory of social action. On the one hand, the inability to conceive social action in appropriate terms means that its productive, innovative and contingent characteristics go unperceived, so paving the way for the resort to an absolute structure-determining force; while on the other, structuralist reductionism relieves Marxism of the need to construct a theory of social action, which it replaces with the task of identifying the mechanisms by which social agents implement the determinist dictates of the structure. According to this argument, it is just this that gives rise to the diverse conceptions of social agent that coexist in Marxist texts. They constitute a heteroclite repertory of categories which are resorted to pragmatically and opportunistically to explain why the observed course of social development fits — or, more often, fails to fit — the course predicted on the basis of the fundamental properties attributed to the structure of a given social formation. From the critical viewpoint sketched above, Marxist structuralist reductionism and the lack of a consistent, unified Marxist theory of social action would be just two sides of a single coin.

THE ANTIREDUCTIONIST REACTION AND THE TURN TO ACTION IN MARXIST THEORY

The view described in the previous section is not by any means the whole story. It would be difficult to deny that Marxism has always featured reductionist trends and that a deterministic structuralist component looms large in its theoretic tradition. But it is equally true that from its early years there were attempts to counteract this component and reverse such trends to produce a comprehensive, balanced theory in which structure and action were to be integrated as complementary constituent social dimensions. In this respect, the history of Marxist theory has been, under a variety of changing forms, that of a continual tug-of-war between, on the one hand, a leaning towards essentialism, determinism and structuralist reductionism, and, on the other, the attempts to repair or definitely overcome such deformations.[2] These attempts have in some cases led to the opposite extreme, i.e., to the voluntarist assertion of the omnipotence of action. In fact, both strands of thought have cohabited uneasily in the work of the chief Marxist writers, starting with the duality that exists in the writings of Marx himself between a determinist conception of history as the process of development of productive forces (a process shaped by the correspondence or noncorrespondence between relations of production and productive forces) and, on the other hand, the nondeterminist conception of history as an open-ended struggle between social classes. Similar contradictions can easily be found in the works of authors as varied as Rosa Luxemburg, Trotsky or Althusser.

Awareness of the dangers of reductionism and structuralism in Marxist tradition has been especially acute since about the late 1970s, and has given rise to serious attempts to rethink some of the key concepts of this tradition so as to avoid such dangers and lay the foundations for the construction of theories and analytical frameworks capable of harmonizing the various constituent dimensions of society without giving any single one such absolute priority as to annihilate the reality of the others. As part of this movement, Marxist theory has experienced a radical, sweeping turn towards social action, an "actionalist turn." Though developed in a variety of different directions, this movement has as its central characteristic the emphasis laid upon the reality of social action and upon the demolition of the basic assumptions of the structuralist Marxism of the 1960s and early 1970s.

It would be possible, I believe, to show that there is a direct connection between the "actionward" turn of the theory and external circumstances indicative of the failure of objectivist social and political analysis. These circumstances include the definitive demise of the expectations invested in possible revolutionary transformations born of objective historical trends; the rise of the New Right with the acquiescence or active support of social groups to which an objectively transformational historical role had been attributed; the proliferation of new social conflicts, movements, identities and practices that exhibit very diverse origins and aims and are scarcely predictable from their protagonists' positions in the social structure;[3] and the evident crisis of "Fordist accumulation regime," leading to the advent of what some have termed "disorganized capitalism" (Offe 1985; Urry and Lash 1987; see also Hall and Jacques 1989; from a critical viewpoint, see Callinicos 1989, chap. 5; Harvey 1989, Part 2; Bagguleym 1991). Be that as it may, the central concerns of this essay will be the meaning and theoretical scope of the new Marxist emphasis on social action, rather than the social changes that may have brought it about.

A number of preliminary remarks are in order. In the first place, it is clear that it is not only Marxism that has been affected by a reorientation towards social action. In the 1980s, the downfall of the prevailing structuralism of previous decades led to a change in the direction of sociological theory in general, which came under the sway of the "new 'imperialism' of the theories of social action" (Lash and Urry 1985:95; Sztompka 1991:17 ff.). Social action has now been granted such a central role that structure has become "dissolved" within it. In extreme versions, indeed, society itself is "dissolved" in the "social" and the existence of society as a possible object of theory is denied (Laclau 1983:21–24, 1990:89–92; Laclau and Mouffe 1985: 117 ff.; Pérez-Agote 1989:34 ff.). This change of course may perhaps be considered as just one aspect of the more general rise of "postmodernist" culture, or as a theoretic response to the specific features of "postmodernity" (Arditi 1986:198 ff.). In my view, the turn to social action nevertheless has a special meaning for Marxism, because in opposing the structuralist and determinist elements inherent in Marxist theoretic tradition it has questioned some of the constituent postulates of Marxism as a program of social investigation, in particular its theory of the structure of social relations.

The actionward reorientation of Marxist theory has meant the appearance of a wide variety of theories or analytical approaches that, though stemming from controversies that are internal to Marxist tradition (the opposition of reductionism and antireductionism, determinism and nondeterminism, structuralism and theory of praxis), nevertheless make a clear break with this tradition to inaugurate new lines of investigation (generally by cross-fertilization from other traditions, as in the interpretive paradigm, poststructuralism, or the theory of rational choice). In other words, the "actionalist turn" is the starting point of a plurality of post-Marxist theories whose common factors are the recovery of a social dimension — action — that had been more or less buried by Marxist tradition, and the consequent consideration of social action as the site of contradictions and possessor of causal powers hitherto attributed to social structure. This proposition covers not only such explicitly declared post-Marxist positions as that of Laclau and Mouffe, but also certain recent contributions to social theory and analysis that claim to be Marxist (albeit for no apparent reason other than the wish to assert the emotional continuity with an ethical, political and critical tradition linked with — and often indistinguishable from — Marxist theory).[4] I would even go further, and posit the same proposition retrospectively of the "humanist Marxism" that blossomed in the late 1950s and early 1960s (especially in the field of historiography) and which put up continual opposition to the structuralist interpretations and usage of historical materialism (a paradigm of this school is the work of E. P. Thompson). I believe, indeed, that there is a surprising degree of coincidence between the consequences and implications of humanist Marxism and those of certain recent post-Marxist tendencies that ought superficially to be diametrically opposed to it.

The aim of this article is to argue for the above ideas by briefly reviewing three cases in which the turn to social action leads to a break with certain fundamental principles of Marxism as a program of social investigation. The first is the work of Thompson, an author whose influence can be traced throughout the past 30 years; the other two are widely differing variants of the actionward reorientation of the 1980s, one being what I shall term the "textualist" (or "pan-semiological") post-Marxism represented by Laclau and Mouffe, and the other "analytical" post-Marxism, which I shall discuss with reference to Przeworski and occasionally Elster. It is evidently impossible to do justice here to such rich approaches; my intention is merely to draw on them to illustrate the ideas sketched above, and to support the thesis that all these attempts to overcome the shortcomings of classical Marxism, regardless of how important they may be for our understanding of partial aspects of society and for designing new programs of investigation, lead eventually to a paradoxical return to reductionism. Both Thompson and Laclau and Mouffe oppose the structuralist reductionism of classical Marxism with "actionalist" reductionism. The case of analytical post-Marxists is more complex because they are more aware of the duality between structure and action, but I believe that the inability to digest this duality theoretically has led to the coexistence, within a single discursive web, of two contradictory reductionist tendencies, one being an explicit "actionalist" reductionism and the other a covert structural reductionism inherent in the use of rational choice models; this ambivalence will be seen to be rife in the work of Przeworski.

THE HUMANIST MARXISM OF E. P. THOMPSON[5]

For full appreciation of its content, Thompson's conception of history and society, as expounded in *The Poverty of Theory* and applied in his historiographic work, should be seen in context as a struggle against any kind of objectivist approach to social research, including quantitative history, systems sociology and structuralist Marxism. It is no accident that of all Thompson's writings, that containing his most overt proposal of a program for social research is an attempt to reformulate historical materialism and wrest it from monopolization by Althusser's Marxism, which it virulently attacks. For our present purposes, Thompson's ideas may be summarized as follows.

First, social phenomena are radically historical, in the dual senses of taking place in time and of being produced by human action. This postulate emphasizes the instability and continual redefinition of social relations, institutions and identities: society is involved in a never-ending process of totalization-distotalization-retotalization. The epistemological consequence of this thesis is the need to resort to a logic specifically appropriate to the analysis of social reality. This is a historical logic that uses notions whose particularity lies in their being "definitions from within" that embrace the inherent temporality of both their object and knowledge of their object (Thompson 1978:231, 236, 301–302).[6]

Second, the historical social process is structured but open-ended, and its specific forms and interactions are ultimately undetermined.

Third, the basic element of the social process is social action; history is an "unmastered human practice" consisting in the dynamic interaction between social being and social consciousness.

Fourth, what mediates between being and consciousness in this interaction is human experience understood as "the mental and emotional response, whether of an individual or of a social group, to many interrelated events or to many repetitions of the same kind of event"; through consideration of this productive, creative response, "men and women also return as subjects" (Thompson 1978:199, 356).

Fifth, social agents are conceived as subjects capable of knowledge, reflection and deliberation who are faced with, and experience, a certain human and material medium. On the basis of cultural resources inherited from their past history, social actors construct a universe of meaning, define their intentions and preferences, and act, so creating social reality. By reflective, creative elaboration of their experience they are able to reconstitute their consciousness, their received systems of values and the very universe of meaning in which they are immersed (Thompson 1978:362–363, 1977:II:205).

Sixth, the epistemological consequence of the above is that the social or historical researcher's strategy must be to reconstruct and interpret the sense of the entirety of a certain social process or formation from the representations, intentions and culturally configured actions of the agents in the light of the cultural context in which they moved. The idea is thus to move "beyond the particularities of specific experiences to comprehend totality in motion" (Palmer 1981:73).[7]

Central to the above postulates is the *category of experience*, which must fulfill several basic functions for the approach as a whole to be viable. In the first place, it is the main unifying factor of the social whole and the time in which the historical process occurs, and at the same time guarantees the mutual unreducibility of a society's diverse practices and activities. Society and history are unities, as *human* society and history, insofar as they stem and take their meaning from human experience, its cultural elaboration and the action to which the latter gives rise; the various social spheres are aspects of the social formation whose autonomous reality derives precisely from their being *particular* expressions and elaborations of *manifold* human experience. The notion of experience thus serves as the basis for a pluralistic, relational vision of society, one that denies that society be a stable, hierarchical system of instances, subsystems or levels that are all reducible to a primary level *or* linked together in a given fundamental structure. In place of this, Thompson sees the social sphere as a space in which everything is related to everything else, or "present in everything," making history contingent, social identities unstable and social relations practical-dynamic.

Secondly, experience provides the nexus between social being and social consciousness. It is, as it were, the "material substrate" of action. Experience is what guarantees that the practices — and identity — of the actors are not the mere expression of something already determined, nor the random motion of individuals floating in a vacuum, but instead the effects of interaction between action and structure.

Thirdly, the experience of social agents is the touchstone for the validity of their actions, the only point of view from which the latter can be understood and retrospectively evaluated.

The category of experience is thus the basis of Thompson's version of historical materialism. It underlies its humanistic, interpretive, *verstehende* nature in that experience and the subjective elaboration of experience are respectively the stuff that feeds and the mechanism by which social agents carry out the definition of the universe of meaning that constitutes their social reality and whose reconstruction is the job of the social sciences; it underlies its relationalist, pluralistic nature in that experience and action both unify and differentiate the various dimensions of the social universe; and finally, it underlies its assumed materialism in that experience is postulated as the link between objective materiality and the expression of the social subjectivity.

The logical consequence of awarding the concept of experience this central role is that any theoretic flaws in its formulation or use must undermine Thompson's whole analytical program. And in my view this is just the case. Thompson's theoretic approach is unconvincing because his formulation and use of the category of experience are both fundamentally untenable.

His *characterization* of experience is weak for several reasons. In the first place, a number of different senses of "experience" cohabit in his writings, making the concept unstable or even inconsistent. In particular, it is not clear exactly what its status is in relation to the difference between social being and social consciousness.[8] Thompson's attempts to overcome this difficulty by distinguishing between experience as lived (experience I) and experience as perceived (experience II) just complicate the problem. Thompson is unable to provide concepts that clarify the mechanisms by which social being exerts its "pressure" on social consciousness (Thompson 1984:301–317, 277–286; McLennan 1981:126–128).

Secondly, as Perry Anderson (1980) has shown, Thompson confounds two quite different senses of "experience," one the neutral sense of living through certain events or situations, and the other the positive sense referring to the acquisition of knowledge and the modification of self as the consequence of what has been lived through. The resulting confusion between the moral-existential plane and the practical-experiential plane leads ultimately to the conclusion that all action is absolutely valid to the extent that it is the fruit of what the individual, in his or her universe of meaning, has lived through. This conclusion has a variety of undesirable effects. Firstly, it makes the idea of critical social science inviable, since it leaves no room for social practices to be rationally evaluated by reference to criteria that are external to the representations of the agents being studied. Secondly, it leads to extreme evaluative and epistemological relativism. Thirdly, it implies that social agents are perfectly rational beings for whom social relationships are transparent, since it is assumed that for optimal understanding of a social situation, and consequent adoption of a valid course of action, it is sufficient to live through that situation.

The *use* that Thompson is able to make of the category of experience is equally deficient, since it does not in fact perform its declared functions. In practice, its use leads to the total evaporation of any structural determination of human action, and to the reduction of society to a collection of products of the action as instituting the constitutive meaning of social relations. Thus, Thompson's historical materialism, apart from not being, in any clear sense, materialism, ends up as inverted reductionism. For one thing, as many critics have pointed out,[9] there is in Thompson's historical analysis a tendency to a shift upward: economic relations and conflicts are understood in political and cultural terms. Economy is replaced by "moral economy," so that Thompson narrates a culturalist history whose principal objects are power relations and popular resistance, but he never makes clear the connections between this dialectic between power and resistance on the one hand, and the place of its protagonists in the social structure on the other. More crucially, objective relations, situations and events are replaced by experience in its most elementary, neutral sense, i.e., by subjective involvement in an event or situation. To put it another way, the only form of objectivity that is recognized by Thompson emerges from the subject's attribution of meaning on the grounds of experience, so that social relations are reduced to relations of meaning (which are admittedly intersubjective to the extent that meaning is established in a process involving the mutual interaction of the social agents). Thus Thompson's use of the category of experience leads to social being's disintegrating in experience, and hence to the dialectic between social being and social consciousness being replaced by the interaction between experience and consciousness, i.e., between the subjectivity's experiential and cultural aspects.

Depriving the social universe of its objective status means relinquishing the concept of social structure. Thompson in fact renounces historical materialism as a particular theory of social relations. In its place he puts not an alternative theory, but an eclectic relational interactionism, abstaining from the formulation of any kind of hypothesis concerning the probable ways of structuration of society or the regular patterns of historical development. Instead of these kind of hypotheses, he offers elusive formulae amounting to "the reduction of history to a kaleidoscope of independent variables" (Kiernan 1987:107). The final result is blatant empiricism of a peculiar kind: *verstehende* empiricism.

To sum up, humanism, an interpretive orientation, eclectic relationism and empiricism are all interwoven components of Thompson's approach; together they make for an actionalist reductionism that in actual practice produces culturalist analyses due to the subreptitious introduction of unjustified premises.[10]

THE TEXTUALIST POST-MARXISM OF LACLAU AND MOUFFE

Ernesto Laclau and Chantal Mouffe set out from a position diametrically opposed to Thompson's. Whereas Thompson attempts to offer a humanist alternative to structuralism, Laclau and Mouffe's approach can be regarded as to some extent arising from within structuralist Marxism itself. Their starting point is the recognition that in Althusser's Marxism reductionist and essentialist elements (such as the concepts of "structural causality" and "determination in the last instance by the economy") coexist with profoundly antireductionist elements implying the contingent, open nature of the social universe (such as the concept of overdetermination) (Laclau 1988:11). Laclau and Mouffe develop the latter elements to the point of breaking the bounds imposed on them by their original structuralist setting. With the help of elements taken from Gramscian Marxism, post-structuralist philosophy and other traditions, they pursue the orientation implicit in the category of overdetermination to its ultimate consequences, conceiving the realm of social phenomena as a symbolic space in which all terms or identities are inserted in an infinite "intertextuality" in which their sense is continually redefined and subverted, without any subject governing this process. The concept of the social so arrived at is characterized by what Rorty has called *textualism* (Rorty 1982). Laclau and Mouffe set off from structuralist Marxism and end up with textualist post-Marxism.

Their starting point is the assertion that every object is constituted as such only within a certain discourse, i.e., within a system whose terms are mutually connected by relations of meaning to shape a "differential, structured system of positions." There is thus no distinction between discursive and extra-discursive reality. Now then, there is never just one discourse, there is a variety of them that are mutually irreducible and separate, and which arise from the clash and coupling of a plurality of articulatory practices that by establishing relations among a set of terms modify the identity of the latter. The ultimate horizon of the articulatory practices is the transformation of "elements" in "moments," i.e., the absolute reduction of the identities of the terms to the relations constituting the internal structure of the discourse. But precisely because of the existence of a multiplicity of discourses and articulatory practices, "the transition from the 'elements' to the 'moments' is never entirely fulfilled." On the contrary, "the status of the dispersed entities is constituted in some intermediate region between the elements and the moments." Consequently, "there is no social identity fully protected from a discursive exterior that deforms it and prevents it becoming fully sutured. Both the identities and the relations lose their necessary character" (Laclau and Mouffe 1985:107, 110–111).[11]

Society is thus presented as a symbolic order in which signifiers are constantly overwhelmed by signified and identities are always overdetermined due to the presence of everything in everything else. Each single object is present in all others, modifying their identities so as to convert them in mere nodules of partial, provisional fixation of meaning. In short, society is the product (and arena) of the unending production, fixation and subversion of meaning: "the partial character of this fixation proceeds from the openness of the social, a result, in its turn, of the constant overflowing of every discourse by the infinitude of the field of discursivity" (Laclau and Mouffe 1985:113).

This conception of the social has two obvious implications that it is convenient to emphasize. In the first place, it has no room for the differentiation and hierarchical ordering of social spheres, and hence no room for the identification of determination or causal relations among them; it in fact makes it impossible to speak in terms of a stable matrix of social relations. Secondly, it abolishes the category of subject, at least in the sense in which a subject is a unitary, rational, self-reflexive agent, since this category suffers from the same polysemia and incompleteness common to all other identities. Subjects are now functions of the discourse: on the one hand, there exists a disperse multiplicity of "subject positions" in a diversity of social relations; on the other, it is impossible to identify *a priori* what the unifying mechanism or the point in which will take place the transitory suture of these positions are. Their fusion in a subjective identity is the product of their mutual overdetermination, of the collision between opposing articulatory practices, and of their provisional, relative articulation by one of the practices that exerts an ephemeral hegemony. This means that the unity of the social agent (i.e., the closure of his or her disperse set of subject positions) is essentially precarious, being subject to a never-ending process of discursive articulation, disarticulation and rearticulation. "Subjects cannot, therefore, be the origin of social relations — not even in the limited sense of being endowed with powers that render an experience possible — as all 'experience' depends on precise discursive conditions of possibility" (Laclau and Mouffe 1985:115).

In general terms, the social theory put forward by Laclau and Mouffe leads to the reduction of classes, subjects and institutions — of the social universe in general — to the unfolding and interplay of opposing articulatory practices. Society is dissolved in action, but not in the intentional actions of human subjects but in a *subjectless discursive action*.

FROM ONE KIND OF REDUCTIONISM TO ANOTHER

In spite of the wide differences between the positions of Thompson on the one hand and Laclau and Mouffe on the other, in my view they share a substantial core of theoretical assumptions directly related to what I have called the actionalist turn in Marxist theory. To bring out this underlying kinship, I shall start by focusing on precisely the area in which their differences might appear to be insuperable, the philosophical premises upon which they are based.

As has already been made clear, Thompson's is a humanistic, historicist philosophy of the subject based on two postulates: the historicity of the social, and the principality of human action as the source of social relationships *qua* universe of meaning. The subject is endowed with an inherent capacity to generate meaning that is actualized on the basis of the experiences lived through. It is not totally clear what status language or sign systems in general have in this scheme; Thompson appears to waver between asserting the utter primacy of the subject and recognizing the autonomy of the symbolic order in which the subject is immersed. His most explicit writings on this subject nevertheless seem to refer all meaning to an originating subject.

At this point Laclau and Mouffe's post-Marxism deeply differs from Thompson's view. Rather than founding meaning on the productive capacity of subjects, they assert the primacy of discourse, conceiving subjects as discursively constructed entities and hence as susceptible to continual deconstruction and reconstruction. Unfortunately, the development of this notion leads them to deny social agents all reflective, deliberative and evaluative capacity, i.e., to ignore human capacity for choice and for conscious, autonomous action. Subjects and their actions become the forms assumed partially and transiently by transcendent discursive practices. The actions of human subjects are dissolved in subjectless discursive action.[12]

The differences between Thompson on the one hand and Laclau and Mouffe on the other are acutely evident at this point. Thompson attempts to avoid the inherent instability of the Marxist theory of action, but employs an ingenuously humanistic conception of the subject that fails to take into account the influence of language on the subject's configuration as such. Laclau and Mouffe introduce the necessary "linguistic consciousness," but do so by adopting a point of view that denies both the autonomy of human action and the efficacy of structure, which are replaced by the primacy of a subjectless, meaning-originating discursive action.

We can now begin to appreciate the underlying similarities between these two approaches. Via theories of action and meaning that differ widely, the arguments of Thompson and of Laclau and Mouffe both end up by *reducing the social to action*, specifically to action that originates meaning. From this viewpoint the parallel articulations of their social theories become intelligible; in particular, there is an evident homology between the two theories as regards the functional relationships among their terms.

The central aim of both enterprises is thus the reduction of the social universe to action: in Thompson's case, to the action of human subjects; in Laclau and Mouffe's, to subjectless discursive action, the action of a code under the free play of the signifier, its constant shifting and the consequent production and subversion of meaning. In both cases, it is action that institutes social meaning. From this point of view, society is a reality characterized by its meaningfulness: according to Thompson, because of the meaning of social relations as experienced by the social agents, while for Laclau and Mouffe it is an immanent meaningfulness governed by a certain system of rules that constitutes and defines social relations themselves insofar as they are the products of discursive practices. For Laclau and Mouffe, "to speak of discourse is to speak of practice and of the 'social' universe as opposed to the 'natural'" (Laclau and Mouffe 1984:148); analogously, for Thompson, to speak of experience and consciousness is to speak of the action of human subjects and of the sociohistorical universe as distinct from the natural universe.

The classical distinction between structure and action is thus demolished by "dissolving" the former in the latter. This has serious consequences. To begin with, it leads to a conception of action — human action according to Thompson, the action of the code according to Laclau and Mouffe — in which, in the last instance, it is absolutely nondeterminate (or, more precisely, the only constraints upon a course of action are other actions); social agents thus inhabit an institutional vacuum.[13] Secondly, it ignores the thorny problem of the relationship between, on the one hand, the objective position of social agents in the structure of social relations (which can be determined independently of their consciousness or of the discursive articulation of their identity) and, on the other, their constitution as active subjects, their aggregation in collective actors, the formation of cultural and ideological communities, observable patterns of action, and so on. The evasion of this problem is evidenced in Thompson's theory by the redefinition of classes in terms of consciousness instead of objective position, and in Laclau and Mouffe's by the utter denial that the concept of class is of any analytical use at all. This leads to radical subjectivism — humanist subjectivism in Thompson's case, and in the case of Laclau and Mouffe a paradoxical "subjectless subjectivism" that involves the simultaneous abolition of the categories of subjectivity and objectivity (and hence of their reciprocal relationship) and thus "inverts" structures until they are in fact subjectivized in the sense of being attributed a self-founded, self-generated active nature that abandons them to their free interplay in an indeterminate space.[14]

The implausibility of this position and indeed its *reductionist character* often pass unnoticed. It is in fact not uncommon for it to be presented as an antireductionist theory that succeeds in overcoming the limitations of historical materialism. In my view, this is due to the obsession for criticism of economic, structural reductionism, an obsession that leads to its being forgotten that the essence of reductionism is the illegitimate suppression (by removal of one of its poles) of the necessary contrast between structure and action. Structure and action are strictly complementary dimensions of the social universe; being qualitatively distinct, they are not susceptible to translation one in terms of the other. Action is the mechanism by which structure is reproduced and/or transformed; structure is both the matrix that positively or negatively configures action and, looked at from the opposite viewpoint, the result of action. The existence of this mutual systematic relationship between structure and action, far from justifying their mutual identification or their joint immersion in a levelling discourse or an ontological continuum, in fact rules out any such confounding of the two. They are, as Giddens (1984:25–28) and Bhaskar (1979:43–46; Bhaskar 1986:123)[15] put it, the terms of the duality that constitutes social reality (the duality of the structure). Their relationship is not pure identity or pure diversity, but rather that of a difference made possible by a subsistent unity. Ignoring this, Thompson and Laclau and Mouffe practice an actionalist reductionism that their lack of awareness makes all the more extreme.

Given their reductionist postulates, for Thompson or Laclau and Mouffe it is obviously absurd to distinguish among different social levels or spheres and to establish, even hypothetically, deterministic or causal relationships among them. Since any conception of the social universe in terms of structure or a structured whole is eschewed, all that can be said is that society consists of a relational space in which each term is linked into the whole by relations of meaning. These relations are originated either by human action (in Thompson's version) or by the mutual overdetermination of the terms themselves — neither pure elements nor pure moments — in their ongoing discursive rearticulation (in Laclau and Mouffe's). In other words, the concept of society as structured gives way to an *eclectic relational interactionism*. Logically, this leads to giving up assumptions such as the existence of objective contradictions, and to the irrelevance of distinguishing theoretically between primary and secondary conflicts or among forms of domination of different social efficacy. Such notions are replaced by the *pluralist* principle that society possesses a multiplicity of contradictions, conflicts and domination relations that have a distinct significance only insofar as they are actually perceived by the subjects involved (in Thompson's version) or are articulated in a discursive formation that assigns them their meaning (in Laclau and Mouffe's). This means that the (ultimately symbolic) weight of each element can be determined only by analysis of specific social situations, without its being legitimate — and this is the nub of the problem — to establish theoretical hypotheses or proceed to macrohistorical generalizations regarding the existence of certain patterns of social determination (and hence of hierarchical ordering of importance among the various kinds of struggle involved in structuring the social universe).

This conception is often presented as freeing theory from the dogmatism of deterministic models,[16] and it may indeed at times have a healthy uncorseting influence. At bottom, however, as a kind of eclecticism *sensu stricto*, its effect is to numb rather than loosen theoretic sinews. Its origin lies in the failure to distinguish between the *use* and *abuse* of certain concepts and principles that are basic to scientific thought. The consequence of this lack of discernment is that the attempt to overcome certain dogmatic deformations ends by relinquishing all efforts to construct substantive theories of social relations and their connection with forms of social action and consciousness. This becomes particularly clear when one perceives the link that exists between this eclecticism and a certain *radically antinaturalistic epistemology* that rejects causal analysis in favor of an interpretative conception. I have already illustrated the presence of this interpretative epistemology in Thompson's work, and it is also explicit in the writings of Laclau and Mouffe. For them analysis consists in reconstructing the systematic organization of symbolic relations (the web of discursive formations making up the social space) from elements that are absolutely opaque (they neither refer to an underlying reality or system of essential relations, nor are susceptible to full conceptual apprehension), but whose very opacity is a sign of their own evidence as the substance of the social. For both Thompson and Laclau and Mouffe, the task to be undertaken is that of relating disperse social elements to a unitary meaningful organization that endows them with sense. That unity is based either on the human subject as origin (Thompson) or on its very dispersion "insofar as it is governed by rules of formation, by the complex conditions of existence of the dispersed statements," i.e., insofar as there is "regularity in dispersion" (Laclau and Mouffe 1985:105).

What needs to be stressed is that according to Thompson and Laclau and Mouffe, the work of reconstruction, the work of inserting the social elements in a systematic organization, is to be carried out without subjecting the experiential or discursive substance of social phenomena to the constraint of an analytic framework involving assumptions about the probable forms of their structuration. This is sheer *empiricism*, albeit with the distinctive feature that the discrete events or facts handled are not to be inductively arranged in causal chains, but instead composed in a meaningful whole.

The actionalist reductionism of Thompson and Laclau and Mouffe also leads them to radical *historicism*, and in two senses. Firstly, since both objective and subjective identities are undermined, change becomes absolute. Thompson formulates this in terms of his philosophy of the subject: the principle of instability represents the infinite productivity of subjects who are immersed in the stream of time and subjected to a continuous deluge of experiences. For Laclau and Mouffe, unceasing mutation derives from the infinitely dynamic nature of discourse, the Brownian interlacing of opposing discursive practices with uncertain effects. Secondly, there is historicism in Althusser's sense to the extent that all agents, relationships and institutions are, as it were, temporarily frozen figures acting momentarily as the objectivation of processes of action founded on constitutive principles whose unfolding is the origin of social phenomena. In the one case, identities are expressions of the current totality of human action, and in the other effects of the free interplay of signifiers.

This historicism has the paradoxical consequence that it becomes impossible to distinguish between different social dimensions. One has to relinquish the possibility of discerning aspects of society with specific, relatively autonomous histories (what Althusser would call differential histories) exhibiting distinct rates of change and degrees of stability. Further, one must refrain from investigating one of the constituent features of society, the duration and resistance to change of the institutional complexes that it comprises (Mouzelis 1988:113–114).[17] Finally, the avoidance of any analysis of structural conditions contributing to the configuration of social practices (the conditions bestowed upon social agents prior to all experience or action) means that history becomes the arena of the *absolutely* contingent.[18] The obvious consequence is that it is simply out of place to attempt any explicative causal reconstruction of history, let alone predict probable patterns of development; all that is possible is narrative recomposition.

Thus both Thompson and Laclau and Mouffe begin by criticizing mechanicism and end by throwing out the concept of cause itself and giving up the investigation of causal patterns present in a particular society and/or generalizable over a certain region of time and space. They begin by decrying determinism, and end by denying the distinction between different modes of determination and by relinquishing the construction of theoretic models of determination. Starting out from a praiseworthy rejection of economicism (i.e., the presentation of all social elements as mere expressions of a privileged, foundational moment, the economy), they go on to confuse it with — and so to anathemize — the legitimate hypothetical postulation of the primacy of economy in the configuration of social relations.[19] They begin by expelling vulgar materialism, and end by banishing materialism in any form. They recognize the constitutive historicity of the social, but on this basis construct an ultimately ahistorical theory that glorifies mutation and contingency to the point of excluding such order and stability as do exist in social reality. Finally, Thompson and Laclau and Mouffe begin by championing the necessity of flexibility in analytical categories, and end by asserting the constituent opacity of reality, the impossibility of grasping reality conceptually. I have tried to show that the origin of all this illegitimate backsliding is the reduction of the social to action.

THE AMBIVALENCE OF ANALYTICAL POST-MARXISM

Analytical post-Marxism[20] would appear to provide an alternative to structural reductionism that is likewise able to elude the snare of the action-based reductionism inherent in the theories of Thompson and Laclau and Mouffe. The various currents within this variegated movement implicitly or explicitly recognize the inevitable duality of structure and action. Structure is understood to be the network of social relations configuring a system of options available to the social agents, and so putting limits to the range and scope of social practices; action is the result of the effective choice of one or another option by the agents involved, and implies their ability to reproduce or transform their initial conditions. The structure of society at any given moment is thus the result (to a large extent the unforeseen and unintentional result) of prior actions.

It is true that a central characteristic of analytical post-Marxism is its insistence on the search for microfoundations upon which to base social macroprocesses, which implies a leaning towards action-based analysis. However, this search for microfoundations, though contrary to methodological holism, does not necessarily entail the acceptance of strict methodological individualism, which is in fact rejected by such leading members of this school as Cohen, Wood and Wright (Cohen 1982; Wood 1986; Levine, Sober and Wright 1986; Wright 1989). Moreover, even those who, like Elster (1982), Roemer (1982) and Przeworski (1985b), do fully accept methodological individualism and the theory of rational choice, do so in a way that clearly differentiates their stance from crude atomism, stressing that analysis must necessarily take into account the structural framework in which social agents move.

Apparently, then, analytical post-Marxism recognizes both that structure is objective and determinant (in the sense that it is able to impose constraints) and that social actors possess a real capacity for true choice and for exerting a causal influence on their situation. I nevertheless find this picture less than totally convincing. I believe that analytical post-Marxism does point in the general direction in which a balanced solution to our problem is to be sought. However, it also seems to me that there is considerable ambiguity in the particular forms of analytical post-Marxism developed by some of the movement's leading figures — particularly those who can be classed as subscribing to the "[post]-Marxism of collective action" (Lash and Urry 1984).[21] Rather than harmoniously integrating structure and action, some of these theorists would appear to be more appropriately described as wavering ambivalently between the covert maintenance of structural reductionism and support for the fashionable actionalist reductionism that I have already discussed. To illustrate the way in which such contradictory traits manage to coexist, I shall briefly consider the writings of Adam Przeworski, with occasional reference to Jon Elster.[22]

Przeworski's use of the concept of class is a particularly clear-cut example of teetering between structuralist and actionalist reductionism.

The Marxist problematic of the transformation of a "class-in-itself" into a "class-for-itself" is rejected by Przeworski on the grounds that it presupposes an unacceptable objectivism in the definition of classes. In his view, classes cannot be thought of as the compartments of a formal classification, or as positions in a matrix of objective relations, or as sets of occupiers of such positions; instead, they are "historical actors (classes-in-struggle)." Classes are to some extent indeterminate effects of processes of struggle[23] that are structured in terms of the totality of the prevailing economic, political and ideological conditions. Thus the question of the relationship of determination between classes as sets of objective positions and classes as agents (or class actors) is completely discarded. In its place, Przeworski is concerned with an analysis of the ways in which conflicts, politico-ideological projects and the practices of corporative actors such as political parties and trade unions together *construct* classes out of a set of individuals located in different positions in — or even outside — the system of production. Essentially, it is denied pointblank that it makes sense to talk of the objective, real existence of a structurally defined "class-in-itself"; instead, the whole notion of class is reduced to that of "class-for-itself."

Przeworski is by no means alone in taking this direction. As I pointed out before, a basic postulate of textualist post-Marxism is that classes, to the extent that they are agents, are like all other agents the product of articulatory practices; there is no objective structure in which they are anchored. The rejection of the "in-itself/for-itself" problematic, and the identification of "class" with "class-for-itself" are likewise, in different ways, among the central tenets of authors such as Thompson, Stedman Jones or Sewell. Przeworski differs from Thompson in considering classes as formed chiefly by extrinsic factors, in particular the practices of collective political actors, whereas Thompson thinks in terms of a process of self-formation driven chiefly by shared experience. Stedman Jones and Sewell, in their turn, stress the role of symbols, discourse and the "languages of class" in class formation.[24] But they all share an anti-structural, dynamic, action-based view of class.

To my mind, this attitude effectively does away with the project of class analysis, as Przeworski's treatment shows.

It is true that, in its classical form, the distinction between "class-in-itself" and "class-for-itself" goes hand in hand with a conception of the relationship between classes as objective positions and classes as social agents that is unacceptable for various reasons. First, on account of the very ambiguity imposed on the term "class," which is used to denote two constitutively different realities corresponding to the two mutually irreducible dimensions of the social universe. Second, because it involves the unacceptable notion that classes ("classes-for-themselves") are agents *sensu stricto* (which is quite different from the proposition that there exist class-based actors, or that the constitution of classes as agents works as an imaginary horizon that governs the formation of class-based actors) (Therborn 1986). Thirdly, because the relationship between classes (as objective positions) and (classes as) social agents is presented as an obvious correspondence that, even in the absence of precise empirical support, is guaranteed as a general rule by the developmental laws of the mode of production (and on another plane by a highly simplistic concept of interest).

Along with these improper ideas, the "in-itself/for-itself" duality nevertheless implies recognition that analysis must take into account the unsurmountable tension between the mutually irreducible poles constituted by the web of objective class relations in which individuals are immersed (relations of property, production, exploitation, domination) and the forms of organization and kinds of practice in which the same individuals are collectively involved. To recognize this tension is not to deny the evidence that the structure of relations that exists at any given moment is the product of prior practices; but while accepting this evidence, it likewise implies being conscious that analysis of any given situation must take structure as given and autonomous and endowed with causal efficacy, *durée* and, as it were, its own differential ontological density. The "in-itself/for-itself" duality, when suitably reformulated in Weber-cum-Marxist terms as the distinction between classes and collective actors, in fact allows great clarity in posing one of social theory's basic problems, the forms of the connection between social structure and social practices, be it specific instances, empirical regularities or abstract general mechanisms that are considered.

These remarks do not mean that it is not necessary to supersede the "in-itself/for-itself" problematic. Rather, they mean that although the solution may be implemented in either of two ways, only one is truly satisfactory. The sound way is to allow that the "in-itself/for-itself" issue reflects real duality between two different poles of the social; the specific manner in which the relationship between the two poles was presented in the classical Marxist formulation is rejected precisely so as to accentuate the mutually *irreducible distinctness* of the two dimensions represented. This involves de-trivializing their relationship by including in the analysis a gamut of considerations whose exact role must be specified: the strictly potential nature of objective interests; the ever-present possibility of alternative forms of articulation of objective interests; the inevitability of a greater or lesser degree of incoherence and incompatibility among the potential interests of the members of a particular social category; the availability of discursive resources, means of calculation or modes of reasoning that mediate in the relationship between agents and their objective positions; and so on. The basic question posed by analysis, and which the various contending research programs attempt to answer, is now twofold. On the one hand, how is it that the (class) structure contributes to configuring the formation of (class-based) agents? What are the limits of its determinant power? By means of what mechanisms does it work? On the other, how do the practices of the agents tend to reproduce and/or transform structural frameworks?

The way of superseding of the "in-itself/for-itself" problematic that I have just sketched emphasizes the radical heterogeneity between the twin poles of "in-itself" and "for-itself." Przeworski adopts the opposite procedure, denying any such heterogeneity by identifying or fusing those poles (more precisely, as we have seen, by *reducing* class to "class-for-itself"). Such identification means both that it becomes impossible to ask how class structure relates to class action (since the former vanishes as a thinkable object), and that this question is replaced with the task of analyzing the specific processes by which agents/classes are created; and although this change of focus might appear to be a victory over structuralist reductionism, I believe that it in fact involves shuttling between structuralist and action-based reductionism.

The presence of a leaning to actionalist reductionism in Przeworski's analysis is readily appreciated in view of what we have already seen: at bottom, the objectivity of the positions created by social relations is counterfeit, since they are defined internally to one or another politico-ideological project[25] without real reference to a solid, extradiscursively extant ontological anchor-point; there are no classes that are structural positions governing action (albeit partially), only "positions-in-action."

Paradoxically, however, Przeworski's approach is strikingly weak precisely in its characterization of social agents. In the first place, in spite of attempting to get away from the "in-itself/for-itself" problematic (or rather, on account of the way in which this attempt is made), Przeworski retains one of the most questionable premises of this problematic: i.e., that classes are agents. However loosely one employs the concept of agent, it seems difficult to count as such collectivities such as classes, which lack specifiable mechanisms for deliberation, decision and action. Though it is tenable that the class structure is a matrix which configures action, and that class-based actors exist, classes *sensu stricto* lack the minimal attributes proper to an agent (Hindess 1986, 1989; Harré 1981) — and this ought to be obvious to someone who explicitly and radically accepts, as Przeworski does, the principle of methodological individualism. Secondly, though Przeworski apparently grants action great autonomy, his analysis in fact deprives individual agents of all substance. Their identity and their perception of their situation are assumed to be constructed externally to them; they are products of the practices of corporative actors that create classes from individuals located in a variety of positions. The individuals themselves are mere personifications of a model of identity and of self-representation of their interests that is donned passively upon reception from outside.[26] Thirdly, in open contradiction with his declared antireductionist stance, Przeworski conceives the agents involved in and produced by social conflict and practices in class terms. As we have seen, he denies a structural foundation to the notion of class: it is accordingly hard to see then why such agents must be thought of as classes. In other words, it is not clear what may be meant by calling such agents "classes."

If previous steps in Przeworski's argument are accepted, at this point there are only two avenues left open. One is to treat the concept of class as meaningless and postulate that the only real problem is the analysis of the multiplicity of factors, conditions and practices that result in the formation of social actors. This option involves adopting a radically actionalist, pluralist approach in which it is accepted that the forms assumed by historical actors are generically indeterminable, that they are subject only to case-by-case analysis, and that they are never to be accounted for by any prior principle of objectivity.[27] The other alternative is to retain the idea that historical actors are classes by reintroducing some principle upon which to base their objective primacy, a principle that must necessarily be external to the process in which the agents are created. That this is the alternative chosen by Przeworski is evident in his explaining the formation of the working class by appeal to an objective "commonality of interests" arising from the separation of the means of production (Przeworski 1985a:91), and in his justifying the idea of historical actors as classes in terms of their involvement in the lawfully governed dynamics of the development of productive forces and the accumulation of capital.

The trouble is that this return to a principle of objectivity is totally *inconsistent* with the general gist of Przeworski's approach. What is more, since he has turned away from the problematic of the relationship between class structure and class actors, the reintroduction of a principle of structural objectivity (such as the form of property relationships or the principles of accumulation of capital) takes place in a theoretic context in which it is impossible to formulate the mechanisms by which the determinant power of the structural principle is exerted within certain limits imposed by a diversity of mediating factors. This becomes manifest, for example, in the dogmatic assertion that "all conflicts that occur at any moment of history can be understood in historical terms if and only if they are viewed as effects of and in turn having an effect upon class formation" (p. 80). This proposition amounts to reintroducing the crudest kind of class reductionism: instead of it being acknowledged that class conflicts or class actors are just a particular — though perhaps the most important — kind of social conflict or social agents, all social conflicts whatsoever are to be subjected to an essentialist interpretation in terms of direct or indirect class conflict. Recognition that not all social conflicts are class conflicts, which is the necessary starting point of any nonreductionist class analysis, is impossible for Przeworski precisely because of his antistructuralist motivation. This has led him to abolish categories which are essential for representation of the multidimensionality of the social universe in a way that gives the objectivity of structure a role that is both effective and limited. Hence, when structure reenters his analysis, it must perforce do so enshrouded in the very essentialist objectivism that he aimed to avoid; within his overt action-based approach there lurks latent structural reductionism.[28]

This is the ambivalence to which I referred previously. One of the most striking manifestations of the flaws that I have been pointing out is the formalistic, ahistorical nature of some of the models used by Przeworski in explaining the social democratic orientation of working class political practice — models whose merits in many respects are unquestionable. Przeworski analyses in detail the strategic dilemmas of the working class and the possible courses of action that it must choose among, evaluates the consequences of the possible alternatives, and explains the choices made in terms of their rationality. Unfortunately, at no point is any effort devoted to analysis of the cognitive contexts, modes of calculation, deliberative instances, organizational forms or decision systems involved in the choices. It is never even explicitly stated *who or what* the agent class supposed to choose and act really is, nor how it really makes its choice. Przeworski's models feature only mythical homogeneous agent classes endowed with self-identity and with a formal rationality that allows strategic calculation and decision taking; their initiative is really limited to the actualization of the patterns of action that lie latent in the structure of their situation awaiting execution by a rational agent. Przeworski stresses, of course, that these agent classes are not structurally definable or "natural" entities but the effects of prior practice, and he is aware that classes are not empirically observable actors in the way that individuals, political parties, trade unions and other organizations are. But the entities that are supposed to choose and act in his explicative models are called "the working class" or "the workers," and "capital" or the "capitalists"; the conception of agents as the personification of social relations has crept back in when least expected.

The shortcomings and paradoxes that I have pointed out here are not peculiar to Przeworski's work. They can equally be found in that of other analytical post-Marxists, especially, as I suggested earlier, those who have been most directly concerned with the analysis of "collective action." In Jon Elster's work, for example, it is possible to find some of the same paradoxes, though in more general form; in particular, he too ignores the substantiveness of individual agents and surreptitiously reduces their actions to effects of social relations. Though I must abstain here from subjecting his work to the detailed examination that this highly fecund writer undoubtedly deserves,[29] it is perhaps worth while to sketch briefly, by reference to Elster, how my criticisms of Przeworski might be extended to other analytical post-Marxists of collective action. To this end I shall make use of Barry Hindess's objections to the Marxist reappropriation of elements of the theory of rational choice (Hindess 1988:22 passim).

As in Przeworski's arguments, problems begin to show up in Elster's as soon as it is realized that his idea of the relationship between structure and action entails ignoring the role played in the determination of individual and collective action by the discursive resources, computational procedures and modes of reasoning available to the agents. This negligence is tied in with the adoption of a startlingly simplistic concept of objective interest. Both features derive from Elster's use of the model of actor that he borrows from the theory of rational choice.

Elster assumes that, within the limits imposed by the social relations in which they are involved, social agents choose the option that, according to their criteria, best suits their interests. This idea, which in principle is quite unobjectionable, in practice — Elster's practice — suffers from two flaws. First, Elster tends to think that an option being the most suitable for the agents concerned is purely a matter of universal formal, strategic rationality; in other words, that in a given situation the choice of one or another option is decided on by the agents, after more or less complex calculations, by exercising the rationality attributable to them as human agents. Second, he obviates the problem of the "incoherence" and "incompossibility" of interests by simplistically assuming that for the agents involved in each social situation it is possible to define a set of objective interests that are given from without and characterized by a high degree of unity and univocity.

These two features of Elster's theories lead in contradictory directions and end in paradox. On the one hand, the concept of action associated with the notion of universal formal rationality implies that agents have full autonomy to choose among the various structurally possible courses of action. Consideration of the limitations imposed on agents by their discursive, cultural and moral resources is thereby ruled out, and the role played by modes of calculation and reasoning, which likewise limit the alternatives perceived by the actor as really feasible, is replaced by a generic principle of rationality. The agents' capacity for choice is accordingly overestimated, since without such limitations it encompasses all alternatives that are not excluded on structural grounds, regardless of whether the actors are in possession of the discursive means required for the perception of these courses of action as actually open to them. In short, the existence of duality between situational structure and action is acknowledged, but no account is given of factors that play an important role in mediating the relationship between one and the other, and that control or relativize both the determinant efficacy of the structure and the autonomy of action.

Paradoxically, considered from another point of view, Elster's apparent exaggeration of the autonomy possessed by agents in their choice of the most desirable course of action entails the conclusion that the act of choice is in itself insignificant. For, interests being univocal properties and choice being a matter of the formal rationality common to all human beings, the brushing aside of cultural and moral context and of specific mechanisms of calculation and deliberation results in confusion between the structural conditions of choice and the options available to the chooser, since the set of alternatives is supposed to be fully defined in structural terms, not redefined by the agents with the cognitive resources at their disposal. It follows that since agents are in effect *interchangeable*, being merely "formally rational" beings, their different patterns of action must be the consequence of applying the same rational calculus to different sets of interests associated with different positions in the social structure. Similarly, the formal rational calculus implies that actors occupying the same structural position not only share certain interests but also act in essentially identical ways. This, in turn, requires the assumption that those actors share a common view of their situation because their specific ways of thought and deliberation are determined by their social position. Thus, although Elster appears initially to condemn to oblivion the role played by the discursive resources of the agent in the configuration of action, he actually reintroduces these factors as part and parcel of the social position occupied by the agent. The final result is that the conditions of choice totally determine what is chosen, and choice is an algorithmic process. In other words, we come back to the structural reductionism from which we were trying to escape.

SUMMING UP

In this paper I have argued the following theses. First, that since the late 1970s, reaction to earlier structuralism has led to an actionalist turn in social theory. Second, that this "actionward" turn has had a profound influence in Marxist circles, in which it has adopted a variety of forms (some of which, the humanist theories for example, have preexisting roots in Marxist tradition; while others, such as the textualist and rational choice approaches, draw on external theoretic sources). Third, the effect of the actionalist turn on Marxist theory has not been merely a change of accent, or a critical purge of its reductionist, structuralist and objectivist elements, but rather a reappraisal of some of its central, defining theoretic characteristics. The result of this reappraisal has been the emergence of new programs of social research whose aim is to supersede Marxist theory from within. The actionalist turn is thus a common feature of the variety of post-Marxisms that have arisen over the past decade. Fourth, the extremism of this reorientation is at the bottom of certain flaws shared by the foremost attempts to avoid structural reductionism by means of post-Marxist positions. Fifth, these flawed programs come in two main varieties differentiated by the thoroughness and coherence with which the turn to action is effected. On the one hand are those that avoid Marxist structuralism, not by means of a balanced representation of the social universe in terms of the mutual irreducibility of structure and action, but by utterly reducing this universe to a single one of its dimensions, action. On the other are those which both declare themselves as oriented towards action and attempt to attain the desired equilibrium, but which sadly end in ambivalence or in continual oscillation between the Scylla of actionalist reductionism on one side and the Charybdis of a new, more complex form of structural reductionism on the other.

BY WAY OF CONCLUSION

Clearly, these criticisms do not contain constructive theoretic proposals. Nor, however, is it their aim to condemn all post-Marxist trends and revindicate the virtues of some kind of imaginary Marxist orthodoxy. My hope, in exploring the paradoxes led to by some of the attempts that have been made to revitalize or break with classical Marxism, has been that this analysis perhaps may help others to avoid such pitfalls, and so contribute to the construction of a *post-Marxist historical materialism* in which both structure and action occupy their proper place. It is not possible actually to pursue this program here, but in order not to end on a purely negative note, I will recall a few of the directions such a program might take.

The flaws that I have shown in both classical Marxism and certain neo-Marxist or post-Marxist schools affect two complementary aspects of their theories. The first is the way in which social action is conceived; the second the way in which the nexus between action and structure is conceived.

With regard to the way in which action is conceived, it is characteristic of classical Marxism that it is unable to construct a unified, consistent theory in this respect. As we have seen, there is a co-presence of different views of action, stressing its various dimensions, but these diverse views are not integrated in a systematic theoretic framework. The result is an *inarticulated* — and hence contradictory — *multidimensionality*. In the case of the contemporary approaches that I have examined here, quite the opposite problem arises: these approaches are manifestly *unidimensional* due to their overestimate of one of the constituent aspects of action with exclusion of its other components.[30]

With regard to the relationship between action and structure, which has been my main concern, we have seen that in classical Marxism there is a characteristic tendency towards structuralist reductionism. Beside it, the works of Marx also feature voluntarist moments, but they do not suffice to constitute an alternative to the predominant model.[31] The (post-)Marxist approaches I have examined, on the other hand, are characterized by either actionalist reductionism, or by continual vacillation between action-based reductionism and traditional structuralist reductionism. In both cases, the root of the problem is the suppression of one of the terms of the action-structure dichotomy by its reduction to, or fusion with, the other term.

At bottom, all the flaws discussed above consist in *unidimensionality* or the *inarticulate superimposition of different dimensions*; this is true, whether it be the various aspects of action that are in question or action and structure as components of social reality. I accordingly believe that the key to overcoming these defects must be sought in the reversal of these basic tendencies in order to endow the theory with a *systematically articulated multidimensionality*.

There would seem to be two possible strategies oriented to achieve this articulation, depending on its nature being *internal* or *external*. In the former case (internal articulation or integration), the aim would be to construct a *synthetic* theory that integrates the various dimensions in a unitary conceptual framework while respecting the distinctive nature of each. In the latter (external articulation), the strategy pursued would involve the acceptance of a *principle of complementarity* among various facets, each of which is recognized as partial and limited, but as fulfilling a certain function in the division of theoretical work.[32]

Regarding the way in which action should be conceived, the adoption of a synthetic viewpoint, i.e., the pursuit of internal articulation, implies the need to clarify the importance and mutual relationships of four critical elements: objective interests, discursive and symbolic contexts, identities in construction, and the reflectivity of the agents. Sam Bowles and Herbert Gintis (1986:126) have put forward an appropriate starting point for this program with their formulation of what they call the "becoming-by-acting model of human choice," according to which agents (re-)define themselves through the choices they take when they act within an objectively given system of constraints. This position, which unites some of the most valuable insights of the authors discussed in this article, stands upon three basic principles. First, that agents are strong evaluators, and thus possess a capacity for second-order desires and for choice among alternative normative systems.[33] Second, that their evaluations imply, among other things, the possibility of conscious reconstitution of the agents' own identity through their own (inter)action: "individuals enter into practices with others not only to achieve common goals, but also to determine who they are and who they shall become as social beings" (Bowles and Gintis 1986:150). And third, that both the actions and identities of the agents are always subject to certain symbolico-discursive conditions of existence.

The main difficulty with Bowles and Gintis's proposals lies in what appears to be an unjustifiable rejection of the objective determination of interests, or at least a considerable decrease in the analytical value granted the category of interests in the explanation of social action. This characteristic is unobjectionable to the extent that it avoids the objectivism of the traditional Marxist view of interests; but at times Bowles and Gintis go too far in arguing for the "constructed" nature of interests, which come to be presented merely as an artifact of ongoing struggles and discourses (Wright 1987:752).[34] To my mind, their model would gain in scope and analytical power if interests were recharacterized as attributes that are *objective* (i.e., identifiable without reference to the awareness of the agents) though not necessarily *actual* (i.e., not necessarily incorporated into actual social practice), and which only exist forming *complex matrices* (i.e., combinations that are in general affected by internal inconsistency and comprise a variety of different temporal perspectives) in which they possess differing degrees of *compossibility* (i.e., the various combinations of potential interests have different probabilities of actualization in social practice, and different degrees of relative stability if actualized). Considered in this way, the category of interests would contribute to the definition of a position intermediate between objectivism and voluntarism. Be that as it may, it is only right to acknowledge the value of Bowles and Gintis's thesis as a suggestive framework for the construction of a post-Marxist social theory capable of resolving some of the paradoxes discussed in this article.[35]

The same goal may also be contributed to by certain other approaches that have devoted more explicit attention to the problem of the relationship between structure and action. In recent years there has been considerable concern about this issue, and a consequent spate of proposals dealing with either the synthesis (or internal integration) or complementarity (or external articulation) of structure and action. The synthetic proposals that have been put forward are emblematically exemplified by the notions of "duality of structure" and "duality of praxis" that have been formulated by Giddens and Bhaskar.[36] The proponents of external articulation have defended an "analytic dualism" which involves conceptualization of the ways of combination, interaction or interplay between the properties of agents and the properties of social structures, systems and subsystems, but which stops short of their integration in a unitary theoretic construct. This view implies the rejection of the integrationist thesis that claims that structure and agents are mutually constitutive.[37] Finally, midway between "duality" and "dualism," Piotr Sztompka has suggested a synthetic approach based on "the characterization of social reality as a *living socio-individual field in the process of becoming*" (Sztompka 1991:95); Sztompka considers that "the levels of structure in articulation and of agents in actions" are neither analytically separable nor mutually reducible, but that the basis and mode of existence of both is the "unified socio-individual field."

It is impossible to tell which of the above avenues will eventually prove to be most fruitful. What I believe can be said with some confidence is that these directions point towards a solution of the paradoxes of the (post-)Marxist treatment of social action.

It would also, of course, be possible to choose a different path, namely, to search the Marxian *corpus* or Marxist tradition for principles allowing the development of a multidimensional theory of action. This idea is typically understood as meaning resort to the political and historical writings of Marx, in particular *The Eighteenth Brumaire of Louis Bonaparte*. This work contains an analysis that grants important roles both to the social agents' objective interests and to collective normative frameworks, political traditions, symbols and values. Political struggles are seen in terms not only of the force of the contending groups but also of the role of competing normative complexes. The various class groups are presented as constituting themselves through resort to culturally situated significations (Rundell 1987:161). The result is an unusually complex and subtle analytical perspective whose clarification and development might seem to promise a solution to the thorny problem of the relationships among the several components of action and between action and structure. In the end, however, Marx's analysis in *The Eighteenth Brumaire* turns out not to be free of his historicist and reductionist postulates, and is in fact pregnant with the structural tension that pervades all Marx's work and which is the root cause of his inability to put together a plausible theory of action.[38]

To conclude, I believe that the way to tackle this defect must emerge from detailed critical dialogue between Marxism on the one hand and, on the other, traditions and approaches that hitherto have largely been foreign to Marxism.[39] This may well lead to some blurring of the boundaries that distinguish Marxism from conventional social science; but it is now unquestionable that such blurring is a price that must inevitably be paid by any attempt to uphold and maintain the contemporary relevance of the tradition initiated by Marx.

Notes

1. The most powerful critical analysis of the shortcomings of Marxist theory of action can be found in Lockwood (1981, 1992). Cf. Benton (1984:215 ff.), Callinicos (1987:115 ff.) and Bowles and Gintis (1986:18 ff., 145 ff).

2. A rather similar conception of the history of Marxism can be found in Laclau and Mouffe (1985, chaps. 1, 2). This view receives further elaboration in my forthcoming *Marxismo, posmarxismo y teoría de clases*.

3. This situation has given rise to an influential actionalist approach to social movements, which is concerned "with the reconstruction of frameworks of action and identity which may evolve during social conflict" (Eyerman 1984:80).

4. Good examples of this are by one side so-called "analytical Marxism" and by the other side the work of Hirst and Hindess. See, for illustrative statements of their conception of Marxism — and of themselves as Marxists — Elster (1985:531) and Hirst (1985:128–129).

5. Sections 3, 4 and 5 of this paper draw heavily on materials previously included in my essay "Clase, acción y estructura: de E. P. Thompson al posmarxismo" (Cainzos 1989:1–69).

6. Thompson borrows the category of "notion" from Sartre (see Sartre 1977:12–13, 1966:30). In *The Poverty of Theory* (Thompson 1978) there is a recurrent presence of Sartrean resonances that has not received as much attention as it deserves. See a few comments on Thompson and Sartre in Soper (1990:213–214).

7. At this point it is especially evident the paralellism between Thompson's "historical logic" and Clifford Geertz's interpretive analysis, as has been pointed by Trimberger (1984:226–227) and Geertz (1973:26–27).

8. In Thompson (1978) there are passages leading one to believe that experience forms part of social consciousness (p. 199); others suggesting that experience is equivalent to social being (pp. 199, 298; cf. Wood 1984:71); and others again that identify experience as the external nexus between the two — but without specifying its own ontological status (p. 363).

9. A paradigmatic example of this kind of critique is Johnson (1983:52–85, esp. 73 ff.).

10. In "Clase, acción y estructura..." (Cainzos 1989) I have shown in some detail how the flaws in Thompson's ideas show up sharply in his analysis of class formation, leading him effectively to abandon any significant use of the concept of class and the genuine project of class analysis altogether.

11. An epistemological consequence of this conception is that the social cannot be conceptually cognoscible. In fact, Laclau and Mouffe argue

that the postulate of the opacity of social reality to concepts is a constitutive feature of any materialist position. See Laclau (1984:39–42) and Laclau and Mouffe (1987:87).

12. One of the consequences of adopting this attitude is to waste the potential of Laclau and Mouffe's reinterpretation of politics as a struggle for the formation of identities. Their abolition of reflective action prevents their analysis from including an understanding of the crucial role played in this struggle by agents' desires, intentions and conscious projects concerning the reconfiguration of their own identity in a certain direction. Cf. the approach to this factors outlined by Bowles and Gintis (1986:152 ff.) and Callinicos's (1987:117 ff.) Marxist defense of a theory of action based on Taylor's concept of strong evaluation. And see the last section of this paper.

13. The most elaborated statement of this point can be found in N. Mouzelis 1988 (also Mouzelis 1990, chap. 2). Laclau's reply to this criticism can be found in *New Reflections on the Revolution of Our Time* (1983:222–224). See also Torfing (1991:212).

14. On this point, I draw on Anderson's critique of post-structuralism, which can be extended to other textualist positions. See Anderson (1983).

15. Of course, the idea of "duality of structure" is not free of problems. See, for instance, from different viewpoints: Urry (1982:100–106), Callinicos (1987:85; 1985:133–166), Archer (1990:73–84) and Mouzelis (1991, chap. 2).

16. See Laclau and Mouffe's explicit defense of pluralism in *Hegemony and Socialist Strategy* (1985:131 ff.) and a positive evaluation of the pluralism present in Thompson's analysis, in Albert and Hahnel (1981:11).

17. See also Rustin (1987:159), and the apt remarks of Paramio 1990, p. 69. This point has been conceded even by some followers and sympathetic readers of Laclau and Mouffe, who do not see in it a symptom of "inherent deficiencies in discourse analysis" but only "areas of neglect in a young, ambitious and rapidly expanding programme of research" (Torfing 1991:35–36). See also Jowers (1989:92), who thinks that "Laclau and Mouffe overemphasize the fluidity of the social by taking only one moment of the Derridean argument."

18. On this point it is very illustrative the following statement by Laclau: "By articulation we understand the creation of something new out of a dispersion of elements ...; the moment of creation is radical — *creatio ex nihilo* — ... Articulation, in that sense, is the primary ontological level of the constitution of the real." (Laclau 1988:16). And compare the distinctive and much more nuanced position of Stuart Hall: "I do not believe that just anything can be articulated with anything else... All discourse has conditions of existence which ... set limits or constraints on the process of articulation itself. Historical formations, which con-

sist of previous but powerfully forged articulations, ... *are* deeply resistant to change, and do establish lines of tendency and boundaries which give to the fields of politics and ideology the 'open structure' of a formation and not simply the slide into an infinite and neverending plurality" (Hall 1988:10).

19. I think that this principle cannot be rejected on merely logical grounds, as both Thompson and Laclau and Mouffe intend to do. On the one hand, it is susceptible of a high degree of conceptual and formal refinement, as the analytical Marxist literature has proven. On the other hand, its validation or falsation has to be given in terms of its long-term ability to account for the available empirical evidence better than alternative principles.

20. This label seems to me more appropriate than the usual "analytical Marxism" because it points to the ambivalent relationship between this school of thought and Marxist tradition, from which it departs in fundamental respects while preserving — at least partially — its research agenda and motivating values. Roemer himself acknowledges in his presentation of *Analytical Marxism* (1986:2) that he is not sure whether this kind of work ought to be called Marxist, though his final inclination is towards an affirmative answer.

21. My criticisms are aimed specifically at the authors most directly involved in this form of analytical post-Marxism, not at analytical post-Marxism as such. On the contrary, I believe that, thanks to their epistemological and methodological flexibility and concern for structural analysis, authors such as E. O. Wright hold out the promise of a genuine means of avoiding the errors of some of their companions.

22. The subsequent remarks draw extensively on Hindess's critique of rational choice analysis and its appropriation by "analytical post-Marxism" (see Hindess 1988, 1989). Nonetheless, I do not accept Hindess's own global position.

23. Przeworski (1985a:66 ff., 47, whole of chapter 2).

24. See Stedman Jones (1983). Also, see the critical reconstruction of Thompson's argument made by Sewell, who emphasizes the significance of symbolic elements in the process of class formation (Sewell 1990:50–77).

25. Przeworski's *Capitalism and Social Democracy* (1985a:67) "the very theory of classes must be viewed as internal to particular political projects." Cf. Abercrombie and Urry (1983:130) and McLennan (1989:110–111).

26. See the brief but insightful remarks of Burawoy on this point (1989:3).

27. The most extreme defense of this position that I know can be found in Johnston 1986.

28. This inconsistent reintroduction of objectivism and essentialism has been criticized, from different viewpoints, in Johnston (1986:105–106) and McLennan (1986:111).
29. Most relevant references in this context are Elster (1982, 1985) and Roemer (1986).
30. From what I have said, it is clear what the overvalued aspects are. In Thompson's case, it is the founding nature of the subject that is exaggerated; in particular, too much weight is given to the mediating function attributed to experience. In the case of Laclau and Mouffe, too much emphasis is placed on the autonomy and constituent efficacy of discursive orders and of social processes of power acquisition. Finally, Przeworski exhibits a one-sided concern with the means-ends rationality of individuals. Cf. Hönneth (1991:65).
31. In *Marxism, Post-Marxism and the Theory of Classes*, I have argued that the duality between structuralist reductionism and residual voluntarist elements is one aspect of the structural tension between historicism and antihistoricism that imbues not only the work of Marx but the whole of nineteenth-century social thought.
32. In the field of Marxism, the principle of complementarity has been quite frequently resorted to in connection with a variety of problems. See, for example, Albert and Hahnel (1981:26–27;), McLennan (1989: 262–264) and Jessop (1990:304).
33. Cf. Callinicos (1987:117), in which he follows Taylor (1985).
34. Wright has shrewdly pointed out that in their soundest arguments and their concrete analyses, Bowles and Gintis show little of the voluntarist radicalism of some of their less well-founded theses, including the wholesale rejection of the category of interests. An additional proof of this is the defense of an "interest-based concept of power" that they have made in another text (Bowles and Gintis 1990:173, 211), which leans heavily on the category of interest.
35. As I have already recognized, one alternative to this attempt to construct a synthetic approach to action would consist in the *external* articulation of complementary views. As I understand it, this is what has been done, in the field of class theory, by Erik Wright and Kwang-Yeong Shin, whose starting point is precisely some of the ideas of Bowles and Gintis. Wright and Shin distinguish between structural and processual views of classes, and in the light of a comparison of the effects of class structure and class trajectories in Sweden and the United States suggest that each has its distinctive explanatory value. See Wright and Shin (1988).
36. Though they lie in the same general direction, the approaches of Giddens and Bhaskar are not strictly identical. As has been pointed out by (among others) Anderson (1990:54), Giddens's work lays relatively more emphasis on explanation from the point of view of action, the

consequence being "to understate considerably the typical pressure of social determinations." Bhaskar draws a more balanced picture, and in particular his "transformational model of social activity" stresses more vigorously the mutual irreducibility and distinctive nature of structure and action, society and agents, between which there is an "ontological hiatus" (see Bhaskar 1979:46, 1986:123–124). Cf. Collier (1989:90 ff.).

37. See Archer (1990; also 1988). And from a very different (rational-choice) viewpoint, Taylor (1989:118).

38. In Chapter 6 of his *Origins of Modernity*, John Rundell offers a suggestive exegesis of the Marxian "paradigm of class action" in *The Eighteenth Brumaire*, showing both its oscillations and how it finally falls back upon historicist essentialism.

39. Among them must be included those theoretic constructions that have arisen within the rational choice paradigm intending to overcome its most serious flaws, and which aim to integrate dimensions that are typically excluded from the rational choice approach (in particular the consideration of normative orders). A noteworthy example is Jon Elster's recent work, which unfortunately suffers from a somewhat disdainful neglect of the contributions of "mainstream sociology." See Elster (1989).

Bibliography

Abercrombie, N., and J. Urry (1983). *Capital, Labour and the Middle Classes*. London: Allen & Unwin.

Albert, M., and R. Hahnel (1981). *Marxism and Socialist Theory*. Boston: South End Press.

Anderson, P. (1976). *Considerations on Western Marxism*. London: Verso.

_____ (1983). *In the Tracks of Historical Materialism*. London: Verso.

_____ (1990). "A Culture in Contraflow, I." *New Left Review* 180.

Archer, M. (1988). *Culture and Agency: The Place of Culture in Social Theory*. Cambridge: Cambridge University Press.

_____ (1990). "Human Agency and Social Structure: A Critique of Giddens." In: *Anthony Giddens: Consensus and Controversy*, eds. J. Clark et al., pp. 73–84. London: Falmer Press.

Arditi, B. (1986). "Una gramática posmoderna para pensar lo social." *Zona Abierta* No. 41/42, pp. 184–206.

Bagguley, P. (1991). "Post-Fordism and Enterprise Culture: Flexibility, Autonomy and Changes in Economic Organization." In: *Enterprise Culture*, eds. R. Keat and N. Abercrombie, pp. 151–168. London: Routledge.

Benton, T. (1984). *The Rise and Fall of Structural Marxism*. London: Macmillan.

Bhaskar, R. (1979). *The Possibility of Naturalism*. Brighton: Harvester.

_____ (1986). *Scientific Realism and Human Emancipation*. London: Verso.

Bowles, S., and H. Gintis (1986). *Democracy and Capitalism*. London: Routledge & Kegan Paul.

_____ (1990). "Contested Exchange: New Microfoundations for the Political Economy of Capitalism." *Politics and Society* 18(2).

Burawoy, M. (1989). "Reflections on the Class Consciousness of Hungarian Steelworkers." *Politics and Society* 17(1).

Cainzos, M. (1989). "Clase, acción y estructura: de E. P. Thompson al posmarxismo." *Zona Abierta* 50:1–69.

Calinicos, A. (1985). "Anthony Giddens: A Contemporary Critique." *Theory and Society* 14:133–166.

_____ (1987). *Making History*. Cambridge: Polity Press.

_____ (1989). *Against Postmodernism: A Marxist Critique*. Cambridge: Polity.

Cohen, G. (1982). "Reply to Elster, 'Marxism, functionalism and game theory.'" *Theory and Society* 11:483–496.

Collier, A. (1989). *Scientific Realism and Socialist Thinking*. Brighton, Harvester.

Elster, J. (1982). "Marxism, Functionalism, and Game Theory: The Case for Methodological Individualism." *Theory and Society* 11: 453–482.

_____ (1985). *Making Sense of Marx*. Cambridge: Cambridge University Press.

_____ (1989). *The Cement of Society*. Cambridge: Cambridge University Press.

Eyerman, R. (1984). "Social Movements and Social Theory." *Sociology* 18(1).

Geertz, C. (1973). *The Interpretation of Cultures*. New York: Basic Books.

Giddens, A. (1984). *The Constitution of Society*. Cambridge: Polity.

Hall, S. (1984). "En defensa de la teoría." In: *Historia popular y teoría socialista*, ed. R. Samuel, pp. 277-286. Barcelona: Crítica/Gijalbo.

Hall, S., and M. Jacques (Eds.) (1989). *New Times: The Changing Face of Politics in the 1990s*. London: Lawrence and Wishart.

_____ (1988). *The Hard Road to Renewal*. London: Verso.

Harré, R. (1981). "Philosophical Aspects of the Micro-Macro Problem." In: *Advances in Social Theory and Methodology*, eds. K. Knorr-Cetina and A. V. Cicourel. London: Routledge & Kegan Paul.

Harvey, D. *The Condition of Postmodernity*. Oxford: Blackwell, 1989.

Hindess B. *Politics and Class Analysis*. Oxford: Blackwell, 1986

_____ (1988). *Choice, Rationality, and Social Theory*. London: Allen & Unwin.

_____ (1989). *Political Choice and Social Structure*. London: Edward Elgar.

Hirst, P. (1985). *Marxism and Historical Writing*. London: Routledge & Kegan Paul.

Hönneth, A. (1991). "Lógica de la emancipación. El legado filosófico del marxismo." *Debats* 37.

Jessop, B. (1990). *State Theory: Putting Capitalist States in their Place*. Cambridge: Polity.

Johnson, R. (1983). "Edward Thompson, Eugene Genovese y la historia socialista-humanista." In: *Hacia una historia socialista*, pp. 52-85. Barcelona: Ediciones del Serbal.

Johnston, L. (1986). *Marxism, Class Analysis and Socialist Pluralism*. London: Allen & Unwin.

Jowers, P. (1989). "Defending Theoretical Openness: Deconstruction and Post-Marxism." In: *Approaches to Marx*, eds. M. Cowling and L. Wilde. Milton Keynes: Open University Press.

Kiernan, W. (1987). "Problems of Marxist History." *New Left Review* 161:107.

Laclau, E. (1984). "The Controversy over Materialism." In: *Rethinking Marx*, eds. S. Hännine and L. Paldan, pp. 39-42. Berlin: Argument Verlag.

_____ (1988). "Building a New Left: An Interview with Ernesto Laclau." *Strategies* 1:10-28.

_____ (1983). "The Impossibility of Society." *Canadian Journal of Political and Social Theory* 7:21-24. (Now in E. Laclau: *New Reflections on the Revolution of Our Time*, pp. 89-92. London: Verso, 1990).

Laclau, E., and C. Mouffe (1984). "Hegemonía y nuevos movimientos sociales. Entrevista de D. Plotke a Laclau y Mouffe." *Zona Abierta* 30:148.

_____ (1985). *Hegemony and Socialist Strategy.* London Verso.

_____ (1987). "Post-Marxism without apologies." In: E. Laclau, *New Reflections on the Revolution of Our Time*, pp. 106–107.

Lash, S., and J. Urry (1984). "The new Marxism of collective action: a critical analysis." *Sociology* 18(1):33–50.

_____ (1985). "The Dissolution of the Social?" In: *Sociological Theory in Transition*, eds. M. L. Wardell and S. P. Turner. London: Allen & Unwin.

Levine, A., E. Sober, and E. O. Wright (1986). "Marxismo e individualismo metodológico." *Zona Abierta* 41–42:131–157.

Lockwood, D. (1981). "The Weakest link in the chain? Some comments on the Marxist theory of action." *Research on the Sociology of Work* 1:435–481.

_____ (1992). *Solidarity and Schism: "The Problem of Disorder" in Durkheimian and Marxist Sociology.* Oxford: Clarendon.

McLennan, G. (1981). *Marxism and the Methodologies of History*, pp. 126–128. London: Verso.

_____ (1989). *Marxism, Pluralism and Beyond.* Cambridge: Polity.

_____ (1988). "Marxism or Post-Marxism?" *New Left Review* 167:107–124.

_____ (1990). *Post-Marxist Alternatives.* London: Macmillan.

_____ (1991). *Back to Sociological Theory.* London: Macmillan.

Offe, C. (1985). *Disorganized Capitalism.* Cambridge: Polity.

Palmer, B. S. (1981). *The Making of E. P. Thompson: Marxism, Humanism and History.* Toronto: New Hogtown Press.

Paramio, L. (1990). "Ideología y dominación en la sociedad actual." In: *Socialismo y cultura*, eds. A. Guerra et al. Madrid: Sistema.

Pérez-Agote, P. (1989). *La sociedad y lo social.* Bilbao: Servicio Editorial de la Universidad del País Vasco.

Przeworski, A. (1985a). *Capitalism and Social Democracy.* Cambridge: Cambridge University Press.

_____ (1985b). "Marxism and Rational Choice." *Politics and Society* 14(4):379–409.

Roemer, J. (1982). "Methodological individualism and deductive Marxism." *Theory and Society* 11:513–520.

_____ (1986). *Analytical Marxism* Cambridge University Press.

Rorty, R. (1982). "Nineteenth-century idealism and twentieth-century textualism." In: *Consequences of Pragmatism*, pp. 139–159. Brighton: Harvester.

Rundell, R. F. (1987). *Origins of Modernity*. Cambridge: Polity.

Rustin, M. (1987). "Absolute Voluntarism: Critique of a Post-Marxist Concept of Hegemony." *New German Critique* 43.

Sartre, J.-P. (1966). "Jean-Paul Sartre répond." *L'Arc* 30:94.

_____ (1977). *Situaciones*, Vol. 10. Buenos Aires: Losada.

Sewell, Jr. W. H. (1990). "How Classes are Made: Critical Reflections on E. P. Thompson's Theory of Working-Class Formation." In: *E. P. Thompson: Critical Perspectives*, eds. H. J. Kaye and K. McClelland, pp. 50–77. Cambridge: Polity.

Soper, K. (1990). "Socialist Humanism." In: *E. P. Thompson: Critical Perspectives*, eds. H. J. Kaye and K. McClelland, pp. 213–214. Cambridge: Polity.

Stedman, Jones G. (1983). *Languages of Class*. Cambridge: Cambridge University Press.

Sztompka, P. (1991). *Society in Action: The Theory of Social Becoming*. Cambridge: Polity Press.

Taylor, M. (1985). "What is Human Agency?" In: *Philosophical Papers*, Vol. 1: *Human Agency and Language*, ed. C. Taylor. Cambridge: Cambridge University Press.

_____ (1989). "Structure, Culture and Action in the Explanation of Social Change." *Politics and Society* 17(2):118.

Therborn, G. (1985). "The rise of social scientific Marxism and the problems of class analysis." In: *Macro-Sociological Theory*, eds. S. N. Eisenstadt and H. J. Helle, pp. 135–167. London: Sage.

_____ (1986). "Class Analysis: History and Defence." In: *Sociology: From Crisis to Action?* ed. U. Himmelstrand, Vol. 1, pp. 96–132. London: Sage.

Thompson, E. P. (1977). *La formación de la clase obrera inglesa*. Barcelona: Laia.

_____ (1978). *The Poverty of Theory and Other Essays*. London: Merlin Press.

_____ (1984). "La política de la teoría" In: *Historia popular y teoría socialista*, ed. R. Samuel, pp. 301–317. Barcelona: Crítica/Gijalbo.

Torfing, J. (1991). "A Hegemony Approach to Capitalist Regulation." In: *State, Economy and Society*, eds. R. B. Bertramsen et al., p. 212. London: Unwin Hyman.

Trimberger, E. K. (1984). "E. P. Thompson: understanding the process of history." In: *Vision and Method in Historical Sociology*, ed. T. Skocpol, pp. 226–227. Cambridge: Cambridge University Press.

Urry, J. (1982). "Duality of Structure: Some Critical Issues." *Theory, Culture and Society* 1(2):100–106.

Urry, J., and S. Lash (1987). *The End of Organized Capitalism*. Cambridge: Polity.

Wood, A. W. (1986). "Historical Materialism and Functional Explanation." *Inquiry* 29:11–27.

Wood, E. M. (1984). "El concepto de clase en E. P. Thompson." *Zona Abierta* 32.

Wright, E. O. (1987). "Towards a Post-Marxist Radical Social Theory." *Contemporary Sociology* 16(5):??–??.

_____ (1989). "Rethinking, Once Again, the Concept of Class Structure." In: *The Debate on Classes*, eds. E. O. Wright et al., p. 276. London: Verso.

Wright, E. O., and Kwang-Yeong Shin (1988). "Temporality and Class Analysis." *Sociological Theory* 6:58–84.

Chapter FIVE

Hermeneutics and the Theory of Social Action

Franco Crespi

THE REDUCTION OF ACTION TO MEANING

Summarizing the conclusions of his critical appraisal of different contemporary sociological theories of action (Parsons, Luhman, Habermas, Touraine), Rüdiger Bubner writes: "The concept of action has been defined, without exception, through another concept, which is now at the centre of attention... The term replacing the concept of an action is always that of 'meaning,' even if the latter may refer, according to the circumstances, to completely different things" (Bubner 1976:52).

An analysis of the most important theoretical approaches to social action in contemporary sociology shows a common orientation towards the critique of the merely objectivistic approaches, stressing the creative dimension of action; but there is also a common tendency to overevaluate the determinate symbolic-normative dimension of action, and to disregard the indeterminate dimensions of it more directly connected to life experience.

When society is mainly analyzed in terms of values and patterns of behavior, the impact of cultural elements is inevitably overestimated to the detriment of interpretation of actual social relations which, although they are largely the product of the observance of norms and codified social models, can also be regarded as the result of a constant infringement of such norms and models.

There certainly is a connection between the tendency to stress the cultural-normative concept of social reality and the concept of science as knowledge mainly based on predictability and control, that is, analysis more oriented to understanding than to causal explanation. Stressing the anonymous character of codified habitus, tradition, values, internalized rules, etc., undoubtedly leads to a clear determination of the sociological field, while consideration of the subjective dimension of action makes the object of sociological analysis far less precise. As Levi-Strauss rightly argued, to obtain an exact science one must *repudier le vecu* (Levi-Strauss 1955:50). But how could we reach a real understanding of social dynamics by ignoring the specific character of action?

I believe that sociological analysis can develop only through recognition and interpretation of the ambivalent character of the relation between action and symbolic order. Here lies, of course, a challenge for sociological knowledge, for life experience as such necessarily escapes empirical observation. As the latter has to be developed through a partial selection of aspects from a stream of complex relations, the particular contribution of sociology must take place in the intermediate point between the opposite extremes of absolute abstraction and total concreteness, revealing, within a constant oscillation between these two poles, some aspects of reality which otherwise would be ignored.

I believe that an adequate understanding of action should take into account first the fact that the cultural forms are generated by action before orienting it; second, that the unmeasurable dimension of action, although limiting our capacity of predictability and understanding, is an essential reference to prevent losing sight of the specific character of the social situation.

In this paper I shall briefly try to show that an adequate theory of social action should free itself from every totalitarian pretension characteristic of the teleological paradigm of our cultural tradition. As stressed by Heidegger's hermeneutical analysis, the primacy attributed within that tradition to cognition and purposive rationality has removed the "ontological" dimension: when the latter is duly recognized it then appears that action cannot be interpreted only by means of causal factors or normative principles, but it emerges as a multidimensional reality "having no reason," and as previous to any conscious determination of intentionality and values (see Schürmann 1982).

When perceived against the background of the ontological dimension, the unmeasurable character of action explains, on the one hand, the capacity of the social actor to transcend to a certain degree the symbolic-normative orders to the point of contrasting "reality," while on the other hand, the pre-predicative character of action can be interpreted in terms of the social actor's belonging to a sociocultural context which defines the horizon of his or her concrete possibilities. In this way the fallacies of traditional individualism can be avoided.

The unobjectifiable character of life experience shows that action is a borderline concept for sociological theory, reference to which is however essential for a nonreductive empirical analysis of social reality. This analysis can be developed only by taking into account the particular position of the individual in his relation with the practical determinations of action and the forms of symbolic-normative mediation.

On the basis of these presuppositions, the problem of the theory of action can be developed through a confrontation with the contemporary experience of hermeneutics, as long as that experience appears grounded on the relationship between life experience and cognitive forms as well as on the interrelation between action and language.

ONTOLOGY OF UNDERSTANDING, SUBJECTIVITY, ACTION

Ricoeur has pointed out that Heidegger's ontological research puts an end to the characteristic "predominance of epistemology" of Dilthey's hermeneutics. Dilthey was interested above all in establishing the autonomy of the "sciences of the spirit" as opposed to the "sciences of nature." Through distinction between understanding and explanation and by stressing the capacity of the individual to grasp empathically the psychological experience of others, Dilthey intended to guarantee both the dignity and the specificity of historical and social sciences (Ricoeur 1987).

In Dilthey, however, the rationalistic and positivistic conception of science still predominates, and the "sciences of the spirit" are mainly conceived with reference to that model. Thus, for Dilthey, understanding continues to have priority on being.

Heidegger instead stressed the ontological dimension by considering the nature of the human subject as a being who formulates questions about Being. In this perspective, understanding is interpreted as "a distinctive character of being-in-the-world" (Ricoeur 1987). In *Sein und Zeit*, *Dasein* (existence) is conceived as thrown into the world, as involved from the very beginning in the essential situation characterized by affectivity, anxiety and care (*Sorge*) (Heidegger 1927). The involvement of Dasein in the existential situation shows the pre-predicative character of our relation to the world, the existential prior-structure which anticipates all cognition and self-awareness. It is precisely from this prior-structure that action develops as a dimension directly connected with being-in-the-world, prior to any conscious understanding or interpretation.

The situation into which the individual is projected is characterized by reflexive comprehension, but the latter is deeply conditioned by the situation itself; that is, by that pre-predicative relation to what is an image of action ready-to-hand (*zuhanden*) which is already intrinsically a form of understanding and interpretation (Heidegger 1927). The Heideggerian concept of prior-structure is, as Derrida has pointed out, an essential dimension referring to the fact that the individual is from the very beginning engaged or involved in a situation before he makes any conscious choice (Derrida 1987:153).

Heidegger's criticism of the traditional concept of consciousness correctly stressed that consciousness does not have a founding function. The specific self-understanding of consciousness appears as essentially limited, constantly prone to error and self-deception and, in the final analysis, doomed to fall short of its project of total transparency.

In this context, self-consciousness can be essentially understood as the capacity to negate objectivized forms. To be self-conscious does not mean knowing who we are, but knowing who we are not: It is characteristic of the Ego to differentiate itself not only from external things, but also from internal objectivizations which constitute its own Self or identity.

George Mead and Sartre's different analyses of the process through which the Self is constructed show that both the dimension of identification with and differentiation from the other are equally important for the development of self-consciousness (Aboulafia 1986).

Identity thus appears only as part of self-consciousness, the latter also being always comprehensive of nonidentity, that is, of the capacity to differentiate from any form of determinacy. "Man is the being who can say no" (Scheler 1927): the capacity of negation and differentiation lies at the basis of the essential insecurity and weakness of the human being stressed by Gehlen. Self-consciousness produces a reflexivity which breaks immediacy, that simple harmony of the living individual with himself, thus creating an irretrievable gap between the individual and his instinctual drives. At this point, a new settlement based on symbolic mediation becomes necessary. What before was lived with the immediacy of an instinctual response now has to be elaborated by means of a system of symbolic meanings; that is, through those expressive and normative forms that sociologists call culture. The instinctual mechanism is thus replaced by representations, values and rules, which orient the action of the individual as well as that of collectivities.

In this perspective it appears that two conditions mainly characterize the dimension of action. The first is connected with the breaking of the direct relation between behavior and its meaning. Action always has a symbolic meaning related to the inner world of the actor, a meaning which cannot once and for all be taken for granted, but has to be verified anew each time.

The second condition concerns the constant oscillation between the need of determinacy (social predictability necessary for social life, reinforcement of identity both at the individual and the collective level, etc.) and indeterminacy due to the capacity of negation and to the complexity of life experience and its necessary adaptation to ever-changing material or cultural conditions in the natural and social environment. Being determinate, the forms of symbolic mediation are in fact always reductive of the complexity of action and, in the final analysis, turn out to be inadequate for the different needs which emerge in life experience (Crespi 1982, 1985, 1992).

ACTION AND LANGUAGE

The theory of social action has not until now adequately exploited the implications of the acknowledgment that action emerges in a prelinguistic and prereflexive situation. On the contrary, in recent years there has been a tendency to consider hermeneutics only with reference to language and symbolic order, thus removing the specific ontological dimension of Heidegger's thought.

As it is well known, even Heidegger progressively abandoned phenomenological analysis of the existential situation, seeking in poetical language a different way of referring to Being. This turning point in Heidegger's thought may be justified by the intent to consider Being as independent from Dasein, thus minimizing the subjective decisionist dimension developed in *Sein und Zeit* within the problem of life authenticity. But at a different level of sociological theory, the phenomenological analysis of Dasein by the early Heidegger still remains valid.

In Heidegger and in Gadamer, language always has an ontological character: language reveals, and at the same time conceals, Being; language brings in itself Being, but it is also that which alludes to Being, thus showing that language is not commensurate with Being itself.

In particular, the relation to tradition still has in Gadamer that dimension of ontological belonging which both Apel and Habermas, by stressing the critical attitude towards tradition and by reestablishing the priority of cognitive and communicative procedures as a basis of formal rationality, tend to eliminate. The fact that interpretation belongs to the horizon of subjective experience is submitted by Habermas to the criteria of communicative rationality and to the validity claims pertaining to an ideal linguistic situation. In so doing, Habermas reestablishes the priority of transcendental reflexivity over the existential situation and reduces life-world to merely cultural or communicative reality.

The opposition between Gadamer and Habermas is based precisely on the different relevance attributed to the ontological dimension of preunderstanding with regard to reflexivity and communication. If Gadamer's attitude towards this aspect appears at times ambivalent, in his approach there remains the possibility of recognizing the essential limits of language in its relation to Being. To consider language as a fundamental ontological horizon does not necessarily imply that language can exhaust the entire reality. According to Gadamer, historical being-in-the-world, although it dwells in language, is never revealed as such by language: the historical being remains concealed in language since the nature of language itself remains essentially unknown to us (Gadamer 1971). This shows that Gadamer conceives language in terms of a reality having the same elusive character of Being; that is, in quite different terms from the analytical approach to language in Habermas and the current philosophy of language. Gadamer's reference to the reductive character of language is even more explicit when he states that if "Being that can be understood is language," not all Being can be understood. Gadamer also stresses that the awareness of effective-history is "unavoidably more Being than consciousness" and that self-knowledge can never be complete: this shows that life experience always transcends understanding (Gadamer 1969:352, 536).

Habermas instead refers to communicative rationality as a deep structure which emerges once the coercions and distortions of the authority of tradition are eliminated. By referring to an ideal model of rational transparency which overcomes every contradiction in a free communicative exchange, the Habermasian approach appears to be a new, more sophisticated version of the utopia of freedom from all coercion and conflict, thanks to a self-evident reason. Even if, stressing the function of the critique of ideology, Habermas implicitly recognizes the relevance of the capacity of negation as specific to subjective consciousness; he tries to positively establish rationality by reducing the pre-predicative structure of life-world to a merely cultural dimension, and he lapses into a sort of absolutization of the communicative structure. This attitude is obviously antithetic to Heidegger's and Gadamer's hermeneutics as well as, at least under certain aspects, to Wittgenstein's language-games theory. All these different approaches stress in one way or another the limitations of understanding and the priority of experience as compared to forms of rationality.

To remain in the hermeneutic perspective, it is necessary, on the one hand, to recognize that life experience is not exhausted by the linguistic dimension, while not ignoring the constitutive character of language for the construction of reality. On the other hand, besides our belonging to tradition and to the Husserlian "natural experience of life" (Lebensfahrung), it is also necessary to stress the capacity of the individual to negate the cultural objectivizations, thus laying himself open to ever new forms of life experience.

The last issue can be developed from Gadamer's concept of experience as an initial experience of nonentity; that is, the perception that "things are not what we thought they were" and the development of self-consciousness as a unit through the acknowledgment of what is alien to it. This occurs mainly through a distinction between the horizon of the past and that of the present: the fusion of horizons, according to Gadamer's terminology, becomes possible thanks to the awareness that we are alien to the past, and at the same time, our capacity of establishing a relation with the past through the specific interpretive horizon of our time (Gadamer 1960:356).

Thus the connection with tradition also allows a dialectic approach which, through the fusion of horizons, creates ever new perspectives: "Experience as such can never be merely knowledge ... true experience is always a reference to the possibility of new experiences. When we consider somebody to be an 'expert,' we never consider merely that he has become such through the experiences he has made, but also we imply that he is open to new experiences" (Gadamer 1960:411). The expert is essentially an undogmatic person capable of learning from experience: "The dialectic of experience does not end with acquired knowledge, but with that opening to experience which is a product of experience itself" (p. 411).

An essential feature of experience is in fact the capacity of releasing oneself from the prison of established things through a sort of dislocation which, by involving the actor in the game of action, brings him "out of himself" (Vattimo 1981:72-73).

Experience means acknowledgment of human limits, of the fact that we are not in control of time, that our capacity of prediction is scant, our projects are always uncertain and, above all, that "the question always prevails on the answer."

In spite of the fact that awareness of effective-history is "more Being than consciousness," the latter, according to Gadamer, is also that which permits escape from ideological rigidity and "to decide freely as to the soundness or unsoundness of my preunderstanding." In this way the inevitable prejudices which determine my preunderstanding can be transformed: the capacity to develop new preunderstandings through any available information explains the relentless strength of experience (Gadamer 1979).

Besides the initial dimension of belonging to tradition, in Gadamerian hermeneutics there is the possibility of a critical distanciation from objectivized forms. It is precisely with reference to the oscillation between distanciation and belonging, stressed — as we shall see further on — by Ricoeur, that we shall manage to understand better the ambivalent character of the dynamic relationship between action and symbolic order.

ACTION AS AN EVENT: IDENTIFICATION AND DISTANCIATION

Paul Ricoeur's critical analysis of the relation between existential phenomenology and hermeneutics has made an important contribution to the understanding of the specific character of social action in its relation to the symbolic-normative order.

Our comprehension of social action develops through analysis of forms of expression (language, social representations, etc.) and of cultural documents or "texts" into which life experience is objectivized. However, in its connection with phenomenology, hermeneutics is never merely a semantic analysis of meaning. When language is considered only semantically as a closed self-referential system, the fundamental function of the sign — the fact that it stands for something else, that it is allusive — is forgotten: "Language in itself, as a meaningful system, has to be referred to existence" (Ricoeur 1965:29).

Ricoeur considers the symbolic order to be a structure of significance where a direct, primary, literal meaning refers to another indirect, secondary, figurative meaning which can be grasped only through the first. For this reason, hermeneutics is not merely an epistemology of interpretation, but also an ontology of understanding: the comprehension of symbolic multivalent expressions is always an interpretation of life experience and of the Self.

The individual who, by means of signs and symbols, develops a reflexive interpretation of himself, is in the hermeneutic perspective no longer considered as the Cartesian subject establishing in the Cogito an immediate relation with himself; he is rather somebody who, through the exegesis of his life, discovers that he has been put into being before any self-consciousness (Ricoeur 1969:33).

In this perspective Ricoeur makes a distinction between the semantic level, where interpretation is considered to be the recognition of the different levels of significance and as the decoding of hidden meanings, and the reflexive level, where — presupposing the need to refer language to experience — the connection between signs and comprehension of Self is established.

As stressed by Marx, Nietzsche and Freud, "immediate" consciousness is merely a "false" consciousness: reflexivity is above all a critique of false consciousness, which follows the principle "to lose Self in order to find Ego." Consequently, reflexivity appears to be doubly indirect, as on the one hand, existence can be grasped only through texts or documents and, on the other hand, immediate consciousness is false (Ricoeur 1965:31).

Given these presuppositions, hermeneutics is released from the traditional foundation of subjectivity and "restored" in the existential dimension of desire. Taking into account the relevance for Freud of the relation between meaning and desire, sense and energy, language and life, we can understand, according to Ricoeur, that the individual is far from being self-sufficient and self-founding. Although we can never reach desire directly, by deciphering the illusions of desire we can probe more deeply into the relation between reflexivity and meaning, but only through the interpretation of signs and symbols (see Ricoeur 1965:33).

The fact that desire has to be guessed "behind the enigmas of consciousness" without ever being grasped in itself, prevents falling into a sort of "mythology of pulsions" and reveals the difference between hermeneutics and any form of vitalism.

With Ricoeur's approach to the authentic meaning of hermeneutics, we can also throw light on the context of a nonreductive theory of action. To do so, we must make a distinction between objectivized forms of symbolic mediation, constitutive of the "texts" of life which are susceptible to structural analysis, and the existential dimension, whose recognition — albeit always indirect and partial — cannot be avoided. Indeed, as mentioned above, existence is a constant reference of the symbolic order. Only through recognition of the tension within this reference, can one pay due attention to the contradictions of social action. Although Ricoeur stresses the autonomy of the text and the possibility of considering an accomplished action as text, he conceives structural text analysis as only part of a broader interpretive process which, in the final analysis, must refer to the existential dimension of action (Ricoeur 1986:183)

While we can analyze action empirically through its objectivized forms or traces, we should not forget that action is also an event: from a theoretical standpoint it is important to take into account that any fixing of an event (written text as compared to live talk, "traces" as compared to actual action, etc.) entails a certain degree of loss (Ricoeur 1985:171). Ricoeur's concept of trace as an "effect-sign" refers to the meaningful relation between action as an event and the signs it has left. In the latter perspective, the connection, stressed by Ricoeur, between action and desire permits taking into account many symbolic meanings of social action.

Ricoeur's distinction between belonging ("l'appartenance") and distanciation is also relevant for the theory of action. This distinction in fact corresponds to that between identification with and negation of the objectivized forms which we have already considered as a capacity of consciousness.

Referring to the foundation of the critique of ideology, Ricoeur justly underlines the dialectic character of the relation between experience of belonging to a tradition or a sociocultural context, and experience of distanciation, i.e., of becoming estranged (Verfremdung) from that same tradition or context (Ricoeur 1986:365). Without expounding here Ricoeur's theory, I shall just recall that his distinction fits neatly into the controversy between Gadamer — accused of ontologizing hermeneutics to the point of attributing preeminence to historical tradition over judgment, and Habermas's critical approach, which instead gives preeminence to rational reflexivity over any historical conditioning.

Ricoeur's attempt is correctly oriented to avoid both extremes: on the one hand, that of stressing the dependence of the individual from historical-cultural tradition to the point of denying any possibility of dissent from the prevailing social order on which even hermeneutics would appear to depend; and on the other hand, of univocally stressing the dimension of distanciation, thus lapsing into a new form of idealism, by assuming — as in Habermas's theory of communicative rationality — the possibility of judging the contextual relativity of interpretations from a superior point of view, free from any connection with tradition. The former issue does away with the negative dimension of distanciation, while the second tends to ignore the fundamental hermeneutic assumption that being-in-the-world is prior to consciousness and knowledge.

Only through consideration of the radical limit arising from the unavoidable dependence of our understanding on tradition and prejudice, can one establish a correct critique of the different objectivized forms. In fact, such critique stems from the impossibility of considering the definite reductive forms of symbolic mediation as absolute truth, and at the same time, from awareness that these forms — precisely inasmuch as they are definite — always tend to assume an absolute character. In this context the critique of ideology appears, in the final analysis, to be recognition of the inevitable "ideological" character of any form of representation and interpretation of reality (Crespi 1987).

Distanciation is thus eminently negative as it does not lead to absolute overcoming of prejudices, but instead leads to their transformation through the gradual shifting from one form of interpretation to another. In this way neither form is dogmatically confirmed, thus becoming functional to power: power, seeking its own absolute legitimation, always makes use of ideological forms which are not recognized as such.

Instead, when distanciation is considered as a positive capacity of giving up prejudices and of developing "nonideological" forms, there is the risk, by giving priority to understanding, of falling into a form of ideology precisely because one aspires to establish an entirely nonideological point of view.

In the hermeneutic perspective there is no transparency of meaning, nor is any "exclusive possession of the true opinion" possible, communication is therefore conceived as a "reciprocal testing of different prejudices" (Gadamer 1979:301, 305).

Ricoeur's theory of the dialectic relation between belonging and distanciation shows that recognition of the impact of tradition and prejudice on our understanding does not necessarily lead to blind submission to the prevailing sociocultural orders. As Gadamer has pointed out, all change, as well as any attitude opposed to change, inevitably takes place in relation to tradition. Such dialectic, which corresponds to the aforementioned relation between identification with and negation of the objectivized forms, reveals the social actor to be both a product and an active producer of social reality.

HERMENEUTICS AND PRAGMATISM: ACTION AND SOCIAL PROJECT

Richard Rorty, in an attempt to develop a new approach to pragmatism, has compared the theoretical perspectives of John Dewey and Martin Heidegger, and stressed some common points between the two (Rorty 1982:67).

Without entering here into the legitimacy of Rorty's approach, I believe we should recognize that, at least to a certain extent, comparison between hermeneutics and pragmatism can be useful for the theory of action.

Both for hermeneutics and pragmatism, knowledge is an interpretive process which, stemming from concrete historical contexts and intersubjective practical experience, leads to results which are continuously susceptible to revision. The priority of being-in-the-world on understanding appears to be confirmed by pragmatism, which is also oriented to consider action both in its connection with the conditions of the historical and social situation and as a creative dimension.

However, concerning pragmatism, the most important contribution to sociological theory of action was of course George Mead's analysis of the relation between "I" and "me." If "me" is the organized unit of social codified attitudes, the "I" is the response to these attitudes, the typical individual reaction to the socially organized "me".

When he makes a distinction between "I" and "me", Mead seems implicitly to recognize the dynamic between identity ("me") and nonidentity ("I") which I defined above as the negative capacity proper to consciousness. The "I," as an active and relatively autonomous response to the codified attitudes of "me" as a social product, has a creative character: "reducing to a minimum" the conventional form of "me," the "I" can actively introduce changes in society itself (Mead 1934:218 ff., 326).

Even if intimately connected with pragmatism, Mead also studied with Dilthey and was "familiar with the latter's intellectual aims" (Joas 1985:41). His experience thus appears as the point of intersection between pragmatism and hermeneutics. This explains why Mead has made an important contribution to better understanding of the relation between action and cognition, between action and the determined forms of symbolic-normative mediation.

Moreover pragmatism has revealed dimensions which risk being overlooked by the hermeneutic perspective. I am referring in particular to the practical problem of founding a social project which, while denying any absolutization of the forms of the symbolic-normative order and social institutions, would develop beyond any abstract scheme as a capacity of attention to concrete situations, and of dealing with their inevitable contradictions.

In this same direction one could develop a nonreductive pragmatism, since the tendentiously instrumental character of pragmatic action can expand with reference to the indeterminate dimensions and changing requirements of life experience, thus stressing the creative potentialities of action. It is evident that the priority given to the negative dimension of consciousness by no means excludes the possibility of a positive social project. The critique of the established social order can develop concretely only through a constructive proposal based on evaluation of the contingent situation and selection of its actual possibilities.

The connection between the negative dimension of consciousness and the positive social project eliminates from the latter any trace of voluntaristic imposition. By making concrete choices in full awareness of the inevitably reductive nature of any type of selection, the social project thus appears to be qualified by the constant capacity of reflexive adjustment by means of trial and error. Thus the "violence" inflicted on reality, which, at least to a certain extent, is implicit in any reduction of complexity or determinate form of interpretation, would be attenuated.

CONCLUSION: DETERMINACY AND INDETERMINACY OF ACTION AND THE FUNCTION OF SOCIAL RESEARCH

In this paper I have merely attempted to sketch the general lines of the relevance of hermeneutics in the theory of social action when we consider the former as against its edulcorated translation in the current "linguistic" approach, and when we take into account the non-reductive ontological perspective attributed to hermeneutics by the early Heidegger.

I shall not attempt to analyze here all the possible consequences of such reference, but in concluding, I should like to recapitulate some of the results which I consider of importance for further steps towards a theoretical discourse "beyond polarization". (For a fuller analysis of this problem, see Crespi 1992.)

In the hermeneutic perspective, truth appears as the result not only of scientific methods, but also of the lived experience within which scientific work becomes possible and from which emerge the choices which orient theories and research methods. In this context, any form of knowledge appears to be reductive when compared with the complexity of experience (Erlebnis), which in itself appears inexhaustible.

The importance of the preconscious, pre-predicative dimension establishes hermeneutic knowledge as a translation (which is intrinsically in some way also a shift from the original meaning) stemming from a historical and cultural tradition, and as a fusion of different horizons. In this way, the idea of truth as a mirror of reality is completely done away with.

Showing the relations among interpretation of a written text, theory of action and historical knowledge, Ricoeur considers both understanding (Verstehen) and explanation (Erklären) as necessary parts of the process of interpreting. If, at a strictly epistemological level, the scientific method is represented only by casual explanation, understanding appears as the "non-methodic" moment which precedes, accompanies and follows any explanation. Understanding gives a specific contribution whether to the deciphering of the signs in the theory of the text, or to the interpretation of motivational intentions in the analysis of action, or as the capacity to follow a narration in the theory of history (Ricoeur 1986:181). Verstehen in this perspective is related to our belonging to Being, prior to any distinction between subject and object and to any objectivization resulting from explanation. However, as we have seen, the dimension of belonging does not exclude the possibility of distanciation, which develops through the objectivizing method of science. If Verstehen includes explanation, the latter is a partial analytic translation of the former. The possibility of objectifying and of analytically explaining reality appears thus as a specific linguistic game which, as any other linguistic game, can only develop thanks to the pre-predicative belonging to a form of life.

I believe that sociological theory of social action entails maintaining a special tension between the method of explanation, peculiar to analytical sciences, and the understanding linked to practical experience of everyday life. Any interpretation of social action, even of the more reductive type, as the utilitarian model, holds (at least implicitly) a reference to the entire existential situation. If this is true for the concept of intentionality even when used in connection with instrumental rationality, it is all the more so when we deal with the Weberian concept of rationality oriented to value, where the reference to the entire horizon of lived experience is inevitable.

At an empirical level, the ontological dimension of action explains its relative opacity to any type of interpretation, since action is reducible neither to meaning nor to intentionality. Thus action should be considered, as mentioned earlier, as a borderline concept of sociological theory referring to a reality which can be grasped only indirectly, and never entirely comprehended by means of interpretive paradigms. Recognition that action is not reducible to meaning, to the rules of communication or to the symbolic-normative order permits awareness of the fundamental contradictions of social action in its relation to the institutional structures of the social system. This explains why reference to the borderline concept of action is essential for an adequate theory of society.

The acknowledgment of the pre-predicative dimension of action shows, on the one hand, the contradictory relation existing between action and the determinate forms of symbolic-normative order along the lines described above of identification ("belonging") and distanciation, identity and nonidentity. On the other hand, it shows that the practical necessity of dealing with that contradiction is a fundamental drive of social action.

In this perspective, which takes into account both the indeterminacy and the determinacy which characterize action, the analysis can develop as interpretation of the internal coherence of one specific action without dogmatically applying external models of instrumental or axiological rationality formulated by the social scientist. The interpretation should attempt to reach the meanings peculiar to the actor's situation, both with reference to the general categories of action in its relation to the contradiction connected with being-in-the-world, and to the material and cultural conditions of the specific contingency considered. In this way, reference is no longer to an abstract model of rationality, but to the internal "logic," conscious or unconscious, of that particular social experience.

Following Ricoeur's analysis of the text, social research in a hermeneutic perspective develops through taking into account, on the one hand, those concrete objectivized forms or "traces" which action inscribes in history, and on the other hand, the fact that these traces, as we have seen, lead to the manifold meanings of action as an "event."

At the same time a concrete product and a sign related to something else, the trace has a dual nature: as objectivized form it can be analyzed in terms of cause-effect in relation to a concrete sociocultural reality; as a sign it has also to be analyzed with reference to the ambivalent relation between action and the symbolic normative order. In this context, the social actor can be seen both as a product of the social system and as an active capacity through reflexive distanciation and negation of objectivizations, able to transform through continuous shifting, prevailing social models and values, and institutional social structures.

In this same perspective we can identify the social function of sociological research which appears as exchange between the different interpretations made by social actors and social scientists.

Considering the linguistic dimension (Sprachlichkeit) as the essential medium of life experience, Gadamer stresses both the limits of language as a definite code and its limitless capacity of creating ever new meanings. Thus, critique of ideology is grounded in recognition both of the finite character of determinate forms of expression and of the opening dimension of language as such: Any form of culture which conceals the reductive character of symbolic mediation is ideological inasmuch as it is an attempt to cancel that opening dimension through absolutization of the current form of expression — a removal which, in final analysis, is always functional to repressive domination.

The essential function of social research is therefore denunciation of all crystallized forms of symbolic mediation and revelation of the gap between the institutionalized social order and the true requirements of social action; it also gives voice to voiceless people still deprived of social recognition. Through self-criticism and the promotion of social communication, social research opens up social action to new prospects.

In this context, social research has mainly the cognitive function of letting the unseen and the unknown emerge, thus favoring the shifting from one form of symbolic-normative order to another, and forbidding any determinate historical form to be assumed as perfect or final.

As an essential hermeneutic exchange at a collective level, social research develops an active dialogue within society among all the various social actors in order to acquire a better understanding of the deep elements and contingent mechanisms underlying social processes. Thus, social research reveals itself to be pragmatically oriented towards the renewal of culture and society in a perspective of freedom.

Bibliography

Aboulafia, M. (1986). *The Mediating Self New Haven*. New Haven: Yale University Press.

Bubner, R. (1976). *Handlung, Sprache und Vernunft*. Frankfurt: Suhrkamp.

Crespi, F. (1982). *Mediazione simbolica e società*. Milano: Angeli.

_____ (1985). *Le Vie della sociologia*. Bologna: Il Mulino.

_____ (1987). "Ideologia, potere e analisi del linguagio." In: *Ideologia eproduzione di senso nella società contemporanea*, ed. F. Crespi. Milano: Angeli.

_____ (1992). *Social Action and Power*. Oxford: Basil Blackwell.

Derrida, J. (1987). *De l'esprit — Heidegger et la question*. Paris: Ed. Galile.

Gadamer, H. G. (1960). *Warheit und Methode*. Tübingen: Mohr.

_____ (1979). "Retorica, ermeneutica e critica dell'ideologia." In: *Ermeneutica e critica dell'Ideologia*, ed. G. Ripanti. Brescia: Gueriniana.

Heidegger, M. (1927). *Sein und Zeit*. Halle: Niemeyer.

Joas, H. (1985). *G. H. Mead — A Contemporary Reexamination of his Thought*. Cambridge: MIT Press.

Levi-Strauss, C. (1955). *Tristes Tropiques*. Paris: Plon.

Mead, G. (1934). *Mind, Self and Society*. Chicago: University of Chicago Press.

Ricoeur, P. (1965). *De l'interpretation*. Paris: Seuil.

_____ (1985). *Le Temps raconte*. Paris: Seuil.

_____ (1986). *Du texte à l'Action-Essais d'herméneutique, II*. Paris: Seuil.

_____ (1987). "Logica ermeneutica?" pp. 217–218.

Rorty, R. (1982). *Consequences of Pragmatism*. Brighton: The Harvester Press.

Schürmann, R. (1982). *Le Principe d'Anarchie — Heidegger et la question de l'agir*. Paris: Seuil.

Vattimo, G. (1981). *Al di la del soggetto*. Milano: Feltrinelli.

Chapter SIX

Away from Structuralism and the Return of the Actor: Paradigmatic and Theoretical Orientations in Contemporary French Sociology

Francois Chazel

Nowadays sociology no longer enjoys the exciting climate of the 1960s. Sociology has ceased to occupy a central position in the guided transformation of society and the sociologist is no longer seen as a herald of modernism or post-modernism, a favorite adviser to the prince. Uncertainty about the future, whether on a professional, national or even European level, has generated a wave of nostalgia which has given a real boost to history, and not only to the prestigious tradition of university history. These various factors have combined to weaken the overall position of sociology, which remains fragile despite the unquestionable developments which have taken place in the discipline. And yet this situation hardly warrants, in my view, a pessimistic diagnosis of the present or future state of the discipline, given the new directions currently shaping up.

THE TRANSFORMATION OF THE INTELLECTUAL CLIMATE AND THE CRYSTALLIZATION OF NEW RESEARCH DIRECTIONS

For a variety of reasons, connected both with the collapse of the Soviet model, and with the domestic failure of successive governments to resolve the major problems posed by the recession, the last decade has seen a progressive and increasingly adamant rejection of global ideologies. Marxism, which previously occupied a dominant position in intellectual life, and whose general influence was felt far beyond the small circle of academic Marxists, has been the first to experience the full blast of this shift in direction: it has now ceased to be a major reference point against which to situate individual social scientists. In its fall, it has been accompanied by other ideologies — such as Third Worldism — with which it was more or less closely associated and which, although of less general importance, are often quite significant in the social sciences.

In this connection, it is important to note that while all types of Marxism have been hit by this deep-rooted disillusionment, the previously dominant version, structuralist Marxism, has been more specifically and durably affected, so much so that it has experienced a virtual collapse. The approach and themes developed by Althusser, who was one of the leading protagonists of intellectual debate in the former period, or by Poulantzas, the main champion of structuralist Marxism in the field of sociology, have rapidly lost whatever influence they ever had. This has led to a somewhat paradoxical situation: if their ideas have any currency at all today, it is to be found neither in France nor even on the continent of Europe, where they were developed, but in the Anglo-Saxon world, in Great Britain and especially in the United States.

But in France, the structuralist approach, which underlay this current and which, in a variety of more or less radical or explicit forms, constituted one of the dominant characteristics of the social philosophy and of the sociology of the two preceding decades, has now been fundamentally challenged. And in such a context it was virtually inevitable that the thought of Michel Foucault, another major representative of the previous period, would eventually be tarred with the same brush. Some have called for Foucault to be "forgotten"

(Baudrillard 1977). In fact, what is happening is a break with Foucault.

The combined insights of Althusser and Foucault so dominated the previous period that it is possible, on the basis of these two approaches alone, to identify the former overriding tendencies in sociological research. Sociologists were recommended, if not actually required, to think in terms of structured totalities (whether these were social formations or epistemological systems) themselves subjected to modes of structural causality, in a perspective which aimed to supersede existing theories of the science of man. The flavors of the month were structuralism, determinism, anti-humanism and holism. In such a climate, sociologists were more attentive to synchronic than to diachronic criteria, became obsessed with the problem of the reproduction (Bourdieu and Passeron 1970) of social systems and paid scant attention to the analysis of social change. Their constant preoccupation was in apprehending structural determination, they tended to attach little or no significance to the degree of autonomy enjoyed by the agents they were studying, these being sometimes reduced to mere "structural support systems" (as put by Althusser). Sociologists were expected to steer clear of lapses into any philosophy of the subject and in so doing to neglect the specific impulses of different social actors. Finally, they were prone to postulate the existence of a total social control whose ramifications the disciples of Foucault (in the light of their master's work, Surveiller and Punir 1970) had the task of denouncing (e.g., Meyer 1977).

Today's sociology is based on a totally different set of characteristics. The structuralist and post-structuralist wave has broken. Structuralism is no longer a first source of inspiration, even if it still represents a type of thinking against which some sociologists find it useful to situate themselves. The obsession with social control has gradually faded and with it has disappeared a fundamentally naive if not actually caricatured vision of the phenomena of domination. Determinism is regularly challenged, and even when it is not rejected outright, there is much greater reluctance to accept that it can have a massive or unilateral impact. As for anti-humanism, the new direction is much less clear, but the concept itself is considered outdated and the major protagonists on this question would not use the same type of language. Where sociology is concerned, it is therefore possible to speak of a complete turnaround in thinking. It would, of course, be too simplistic to see this merely as a return swing of the pendulum: sea changes in the intellectual landscape never entirely respect the neat patterns of periodization, nor does the emergence of new directions in research generally happen overnight or without encountering resistance.

The turnaround is characterized above all by the appearance on the French sociological scene of methodological individualism, an astonishingly late development when compared with Anglo-Saxon countries.[1] The event itself was invested with a degree of solemnity on the publication of Raymond Boudon's and Francois Bourricaud's veritable manifesto, the *Dictionnaire critique de la sociologie* (1982). The two authors situate their work in the tradition of Max Weber, at any rate the Max Weber who, in a letter to Robert Liefman (1920), expressed his utter hostility to exercises based on collective concepts in sociology. That sets the tone; Boudon and Bourricaud express their rejection of totalitarian realism, propose to treat social facts as "aggregate phenomena ... resulting from the coming together of individual actions" and assert that the principle of methodological individualism must be regarded as a fundamental principle, not only of economics but of all the social sciences (1982:287). Clearly, a work of this type could not be received without reticence and reservations, but its publication and its impact bear witness to the new climate which I believe can be characterized by three basic traits: an interest in the economic paradigm, a mistrust of determinism, and an insistence on the rational dimension behind human and social behavior.

The economic paradigm, which for years aroused the hostility of most French sociologists, and which had in fact been more or less ignored by them, began to attract attention through partial borrowings (Simon's theory of limited rationality) or shared insights (the importance attached to game theory) in seminal works such as Crozier and Friedberg's *L'Acteur et le système* (1977) or Adam and Reynaud's *Conflits du travail et changement social* (1978), both of which offer a model of strategic analysis. And this new interest was reinforced by translation of the works of professional economists which nevertheless dealt with problems the sociologist could not ignore, such as Olson's *Logique de l'action collective*, published with a preface by Raymond Boudon (1978). Thus the problem of the relationship between economics and sociology was gradually formulated — or rather reformulated. In this respect it is interesting to note the relatively successful organization, under the aegis of the Société Francaise de Sociologie, of colloquium on Economy and Sociology in 1987. Such an event would have been difficult to imagine twelve or even ten years ago. The publication of the collective work *Sur l'individualisme* (Birnbaum and Leca 1986) is also an indication of these recent preoccupations, although, as Pierre Birnbaum and Jean

Leca indicate in their general introduction, individualism is approached from three distinct directions: descriptive, justificatory and explanatory (1986:13) of which only the latter need concern us here. But it is nevertheless revealing to see several authors pondering (and this is sometimes the central theme of their article) on the specific contribution of methodological individualism to the apprehension of social and political phenomena. It should be stressed that the conclusions to such studies are not always positive. The present writer suggests that, in the final analysis, the utilitarian perspective does not offer an adequate basis on which to build a genuine theory of social-political mobilization (Chazel 1986). George Lavau even expresses serious reservations about the economic explanations of electoral behavior (1986). More generally one might say that methodological individualism has aroused more interest than genuine conversion, but this interest has, as we shall see, helped incubate a number of significant developments.

Mistrust of determinism finds its strongest expression in Raymond Boudon's *La Place du désordre* (1984). This work is a resounding plea for the recognition of at least partial indeterminism in social phenomena. Specialists in these fields, Boudon insists, should prefer rather more cautions formulations than those which they have usually adopted: determinism has now been quite considerably relativized. Here Boudon is translating into his own language themes which remain vague, though nevertheless implicit within the sociological community: the futility of any research into primary causes of social change; skepticism about the nomothetic pretensions of sociology, which were nevertheless proclaimed by the founding fathers; weariness, in the wake of the more excessive (and often also the more degraded) versions of structuralism, with any presumptuous, generalizing theoretical constructions. But a good many sociologists would refuse to go further than this partial realm of agreement. In particular, they would not agree to base the analysis of social change solely on the principles of methodological individualism. And, despite the well-known abuses resulting from theoretical generalization, they would not systematically reject any general theory. Whatever the state of these differences of opinion, there is broad agreement around the notion of a diversified set of determining factors, as opposed to one massive determinism: Boudon's warnings about epistemological caution appear to have been heeded, although it would be fairer to say that they were already shared by many. Researchers are now better equipped to pay attention to the plurality of situations, as can best be seen by the renewal of interest in local studies. Sixty local areas have recently been subjected to an in-depth study under the impressive research program "observation of social change," which has brought together several teams under the joint direction of Jacques Lautman and Henri Mendras. The synthesis resulting from these projects bears witness to a new understanding of the "local" phenomenon which is now understood less as a "visible" community and more as a complex whole made up of action systems (Lautman and Mendras 1986). This complexity can be usefully studied at the level of sociability: as Alain Degenne (1983) has shown, researchers are now looking more specifically at networks of relationship and are thereby rediscovering the interest shown by Celestin Bougle (1870–1940), or even Georg Simmel (1858–1918) in social circles; at the same time, they can benefit from the techniques for analyzing social networks which have been developed in the United States. In this way, these new directions can give rise to methodological progress or at the very least, as a first step, to new methodological depths. The same point could be made about other objects of study, for instance "social trajectories." We are beginning to see more concern for the duration of phenomena, whether in the context of an individual biography or a collective history, a family of several generations. This reformulation of the aims and objectives has brought about shifts in methodology, which is now required not so much to serve up samples or cross sections but to come to grips with processes, both in their specificity and in their development. This explains the keen interest in biography and longitudinal analyses.

In these new approaches, whether motivated by a desire to break with determinism or simply by a recognition of the occasionally contradictory plurality of determining forces, individual social actors can no longer either be ignored or neglected, and this reassessment has given rise, in certain instances, to an insistence on the rationality of behavior. Of particular relevance in this connection are the rich insights to be drawn from the application to the sociology of organizations of Michel Crozier's model of strategic analysis. Francois Dupuy and Jean-Claude Thoenig (1983, 1985) have succeeded in showing how, in the context of French administration, the same civil servant can at the same time rationally play two seemingly contradictory games: he can avoid any trespassing on his own patch by fostering relationships of avoidance (évitement) both with his superior and with his own staff, as well as a relationship of noncommunication with his colleagues, while all the time looking for an "arrangement on the margins" with his external associates. It is therefore correct to suggest that the state administration suffers from bureaucratic rigidity, but only if it is also recognized that the same administration is constantly adapting itself to the environment through specific arrangements negotiated on a case-by-case basis. Such an approach, which it would not be inappropriate to call relatively rational, is easily transported from the specific sphere of organizations to that of public policy, and it is no surprise to note that these two authors, especially Jean-Claude Thoenig, have clearly set their sights in that direction (e.g., Grawitz and Leca 1985).

In a totally different field — collective behavior — Pierre Birnbaum (1984) has argued the case for the (at least partial) value of utilitarian perspectives. From general principles, he moved to specific examples by stressing the rational individual components of working-class strategy (Birnbaum and Leca 1986). But once again it was Raymond Boudon who emerged as the most ambitious — and the most reckless — theoretician in putting forward, in a 1986 book, a "rationalist theory of ideology" (Boudon 1986). As Boudon himself admits, classical theories, whether or not they are Marxist in inspiration, see ideology as a body of false ideas which people cling to for passionate (in other words, irrational) motives, while modern theories, like those of Geertz, tend rather to see in ideology a meaningful interpretation of the world which refuses to fit into criteria of truth or falsehood. But Boudon sees the analysis of ideologies quite differently: they may well be based on false premises, but it can be quite rational for the individual to adhere to them. The central part of Boudon's book is devoted to an explanation of this paradox. It must be stressed that, in order to do this, Boudon adopts a very broad definition of rationality: he is concerned with bringing out the correct reasons which have led an individual to cling to false ideas without restricting himself to a utilitarian interpretation of rationality or even to the Weberian framework of *Zweckrationalitat*. On the other hand, Boudon seeks to clarify the relationship between ideology and science, categories which he is careful not to set up in naive opposition to one another. Indeed, for Boudon the problem is precisely to explain how false ideas can be backed up by the authority of science, and the explanation lies at the heart of his "restricted theory of ideology." Boudon himself recognizes the limits of his own theory, but even so one has to ask whether this analytical approach, which is influenced by the sociology of knowledge and is, in that sense, very exciting, can in fact offer an explanation of the intensity of the hold which ideologies, particularly political ideologies, can exert over social actors. On a more epistemological level, the reader would like Boudon to develop in more depth his concept of rationality.[2]

Boudon clearly understood the challenge and that is why his last book, *L'art de se persuader des idées douteuses, fragiles ou fausses* (1990), is, in some respects, "a contribution to the theory of rationality." Boudon dwells on the importance of the notion, worked out by Simon, of subjective rationality and tries to clarify its meanings: actors may have good reasons, from a subjective point of view, to choose a wrong solution to a cognitive problem and more generally to adhere to false ideas. In other words, good reasons are not to be reduced to objectively valid reasons. The main examples, borrowed by Boudon from philosophy and sociology of science, are intended to reveal one and the same pattern: their conclusions are derived from an explicitly solid argument and yet are false or, at least, doubtful, because they are contaminated by implicit *a priori*, whether these *a priori* are of a logical, epistemological or linguistic kind. Human thought is guided by metaconcious frames and the whole book is built upon this theme, adumbrated by Simmel but articulated by Boudon in what he deferentially calls "Simmel's model." Therefore a clear demarcation has to be drawn between a relativistic theory of knowledge in Simmel's use of the word which only means that human and social knowledge is perspective — constrained and the modern and now fashionable relativism which denotes a pure skepticism. And throughout the book Boudon argues the case for developing a broad program of cognitive sociology, focused upon means and ways of adhering to ideas, which stands out against the narrower field of sociology of knowledge, restricted to the social causes of types of thought and beliefs. *L'art de se persuader* is in many aspects, as Boudon himself notes, in his "Préface à la nouvelle édition" (1991), a companion volume to *L'idéologie* but at the same time opening up new avenues of research. Beliefs and not only decisions must be studied in terms of subjective rationality, and sociology as well as psychology and philosophy has to contribute to the understanding of processes of cognition.

This stress on rationality (at least partial rationality) is symptomatic of the growing attention which is now being paid to the meaning of behavior patterns. Can we now speak of a "return of the actor," to use Alain Touraine's expression? (Touraine 1984) The work of Touraine and his colleagues, whether dealing with the strengths and weaknesses of the new social movements (students, regionalism, anti-nuclear) or with the overall decline of the labor movement (Touraine, Wieviorka and Dubet 1984; Touraine et al. 1978, 1980,

1981), suggests that the expression is appropriate. They have shown that any in-depth analysis of social movements cannot avoid coming to grips with the meaning and intentions of action, even if their particular method — sociological intervention — gives rise to serious reservations. In the same way, Francois Dubet's appropriately titled *La galère: jeunes en survie* (1987) shows how certain categories of particularly disadvantaged young people cannot be satisfactorily defined in terms of domination and exclusion (as the "received wisdom" of the 1970s would have put it), or even in terms of disintegration, following the principles of classical sociology, but in fact show signs (often rather fleeting) of autonomy and resistance. Towards the end of his book, Dubet is led to speculate about the symptoms of "a nascent social movement." In *Le retour de l'acteur*, which admittedly sees itself as a sociological essay with a much broader sweep, Touraine goes even further in asserting that "a new type of subject is beginning to emerge." "This book," he continues, "ought perhaps to have been called *Le retour du sujet*, because the subject is the name we give to the actor who is engaged in historical processes, in the production of the great normative directions of social life" (1984:15). Despite the brilliance of this formulation, I personally am worried by the equivalence (even partial) between actor and subject, which I fear runs the risk of creating confusion. It is essential to draw a rigorous distinction between the analytical and the empirico-historical. The return of the actor, in the sense in which we would use the term, can be used, in the current context, to refer to a more positive reassessment of the place of the actor in the interpretation of social life, a reassessment which owes a great deal to the Touraine school. The return of the subject, on the other hand, if we have to use this type of language, is a concept which only acquires its full meaning with reference to concrete sociohistorical change. If we accept the validity of this distinction, we would expect the expression "return of the actor" to be reserved for a certain type of transformation, observable via the paradigms and analytical modes of sociology, independently of any hypothesis or forecast about social evolution. Thus the actor (with a small "a") as an analytical concept in sociology would be totally dissociated from the historical Subject, a beast both the sociologist and the citizen have every reason to steer clear of.

AGAINST THE TIDE?

Pierre Bourdieu and his followers have, at any rate, engaged battle against the illusions of a philosophy of the subject and steadfastly oppose the drift of sociological research towards subjectivism. The principal concerns of the Bourdieu camp hardly seem in tune with the evolving trends I have tried to identify. Admittedly Bourdieu has always been at pains to distance himself from structuralism, in particular the Marxist variety, which he regularly accused of having done away with all agents (Bourdieu 1980:70). Very probably it was his rejection of Althusser's reduction of historical agents to the simple function of structural "supports" at the heart of Bourdieu's notion of "habitus." The habitus, a "system of lasting and transposable dispositions" (1980:88), allows for mediation between the realm of social determination and the realm of practice. But it must be stressed at once that the habitus is the product of objective conditions, more precisely "of the material conditions of existence characteristic of a social class" (Bourdieu 1972:175) and, as such (necessity becomes a virtue), it gives rise to aspirations and practices which are objectively adjusted to meet the situation. Bourdieu's agents are therefore very far from being subjects, and while the mediation of the habitus can be effective in so far as it is self-modifying in response to practical reality, it is in fact illusory, at least as far as the actor is concerned, since he is credited with no real autonomy. Only the deficiency of these habituses, that is to say the extent to which they lag behind present reality, allows us to escape the dominant logic of reproduction, and it is only in this indirect way, and therefore to a very limited extent, that the habitus can be regarded, *stricto sensu*, as a "principle of invention" (Bourdieu 1980:135). Such a concept, I feel recognizes (*reconnaître*) the role of agents, but to paraphrase Bourdieu's language does misrepresent (*méconnaître*) the importance of the social actor.

It is therefore hardly surprising if, in the new context of the 1980s, Bourdieu's theoretical constructions have been subjected to serious criticism, directed in particular at his two major notions: educational reproduction and symbolic domination. Bourdieu's model of reproduction through schooling, and the systematic opposition which he posits between democratization and reproduction, have been accused of amounting to the "effect of a theoretical closed shop." The static features of his theory — at least in the early version — have also been deplored (Cherkaoui 1983:22, 91). But it is the criticisms which have been levelled at the most recent formulation of the theory which seem to me to be the most relevant and significant. Pierre Bourdieu has now modified his theory in an attempt to take account of the changes in the French educational system over the last two decades and in particular the explosion in student numbers. According to Bourdieu, the real detonator of this phenomenon is to be sought in "a transformation in the reproductive strategies of those sections of the upper and middle classes with the greatest quantities of economic capital" (Bourdieu et al. 1973). In order to maintain their position in a new economic system, which implies a new type of industrial management, where degrees and diplomas become crucially important, these sections of the upper classes have, according to Bourdieu, converted their "economic capital" into "educational capital" and, as a result of their own intense usage of the education system, they have forced all the other classes to increase very substantially their own investment in education. This offers an explanation for the concurrent phenomenon of inflation and devaluation of educational qualifications. These "conversion strategies" thus amount to little more than "changing in order to conserve," competition in the educational field being quite simply translated into educational achievement rates as between the different classes and strata. In the end, "this peculiar form of class struggle" contributes massively to the reproduction of the status quo (Bourdieu:176–185). This original thesis, which draws attention to the relationship between shifts in the structures of industrial management and the educational itinerary of elites, does not stand up to close scrutiny, as Cherkaoui has shown (1983:90–97). Instead of there being prior intensive use of the education system by those with most economic capital, Cherkaoui has shown a simultaneous demand for education across all social groups. Moreover, far from there being a parallel evolution in educational attainment rates, he has discovered differential growth according to social categories. More generally, Cherkaoui emphasizes the limitations of this type of explanation which only brings in factors exogenous to the educational system itself and which therefore seem to him to be reductionist. Through his insistence on endogenous factors and through his concern to develop a sociology of change, Cherkaoui is in effect pleading for a new analysis of educational phenomena which is poles apart from the previously dominant tradition, of which Bourdieu is the principal representative.

The break is certainly less dramatic in the area of the sociology of culture, if only because Bourdieu's early project — to demonstrate the social stratification of cultural practice — is perceived, even according to the preestablished notion of the discipline, as being taken for granted. But if there is agreement on the basics of his study, there is little chance of agreement on the extreme conclusions which Bourdieu feels can be drawn from them, nor on the theoretical interpretation of the survey data which Bourdieu proposes. Indeed, there are very few people, including sociologists, who would accept the pure and simple substitution of the social critique of judgment for the Critique of Judgment, or who would bestow upon the sociologist (no prizes for guessing which one...) the eminent position previously occupied by the philosopher (in this case, Kant)! At a more basic level, Bourdieu's interpretation has been attacked, less, it must be said, because of its concentration on cultural domination than because it offers a reductionist vision of that domination. According to Claude Grignon and Jean-Claude Passeron (1984) Bourdieu is guilty of "legitimism," of only viewing the tastes of the middle classes and even more so of the popular classes through the prism of dominant tastes: to have popular tastes, in this view, is to have no taste for things which are inaccessible and reserved for others (Grignon 1987:21). Such a negative definition of popular culture, which is seen in terms of what is lacking, in effect prevents it from being studied seriously. If popular culture has its absences, middle culture is truncated: Bourdieu only comes at it from the angle of "cultural goodwill," which amounts to aping, more or less successfully, the genuine distinction which is the preserve of the dominant class. Inevitably, therefore, in Bourdieu's view, it lacks both autonomy and creativity (see Schweisguth 1983).

However, as far as the critique of Bourdieu and his disciples is concerned, it is insufficient simply to refer to a sociological approach which is rather old-fashioned in some of its expressions (sociology of education) or challenged in its hard core (sociology of culture). It must be pointed out that Bourdieu himself and some of his close collaborators have made efforts to adapt to some of the new prevailing trends. Three main aspects deserve mention here. First, Bourdieu has often adopted a strategy of defensive adjustment which, as we have already seen with the reformulation of the theory of reproduction, is not devoid of a genuinely scientific dimension, even if it is not as successful as had been hoped. There is a particularly striking illustration of this in *Choses dites*, a collection of texts and interviews where Bourdieu stresses "the idea of strategy as an orientation of practice" (pp. 33–34). This now seems to have replaced habitus as the cornerstone of Bourdieu's theoretical edifice. Second, we have been witnessing a redefinition of priorities: previously, despite the well known formula which defined habituses as "structured structures with a predisposition to function as structuring structures" (Bourdieu 1979:175, 1980:88), this type of sociology tended to see societies first and foremost as structured; whereas today it tends to attach more importance to the other side of social reality and to rediscover the significance of the structuring element. The most influential application of this new approach is Luc Boltanski's work on cadres (1982). The author, who then was one of Bourdieu's best-known disciples, devotes himself to the task of highlighting the progressive construction of an identity, to teasing out the processes of social formation from a universe of representation. But sometimes Bourdieu's influence can be felt in a less obvious way. In a book which is bubbling with original insights, and which seeks to elaborate a *Sociologie des crises politiques* from the standpoint of strategic interaction, Michel Dobry (1986) attempts to reconcile this major approach with a hypothesis about regression towards habitus in times of crisis, which effectively exposes his attempts at theoretical construction to extra difficulties, which in my view are futile. Such a construction poses relatively acutely the problem of the compatibility between profoundly different models, which is perhaps not very surprising at a time when interests are being redefined. Dobry's position is also significant in another way: institutionally, he belongs to a political science department, but professionally, he sees himself as a sociologist. He is far from being alone in this respect among the new generations of political scientists, who are strongly, although not exclusively, influenced by Bourdieu.[3]

This brings me to my third and final point: the displacement of Bourdieu's influence. Formerly dominant in the fields of sociology of education and culture, it is now more in evidence in political science among the younger researchers who are struggling, within their institutions, for full recognition to be granted to political sociology.

This displacement of influence is perhaps, in my opinion, to be observed from an other point of view. Bourdieu's inner circle has recently lost in France some of its outstanding representatives. Boltanski's recent book (1990) in which he gives an account of several years of research work, deserves in this respect to be referred to. Boltanski openly challenges the paradigm of "critical sociology" which, though it is improperly linked up with the approach of the classical sociologist, obviously is Bourdieu's own, disclosing at the same time the delusions under which social actors live and their postulated unfairness (*mauvaise foi*); he objects to "this universal clue" and does not grant the adequacy of the assumption of "a complete gap between self-conscious understanding of persons and realities of the social world in which they live" (1990:50). But we must not either lose sight of the fact that Bourdieu's work has now come to the fore in the Anglo-Saxon context: a recent book, in which he upholds his thought and cause in answering questions by Loic Wacquant, is clearly intended to publicize and promote his sociological method among American scholars (Bourdieu 1991); thus, he found Wacquant's help (who is used to a gatekeeper role between the two scientific communities) valuable.

TOWARDS A RECONSTITUTION OF THE SOCIOLOGICAL LANDSCAPE

Such, at any rate, are the indications suggested by the main trends we have just outlined. But one must beware of oversimplification: it would be too simplistic, for example, to say that we are moving from a collectivist to an individualist world view, or in ideological terms, from left-wing to right-wing sociology. As we have seen, it would be an exaggeration to consider methodological individualism as the dominant current, even though its influence is beyond dispute. Moreover, although this school's main protagonists in France have been conservative in sympathy, methodological individualism is in no way tied to a particular political ideology. If proof were required, one needs to remember that it was seen in the 1970s, in the United States, by the younger generation of sociologists as a protest against the then dominant academic tradition, which was accused of being conservative (when in reality it was closer to liberalism). The case of Jon Elster (1985), who claims to be both a Marxist and a methodological individualist, suggests that alignment with a particular school or paradigm can also be based on a specific interpretation of Marx.

To return to the French context, I believe it would be more accurate to say that we have witnessed the rapid breakup of a reifying vision of society, which threatened to impose upon sociology a type of jargon which came close to paralyzing the discipline. This collapse was the result of the combined efforts of various critiques, prominent among which were those of the methodological individualists. In some ways, the present situation can be seen as a period of transition. Sociology will henceforth be more open, which is a considerable blessing, but it is still difficult to say what the future holds. It is probable, given the general evolution of society, that the crude labels of right and left will be less and less relevant or appropriate as yardsticks for judging the opposing camps within the discipline. That is not to say that sociology is gradually joining the "end of ideology" model. But beyond this global sense that ideological spectacles are inadequate instruments with which to examine the new developments in the discipline (and a good number of sociologists would agree with that), there is likely to be little agreement on the shape of the sociology to come.

This uncertainly is reinforced by two factors: first by the characteristics of the present time which, as befits periods of transition, has first opened up avenues for the reconstruction, on new bases, of sociological knowledge; but secondly as a result of the institutional fragility of sociology in France. French sociology is lacking — in a general sense — the great debates and their attendant excitement. I am not talking about the pseudo-debates which are drummed up by the media or around popularized issues (Heidegger's links with Nazism). I am thinking of the lack of any really rigorous discussion in the scientific journals or in scholarly works. There has been, in France, no equivalent of the controversy between Habermas and Luhmann in Germany. In my opinion, the exemplary nature of that particular clash lay less in its specific content than in the mutual recognition and respect in which the protagonists held each other, over and above the real differences between them. Such conditions for debate have usually been lacking in France. Furthermore, although sociology in France has not escaped the general tendency towards institutionalization (even if it happened later than in the Anglo-Saxon countries), the professionalization which necessarily must follow has not yet been fully taken on board. There is still, quite visibly, a strong tendency towards more or less impressionistic essay writing. This is all the stronger in that the different types of intellectual production all have their specific markets and that this outlet allows the public access, with minimal outlay, to a symbolic form of gratification. I am not suggesting for a moment that the sociologist should be denied the use of a genre (the essay) or prohibited from following his or her intuition, especially in new or relatively peripheral areas of the discipline. But there are two major risks to be avoided if this path is pursued. Essays, by definition, tend to lack clear content definition and it is perhaps no accident that certain essay writers, including some of the most lucid, like Jean Baudrillard, have progressively drifted away from their disciplinary moorings.[4] At the same time, essayists often tend to overestimate the importance of their contribution to the social sciences. They fail to recognize that an essay is no substitute for authentic research, even if it can prepare for or put the finishing touches on research. Professionalization is also incomplete for a quite different reason, one which is less often noticed: the fact that researchers and scholars often have too narrow a conception of the "professional." The rapid expansion of demand for social (but in fact administrative) knowledge has brought about an increase in resources for applied research and an upsurge in surveys. One of the strongest (and therefore least controlled) tendencies has been to go for low-cost utilization of these new opportunities by acquiring a basic technical skill which can be readily adapted to different survey areas. In this way we have witnessed the development of a short-term expertise, too deeply involved in conducting raw surveys to bother about interpretive depth or methodological creativity. True sociological research has thus had to steer a narrow path between the mirage of impressionism and the illusion of technicity. And today it also has to protect itself against a number of ingenious projects in which banal variations on well-known themes are cleverly dressed up in technical jargon.[5]

But there are reasons for optimism. The transitional period we have just been through can be seen as the first stage of a reconstruction which has been marked by intensive criticism of the past and the crystallization of new directions. The conditions clearly exist for pursuing this task of reconstruction. One promising development is the increasing participation of (often younger generation) sociologists, in the work of the major research bodies, INSEE and INED. As a result, a mass of specifically sociological data is now available for use by researchers across a range of disciplines. In recent years there has also been a serious effort in translation, although it must be said that there was a considerable backlog of major works demanding attention. In the first instance we have seen translation of the classics, in particular Georg Simmel,[6] who has remained little known in France, and of well-known and relatively early works like Nisbet's *The Sociological Tradition*, Lewis Coser's *The Functions of Social Conflict*, or Howard Becker's *Outsiders*, as well as others.[7] This effort, which several publishers have helped promote, is symptomatic of a new state of mind, of a new curiosity about work carried out abroad, and of a further retreat for outdated "Hexagonalism."

This optimism would be misplaced if I failed to point out that there are serious obstacles to achieving full disciplinary autonomy. For instance, increased sensitivity to the historical dimensions of social phenomena, which has led to a transcendence of the artificial boundaries between sociology, perceived uniquely as a science of the present, and history, has not always been accompanied by a sufficiently clear consciousness of the specificity of each discipline. Sociology can derive great benefit from social history, but cannot be reduced to it. It is also becoming essential to rethink the links between sociology and philosophy. From an initial position of undue mistrust (in the early positivist period), sociology moved to one of undue dependence (as in the 1970s when certain philosophers — Althusser, Foucault — became major models of reference). This problem is now again with us. Boudon's work contributes to this reconsideration when he critically surveys the argument of some distinguished philosophers of science, and the question is explicitly aimed at by Boltanski and Thevenot in *Economies de la grandeur* (1987) when they draw upon political philosophy to build up their model of six different but principled cities, as well as, more implicitly, by the reflections of a group of sociologists who take their inspiration from Habermas and also in part from ethnomethodology. But there is still extensive work to be done in this area.

All things considered, it seems to me that the present trends are in the direction of a model of sociology which is pluralist, attentive to foreign work, without relinquishing its own specificity, and finally autonomous in the sense indicated above. But a last problem must not be dodged. Is not then French sociology going to incur the risk of splitting up into incommensurable outlooks and research? Are there any remaining links, on the one hand, between the program of cognitive sociology developed by Boudon and the theology — inspired inquiry of Boltanski into "agape" as a form of peace and on the other hand between Jean-Daniel Reynaud supporting the case of a "sociology of social regulations" (1989, 1991) which would combine Durkheimian concerns with a decision-oriented approach and younger scholars mainly dedicated to the investigation of different kinds of "social experience" by the method of sociological intervention? In spite of obvious differences, these approaches share some basic, theoretical as well as metatheoretical, orientations. First, they all rule out deterministic explanations of social behavior. Second, they pay much attention to actors ability and competence in facing their situation, cognitive and argumentative competence in Boudon's work (and in other respects in Boltanski's model of justice) decision-making capacity in Reynaud's or Crozier's approach and prospects of "historical action" in the Touraine group. Third, they state that the way is now paved for the developing but many-faceted paradigm of a sociology of action.[8] There is enough common ground for debate and I hope French sociology will profit by this intellectual context[9] to become more open, that is to say able to discuss from within its own ranks the diversity of its approaches.

Notes

1. The debate about methodological individualism took place in Great Britain in the 1950s and the early 1960s.
2. This concept appears in his work only in a long footnote at the end of chapter 1 (pp. 294–295, n. 14).
3. To give but one example, Badie (1978, 3rd ed., 1984) and Badie (1986), is totally unaffected by Bourdieu's influence.
4. The intellectual itinerary which led Baudrillard from Baudrillard (1970) to Baudrillard (1987), is in this context highly significant.
5. See, e.g., Bernard Cathelat (1985). For a useful update on this, see the critical notes by Nicolas Herpin in *Revue Francaise de Sociologie* 27:256–272 (1986).
6. We have seen the publication, in the collection *Sociologies* directed by Raymond Boudon and Francois Bourricaud, with Presses Universitaires de France, of Simmel's *Sociologie et épistemologie* (1981), *Les problèmes de la philosophie de l'histoire* (1984) and *Philosophie de l'argent* (1987). More recently, Max Weber's *Histoire economique: Esquisse d'une histoire universelle de l'économie et de la société*, and Troeltsch's *Protestantisme et modernité* have been published, both with Gallimard in 1991.
7. Mention should be made, among others, of Giddens (1987), Hirschman (1983) and Habermas (1987) in the collection edited by Birnbaum. Also the volumes by Becker (1988) and Goffman (1991) have come out recently.
8. In the introduction to a recently published *Traité de sociologie*, Raymond Boudon, the editor of the book, dwells on a common frame of reference to the contributors which he calls *actionnisme*. Such a frame of reference means first and foremost that actors must be taken seriously.
9. I should add that this overview is by no means complete. We have hardly mentioned the history of sociology, which has seen some well received works, such as Lamberti (1983), Besnard (1987) and Valade (1990).

Bibliography

Adam, G., and J.-D. Reynaud (1978). *Conflits du travail et changement social*. Paris: Presses Universitaires de France.

Badie, B. (1986). *Les deux Etats: Pouvoir et société en Occident et en terre d'Islam*. Paris: Fayard.

_____ (1978). *Le developpement politique*. Paris: Economica (3rd ed. 1984).

Baudrillard, J. (1970). *La société de consommation*. Paris: SGPP.

_____ (1977). *Oublier Foucault*. Paris: Galilée.

_____ (1987). *Cool Memories: 1980–1985*. Paris: Galilée.

Becker, H. (1988). *Les mondes de l'art*. Paris: Flammarion.

Berthelot, J.-M. (1982). "Réflexions sur les théories de la scolarisation." *Revue Francaise de Sociologie* 23:585–604.

Besnard, P. (1987). *L'anomie*. Paris: Presses Universitaires de France.

Birnbaum, P. (1984). *Dimensions du pouvoir*. Paris: Presses Universitaires de France.

Birnbaum, P., and J. Leca (Eds.) (1986). *Sur l'individualisme*. Paris: Presses de la Fondation Nationale des Sciences Politiques.

Boltanski, L. (1982). *Les cadres: la formation d'un groupe social*. Paris: Editions de Minuit.

_____ (1990). *L'amour et la justice comme compétences: Trois essais de sociologie de l'action*. Paris: Editions Metailié.

Boltanski, L., and L. Thevenot (1987). *Les économies de la grandeur*. Paris: Presses Universitaires de France.

Boudon, R. (1978). "Preface." In: *Logique de l'action collective*, ed. M. Olson, pp. 7–20. Paris: Presses Universitaires de France.

_____ (1984). *La Place du désordre*. Paris: Presses Universitaires de France.

_____ (1986). *L'idéologie ou l'origine des idées recues*. Paris: Fayard.

_____ (1990). *L'art de se persuader des idées douteuses, fragiles ou fausses*. Paris: Fayard.

_____ (1991). "Préface a la nouvelle édition," to his *L'art de se persuader des idées douteuses, fragiles ou fausses*, 2nd ed. Paris: Fayard.

_____ (Ed.) (1992). *Traité de sociologie*. Paris: Presses Universitaires de France.

Boudon, R., and F. Bourricaud (1982). *Dictionnaire critique de la sociologie*. Paris: Presses Universitaires de France (2nd ed. 1986).

Bourdieu, P. (1972). *Esquisse d'une théorie de la pratique*. Geneve: Droz.

_____ (1979). *La distinction*. Paris: Editions de Minuit, pp. 176–185.

_____ (1980a). *Le sens pratique*. Paris: Editions de Minuit.
_____ (1980b). *Questions de sociologie*. Paris: Editions de Minuit.
_____ (1987). *Choses dites*. Paris: Editions de Minuit.
_____ (1991). *Réponses*. Paris: Edition du Seuil.

Bourdieu, P., and J.-C. Passeron (1970). *La reproduction*. Paris: Minuit.

Bourdieu, P., with L. Boltanski and M. de Saint-Martin (1973). "Les stratégies de reconversion." *Information sur les Sciences Sociales* 12:61–113.

Cathelat, B. (1985). *Styles de vie*, Vols. 1 and 2. Paris: Ed. d'Organisation.

Chazel, F. (1986). "Individualisme, mobilisation et action collective." In: *Sur l'individualisme*, eds. P. Birnbaum and J. Leca, pp. 244–268. Paris: Presses de la Fondation Nationale des Sciences Politiques.

Cherkaoui, M. (1983). *Les changements du système éducatif en France 1950–1980*. Paris: Presses Universitaires de France.

Crozier, M., and E. Friedberg (1977). *L'acteur et le système*. Paris: Seuil.

Degenne, A. (1983). "Sur les réseaux de sociabilité." *Revue Francaise de Sociologie* 14:109–118.

Dobry, M. (1986). *Sociologie des crises politiques*. Paris: Presses de la Fondation Nationale des Sciences Politiques.

Dubet, F. (1987). *La galère: jeunes en survie*. Paris: Fayard.

Dupuy, F., and J.-C. Thoenig (1983). *Sociologie de l'administration francaise*. Paris: A. Colin.

Dupuy, F., and J.-C. Thoenig (1985). *L'administration en miettes*. Paris: Fayard.

Elster, J. (1985). *Making Sense of Marx*. Cambridge: Cambridge University Press.

Foucault, M. (1970). *Surveiller et punir: naissance de la prison*. Paris: Gallimard.

Giddens, A. (1987). *La constitution de la société*. Paris: Presses Universitaires de France.

Goffman, E. (1991). *Les cadres de l'expérience*. Paris: Editions de Minuit.

Grawitz, M., and J. Leca (Eds.) (1985). *Traité de Science Politique*, Vol. 4. Paris: Presses Universitaires de France.

Grignon, C. (1987) "Quelle sociologie des pratiques culturelles." In: *Pratiques culturelles et politiques de la culture*, ed. F. Chazel. Bordeaux: Maison des Sciences de l'Homme d'Acquitaine.

Grignon, C., and J.-C. Passeron (1984). "Sociologie de la culture et sociologie des cultures populaires." *Documents de GIDES*, No. 4.

Habermas, J. (1987). *Théorie de l'agir communicationnel*. Paris: Fayard.

Hirschman, A. (1983). *Bonheur privé, action publique*. Paris: Fayard.

Lamberti, J.-C. (1983). *Tocqueville*. Paris: Presses Universitaires de France.

Lautman, J., and H. Mendras (Eds.) (1986). *L'esprit des lieux. Localités et changement social en France*. Paris: Ed. du CNRS.

Lavau, G. (1986). "L'électeur devient-il individualiste?" In: *Sur l'individualisme*. eds. P. Birnbaum and J. Leca, pp. 301–329. Paris: Presses de la Fondation Nationale des Sciences Politiques.

Maffesoli, M. (1985). *La connaissance ordinaire*. Paris: Librairie des Meridiens.

Meyer, P. (1977). *L'enfant et la raison d'Etat*. Paris: Seuil.

Olson, M. (1978). *Logique de l'action collective*. Paris: Presses Universitaires de France.

Reynaud, J.-D. (1989). *Les régles du jeu: l'action collective et la régulation sociale*. Paris: Armand Colin.

_____ (1991). "Pour une sociologie de la régulation sociale." *Sociologie et sociétés* 23(2):13–26.

Schweisguth, E. (1983). "Les salariés moyens sont-ils des petits bourgeois." *Revue Francaise de Sociologie* 14:679–704.

Touraine, A. (1984). *Le retour de l'acteur*. Paris: Fayard.

Touraine, A., with M. Wieviorka and F. Dubet (1984). *Le mouvement ouvrier*. Paris: Fayard.

Touraine, A., et al. (1978). *Lutte étudiante*. Paris: Editions du Seuil.

_____ (1980). *La prophétie anti-nucléaire*. Paris: Editions du Seuil.

_____ (1981). *Le pays contre l'Etat*. Paris: Editions du Seuil.

Valade, B. (1990). *Pareto: La naissance d'une autre sociologie*. Paris: Presses Universitaires de France.

III.

Dimensions of Agency and Structure: Toward a Theoretical Convergence

Chapter SEVEN

Postmodernism as Pseudohistory: Continuities in the Complexities of Social Action

Craig Calhoun

AGAINST POSTMODERNISM

Problems of historical and cultural specificity have returned recently to the foreground of sociological discussion, propelled in large part by debate over modernity and postmodernity, modernism and postmodernism. Though in recent years this debate came to sociology largely from outside, it is a worthy renewal of some of the key concerns of the classical social theorists who struggled to identify the core feature distinguishing modern Western society from other epochs and sociocultural formations.

As it has been cast so far, the debate often has been regrettably vague about cultural and historical specificity, and relatedly problematic for practical social action. On the postmodernist side in particular, the use of the prefix *post* and the proliferation of contrasts to putative modernity or modernism introduces a kind of pseudo-specificity. Such contrasts sometimes point to significant variables differentiating social practices. They are seldom developed as very precise categories, however, or concretized in serious historical or cross-cultural analyses. Rather, the Enlightenment is evoked as though it were the archetype of a unidimensional and uncontested modernity, or the non-Western or Third World is posed as a critical vantage point on the West in an ironic new Orientalism, without consideration of the enormous internal heterogeneity of those constructs. In each case, a crucial question is how a social change has shifted the conditions and capacities for human action. The broad postmodernist discourse obscures this issue, however, by positing an end to subjectivity or rendering it universally problematic rather than addressing the ways in which agency and subjectivity are constructed in specific historical and cultural situations.

In the present paper, I want to question how much the genuinely dramatic cultural changes that are going on around us are a real departure from previous trends, the extent to which they are, and whether this is part of a social transformation sufficiently basic to warrant an argument that modernity is dead or dying. I will argue generally against the postmodernist view. Though changes are real and major, they do not yet amount to an epochal break. Indeed, many of them reflect continuing tensions and pressures which have characterized the whole modern era.[1] Underlying my account of the problems of the claim that postmodernity is upon us are two counter claims. First, the two basic organizing forces in modernity — capitalism and bureaucratic power — have hardly begun to dissolve. Second, the problems of self and agency are neither new to a postmodern era nor obsolete because neither has been superseded either historically or theoretically; they continue to shape our lives and thought as they have shaped them throughout modernity. Rather than narrowing our notion of the modern in order to justify the use of the prefix *post*, I will argue that we need to incorporate the insights of postmodernist thinkers into a richer sociological approach to the entire modern era.

In the first part of the paper, I will briefly introduce the notion of a postmodern condition. Since this is a position argued by a variety of thinkers on somewhat different grounds, and since some scholars — like Foucault — are claimed as part of the movement though they never proclaimed themselves postmodernists, my sketch will inevitably conceal a good deal of complexity. I will also ignore a number of crucial topics in the debate over postmodernism. Two key issues, for example, are the difficulty postmodernist theories have in accounting for the genesis of novel forms of cultural productivity — in other words, an absence of dynamism; and their difficulty in finding a vantage point for comparative analysis (as distinct from mere celebration of difference or syncretism). Closely linked to this second issue is the difficulty of reconciling the normative positions of postmodernism (e.g., extolling the virtues of difference and condemning the vice of repressive normalization) with its generally relativist theoretical orientation. Performative contradictions abound as postmodernists issue authoritative pronouncements on the basis of theoretical positions that deny any nonarbitrary basis to authority.[2]

Constrained by space not to go into all the ramifications of the postmodernist argument or its implications for sociology, in the second part of this paper I will take up one particular instance, the conceptualization of new social movements. It is an advantageous one for discussion because it links nearly all the different discourses contributing to the postmodernist potpourri and has been a topic of discussion outside of the postmodernist debate as well. As in my more general treatment of postmodernism, I argue here that novelty is being overstated and the modern era itself poorly conceptualized by a picture which flattens out its own internal diversity. The "new" social movements appear to be quite new only because they are understood in contrast to a one-sided, hypostatized account of the "old" labor movement.

THE POSTMODERN CONDITION?

What then are we to make of the frequent declarations that we have entered a postmodern age? Is this something that has happened to architecture, but not to society? Or have cultural analysts noticed something that has eluded the attention of sociologists? A little belatedly, a self-declared postmodernist sociology is being forged, absorbing previous arguments about, for example, new social movements, postindustrial society and claims to the autonomy of cultural change (see, e.g., Lash 1990; Rosenau 1992).[3] This postmodernism is widely dismissed or attacked with vitriolic ill-humor and a curious anxiety. I will suggest, however, that there is much of value in many of the specific arguments and interpretations grouped together as postmodernism, even while I challenge its overall conceptualization. Indeed, I will claim that thinking of these specific points in terms of the general claim that we are entering a postmodern age obscures and detracts from their value. We need to free the insights of postmodernist thought from their loading in a pseudo-historical conceptual framework. Where the insights are sound, they call for changed attention to many historical and crosscultural topics, not only to the most recent changes in advanced societies.

Postmodernism is a confluence of several partially distinct trends:

1. Perhaps with clearest meaning, postmodernism is a rejection of artistic modernism (such as the international style in architecture) in favor of freeing the aesthetic from the functional, putting signification, intertextual reference and self-reflexivity forward as independent goods. While architects like Venturi and Jencks have played a primary role in promoting the conceptualization of postmodernism, related changes are current and self-identified throughout at least the visual and dramatic arts (including cinema) and literature.

2. Postmodernism as a theoretical or critical position derives substantially from poststructuralism. This is a largely retrospective label for a series of French-led shifts in cultural, psychological and social theory, notably the critique of subject-centered reason, monological texts or readings, grand narratives, general truth claims and the normalization of Enlightenment rationality. Central players include Derrida, Foucault (a little ambiguously), Lyotard, Baudrillard, and various American epigones.

3. Closely related to poststructuralism in many accounts is the postmodernist critique of foundationalism in philosophy and theory, at a minimum an extension of the Nietzschean and Heideggerian critique of metaphysics into an attack on all claims to an external standpoint for judging truth. In the work of Rorty (1979, 1982, 1989), for example, a level of necessary theoretical indeterminacy is made the basis for a call to abandon repressive demands for certainty in favor of a "liberal" toleration of diversity on even the most basic epistemological and ethical points. In other hands, antifoundationalism becomes an attack on theoretical systematicity itself.[4]

4. Finally, postmodernism includes sociological and political economic claims to identify a basic transition from modernity to a new stage of (or beyond) history. These emphasize postindustrial — information or knowledge — society as the new societal formation. A new centrality is posited for media, information technology and the production of signification (e.g., culture industry) as an end in itself. Key figures in this line of argument (notably Bell and Touraine, and popularizers like Toffler and Naisbitt) are not directly a part of the postmodernist movement, but their arguments have influenced it substantially. The four lines of influence are not strictly commensurate. In particular, the *post* prefix may oppose modernism as an artistic movement of the late 19th and early 20th centuries, foundationalism as a feature of early modern science and Enlightenment discourse, modernity as an epoch of much longer duration, or the very construction of a progressive historical narrative such as those used to identify modernity in the first place (primarily during the 18th and 19th centuries). Nonetheless, the various strands of the phenomenon draw strength and significance from being intertwined (Harvey 1989; Kellner 1990; Rosenau 1992).

Postmodernism is a recognizable artistic and cultural trend that can be distinguished from (and indeed reacts against) modernism. But this is not the same as saying that modernity has given way to postmodernity. Even in the cultural realm, it is hard to place postmodernism. Surely we can recognize it in recent video and performance art, in the architecture of *pastiche* and in novels whose weight cannot be borne by the narrative of any subject. But are these extensions of early trends or something dramatically new?

The period from the 1890s to the 1920s must be reckoned the glory days of high modernism. Bauhaus architecture, Russian formalist painters, the French and German novelists and English poets of the day seem unquestionably modern. Brecht and Simmel, Joyce and Woolf are paradigmatically modern. Yet they also seem very close to the so-called postmodern. The themes of fragmentation of consciousness, the distance between the intentions and ends of action, the severing of symbol from referent are all felt in the art and social thought of this high modernist era. Robert Musil's *The Man Without Qualities* (1965), written mainly in the 1920s, is strikingly postmodern, an anticipation of Kundera, in its account of the insufficiency of the self as bearer of the weight of modernist subjectivity. If these are all to be embraced as part of the postmodern, then the postmodern must be understood as part and parcel of the modern, and the label must be seen as essentially misleading, perhaps willfully so, perhaps simply conditioned by the general modern sensibility that the new is always better than the established.

It is hard, in this connection, to distinguish the postmodern from the merely antimodern — that is, from the various sorts of oppositions to dominant themes in modernity which have accompanied modernization from its beginning. In this sense, what is new is only the highly modernist stylization of conservatism on the one hand, and the production of sometimes very unconservative antimodernisms on the other. But the issue goes one step deeper. Not just the antimodernism of Catholic conservatives and country squires, or of the scholastic defenders of artistic classicism and traditional iconic languages of representation, accompanied modernism from its inception. So did very modern, but in many ways anti-modernist, figures like Nietzsche. Modernism and modernity have always been internally complex.

The postmodernist critique and the defense of modernity mounted by figures like Habermas (1988b) tends to equate modernity with the rationalist Enlightenment.[5] But the Romantics were as modern and as new as the rationalists. Characters crucial to modernity — most notably Rousseau but also Goethe and some of the English Romantic poets — combined elements of both rationalism and romanticism in their writing and their lives. The individualism we identify as so central to modern experience and culture was shaped by both romantic and rationalist notions, not only by Enlightenment modernism and the other side of modernism represented paradigmatically by Rousseau, Goethe and Nietzsche, but also, only somewhat more ambiguously, by Freud and Simmel.[6] The complexity of interplay across rationalist and romantic lines is important to grasp. Shelley is certainly a paradigmatic Romantic, yet we might recall that Shelley was drawn to Godwin for the very rationalism of his anarchist political theory even before he eloped with his daughter. The late 18th century in many parts of Europe and America saw versions of the circle of connections which knit the Godwins, Wolstonecraft, Shelley and Byron together. There may be an important battle between rationalist universalism and attention to the irrational, between the value of the particular and the repressive, disempowering and deceptive side of individualism. But to equate that with a battle between modernity and its putative successor is to fail to recognize how deeply a part of modernity that whole frame of reference is. And this is only to speak of Western modernity.

The broad themes of postmodernism, then, are not new and do not mark any sharp break with modernity or modernism. What of the more specific claims postmodernism, most notably poststructuralism, makes within the realm of social theory? Perhaps Derrida heralded this turn as much as anyone, publishing three important books in the year 1967.[7] But the poststructuralist turn was much broader than deconstructionism, and includes a number of figures — including Bourdieu — who are not amenable to the postmodernist label. This poststructuralism was not really announced at its birth; it appears only retrospectively in the careers of structuralists who decided that decentering the subject — a central structuralist move — did not require them to abandon critical reflection on the categories of thought. Structuralism had in a sense denied epistemology on the grounds that it could only be pursued in terms of a philosophy of the subject. The poststructuralists sought ways to do a sort of epistemology, an inquiry into knowledge, without basing themselves on such a theory of subjectivity.

The contributions of the poststructuralist tributary into the postmodernist current were first and foremost the absorption of structuralism's critique of subject-centered thought, and the argument that monological statements of truth — originary speech, in Derrida's term — were in some combination misleading, false or repressive. In varying ways, then, the poststructuralists showed the tensions within seeming truths, the difficulties involved even in seemingly ordinary understandings, the constant effort of construction involved in accepted truths, as well as the constant tendency of those truths to break down and reveal their internal inconsistencies and aporias.[8] Some, like Bourdieu, made this crucially a social argument; the tensions involved in understanding derived not simply from textuality, but from interpersonal struggles and fields of power. For many others, materiality, physical embodiment and social relations were lost in treating all aspects of culture and human action as texts. In all versions, the poststructuralist move was for the most part an essentially theoretical shift, not a claim that anything in the external world had changed to necessitate a new theory.

Another sort of argument has been incorporated into the postmodernist position, however, which stems much more from claims about changes in the empirical world. This is the claim that we need a postmodernist theory because we live in a postmodern age. The proliferation of such labels was a particular feature of the 1970s and

1980s. Daniel Bell's and Alain Touraine's different accounts of post-industrial society marked early versions. The postmodernists posed much more radical claims about the implications of computerization, new communications media and related sociotechnical changes. Bell (1973) had already joined Habermas and other thinkers in suggesting that the advance of information processing and automating technologies meant that labor should no longer be privileged (in the Marxist sense) as the basic source of value.[9] Jean Baudrillard (1975, 1977, 1981), among others, has argued that the whole form of social organization based on production relations and power has given way to a society and economy organized on the bases of consumption and seduction, for example by advertising. In such a postmodern society, the sign becomes the autonomous source and form of value, the signifier is detached from the signified. The structure of relations which now matters is not that by which capital dominates labor, or centers of power grow and eliminate the territorial organization of power. Rather, the structure of relations which now masters is among signs. The representations are more real than the things represented. People are exteriorized into a technoculture of hyperreality where significance replaces reification and we know only the simulacra of mass existence. Or as Guy Debord put it in *Society of the Spectacle* (1983), the alienation of the commodity form is experienced to such a degree of abstraction that the commodity becomes a mere image detached from its previous ground in human labor or concrete use value. As a result, the critiques based on use value and concrete labor are rendered impotent.[10]

But the positing of an epochal change is problematic. There has undoubtedly been an increase in the role of advertising and the media generally (and not only in the economic sphere, but also in politics and efforts to influence personal decisions, such as about abortion). Consumption has indeed been thrust to the foreground of practical concerns, both for those who attempt to manage it in the business world and for everyone in the organization of everyday life. These genuine changes, however, do not add up to a very conclusive case that production has lost its basic importance or that signification has gained the status of self-production free from any need for creative subjects or material referents.[11] This postmodernist argument against Marx depends on a rather rigid reading of *Capital* in which, among other things, Marx is treated as having underappreciated his own argument as to the importance of abstraction in the commodity form through which labor is rendered into capital in favor of a naturalistic (and therefore transhistorical) understanding of labor.[12]

This issue, however, goes beyond a fight about Marxism. The claim that material production is no longer central to the organization of economic and social life is meant to reveal the postmodern age as free from a whole series of constraints discussed in nearly every version of economic theory — it is meant to have liberated culture from material social determinations. Yet even on the face of things it appears false, mistaking the rising importance of information technology *within* capitalism for a basic transformation *of* capitalism, not just into a new phase but into something altogether different. No evidence is presented that capital accumulation is not basic to economic activity and social power today (though it may never have been as exclusively fundamental as some Marxists have claimed). And though industry employs a declining percentage of the population, this does not mean a decline in all measures of its importance. The very implementation of labor saving technology requires an *increasing* capital investment, and the distributive (consumption, financial, etc.) orientation of business (which has been widely criticized in recent years by supply-siders and more conventional economists and business analysts alike) can still be understood as a response to the problem of utilizing productive capacity. Our cultural orientation, moreover, still seems to be very productivist and focused on the acquisition of material goods. Last but not least, the insight gained from focusing on movement away from productive industry — whether basic or minor — seems hardly able to make sense of an entire economy; at most it may have purchase on that portion of the international economy which is located in the rich — for instance, OECD — countries.

Lyotard has more plausibly suggested that postmodernity "is undoubtedly a part of the modern" (1982:79). Postmodernism in this view is a phase in modernism's constant push to negate the existing and produce the new. This makes sense, though it makes the label misleading. But Lyotard is not altogether consistent, for he also suggests a different sort of basic historical change which provides a grounding for postmodernism's currency.

On this account, postmodernity suffers from a loss of meaning or a meaningfulness which can only be repressively imposed because the great legitimating narratives of modernity have been exploded. Lyotard is hardly the only figure to stress this sort of argument. He gives it one of its most prominent expositions, however, suggesting that this is not just a possible intellectual stance but a basic social transformation:

the old poles of attraction represented by nation-states, parties, professions, institutions and historical traditions are losing their attraction. And it does not look as though they will be replaced, at least not on their former scale. (1979:14)

I have elsewhere tried to show the simple empirical falsity of this argument (Calhoun 1992), evident especially when one looks momentarily outside of the North Atlantic axis. Here it is enough to grasp that Lyotard is claiming that the world has changed such that a sociological analysis focused on these institutions or "poles of attraction" can no longer adequately grasp the state of social life.[13]

Lyotard and Baudrillard both distance themselves from Foucault, though he is claimed by other postmodernists, particularly in America, where postmodernism has taken on more of the status of a movement, allying itself not only with generational politics within academic disciplines but with broader public movements like feminism. Foucault was, first and foremost, an analyst of modernity, albeit one who set the stage for postmodernism with his discussion of historical ruptures and his thematic stresses on the repressive character of modernity, its arbitrary construction of the subject as a disciplinary ploy, and the inescapable mutual imbrication of power and knowledge (Foucault 1965, 1977a, 1977b, 1978). Especially in his earlier work (notably 1966, 1969), Foucault lay great stress on the ways in which internally coherent modes of understanding lost their grip and were superseded, and by showing these breaks both situated modernity and implied criteria for judging what might constitute a fundamental intellectual transformation. But Lyotard and Baudrillard want to go further. Baudrillard (1977) suggests Foucault was still caught in modernity's grasp, just as Marx was (in his opinion) caught in capitalism's. Elsewhere (see 1981, 1983), he declares the death of the social, the end of true social relations and their replacements by the simulacra of hyperreality. Lyotard is much more directly concerned with social arrangements, but he too wishes to break from Foucault. For him, not only the claim that society is a functional, systemic unity is a spurious modern view, so is its main opposite, the view that society is a conflictual field of struggles held together by power. Both of these accounts, on his view, represent unacceptable "metanarratives":

> I will use the term *modern* to designate any science that legitimates itself with reference to a metadiscourse of this kind making an explicit appeal to some grand narrative, such as the dialectics of Spirit, the hermeneutics of meaning, the emancipation of the rational or working

subject, or the creation of wealth... Simplifying to the extreme, I define *postmodern* as incredulity toward metanarratives. (1979:xxiii–xxiv)

It is first and foremost science which has challenged the hegemony of narrative, Lyotard suggests, because the pragmatics — the criteria of acceptance — are different for scientific and narrative knowledge (1979:25–26). Yet for a time it appeared that one might appeal to science itself to save a great legitimating narrative of modernity. But this is not so: since "science plays its own game it is incapable of legitimating the other language games," in fact "it is incapable of legitimating itself" (1979:40). So, though it is powerful, science is ultimately just one more game in a world in which

> all we can do is gaze in wonderment at the diversity of discursive species, just as we do at the diversity of plant or animal species. Lamenting the 'loss of meaning' in postmodernity boils down to mourning the fact that knowledge is no longer principally narrative. (1979:26).[14]

The postmodernist is called upon to "wage a war on totality" (1982:82) because totality breeds terror. This much is reminiscent of Foucault. But where Foucault offered a historical account of this as a dimension of modernity, Lyotard's account is severed from any specific historical contextualization. Lyotard, moreover, tends to reduce the social almost entirely to the linguistic: "the observable social bond is composed of language 'moves'" (1979:11). But he then fails to introduce any account of how participants in different discourses can ever be expected to reach agreements or even mutual understandings (Calhoun 1991b).

This raises the final basic postmodernist point, the importance of difference. This point is associated most especially with Derrida, though he develops it primarily in contexts other than the sociological (see 1978, 1982:1–27). Derrida stresses the ways in which the basic phenomena of distinction and contraposition produce identity, as opposed to essentialist attempts to locate identity in the inherent attributes of any entity — either a subject or an object. Derrida (1967, 1972) positions his argument for the importance of difference (or *differance*) mainly within a dialogue with a Western philosophical tradition that approaches truth monologically, even often as substance. These assertions Derrida deconstructively shows to conceal the play of hidden dialogicality. In doing so he offers a defense of the very complexity of thought itself such that truth or knowledge becomes something much more difficult than we have thought, not therefore something to be dismissed.[15] *Differance*, for Derrida, is really a property of discourse, not subjects, and indeed (following on the structuralist tradition) subjects appear in his work mainly as creatures of discourse rather than speakers able to claim some primacy over it. It is important, though, that Derrida's approach draws attention to difference among subjects not just as multiplications of the same sort of identity, differently situated, but as radically singular.[16]

Difference is also crucial to Foucault. First, he offers an account of the way modern subjects are constituted and disciplined as individuals who experience a simultaneous production of desire and its repressive normalization (1977a). This suggests a certain special priority to human difference. Foucault is ambiguous, for on the one hand he can be read as asserting only that certain kinds of difference among people were subjected to normalizing discipline in the historically specific production of modernity. On the other hand, however, particularly in his later work on sexuality, Foucault (1978–88) appears to ascribe to all humans a kind of natural propensity for resistance to the normalizing tendencies of social life (which also appear as increasingly general rather than historically specific, present in ancient Greece and China as well modern France). Throughout, though it is never clearly articulated in his major works (as distinct from interviews), Foucault implies a normative defense of difference against normalization. If Foucault is ambiguous on this personal aspect of difference, he is clear at least in his early work, and his arguments are crucial on the issue of historical difference. Foucault (1966, 1969) explicates the radical ruptures that separate the epistemological understandings of different ages. Though he links these epistemic breaks somewhat to changes in social life, this is not his major theme. His argument does not rest on shifts in any underlying causal factors such as economy, military power or demography, but rather on the transmutation of systems of knowledge such that they become incommensurable (to borrow Kuhn's 1970 term). In offering one of the most profound articulations of what it means for systems of knowledge to be radically different, and particularly of how such difference can occur historically within a civilization, rather than only cross-culturally, Foucault augments an important discussion of incommensurability with roots in philosophy of science and hermeneutics.[17]

This emphasis on difference is the most valuable and defensible of postmodernist arguments, though it is not defensible on postmodernist terms. Both Derrida and Foucault (and many postmodernist followers) mobilize their arguments about difference as bases for rejection of all grand narratives without any search for a substitute ground for normative discourse. In doing so, they introduce a particularism so extreme that it ultimately (and ironically) results in a decontextualization, an incapacity to place the particular in relation to other phenomena.[18] A particularism so extreme — which is not, I think, what most postmodernists want but what a hastily espoused theory offers — cannot justify even the very value on difference with which it starts. Lyotard thus joins Derrida and Foucault in wishing to show the agonistic element in all culture, but is left with a more or less arbitrary assertion. But even Foucault and Derrida, let alone Lyotard, are left with a program of pure critique, showing the dragons which lie in the way of modernism but offering no real analytic purchase on the problem of analyzing the transformation of power and social structure as it bears on practical action in the modern world.

Treating variations and disputes in artistic style, social consciousness and theory within the frame of epochal historical transformation produce a misunderstanding, even where the changes are of some significance. Postmodernism is a continuation of modernism in aspects of its style (such as the claim to be the latest avant garde, or the self-legitimation of mere novelty). More basically, the crucial dimensions of variation are mostly long-standing, and postmodernism carries on basic themes of all modernity — which indeed produced an internal anti-modernity from the beginning, as well as splits of rationalists from romantics, realists from figuralists, etc. Perhaps the most distinctive feature of postmodernist *theory* is its denial of a basis for critical judgment and moral responsibility, except as the arbitrary reflection of a tradition. This poses basic problems for its own attempt to take cultural difference seriously, since it precludes genuine learning from the Other. It opens postmodernist theorists (and political activists) who attempt to persuade others that they are either committing a performative contradiction or simply exercising a will to power no more legitimate than any other.

In relation to both critical judgment and historical transformation, postmodernist theory at the very least crucially overstates its case. Accounts are needed of epistemic gain which does not imply a sharp opposition of truth and falsehood, and of historical change that does not mean epochal rupture (Taylor 1989; Calhoun 1991b).

HOW NEW ARE THE NEW SOCIAL MOVEMENTS?

I propose to try to make some of this a little more concrete with a discussion of one sort of phenomenon in which recent theory identifies noteworthy change but overstates its novelty. I refer to the so-called new social movements. This purported transformation of the ways in which people try collectively to improve their lives and change society is linked to the broader postmodernist problematic by several joint themes: decentering of the subject, problematizing of identity, rejection of overarching telos or order, and emphasis on experimentation and play.

The idea of new social movements has been brought into currency by a number of authors, both within and outside of the postmodernist movement (Melucci, Touraine, Habermas, Offe, Cohen). In all cases, the concept is defined though the crucial counterexample of the 19th- and early 20th-century working-class or labor movement. This is understood primarily in the singular (while new social movements are plural). The labor movement is reified, hypostatized. It is treated as having an implicit telos, and as having been putatively or potentially transformative for the whole society. However, the day when it held this potential, or could reasonably and widely have been thought to hold this potential, has passed, according to the new social movement theorists.

Several key features are held to distinguish new social movements (NSMs).[19]

1. These movements focus on identity, autonomy and self-realization rather than material benefits, resources and instrumental goals. It is in this sense, in part, that these movements are said to stay largely within the realm of civil society rather than addressing themselves primarily to state or economic actors.

2. Mobilization for the NSMs is as much defensive as offensive, hence less negotiable than more abstract utopian social projects.

3. Membership cuts across class lines because socioeconomic categories are losing their salience, one link to the postindustrial or information society argument.

4. Organizational forms are themselves work objects of movements, which aim to be nonhierarchical with direct democracy as an ideal.

5. Membership is generally only part-time, with potential multiple and overlapping commitments.

6. Activities are generally outside the official legislative system and often use unconventional means.

7. In the new social movements, an attempt is made to politicize aspects of everyday life formerly outside of the political.

8. Finally there is less tendency toward unification under some larger umbrella form or still less a master narrative of collective progress (though this is disputed, with Melucci suggesting that there is virtually no such tendency and Touraine suggesting that this is a temporary transition and such a tendency could yet emerge).

A variety of primary examples inform the conceptualization. Melucci (1988:247) cites the women's movement, ecological movement ("greens"), youth movement (seen as a struggle over the use of time and alternative lifestyles) and peace movement. One could reasonably add the gay and lesbian movements and other struggles for legitimation of personal identity or lifestyle, the animal rights movement and the anti-abortion and pro-choice movements.

Without question there has been a proliferation of social movements in the contemporary era, and the various key characteristics listed do give insight into them. But it is important to reexamine the historical claim of sharp novelty. The 19th- and early 20th-century working class movement (if it even can be described more than tendentiously as a single movement) was multidimensional, only provisionally and partially unified and not univocal. It did not constitute one collective actor in a single social drama. There was mobilization over wages, to be sure, but also over women and children working, community life, leisure activities, the status of immigrants, education, access to public services and so forth. Relatedly, many different sorts of mobilizations have been claimed as part of class struggle, by organizers and analysts both. Thus not only wage laborers in industrial capitalist factories (the Marxian ideal type) but traditional craft and agricultural workers struggling to defend their occupations and communities joined in the struggles which are described as unidimensional in comparison to NSMs.

In other words, the labor movement was itself a new social movement — and this in two senses. First, as Tarrow (1989) has suggested, many of the features of NSMs ascribed to epochal social change are in fact characteristics of new movements — those in the early stages of organization — in any era. Second, the early labor movement was itself engaged in identity politics, trying to promote and legitimate the political and economic claims of workers, trying to gain the commitment of workers to their class identity. Is this not part of what is suggested by the Marxian notion of class consciousness, let alone by the activities of labor organizers who argued for the primacy of class identity over craft, community, gender, ethnicity, religion and a host of other competing claims on individual and group self-understanding and loyalty? NSM theory sometimes suggests that the mobilization of workers was simply a reflection of underlying interests, while the fragmentation of interests in the contemporary era is responsible both for the decline of labor and the rise of rival movements. This misses the extent to which those committed to class struggle had to *make* class identities count, and the extent to which collective action always depends on struggles to forge the capacity for agency as a matter of redefining identity, not merely mobilizing resources.

Throughout the 19th and early 20th centuries (and indeed not only then), a wide variety of social movements flourished. There were, for example, ethnic and nationalist movements, which were never really suppressed by class as Melucci (1989:89-92) suggests, but have ebbed and flowed throughout modernity. Religious awakening, revitalization and proliferation were major themes of the 19th century, as was anticlericalism and free-thinking. Anti-slavery or abolitionist movements were often closely linked to religion but were autonomous from any particular religious organizations. Communitarianism, temperance and various dietary and lifestyle movements attracted hundreds of thousands of adherents in both Europe and America. Popular education was the object of struggle, especially in Britain, where free public schooling was not universal until very late. Last but not least, women's movements are hardly a unique invention of the late 20th century, though they have perhaps had more strength and more success in recent years.

All these 19th- and early 20th-century movements exhibit the key putative characteristics of new social movements. What better exemplifies making a work-object (in Melucci's phrase) of a social movement's own organizational forms than the communal movement of the 1840s? Was identity not crucially at stake in nationalism as it spread throughout early 19th-century Europe? And indeed, did (and does) nationalism not cut crucially across class lines (and derive at least some of its appeal from doing so)? Were the struggles of 18th- and 19th-century craft workers against industrialization not defensive? All manner of direct action outside the official legislative system characterized the struggle against slavery and the saloon-smashing wing of the temperance movement. Did temperance, popular education and many others of these movements not attempt to politicize aspects of everyday life formerly outside of the political? Indeed, were the early labor movements not attempting to politicize aspects of everyday life formerly (and by their opponents) not considered properly political? Finally, was there really much tendency for temperance, nationalism, craft struggle, communitarianism, abolitionism, free-thinking and camp-meeting religion to unify under some umbrella form?

We need, in short, to broaden, enrich and improve our theory and conceptualizations without leaping to a claim of epochal historical transformation. The capacity for collective agency has always been sought on behalf of many claims to identity, moral righteousness and political interest. Agency has always had to be won in a struggle to make movements work, and to make them appeal within a field — richer or poorer — of alternatives. Different periods have nurtured greater or lesser proliferations, but we need to see a continuous generation of movements throughout the modern era. All respond to the weakness, and perhaps the loneliness, of individual action as well as to a mixed and overlapping series of changes in background conditions. In the case of late 20th-century NSMs, at least much of what is novel is only a quantitative increase in number and scale of movements and the introduction of certain new topics and tactics.[20]

MODERNITY REVISITED

Like the postmodernist literature, that on new social movements offers exaggerated claims of novelty. Also like the postmodernist literature it draws our attention to aspects of modern life which had been widely neglected under the predominance of prevailing — largely but not exclusively Enlightenment-based — theoretical tendencies. Analysts — not only Marxists and other supporters — thus ascribed to the social democratic labor movement a capacity to organize divergent interests and identities that it never really achieved. Analysts also commonly neglected the extent to which religion formed the basis of social movement participation (perhaps often seeing it as inherently retrograde and thus both amenable to explanation on the basis of mere endurance from the past and unlikely to hold much of any key to understanding the future). The same could be said of nationalism, arguably more important that any other ideological factor in the major conflicts of the 20th century and yet recurrently relegated to the dustbin of history by social theorists.

The greatest gain offered by postmodernism, in short, is a refocusing of our understanding of modernity, not the analysis of any epochal historical change. There are some qualitative novelties in recent history, but so far these have not been sufficient to overturn basic organizational tendencies of the epoch. Capital accumulation and centralization of power, thus, both continue on a world scale. Efforts to gain effective agency through collective action (including the reformulation of claims to identity and loyalty) must still confront the constraints imposed by the greater power of corporate and state organizations, for example. In the early 19th century, the attempt of workers to reach beyond community to class organizations at the level of the nation-state and its domestic market was in part an attempt to catch up to the level at which economic and political power were already coordinated against them (Calhoun 1987). By the late 20th century, capital was becoming increasingly globalized, and while the state remained both powerful and the crucial arena in which social movements could mobilize to pursue their collective agency, the internationalization of capital and new political forms like the European Community were putting a great deal of power once again out of the grasp of popular agency mediated through social movements.

To reverse the trends towards capital accumulation and centralization of power would indeed be to bring on a postmodern condition. But we need to be careful not to confuse more superficial, if still important, changes for these basic ones. Consider, for example, the claim that information technology has fundamentally altered, or even brought an end to, the modern era. One argument for this claim is the evident dispersal of production relations and other important activities which coordination through telecommunications and computers makes possible. But note the importance of coordination; dispersal of activities serves centralization of power in many cases. When capital flows across borders, this demonstrates rather than reverses centralization of power; it hardly puts an end to the basic drive of capital accumulation. Information technology facilitates further changes of other sorts as well, many of them momentous. But we need to recognize that power was based substantially on knowledge long before microelectronics, and the capacity to control others through organizations run through regularized information flows hardly waited for computers or constitutes a break with modernity (compare Calhoun 1992 with Melucci 1988:249; Keane 1988:8, n. 6).

All this is not to say that nothing has changed, but that changes have been overstated and poorly conceptualized. The expansion of an organizational and technological infrastructure throughout the modern era has, for example, both enhanced state power and transformed it. Revolutionary potential, for example, is diminished in the West, largely because of the spatial deconcentration of power. Whether one wants to call the recent transformations of communist societies revolutions or not, it is important to see the extent to which they depended on the concentration of the institutions of power in capital cities and the underdevelopment of the infrastructures which have dispersed its application in more "modern" societies. But the displacement of power from readily visible individuals into market systems and bureaucratic organizations does not mean that there cease to be social relations of domination, they no longer involve active subjects, or power is not centralized.

Habermas's (Habermas 1984, 1988a)conceptualization of a split between system and lifeworld suggests why these problems are hard to recognize and disempowering of collective agency. Social organization is undertaken simultaneously through directly interpersonal relationships, impersonal or systemic steering media, and large-scale (generally corporate) social organizations which appear from the point of view of everyday social life as autonomous and distant (Calhoun 1991b).[21] Both impersonal, market systems and corporate organizations have grown in importance throughout the modern era. While they organize more of social life — exerting more causal influence over the lives of individuals — they remain inaccessible to most forms of everyday (lifeworld) social knowledge. Markets can only be understood on the basis of statistical reasoning foreign to the conduct of everyday interpersonal relationships.

The omnipresence of "system" — that is, of large-scale market and bureaucratic-corporate influences on our immediate lives — shapes some of the cultural responses problematically identified as postmodern. In relation to problems of collective agency, it encourages two equally disempowering visions. One is of a world out of control, one which does not make sense. The other is of a world all too controlled, but only by distant, hidden actors. Modern consciousness vacillates, I think, between the first — a schizoid chaos of radical and widespread incommensurability (evoked, for example, by Deleuze and Guattari 1983) — and the second, a paranoid worldview understood only by belief in omnipresent conspiracy. Both have roots in the basic split between the lifeworld experiences which give life its basic meaning and the systemic steering and bureaucratic-corporate power which upset the order of the lifeworld but are poorly grasped — indeed necessarily obscured — by the conceptual framework of the lifeworld. It is in this context, for example, that we can see the source of postmodernist critiques of "intentionalist illusions" — putatively spurious belief in the capacity of human subjects to organize significant aspects of their own lives in response to conscious decision. Given the antiuniversalism of postmodernism, however, it is ironic that instead of locating the source of commonly exaggerated faith in intention, and its problems, many postmodernists universalize a critique of intention as fundamentally illusory.

The vision that reality does not make sense and intrinsically cannot make sense is a widespread postmodernist theme. Those who pose claims to demonstrate an order to life and culture must be either paranoid or repressive, or both. Our only legitimate options are to simply accept disorder and uninterpretability or to make highly contingent, local and weakly defensible efforts to bring order to a small part of the world.

This vision of the chaotic, fragmented world is often traced to the breakup of a (implicitly once unified) modern economic or political structure. Yet even here we should be cautious about seeing this as totally new rather than newly prominent. David Harvey (1989) thus has provocatively analyzed the culture of postmodernism as a response to a systemic crisis (but not supersession) of capitalism. Fordist production methods have brought on a crisis of overaccumulation, calling forth a search for new regimes of accumulation (as well as new, post-Fordist production relations). This search fosters new aesthetic movements. Harvey's argument is schematic and somewhat reductionist on the relationship of aesthetics to economics, but powerful in its account of a variety of recent phenomena, not as evidence of the end of the modern era but as aspects of a shift — not the first — in the internal organization of capitalism.[22]

CONCLUSION

Postmodernist reasoning makes it hard to justify any collective response, any attempt at agency, in the face of centralization of power and global capital accumulation accomplished through exploitation. Most postmodernist discourse is normatively incapacitating, even where it is profoundly normative in tone or motivation.

Because processes of power and exploitation are increasingly systemic and removed from the everyday discursive grasp of the lifeworld, however, it is all the more important that a critical *theory* be developed through which to understand them. It is not enough to rely on play, intuition and ordinary experience.

Postmodernist thought has generally been presented in a radical, challenging mode and rhetoric, as though it were a critical theory with clear implications for collective struggle. Indeed, the postmodernist movement has without question informed and in some cases invigorated popular struggles. But it is not equally clear that postmodernist thought can stand very clearly the tests which must be demanded of a critical *theory*.

Ideally, a critical theory ought to provide for an account of the historical and cultural conditions of its own production, to offer an address to competing theories which explains (not just identifies) their weaknesses and appropriates their achievements, to engage in a continuing critical reflection on the categories used in its own construction, and to develop a critical account of existing social conditions with positive implications for social action. Postmodernism contributes to some of these desiderata, but also falls short of them in varying degree.

The postmodernist attention to difference raises the issue of cultural particularity, but difference often is made so absolutely prior to commonality that no basis for mutual engagement or even respect is provided. The theory thus undercuts by overstatement one of its own greatest contributions.

The postmodernist decentering of the subject poses a challenge for a theory desiring to address agency and moral responsibility. Though postmodernist accounts here offer a needed counterpoint to typical individualism, they too often become nearly as much its mirror image as Durkheim. If a critical theory is to hold meaningful implications for action, it must grant actors and action a more significant place.

The postmodernist rejection of grand narratives and other overarching sources of meaning challenges the possibility of a standpoint from which to develop a critical theory (or more generally to defend critical judgments across significant lines of difference). Relatedly, the postmodernist notion of the insularity and incommensurability of traditions of thought suggests that there is inherently no basis other than power or mere persuasion for resolving conflicts among theories.

Finally, the postmodernist claim to represent a historical transformation raises the issue of historical specificity. As I tried to show above, however, it does so largely in a pseudohistorical manner, dependent on oversimplifying notions of modernity to justify premature claims for its supersession.

Among other tasks, any good critical theory must offer a plausible account of the specificity and variation of historical cultural settings for human action. At least superficially, this involves one of the strengths of postmodernist thought. Conversely, failure to attend to this has been one of the central weaknesses of mainstream, especially US-dominated, sociology. Even followers of more historically oriented traditions than the largely functionalist or empiricist mainstream have sometimes been tempted to seek universal reach by dehistoricizing and deculturalizing key concepts. Many Marxists, thus, treat labor as a transhistorical, universal category rather than one specific to capitalism. This undermines the strength of Marxism's own core analysis of capitalism. Similarly, other theorists, recognizing cultural and historical diversity, have attempted to overcome its more serious implications by subsuming it into a common, often teleological, evolutionary framework. Unlike biological evolutionary theories, which stress the enormous qualitative diversity within the common processes of speciation, inheritance, mutation, selection and so forth, sociological theories have generally relied on claimed universal features of all societies — like technology, held by Lenski, Lenski and Nolan (1990) to be the prime mover of evolutionary change — to act as basic, transhistorical variables.

Sociology has been impoverished by its relative neglect of the work of Foucault, Derrida and other major thinkers who have contributed to postmodernism. Their work offers both specific insights and important general emphasis on themes of difference and the problems of subject-centered thought. But even these valuable contributions are undermined by overstatement. And in postmodernist thought (for which amalgam neither Foucault nor Derrida can be held responsible) they come with a great deal of problematic baggage. The apparent historicity of the opposition of modern to postmodern obscures the extent to which this debate is the latest working out of tensions basic to the whole modern era. We need richer, more complex understandings of actual history.

Similarly, I have tried briefly to suggest the advantages to recognizing some of the historical continuities in patterns of social action as well as of intellectual debate. The production of new social movements thus needs to be seen as a continuous feature of modernity, not a sign of postmodernity. More generally, the basic tendencies which have characterized the modern era have not been reversed. Capital accumulation, the centralization of power, and the split between system and lifeworld all proceed apace. Shifts in the specific workings of "time-space distanciation," to follow Harvey (1989) and Giddens (1990) in using this common but inelegant phrase, are very important. Rearrangement of spatial relations of production, extension and intensification of market relations, and severing of place from space all have powerful impacts on the contemporary world. They are not, however, reversals of the most basic tendencies of modern social organization. It is important that we reserve sociological claims for the end of modernity to transformations which do involve such basic changes.

Notes

1. See Calhoun (1991a). In this respect, my argument resembles those of Jameson (1984) and Harvey (1989) to the effect that postmodernism is really a reflection of late capitalism. Their accounts, however, seem to me to border on the reductionist, making the stages and logic of capital too directly determining of cultural forms. Moreover, they neglect many of the similarities of the current era to earlier periods which I want to point up.
2. This paper builds on discussion of these points in Calhoun (1989, 1991a).
3. For the most part, "postmodernist sociology" is still in the business of assimilating arguments developed outside of sociology, especially in French poststructuralism. These are linked to already existing sociological arguments, which are then recast in postmodernist terms.
4. Especially in his more recent works, Rorty's pragmatism is extended beyond a critique of foundationalist philosophy to a series of claims about the virtues of bourgeois, liberal democracy, which are found to adhere not so much in universalistic rationality as in liberal-pluralist openness. Valuable critical discussions of Rorty's extension of his philosophical position to social practice (each of them questioning whether it can be so free of "universalism" as Rorty implies) are offered by McCarthy (1992) and Bernstein (1992).
5. Conversely, much postmodernist and antipostmodernist discourse also overstates the conservatism of hermeneutic thinkers like Gadamer, and accepts too much at face value the claims of Derrida, Rorty and others not to be children of the Enlightenment. In fact, Gadamer (1975) is not hostile to reason or a discourse about truth; as Bernstein (1983) has

suggested, his hermeneutic arguments operate against claims to ahistorical, methodological certainty (and thus coincide with post-Kuhnian philosophy of science and a theme raised in a very different way by some poststructuralist thinkers like Derrida). Conversely, despite their attacks on "logocentrism," foundationalism and universalism, both Derrida and Rorty pose arguments that depend on capacities for generalization and appeal to reason that they share with much Enlightenment discourse and for which they are largely unable to provide alternative theoretical grounds.

6. Frisby's (1985a) account of Simmel, Kracauer and Benjamin brings out this aspect of Simmel rather well.

7. Those of us in the English speaking world, especially in sociology, have been a bit behind the Parisian fashions in this regard. Just as we were assimilating structuralism, especially beyond the dominant influence of Levi-Strauss in anthropology, and therefore including Althusser, Poulantzas, etc. — there was a new turn in dominant intellectual fashion. This was the move beyond structuralism by some of its leading, mostly younger, figures. Lacan and Derrida are perhaps the most paradigmatic thinkers; in different ways both Foucault and Bourdieu made the same sort of move in relation to structuralism.

8. In this, the poststructuralist work resonates very closely with the substantially contemporary work of the ethnomethodologists in English-language sociology.

9. I have criticized such a view (Calhoun 1992a). It is particularly disturbing coming from Habermas, where it marks a willingness to accept systems-theoretical accounts of economic activity without attempting to dereify them to see the role of human action behind production even where self-regulating systems coordinate it, and to see the production of knowledge as itself a form of creativity activity — labor, if you will, though perhaps in a way posing problems for many orthodox Marxist accounts of the labor theory of value.

10. Baudrillard's early work (cited above), like that of Debord, is written as part of a critical social analysis that attempts to theorize the standpoint and conditions of its critique. Baudrillard's later work (1989) increasingly abandons this attempt at critical theory, though he never entirely joins that part of the postmodern current that adopts a fully celebratory style. Much of the best in Baudrillard was in fact anticipated by Debord, whose work is helpfully discussed and situated both in relation to the "Situationalist International" and postmodernism by Plant (1992).

11. In addition, it is not clear that attention to consumption and efforts to influence it through advertising have undergone a qualitative change rather than a quantitative expansion in the post-war years. It may be that a better theoretical revision would focus more of our attention on

the prominence of consumption issues from the beginning of the capitalist (or modern) era.
12. See not only Baudrillard, but also, following his lead, Kroker and Cook (1986:185). For a sophisticated reading of *Capital* treating labor as a historically specific category and properly stressing the role of the dialectic of abstract and concrete labor and time, see Postone (forthcoming).
13. As Giddens (1990) has suggested, though, this is more plausibly read as the completion or radicalization of modernity than as the coming of postmodernity. On this point too, the very fragmentation claimed as distinctive of postmodernity has often been claimed as equally distinctive of modernity.
14. At one level, this talk of "loss of meaning" echoes rather obviously an key theme of earlier modernists. In the terms of my argument below, however, it does perhaps reflect extensions in the severing of the world of practical knowledge and tradition in direct relationships from the coordination of large scale systems of action through indirect relationships.
15. Here again, the similarities between Derrida and Gadamer are worth noting, despite their very different overall approaches; they are due in part, it appears, to their common indebtedness to Heidegger.
16. Derrida does tend to absolutize the notion of difference, and thus to remove the human actor and the concrete social relationship from the discourse. Nonetheless, unlike many other traditions of "alterity" and "other-centered" or "dialogical" understanding, such as that of Levinas, Derrida rejects the idea that this radical otherness precludes treatment of the other as *alter ego*. While it may not be possible in strong senses to have real knowledge of the other, it is nonetheless crucial for Derrida — and in his view the starting point of all ethics — to approach interaction and discourse with "*respect* for the other *as what it is*" (1978:138). There is a good discussion of this in Bernstein (1992).
17. See the helpful review — not, however, including Foucault — by Bernstein (1983, 1992). I have addressed aspects of these issues (Calhoun 1989, 1991a).
18. This is related to deconstructionism's arguments against attempts to discipline the reading of texts by imposition of contextualizing explanations. Yet surely the issue must be not simply to free text from context, but to understand processes of entextualization (Silverstein and Urban 1992) and especially to establish and understand the variable extent to which different discourses attain independence of the contexts of their initial production or of any later deployment.
19. This account is based most especially on Melucci (1988, 1989), Touraine (1977, 1981, 1988), Cohen (1985) and Cohen and Arato (1992, chap. 10).

See also Klandermans, Kriesi and Tarrow, eds. (1988), Tarrow (1989), Scott (1990), Offe (1985), Eder (1985), and Habermas (1984). The last three, along with Cohen and Arato, present views closer to critical theory (and to the present paper) than to the postmodernist assimilation of the idea of new social movements, with its exaggerated notion of a historical break. Just as the present article was going to press, Kenneth Tucker (1991) published a useful examination of the claims of new social movement theory (primarily in its "critical theory" versions) which makes similar points with reference to late 19th-century French examples.

20. Indeed, what is most novel may be the relative bureaucratization and professionalization of the social movement field. This was not altogether absent in the 19th century, when a figure like the journalist-agitator William Cobbett or his sometime friend Orator Henry Hunt could appear as champions of a variety of causes and earn a living primarily from their movement activity (Thompson 1968). Nonetheless, the extent to which formal organizations and professional movement organizers predominate does seem to be a linear (if only ambiguously progressive) trend in the social movement field (Zald and McCarthy 1979).

21. Neither Habermas nor Parsons (on whom he draws) makes clear why power should be considered an impersonal systemic steering medium comparable to money; I accordingly treat corporate bureaucracies as distinct from markets. I would also suggest that it is important to see system and lifeworld as different analytic aspects of social life, not as different realms since it is virtually impossible to give a meaningful account of a lifeworld in modern society that is not deeply influence by systemic factors. What we can see are directly interpersonal social relations that are understandable on bases distinct from the impersonal conceptualizations required by markets and corporations.

22. Jameson (1991) reaches somewhat similar conclusions. Of course, to see capitalism as still a powerful causal factor — and thus a basis for making the world interpretable — need not be to suggest that capitalism explains every aspect of modern social and cultural transformations.

Bibliography

Baudrillard, J. (1975) *The Mirror of Production*. St. Louis: Telos Press.

_____ (1977) *Oublier Foucault*. New York: Semiotext(e).

_____ (1981) *For a Critique of the Political Economy of the Sign*. St. Louis: Telos Press.

_____ (1983) *In the Shadow of the Silent Majorities.* New York: Semiotext(e).

_____ (1989) *America.* London: Verso.

Bell, D. (1973). *The Coming of Post-Industrial Society.* New York: Basic Books.

Bernstein, R. J. (1983). *Beyond Objectivism and Relativism.* Philadelphia: University of Pennsylvania Press.

Bernstein, R. J. (1992). *The New Constellation: The Ethical-Political Horizons of Modernity/Postmodernity.* Cambridge: MIT Press.

Calhoun, C. (1987). "Class, Place and Industrial Revolution." In: *Class and Space: The Making of Urban Society,* eds. P. Williams and N. Thrift, pp. 51–72. London: Routledge and Kegan Paul.

_____ (1989). "Social Theory and the Law: Systems Theory, Normative Justification and Postmodernism." *Northwestern University Law Review* 83:1701–1763.

_____ (1991a). "Culture, History and the Problem of Specificity in Social Theory." In: *Embattled Reason: Postmodernism and Its Critics,* eds. S. Seidman and D. Wagner, pp. 244–288. New York and Oxford: Basil Blackwell.

_____ (1991b). "Imagined Communities, Indirect Relationships and Postmodernism: The Changing Scale of Social Organization and the Transformation of Everyday Life." In: *Social Theory in a Changing Society,* eds. J. Coleman and P. Bourdieu, pp. 95–120. Boulder, CO: Westview Press.

_____ (1992). "The Infrastructure of Modernity: Indirect Relationships, Information Technology, and Social Integration." In: *Social Change and Modernity,* eds. Neil Smelser and Hans Haferkamp, pp. 205–236. Berkeley: University of California Press.

Cohen, J. (1985). "Strategy or Identity: New Theoretical Paradigms and Contemporary Social Movements." *Social Research* 52:663–716.

Cohen, J., and A. Arato (1992). *The Political Theory of Civil Society.* Cambridge: MIT Press.

Debord, G. (1983). *The Society of the Spectacle.* Detroit: Black and Red Press.

Deleuze, G., and F. Guattari. (1983). *Anti-Oedipus: Capitalism and Schizophrenia.* Minneapolis: University of Minnesota Press.

Derrida, J. (1967). *Of Grammatology.* Baltimore: Johns Hopkins University Press.

———————— (1972). *Dissemination*. Chicago: University of Chicago Press.

———————— (1978). *Writing and Difference*. Chicago: University of Chicago Press.

———————— (1982). *Margins of Philosophy*. Chicago: University of Chicago Press.

Eder, K. (1985). "The 'New Social Movements': Moral Crusades, Political Pressure Groups, or Social Movements?" *Social Research* 52:869–901.

Foucault, M. (1965). *Madness and Civilization*. New York: Random House.

———————— (1966). *The Order of Things: An Archaeology of the Human Sciences*. New York: Random House.

———————— (1969). *The Archaeology of Knowledge*. New York: Pantheon.

———————— (1977a). *Discipline and Punish: The Birth of the Prison*. New York: Pantheon.

———————— (1977b). *Power/Knowledge: Selected Interviews and Other Writings, 1972–1977*. New York: Random House.

———————— (1978–88). *The History of Sexuality*, 4 vols. New York: Pantheon.

Frisby, D. (1985). *Fragments of Modernity*. New York: Blackwell.

Gadamer, H.-G. (1975). *Truth and Method*. New York: Seabury.

Giddens, A. (1990). *The Consequences of Modernity*. Stanford: Stanford University Press.

Habermas, J. (1984). *The Theory of Communicative Action, Vol. 1: Reason and the Rationalization of Society*. Boston: Beacon.

———————— (1988a). *The Theory of Communicative Action, Vol. 2: Lifeworld and System: A Critique of Functionalist Reason*. Boston: Beacon.

———————— (1988b). *The Philosophical Discourse of Modernity*. Cambridge: MIT Press.

Harvey, D. (1989). *The Condition of Postmodernity*. Cambridge: Basil Blackwell.

Jameson, F. (1984). "Postmodernism, or the Cultural Logic of Late Capitalism." *New Left Review* 146:53–92.

Keane, J. (1988). *Civil Society and the State*. London: Verso.

Kellner, D. (1990). "The Postmodern Turn: Positions, Problems, Prospects." In: *Frontiers of Social Theory: The New Syntheses*, ed. G. Ritzer, pp. 255–286. New York: Columbia University Press.

Klandermans, B., H. Kriesi, and S. Tarrow (Eds.) (1988). *From Structure to Action: Comparing Movement Participation Across Cultures*. Greenwich, CT: JAI Press.

Kroker, A., and D. Cook. (1986). *The Postmodern Scene: Excremental Culture and Hyper-Aesthetics*. New York: St. Martins.

Kuhn, T. (1970). *The Structure of Scientific Revolutions*. Chicago: University of Chicago Press.

Lash, S. (1990). *Postmodernist Sociology*. London: Routledge.

Lenski, G., J. Lenski, and P. Nolan. (1990). *Human Societies*. New York: McGraw-Hill.

Lyotard, J.-F. (1979–84). *The Postmodern Condition*. Minneapolis: University of Minnesota Press.

——— (1982–84). "Answering the Question: What is Postmodernism?" Appendix to *The Postmodern Condition*. Minneapolis: University of Minnesota Press.

McCarthy, T. (1992). *Ideals and Illusions: On Reconstruction and Deconstruction in Contemporary Critical Theory*. Cambridge: MIT Press.

Melucci, A. (1988). "Social Movements and the Democratization of Everyday Life." In: *Civil Society and the State*, ed. J. Keane, pp. 245–260. London: Verso.

——— (1989). *Nomads of the Present: Social Movements and Individual Needs in Contemporary Society*. Philadelphia: Temple University Press.

Musil, R. [1930] (1965). *The Man Without Qualities*. New York: Capricorn.

Offe, K. (1985). "New Social Movements: Challenging the Boundaries of Institutional Politics." *Social Research* 52:817–868.

Plant, S. (1992). *The Most Radical Gesture: The Situationist International in a Postmodern Age*. London: Routledge.

Postone, M. (forthcoming). *The Present as Necessity: Towards a Reinterpretation of the Marxian Critique of Labor and Time*. New York: Cambridge University Press.

Rorty, R. (1979). *Philosophy and the Mirror of Nature*. Princeton: Princeton University Press

Rorty, R. 1982. *Consequences of Pragmatism*. Minneapolis: University of Minnesota Press.

———————— (1989). *Contingency, Irony, and Solidarity*. Cambridge: Cambridge University Press.

Rosenau, P. M. (1992). *Post-Modernism and the Social Sciences: Insights, Inroads, and Intrusions*. Princeton: Princeton University Press.

Scott, Alan (1990). *Ideology and the New Social Movements*. London: Unwin Hyman.

Silverstein, M., and G. Urban (1992). "Natural Histories of Discourse." Working Paper, Center for Psychosocial Studies, Chicago.

Tarrow, S. (1989). *Struggle, Politics and Reform: Collective Action, Social Movements and Cycles of Protest*. Ithaca: Cornell University Press (Western Societies Papers No. 21).

Taylor. C. (1989). *Sources of the Self: The Making of the Modern Identity*. Cambridge: Harvard University Press.

Thompson, E. P. (1968). *The Making of the English Working Class*. Harmondsworth: Penguin, 1968.

Touraine, A. (1971). *Post-Industrial Society*. London: Wildwood House.

———————— (1977). *The Self-Production of Society*. Chicago: University of Chicago Press.

———————— (1981). *The Voice and the Eye*. New York: Cambridge University Press.

———————— (1985). "An Introduction to the Study of Social Movements." *Social Research* 52:749–788.

———————— (1988). *The Return of the Actor*. Minneapolis: University of Minnesota Press.

Tucker, Kenneth H. (1991). "How New Are the New Social Movements?" *Theory, Culture and Society* 8:75–98.

Zald, Mayer N., and John D. McCarthy (Eds.) (1979). *The Dynamics of Social Movements*. Cambridge: Winthrop.

Chapter EIGHT

Two Conceptions of Human Agency: Rational Choice Theory and the Social Theory of Action

Tom R. Burns

INTRODUCTION: SOCIAL RELATIONSHIPS, ACTION STRUCTURES, AND JUDGMENT SYSTEMS

The rational choice approach, of which classical game theory is a variant, is today probably the dominant mode for conceptualizing human action in the social sciences.[1] Certainly, this theoretical approach can claim the most systematic and elegant formulations of human action models. Also, it has a wide range of applications, among other things: foundations of microeconomic theory, public choice, public policy and politics, social action and exchange models in sociology, group and organizational behavior, and deterrence theory in criminology and international relations.[2] The theory of games (von Neumann and Morgenstern 1953; Luce and Raiffa 1957) deals explicitly with actors in social interaction.

Rational choice is formulated in universalistic terms, abstracted to a large extent from historical and cultural context. A fundamental premise is that each individual human being pursues his or her personal values and self-interest, typically in the context of — and against others — rationally pursuing their own self-interest and their personal values. Such theory emphasizes the volitional nature of human action and the capability of actors to make decisions and to act on the basis of rational calculations of benefit and cost. Individual actors are assumed to be more or less fully informed about their action situations and to choose the best action or means to achieve their ends. In more rigorous formulations, one talks about decisions or actions which maximize (or optimize within defined constraints) some value function such as utility. A major problem with this type of theory consists, on the one hand, in the very simplistic behavioral model which is actually implied and, on the other, the drastically artificial assumptions which have to be made for such a model to be "operational." Indeed, the optimization process, given the information (perfect or less than perfect) that the individual has about his or her "given environment" and about his "feasible set of options," becomes in a certain sense a simple exercise in calculus.

Such a narrow conceptualization of human action allows, of course, very little behavioral freedom to individuals and social agents. The "freedom" they possess is more in deciding their objectives, what and how they value things. But it is precisely these matters that are left unexplained by the theory: "Tastes and preferences" are *given*, or simply assumed. If, on the contrary, a much broader scope is allowed the rational-choice approach, it turns out saying something to the effect that everyone seeks to satisfy his or her own interests even if these include tastes for altruism and solidarity. But in any case, such a theoretical proposition is so general that it is deprived of any operational meaning. In addition, it does not answer the prior question of why people have certain preferences rather than others.

Quite simply, the approach assumes that individuals as rational actors are defined *prior to*, or in a certain sense *outside of*, the society in which they act. Society per se does not exist, or it is only continually emerging spontaneously. Shubik claims that his game theory models derive not only from economics and technology of the situation, but from the sociological, political and legal context as well (Shubik 1982:10). But he offers no systematic or concrete method to proceed from well-defined institutions or cultural forms to specified rules of the game, preference structures and choice principles (see Mirowski 1986). For these as well as other reasons, game and rational choice theories, in spite of their many valuable contributions to social science, are simply unable to take into account or analyze, at least in any systematic way, the social basis of preference structures, action alternatives, decision principles and human interaction patterns at the same time that human agents shape and reshape their social basis part of the historical development of social institutions and societies. These matters are not central to the project of rational choice theory.

Such criticisms have been formulated numerous times and have a long history, especially in sociology.[3] A major challenge concerns the question: Is it possible to construct a systematic, empirically oriented theory of human judgment and interaction that transcends the many serious limitations of rational choice and game theories? To do so implies going beyond a mere critique of these approaches and their substantial limitations. Instead, a framework must be formulated that addresses more effectively — theoretically, mathematically and empirically — many of the same problems to which rational choice approaches are applied. The challenge also implies addressing problems to which rational choice approaches cannot be applied or only applied with great difficulty, such as in specifying and taking into account in decision and game analysis norms, institutions and culture; or dealing with interactions where authority, power and other asymmetric relationships apply; or addressing the problems of human creativity and moral agency.

Field (1984), Hodgson (1986, 1989) and Mirowski (1986) in their critiques of neo-classical economics, and in particular of the basic concept of the abstract, super-rational individual, suggest a perspective where human actors are genuinely social. The social situation — and constraints and possibilities — within which actors interact or play out games are defined by prior, given culture, social structure, social relations and norms. Certainly, a basic truth of modern sociology is that social activity does not take place prior to or outside of social structure. At the same time, social agents may modify or transform social structures or create entirely new structures, but they do this within given social and material conditions.

The social theory of games (abbreviated hereafter as SGT) formulated in this paper rejects the concept of the abstract, super-rational actor underlying rational choice and game theories. Or more precisely, it treats games between rational egoists as only a special, limiting case (see later discussion). SGT assumes, instead, that human rationality, choice, and interaction are *socially embedded* (Granovetter 1985). The focus is on socially constituted agents, their roles, role relationships, cultural and institutional frames that orient and constrain them in their interactions. The theory identifies the organizing principles, social relationships and rules that actors apply to interaction situations and that make for particular *action and interaction logics* (Karpik 1981; Wittrock 1986) or *socially conditioned rationalities* (Burns and Flam 1987). In other words, rationality is a function of the rules, rather than rules being a simple expression of rationality (see Mirowski 1981:604).[4]

The notion of context dependent rationality leads to the categorization and analysis of *institutionally specific rationalities* in, for instance, market, bureaucratic, political, religious, and family interaction settings (Burns et al. 1993). For example, actors with competitive relations in a market setting would behave according to individual decision rules and norms calling for attention to monetary gains and losses for self. In the purest case, social values and norms such as those relating to solidarity and cooperation would not come into play. On the other hand, in interaction settings where solidary relations among equals apply, as in friendship networks, participants would be predisposed to utilize joint or collective decision procedures and to concern themselves with identifying and choosing outcomes that are "right," "fair," or "just" according to distributive norms characteristic of friendship or family networks. Consideration of gains and losses only for oneself would be considered improper and a normative breach of the relationship (see later discussion).

In sum, SGT conceptualizes multiple, context-dependent types of social agency and rationalities and tries to identify the cultural and institutional foundations of some of the more important of these rationalities (Burns and Flam 1987). The SGT framework outlined in this paper and elaborated and applied elsewhere (Burns 1990; Burns and Griffor 1992; Burns et al. 1993) provides a useful point of departure for constructing theoretical models of human social action and interaction. These models stress the culturally defined and regulated nature of human action and interaction, but also its creative and dynamic features, its capability of transforming its own material and sociocultural conditions of action. This perspective is a radical departure from the notion of abstract, rational individuals outside cultural forms, institutional arrangements, social bonds, roles, and normative rules. In a certain sense, one can say that *the theory of games is a cultural or institutional theory of games as opposed to a game theory of institutions* (compare, for example, Schotter 1981).[5] The concepts of

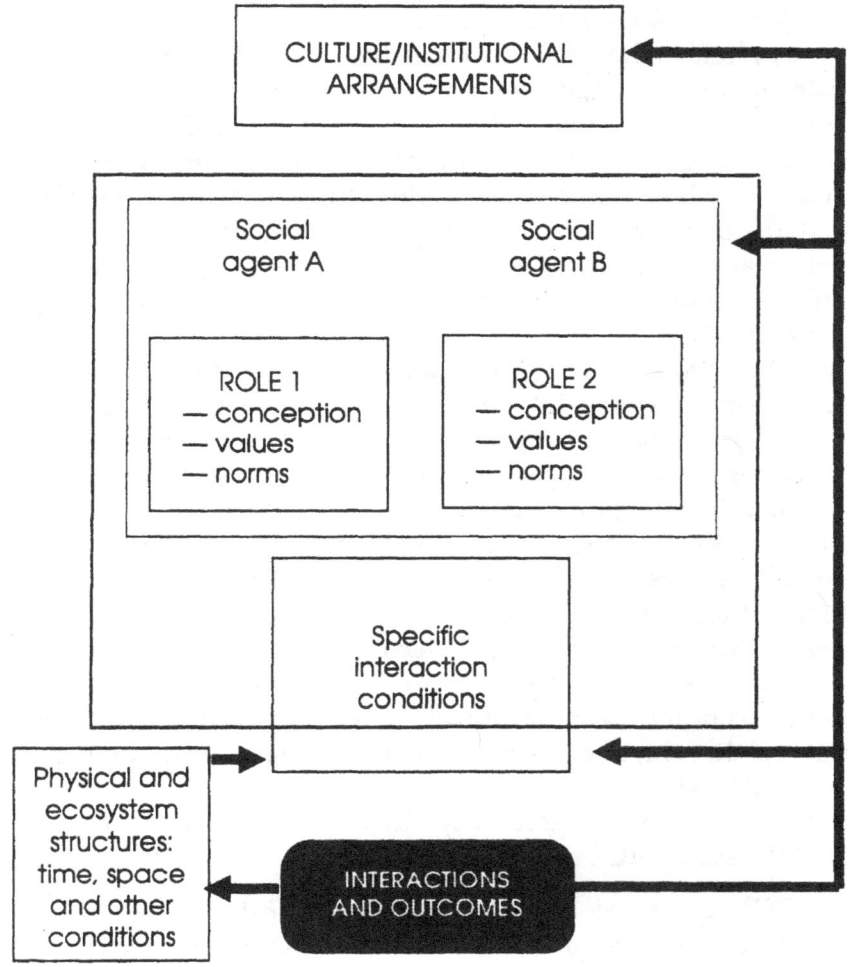

Fig. 1. The theoretical perspective.

culture, institutions, social relationships, roles and norms are readily incorporated into the description and analysis of social interaction and games. At the same time, one is able to significantly expand the empirical scope and power of "game theory" in its application to interaction analysis. The concept of the social embeddedness of games leads one to look for *relationally specific and role based preference* structures, decision procedures, and normative rules that shape and guide actors' behavior vis-à-vis one another (see Figure 1).

Agency refers to the *actors' characteristics and capabilities* in perceiving, interpreting, analyzing, evaluating, and acting as well as affecting the world around them. Rational choice theory (RCT), including game theory and SGT, in theorizing about human action and interaction, conceptualizes human agency. Both theoretical approaches assume that human agents make purposeful choices and that these choices "make a difference," that is that agents exercise power, causing effects in the social and physical environments (Giddens 1984; Sztompka 1991).

The two theories have substantially different conceptions of human agency and its realization in action and interaction. There are three dimensions that concern us here: (1) the sociocultural character of human agency; (2) the normative and moral aspects of human agency; and (3) the creative/destructive capability of human agents.[6] In addition, SGT accepts — and incorporates — the principle that human actors have bounded factual knowledge and computational capability (Simon 1957, 1977). At the same time, of course, actors have extraordinary cultural knowledgeability: knowledge of cultural forms, institutions in the modern world such as family, market, government, business or work organization, hospitals, schools, a variety of social relationships (in the institutional settings) and a number of different roles which they play in modern life.

Let us discuss briefly three key dimensions of human agency which differentiate RCT and STG:

1. RCT assumes an *asocial* (or trans-social) *being* oriented to the consequences of action for self (and only for self). Agency is outside of sociocultural context and outside history. Of course, actors are interdependent, their actions have consequences for one another. But they have no defined social relationships, shared meanings, or cultural forms. SGT, on the other hand, assumes *socially constructed agency*. Human actors are cultural beings, having acquired or learned social rules, institutions, relationships, and roles. Such agency is an historical product, and varies across cultures and civilizations. SGT rejects the notion of a single, universal, utilitarian type of agent, and instead conceptualizes a *role or relationally based concept of rationality, judgment and action*. This implies that there is not one Rationality, that based on utilitarianism, but many rationalities, that is modes or logics of

judging, choosing, and acting. These are linked to actors' different roles, relationships, institutional settings, and cultural frameworks.

2. In RCT norms and ethical considerations are not part of the conception of human agency. The individual actor has subjectively based interests ("self-interest") and concerns himself only with consequences for self. Questions of ethics or of moral sentiments are not of explicit interest. In any case, such sentiments would simply be understood as incorporated into actors' preference structures.[7] In general, matters of morality and ethical behavior have to be raised and analyzed *outside* the theory.[8]

   The socially constructed agency of SGT — stressing the place of human norms and values in social action and interaction — has a relatively well-defined normative aspect; moral sentiments enter into actors' judgment and action processes. Actors' relationships engender notions of fairness and justice, e.g., principles of distributive justice. Their roles function as sources of moral obligation: to obey or to resist; to cooperate or to refuse to cooperate; to help or to expect help (for example, in the latter case, members of a church group or other voluntary organization are expected to help specific categories of persons (the poor, homeless, criminals) but not others (communists, rival religious communities)).

   In general, actors are motivated by — and their judgments and actions biased by — moral and ethical aspects of their relationships with others. Utilitarian or instrumental aspects are not unimportant in the SGT perspective. Indeed, they are often normatively indicated, as in market, technical, or other instrumental settings. Moreover, such considerations find their place in all culture frames. But these aspects of human action must be seen as a part of a complex, multidimensional rationality of human judgment and action, not the only or the main basis for formulating, as in RCT, a universal model of human agency.

3. RCT presumes a type of agent who makes choices according to a single principle (maximization of utility) *within* a given situation — a market setting, a particular game or other interaction setting. This type of agent does not *deviate* from the given principle or action conditions; she does not transform conditions, in short she is neither creative nor destructive.

SGT assumes, in contrast, that human actors have a creative/ destructive capability. They innovate, creating new technologies, new strategies, new rules, institutional arrangements, cultural forms, and, of course, new games and even new types of agents to play the games. They structure and restructure preferences, sets of options, and outcome structures, indeed entire decision and game systems in which they and others participate. Thus, one may speak about the *choice about choice*, or the game about a game, as instances of the *structuring capability of human agents*.

In making and transforming their conditions of actions and interaction — always within certain constraints — actors manifest the dynamic construction of agency. In the course of their actions and interactions, actors modify and reform not only their material and cultural conditions but agency itself. The human development of knowledge, technologies and new action strategies enables agents to overcome or to transcend some, but not all, material and social constraints. Agents exhibit this bounded freedom when they explore and develop new ways of thinking, organizing, and acting, in many instances in response to crisis, predicaments, or emerging problems.

This paper expands on these distinctions, critically examining game theory as a special case of RCT — the one most directly challenging to sociology. The paper outlines the social theory of games and discusses some of the major differences between game theory and SGT. Section 2 briefly describes the rational choice approach, and game theory in particular, pointing out certain basic assumptions and empirical and theoretical limitations. In section 3 I introduce and briefly discuss key SGT concepts and principles. Section 4 presents a few applications of SGT, in particular, the prisoners' dilemma and related games, the identification of social equilibria in interaction settings, and problems of moral agency. The discussion illustrates some of SGT's theoretical and empirical capabilities and its superiority to classical game theory. The concluding section, 5, summarizes the arguments and suggests implications of SGT for a sociology of rationality.

THE RATIONAL CHOICE APPROACH TO SOCIAL ACTION: BASIC ASSUMPTIONS AND LIMITATIONS

Basic Assumptions

Rational choice theories are grounded in the notion that individual actors are fully knowledgeable about their action situations and independently choose the best action or means to achieve their ends. Such choices are made intentionally in the pursuit of individual objectives, and on the basis of expectations about future consequences of current choices (March and Olsen 1984). In the course of the decision process, an actor considers a set of alternatives, ascribes consequences to them, orders these consequences according to their importance and value, and executes an optimal choice among available alternatives (van Parys 1981). One assumes that the actor or actors know all available alternatives, the probability distribution of consequences conditional on each alternative, and the subjective value of each possible consequence. The actor makes a choice by selecting the alternative that maximizes a value function, utility (or more precisely, expected utility).

The theory of games, as formulated by von Neumann and Morgenstern and developed by others, extends a rational choice type of theory for individuals to interacting individuals. That is, game theory is a variant of the general theory of rational behavior. It deals explicitly with actors in social interaction. Each actor rationally pursues his or her own self-interest and personal values against others rationally pursuing their own self-interest and their own personal values (Harsanyi 1977).

Game theory has the following ingredients (von Neumann and Morgenstern 1964; Luce and Raiffa 1957; Hamburger 1979; Jackson 1974): (1) a set of actors or players; (2) the "rules of the game" indicating or specifying which options or sequence of actions are or are not permitted, individually as well as collectively, e.g., in the latter case, communication and negotiation between actors, making binding agreements and making side-bets; also, rules specifying payoffs or outcomes — these may be positive, negative, or zero — to be received by each of the actors. The rules are finitely describable and are fully known to each of the players; (3) the actors' action possibilities or options, that is the actors having a set of given alternatives in the situation, which are known unambiguously; (4) the possible outcomes or payoffs of the options, that is the actors assuming to know all relevant consequences of alternative actions, at least up to a probability distribution; (5) the actors assigning values to the outcomes and having a consistent preference ordering, that is, the consequences of acts can be compared in terms of subjective value; (6) the actors assuming to have a choice principle by which to select a single alternative on the basis of its consequences for their preferences. The objective of each and every player is to choose within certain constraints the maximum "payment" that he or she can obtain.[9]

Most of the games analyzed by game theorists are "games of strategy" with some "competition" among actors. Games of strategy have well-defined rules and objectives for each player. A strategy is a plan or a set of instructions selected by an actor; it specifies each and every move under all thinkable conditions which can arise during the course of the game.[10] Many games can be described as strictly competitive. Such games are also known as zero-sum games, since their payment functions specify that for any play of such a game the sum of the payments received by all players in the game must be equal to zero. In a strictly competitive game, no actor receives a positive payment unless other players receive counterbalancing negative payments. That is, in such games, the actors are assumed not only to be independent beings but to have opposing interests, given the game's payoff structure.[11]

The theory of games identifies optimal strategies, pure or mixed, for the actors. A pure strategy is a single course plan or set of rules, telling an actor what choices she should make for all situations that might arise during the course of a game. In some games the rules specify that choices should (can) be made by chance, in which case the actors are usually given a definite, or at least computable, probability distribution for the various alternatives. In using a mixed strategy, the actor chooses randomly among a set of pure strategies in accordance with the probability assigned to each pure strategy.[12]

In the case of a finite two-person zero-sum game, there exist optimal choice principles, such as the minimax principle, which directs an actor to make his maximum loss as little as possible (that is, he minimizes his maximum loss). The other actor chooses so as to make his minimal assured gain so large as possible (maxmin strategy). Given the complete description of the game, the theory of games provides a computational procedure, capable of determining the correct strategies for all participants in such a game.

Limitations of Rational Choice Theories

There are a number of specific weaknesses of rational choice and game theories as possible empirical theories of human action and interaction.

Agents outside of social structure

These theories treat human agents as social atoms, rationally calculating to further their own self-interests, wholly free from social encumbrances and cultural constraints.[13] Implicitly, a particular type of social relationship is assumed, namely one between egoists, who concern themselves with only their own individual outcomes. This is done despite overwhelming evidence that factors other than self-interest such as institutionalized values and culture generally play a central role in human thinking and action (Sen 1987).

Complete information (but little or no cultural or institutional knowledge)

The players of a game are often assumed to have full knowledge of their own and other players' payoff functions and strategic possibilities. This is far more factual knowledge about action alternatives and game consequences than is usually realistic. Most social interaction does not allow anything approaching perfect or near-perfect information. Indeed, actors are often quite ignorant about their action possibilities and possible outcomes. On the other hand, sociological research suggests that social actors typically have substantial normative, moral, and practical knowledge which they employ in making judgments and acting, and in interpreting and understanding, as well as criticizing, others' behavior. Giddens (1984) refers to the extraordinary knowledgeability of human actors. Analysis of such cultural knowledge, and an understanding of its role in human action and interaction is essential to interaction analysis.

The impossible calculating agent (Hollis 1987)

The game theoretic agent is assumed to have fully ordered and consistent preferences, which are stable over time and space. The rational agent has also unlimited calculating capabilities enabling her to deal with all the information that complete knowledge implies and to process that information in mathematically consistent and effective ways so as to make decisions. Considerable social science research indicates that social agents' preferences are not clearly or consistently ordered in many instances, and may be highly variant over time, space, and social context (Hollis 1987; Burns et al. 1993). Actors' capabilities to think and choose consistently, and to make calculations on the basis of complex information and multiple objectives, are also greatly limited.

Passive, rule-obedient agency

Actors are assumed to engage in social processes programmed *a priori* to behave according to the universal rule of rational, utilitarian calculation. Game theory lacks a notion of the creative/destructive/transformative agent who, among other things, may deviate from some of the rules of the game and, indeed, in some instances transform games, establishing games with new actors, new motives, new action opportunities and payoffs, and new "rules of the game."

Classical game theorists (von Neumann and Morgenstern, Nash, Harsanyi, Howard, among others) invented ways to transform decision structures and games in order to "solve" problems or anomalies. But they never allowed their players to enjoy equal initiative and innovative capabilities. Rather, the theorists typically assumed static models, neglecting the creative and truly dynamic character of human choice and action. Such creativity and transformative capabilities should be a basic consideration in any theory of human action and interaction.

Metaphysical universalism

Game theory and rational choice theory formulate a principle of action — the maximization of utility — that is applied universally, abstracting from all cultural and social contexts, civilizations, historical epochs, cultural forms, institutional spheres, social relationships etc. From the perspective of an empirical social science, this is a serious limitation. One observes that the choice principles or patterns as well as evaluative rules underlying preference structures vary systematically as a function of the social relationship and the institutional setting. One generally does not play a prisoners' dilemma or zero-sum game the same way in a family or friendship network as in a market or labor-management negotiation setting. Friends typically do not try to maximize payoffs for self, but, in general, seek to find mutually satisfying outcomes. They would find it natural or appropriate to coordinate their decision making, either by jointly making decisions or applying a norm to the same effect. They would be predisposed to employ nonmaximizing algorithms, operating, e.g., on complex multidimensional images of the situation or the outcomes. While friends would tend to use joint or coordinating decision procedures, this would not be the case of rivals or enemies — except for purposes of deceit, of course. And actors in an authority relationship, such as in a bureaucratic setting, would be predisposed to utilize a decision procedure where the superior agent makes decisions determining the actions of subordinates and for the collectivity as a whole. Obviously, individual decision making as distinct from collective decision making (joint or democratic, authoritarian, normative)is not the single, universal basis for human decision making.

In sum, traditional game theory is profoundly limited *as a general theoretical framework* for describing and explaining social interaction and related phenomena. It does, of course, allow one to conduct useful, although often highly stilted "thought experiments." As Harsanyi (1977:3), among others, has pointed out, while game theory has had a stimulating influence on the social sciences, it has found only limited applicability in theory development and empirical analysis.[14]

SOCIALLY EMBEDDED ACTORS AND INTERACTION: THE SGT APPROACH

Introduction

A basic sociological axiom, incorporated in SGT, is that social activity does not take place prior to or outside of social structure. Social agents may modify or transform structures or create entirely new structures, but they do this within given social (and material) conditions.

In the SGT approach, games are viewed as embedded in cultural and institutional frames. The latter provide a bases for actors to define what type of situation they are in and what social relationships they have, their roles in the relations, and, in general, the particular rules of the game that should govern their judgments, actions,and interactions in the situation.

A particular social relationship — or normative context — implies particular "rules of the game," including evaluative, decision and action rules (norms, conventions and rituals). The rules of evaluation, decision, and action — the basis of actors interaction logic — will vary systematically across socially differentiated contexts. Thus, one looks for relationally specific decision principles and evaluative rules (underlying actors' preference structures) that derive from the actors' particular social relationship(s) and the wider cultural frame.

Elements of the Theory of Socially Contextualized Games

SGT entails the following distinctive features: (1) Human rationality, choice, interaction and games are socially contextualized.[15] (2) Actors' perception of the game, their preference structures and decision rules derive from their social relationship and the institutional setting in which social interaction takes place. In short, knowledge, preference structures, and decision and action rules are *endogenized*. (3) Actors, through their actions and interactions, not only implement or realize cultural rules but restructure strategically as well as in some instances unintentionally game rules, social relationships and material conditions.

SGT conceptualizes human beings as social actors with certain *social relationships*. Examples of such relationships are friendship, enmity, market exchange, administrative or bureaucratic authority, professional authority, formal relationships between collective actors such as employer associations and labor unions, or between nations, etc. (this list is, of course, not exhaustive, and there are numerous hybrid forms as well as considerable variation in and differing interpretations of any given form).[16] Within a given social relationship the actors have particular *roles*. Actors' purposes are defined within the context of their roles.[17] Each orients her actions within the frame of her role, trying to make a difference, symbolically and instrumentally. The agent is then *causally responsible for an event or development* (Hannerz 1992). In many instances, the purpose of an activity is to express or realize a particular value or norm rather than to achieve a specific material gain or a "payoff." Again, this represents a departure from game theory, and more generally RCT, which assumes that actors focus entirely on the consequences of action; action itself has no intrinsic value or meaning, other than that derived from its consequences.

In SGT actors are conceptualized as social beings who typically — even in highly strategic settings — play specific roles in the context of defined social relationships. Such roles are constituted and regulated by culturally defined organizing principles, norms and values, which are not necessarily consistent. A role consists of two components: specific culturally based *value orientations or goals* and *judgment systems*.

A value orientation or goal expresses desirable properties of actions and/or outcomes. It serves to give priority to relevant values or evaluations indicating which particular value(s) is decisive in case of uncertainty or conflict in judgment and action processes. A judgment system provides a basis for interpreting, reasoning and making judgments in social action and interaction. It consists of rules for describing action and interaction situations, rules for making evaluations of actions, outcomes, and other events, and norms and decision procedures to guide action and choices in the situation. An actor conceptualizes his or her interaction situation, reasons and draws inferences, and makes judgments and acts on the basis of his or her judgment system specific to her role and the social relationship in which she is engaged.[18]

Within the perspective of her judgment system, the actor tries to determine the action(s) that can be expected to realize his or her value orientation or goal, namely her purposeful action or "strategy" in the situation. The latter is, of course, specific to the social relationship in which he or she is engaged with other(s). Such a strategy or "realizer" is not simply an action but a *meaningful action*, one that is conceptualized and justified within the relevant role and its corresponding judgment system. An actor, reasoning in her judgment system, derives judgments such as, for example, that action A_k will realize her (or their) value orientation or goal in the specific interaction situation in which she finds herself (see Burns and Griffor 1991, 1992). In other words, the actor reasons and explains to herself, and possibly others, why she judges action A_k to be such that it will realize the value or goal.

The concepts of social rule and rule system are considerably broader than that of norm familiar to sociologists. Various types of rules and rule systems can be identified and analyzed in terms of their cognitive, behavioral, and institutional status: norms, laws, moral principles, codes of conduct, rules of the game, administrative regulations and procedures, recipes for action, technical rules, conventions, customs and traditions (Burns et al. 1985; Burns and Flam 1987). *Prescriptive rules* including norms are, then, only one type of social rule. Moreover, there are norms of various types, as suggested by everyday distinctions between moral principles, constitutional laws, statutes, administrative rules, informal and local norms. In addition, social actors utilize in their judgment systems *category and descriptive rules* as well as *evaluative types* of rules. Rules of categorization and descriptive rules are used to make distinctions about and to attribute properties to things, people, deeds, and events and their relationships (including causal relationships). They specify what exists, and as a corollary, what does not exist, what, for example, nature, society, men and women are like. This shapes images of what is real and true, what factors to take into account, or to ignore, likely effects of actions and interactions and, in general, the causal linkages between action and outcomes (Czarniavska-Joerges 1988). Evaluative rules assign values to things, people, deeds, events, and states of the world, among other things defining what is "good" and "bad" or acceptable, or what is right, just, beautiful, attractive, enjoyable as well as their opposites — in a word, what actors should strive for or avoid. Values are the basis for generating preference structures.

Category, evaluative and normative (or prescriptive/proscriptive) rules make up and are utilized in judgment systems and help actors organize their perceptions of social and physical reality, define desirable states of affairs, and indicate right or appropriate ways of making choices and, ultimately, acting and interacting. The patterning of social action and interaction in a given situation is more or less predictable — by participants as well as by outside researchers — as a function of the culturally based conception of the relationship (with its specific cultural form and history) and the particular action possibilities and outcomes in the interaction situation (as perceived and analyzed by participants).[19]

Social Contextualization of Games, Rationality, and Agency

SGT views any interaction situation or game as a socially embedded or contextualized game, a *c-game*. In a c-game, each actor conceptualizes the interaction situation within her *judgment system* and is oriented in the situation by her *goal or value orientation*, expressing desirable properties of the activities or outcomes that should be realized in the particular social context. The set of rules that actors apply and derive in their judgment processes makes for particular *action logics* or *socially conditioned rationalities*, resulting in patterned interaction.[20] A *c-strategy* for an actor in a c-game is an action together with a justification (in his/her judgment system) for the judgment that it realizes the actor's value orientation or goal in the situation. Judgments are thus made from the perspective of his or her particular role and its specific judgment system.

An equilibrium in a given social situation consists of a c-strategy for each and every actor in that situation. Our concept of equilibrium is a socially contextualized equilibrium, namely *c-equilibrium*.[21] It refers to a *socially natural state or pattern*, identified or derived within the actors' relationship or cultural form in which they enact their respective roles *vis-à-vis* one another. Particular interaction patterns — both those expected and those enacted and perceived — make sense and derive meaning in these terms. *They "fit," both cognitively and interactionally.* The actors consider the pattern appropriate, proper, "natural," that is consistent with, and indeed, specific realizations of the relational and normative terms on the basis of which they judge their actions (and interactions). Thus, *equilibrium states are specific to the particular social relationship or institutional context in which the actors carry on.* Each social relationship — or more generally institutional frame — is associated with particular equilibrium states or patterns in given interaction settings, although there are combinations of relationships and situations which lack social equilibria (see note 21). Section 4 presents results showing that different social relationships in the same interaction situation imply different social equilibria or stable interaction patterns. Equilibria may be arrived at through complex processes of reasoning and inference generated through actors' judgment processes; they are also arrived at through direct application of norms in the judgment systems, for instance, "generate interaction pattern X, or "distribute a valuable according to principle Z."

The Social Character of Judgment Systems and their Rule Bases

Judgment systems consist to a greater or lesser extent of social rules, that is rules shared within a given cultural population — a type of collective knowledge.[22] Social rules — and their articulation in judgment systems — are historical products of interactions among social agents. Agents cooperate, conflict and engage in power struggles in the course of creating, interpreting, implementing and reforming social rule systems (Burns and Flam 1987). There is a politics and creative dynamics to rule processes. Some agents may seek to reform or replace a rule system that organizes and regulates their economic or political relationships. Others — with strong vested interests in the system — try to defend it. Major struggles in human history and in contemporary society revolve around the formation and reformation of key rule systems: constitutions, core economic institutions including markets, financial institutions and wage negotiation systems; political institutions such as legislative bodies, government agencies and the state generally; family and gender relationships.

Actors' rule based judgment systems provide a more or less common basis on which participants in the relationship can constitute, structure and regulate their interactions.[23] These systems with their common cultural source serve also as "schemes of interpretation," enabling participants to organize their perceptions and interpretations in more or less similar — and also intersubjectively meaningful — ways (Schutz 1962). They can understand what is going on in the settings to which the judgment systems are applied. Finally, these systems provide a common reference frame for talking about and giving accounts of what is or should be going on. Such *collective knowledge* is a major factor in the social construction of specific social realities (Berger and Luckmann 1967) and in the stabilization of perceptions of social order.

Social rules, or better systems of rules, are actors' basis for actors doing the following: (1) To orient to one another and *to organize and coordinate their activities, thereby patterning them and making them predictable to knowledgeable participants*. The actors produce order in terms of known social forms, to which they provide content that is situationally specific and even highly original and unique contributions. (2) To *organize in more or less similar ways the actors' perceptions of choices, activities, and events* and to interpret and understand what is going on as well as to simulate and to predict in more or less common ways the behavior of those involved. Social rule systems provide a basis for *collective knowledge* and a certain *intersubjectivity*. (3) To refer to a *common frame in giving accounts, in justifying or criticizing activities* and, in general, *conductive normative discourse about their activities and interactions*. That is, specific normative and evaluative rules are referred to in criticizing and justifying actions taken or not taken.

Each type of social relationship has its corresponding rule based roles and judgment systems that enable participating actors to constitute, organize, and regulate their interaction. The rules for organizing and carrying out, for example, market exchange obviously differ from those of everyday social exchange between friends and relatives. The basis for interpreting and understanding what is going on and judging what ought to be going on will also differ. The exchange activities are produced and given meanings on the basis of the particular social relationships. The language of normative discourse, the justification and criticism of action and the giving of accounts will also differ accordingly.

Judgment systems are, as suggested above, derived from cultural frameworks but they also vary — not only because actors play different roles in many social relationships varying from egalitarian, solidary relationships to market and authority and status relationships — but because actors often differ somewhat in the ways they have learned (been socialized into) and developed roles and judgment systems through their personal histories and continuing practice.[24]

Social actors follow rules and rule systems because they often make life orderly and predictable; they solve problems of existential uncertainty and double contingency. Many rule systems are learned early in life (early socialization) and, therefore, special value and meaning are associated with them — even personal identity — providing a basis for adherence to and conformity with the systems, e.g., as in the case of male and female roles. Many rules, when adhered to in specific action settings, result in direct payoffs or positive consequences that reinforce or confirm adherence to the rules. For example, technical rules or know-how, relating to operating a machine or dealing with an administrative process are often of this character.

Of course, there are rules such as laws as well as some norms that are enforced through social sanctions. Laws and formal organizational rules and regulations are typically backed up by specific sanctions and specific agents with the responsibility to ensure adherence to the rules. Norms are typically enforced through diffuse social networks — members of a group, community or organization react to norm breaches. Adherence or commitment to a rule system common to a group, organization, community, or social population tends to vary, in general, among members as a function of their socialization, vested interests, capabilities, perceived opportunity structures and social control networks in which they are embedded.

Social Structuring and Creativity

Human actors — individuals as well as organized groups, organizations and nation-states — are active, creative/destructive forces in the making of history. They shape and reshape cultural forms and institutions as well as their material circumstances, as in recent developments in Eastern Europe. Their creative actions are, nevertheless, subject to cultural, social and material constraints. Actors cannot shape their conditions and determine their future as they will. These changes may be brought about intentionally or unintentionally, in the latter case, for example, through mistakes, performance failures and ignorance (for instance, through the aggregate effects of their interactions).[25] Interaction situations lacking social equilibria usually give rise to uncertainty, unpredictability, and confusion, and motivate actors to try, individually or collectively, to restructure the situation.

In their restructuring activities, actors typically engage in reflective processes and make "choices about choice" and participate in games about games, or meta-games (Burns et al. 1993). This includes the capability to structure and restructure their preferences, outcomes and outcome structures, and, indeed, entire decision and game systems in which they participate. Through structuring activity, human agents also create, maintain and change institutions as well as collective or organized agents: organizations, movements, the state, market and bureaucratic organizations. Socially creative/destructive — but constrained — human choice and action plays an important role in reshaping the conditions of social action and cultural evolution (Burns and Dietz 1992).

From the perspective of the SGT framework, institutional arrangements — the social rules and roles of formal organizations, communities, networks, etc. — are continually maintained and reproduced as well as modified through human agency. The modifications are substantial in some instances, entailing shifts between, or transformations of, core organizing principles and particular rules and systems of rules (e.g., the rational-legal bureaucracy, democratic forms, market arrangements) in modern societies. Various social agents are actively and creatively engaged in such processes determining which rule regime or social order is to govern a sphere of activity or social setting (Burns and Flam 1987).[26] Agents with relevant commitments and vested interests struggle to maintain established systems, or to limit changes in them. Others act openly or covertly to modify, avoid or transform the systems.

Even in periods of radical change, however, the actors never start from scratch. They cannot choose a completely different system with alternative futures, since their point of departure is always an ongoing social order in which they are embedded and which conditions their actions and interactions.[27] Rather, they evolve a future through practical activities, experiment and learning, conflict and struggle. The rationality of choice is not a "goal rationality" but a "process rationality," the balancing of human order and freedom. Major social rule systems organize and regulate the interactions among social agents at the same time that actors' interactions realize, maintain, modify or transform the systems of rules.

Conclusion

The SGT conception of social rule oriented, creative/destructive human agency differs radically from the rational choice conception.

By socially contextualizing rationality, judgment, action and interaction, one is able to show systematically how cultural, social relational and normative factors enter into actors' judgment processes, decisions and actions. This is also the basis for a sociological reconceptualization of such key game theory concepts as "action alternative," "choice," "strategy," "game," "solution," "equilibrium" and "rationality."[28]

SGT articulates and elaborates several key concepts important to interaction analysis. The following are worth stressing: (1) Actors' *common knowledge* and their culturally based conceptions of the interaction situation are not taken for granted as in game theory.[29] Actors may have varying structures of perceptions, different socially based knowledge systems, different ways of conceptualizing their interaction situations and also their social relationships, whether relations of kinship, friendship, rivalry, enmity, market or bureaucracy. Such differences play a significant role in their judgment processes and interactions patterns.[30] (2) Actors' *evaluations and preference orderings* in interaction situations are not exogenous, but *endogenous to their social relationships and the cultural frame within which social relationships are conceptualized*. The ways in which actors tend to play the same game or interaction situation will depend on their social relationship and their conception of the situation, both culturally based. Friends will have a perceptual organization and preference ordering different from rivals or enemies in the "same" (at least, structurally the same) interaction situation. Superiors will not perceive the situation in the same way as subordinates. Among other things, actors in these different relationships will categorize, interpret and judge conditions, actions, motives, events and developments differently. Moreover, actors from different cultures will tend to conceptualize an interaction situation differently, generate different preference orders, and utilize different strategies and decision principles (see note 24). (3) *Choice principles and norms of action* vary systematically as a function of actors' social relationship and the cultural frame within which they interact. Maximizing individual payoffs, utility, or some other value cannot be considered in the SGT perspective as a universal decision principle or ultimate rationality.[31] This type of principle applies in certain social relationships and interaction settings such as market exchange among actors unfettered by other social relationships. That is, other values and goals can be assumed to be suspended and rational, egoistic judgment processes become the actual, even the proper, form. Nor would individual decision making as distinct from collective decision making (joint or democratic, authoritarian, normative) be universal.[32]

SGT extends classical game theory by transcending it. The classical theory is a case based on the implicit assumption of a particular social relationship, namely one involving egoists. Each actor is oriented solely toward himself, unconcerned with the other — neither one another's gains or losses, nor with relative gains (between self and other). This case is far to limited an empirical and theoretical base to construct a general theory of human interaction.

APPLICATIONS

In this section we shall briefly explore a few applications of SGT, specifically to an analysis of the prisoners' dilemma game, patterns of social equilibrium, and the question of moral agency.

Prisoners' Dilemma and the Concept of Role or Relationally Specific Rationality

By way of illustrating a specific application of the theory's possibilities, let us consider the well-known two-person prisoners' dilemma (abbreviated PD) game. The game is often referred to as the prisoners' dilemma (and is a prototype for a class of collective action games (Burns et al. 1993)).[33] The formulation presented here is taken from Luce and Raiffa (1957). The payoff matrix is:

		Actor B	
		Not confess	Confess
Actor A	Not confess	(1yr,1yr)	(12yrs,3mos)
	Confess	(3mos,12yrs)	(8yrs,8yrs)

The standard explanation is that the two players are in the custody of the police and are suspected of a crime. The prosecutor is convinced that they are guilty but does not have enough evidence for a conviction. The prosecutor gives the two prisoners the alternatives of confessing or not (note that this is an example of game structuring, as discussed in section 3.5). If neither confesses he threatens to convict them both of a minor charge in any case. If they both confess, they will both be prosecuted but he will recommend a lighter than usual prison sentence. However, if one confesses and the other does not, the one that confesses will get off with a sentence less than that of the minor charge, while the one that does not will receive the longest possible sentence. The reader is invited to interpret the numbers occurring in the "payoff" matrix in this context.

Personal utility in the standard formulation varies inversely with the length of prison sentence and gives rise to obvious preference orderings for the two players (it is only the relative lengths of the prison sentences which are essential here). Game theory presupposes or assumes implicitly a certain social or normative context or relationship between the actors. Namely, they are egotistically oriented to one another or have a mutually egotistic relationship; that is, they concern themselves only with their own outcomes. Given the standard goal or orientation to maximize personal gain, rational actors utilizing maxmin, choice of dominant strategy or other rationality principle for that particular social context results in each choosing to confess (that is, not to cooperate with one another). The interaction outcome is an equilibrium, namely (8yr,8yr) — although it is nonoptimal. The "dilemma" or paradox of the PD game lies in the fact that two "irrational actors" (that is, ones who do not strive for maximal personal gain) achieve an outcome obviously better for both, namely (1yr,1yr), by refusing to confess.

In a social contextualization of this game where another pattern of rationality were possible — for example, one where the two prisoners are friends oriented to taking one another into account and committed to the norm to strive for mutually satisfactory outcomes — the previous noncooperative equilibrium would not be an equilibrium pattern. Friends would be subject to social norms to cooperate and to make sacrifices for one another. This is the social logic or rationality of their relationship. Thus, the outcome that in a rational choice perspective might appear to result from two "irrational" players is a *socially natural state with cognitive and social equilibrium* within the context of the friendship relationship and a PD type interaction situation — this is so at least under a range of conditions (which in SGT become important matters for further research). A status or authority relationship (with one person in a higher position than another) results in a common pattern of preference and judgment where the *asymmetric outcome* is a social equilibrium (e.g., (3mos,12yr) with the higher status person spending only 3 months in jail and the low status person sacrificing 12 years of life, at least under some variants of such a status and authority relationship). Still another case involves enemies who would be expected to find non-cooperation as proper action and the noncooperative outcome as a cognitive and social equilibrium or natural social state within the frame of their relationally derived judgment systems. In general, other variation or changes in actors' relationships — and, therefore, in their goals, conceptions of the situation, outcome preferences, action preferences, and decision rules — yield other equilibria (or no equilibria at all) in the context of the PD game.[34]

Social Roles, Patterning of Interaction, and the Concept c-Equilibrium

Earlier I introduced the concept of a context dependent equilibrium, a *c-equilibrium*, as an outcome which the participating actors — within a given social relationship and cultural frame — judge to realize their respective goals or values. In other words, a c-equilibrium in a game is an interaction pattern or order based on a set of normatively compatible "solutions" (a configuration of actions realizing the various actors' values or goals).

Given a social structure, and their roles and judgment systems in the structure, an equilibrium is understood as a *socially natural state or pattern*. It is a function of the particular relationship between them and the concrete interaction situation in which they find themselves. It fits *cognitively* in that it makes sense, has meaning, is derivable — and justifiable — within the actors' judgment systems. It fits *interactionally* in that it is the pattern which all the actors, from the perspective of their respective judgment systems, applied in the particular interaction context, judge to be proper, right, meaningful. Equilibrium implies stable, predictable interaction patterns. For instance, (1) friends find a common solution — an outcome realizing the values or goals defined within their friendship relationship; (2) rational egoists find a solution that realizes their goals of maximizing personal gains; (3) competitors or rivals try to find an outcome realizing their goals to gain more than one another; this is typically only possible when they have different perceptions of the situation or differing interpretations of the results.[35] (4) persons in a status or authority relationship find common "solutions" which satisfy the goal or expectation inherent in the relationship, specifically that the higher status person should receive more than the lower status person.

Clearly, the right or proper action or "solution" for friends is not that for competitors or enemies. For example, it was argued earlier that in a game situation such as prisoners' dilemma (PD), actors with differing social relationships find *different social equilibria*. The cooperative outcome is a social equilibrium for friends under a range of conditions. The asymmetric outcomes are c-equilibria for actors in a relationship with differentiated statuses. And the noncooperative outcome is an equilibrium for adversaries. Deviating patterns would be judged as normatively wrong, a breach of a norm, role or relationship. Of course, some of many of the actors may reject their roles or relationships, therefore, making uncertain what the basis of their judgments, actions and interactions would be.

C-equilibria are social states defined for the set of participating actors with their particular roles, values, and judgment systems. They contribute to a sense of order, "cognitive order" and "interaction order." Actors in such relationships know that they are oriented to one another in a particular way, and expect certain patterns in their actions and interactions, namely those realizing the value orientations inherent in their particular roles and role relationships.

Social relationships and their specific evaluative and decision rules

Social relationships can be characterized by two of its major rule types:[36] (1) decision principles governing the actors' choice of action in the context of the relationship; (2) value or affective orientations on the basis of which outcomes are evaluated and preference structures are generated. Such rules are endogenous to the actors' relationship and the larger cultural frame. On the basis of this cultural knowledge, actors can understand one another, predict one another's intentions and actions, and organize and coordinate their interactions.

In each type of social relationship, we expect the actors to produce patterned activity with a certain interaction logic. In the case of domination relations, interaction patterns and outcomes would be asymmetric. Egalitarian, solidaristic relationships would be characterized by symmetric interaction, with the actors inclined to coordinate their decisions and actions. Actors in competitive and adversary relationships would also exhibit symmetry in their decision principles, but these would be independent and definitely not coordinative (except for the minimum coordination implied by the "rules of the game"). Actual payoffs or outcomes would typically not be symmetrical, particularly in cases where the participants differ in their resource control, knowledge levels or strategic capabilities.

Status and authority relations, as well as other domination relations, are characterized by *unilateral collective decision principles and rules of asymmetric distribution* (of, for example, prestige and rewards). Dominant actors in these relations not only have the right and expect to make unilateral decisions and exercise much greater influence over collective activities than do those subordinated to them, but they evaluate outcomes in terms of the degree they correspond to a proper asymmetric distribution. (Of course, dominant actors have a strong material and social interest in seeing to it that outcome structures are, indeed, shaped and regulated according to such an asymmetric distributive function).[37]

Egalitarian type relationships are characterized either by bilateral collective decision rules or rules of independent decision making. The particular rule that prevails — along with the distributive rules inherent in the relationship — will depend on the affective quality of the relationship. For instance, actors with a solidary relationship will be predisposed to make decisions bilaterally and evaluate outcomes in terms of the degree to which they are mutually satisfying. They would try to realize outcomes that are symmetric, minimizing differences in gain (or in loss). In contrast, competitors or rivals would tend to make unilateral, self-interested decisions and evaluate outcomes in terms of maximizing relative gains for self. Actors in adversary relationships are oriented not only to unilateral decision making but to maximizing one another's losses.

Social equilibria in the context of defined social relationships and particular interaction conditions

SGT implies that each social relationship — or more generally social structure — is associated with a particular social equilibrium in a given setting or type of game. Among the key results derivable within SGT (Burns and Griffor 1992; Burns et al. 1993), the following are noteworthy (for purposes of our discussion here, actors only have pure strategies, that is no "mixed strategies" (see note 12)).

1. In a given interaction situation, e.g., the prisoners' dilemma game (or "chicken," "assurance," "battle-of-the-sexes," "zero-sum" or other games), social equilibria — the probable, stable interaction patterns — vary with the actors' social relationship.[38] For instance, the social equilibria for asymmetric type relationships such as status or authority relationships are asymmetric outcomes. In general, status differentiated actors expect the lower status actor to make sacrifices and to be

deferential and would find social equilibria in the asymmetric outcomes in the PD game (the outcome (3mos,12yr) in the PD game discussed earlier) and also in such games as "chicken"[39] and "zero-sum."[40]

In contrast, equilibria for egalitarian relationships, whether friends, competitors, or enemies, are *symmetric outcomes* (Burns 1990). Thus, persons with solidary relations find proper social equilibria in the cooperative interactions and outcomes of the PD game (as well as in "assurance" type games).[41] Actors in an enmity relationship find interactions where they punish one another as proper or "natural," namely the noncooperative or confrontation outcome, as in the prisoners' dilemma game (or in confrontation games such as "chicken" and assurance type games, as discussed in, respectively, notes 39 and 41).[42] Pure asymmetric or distributional games provide no social equilibria except for actors in status differentiated relationships.

2. Not every game setup or interaction situation has an equilibrium pattern, given the actors' social relationship. In other words, there are games for which no configuration of actions or interactions is socially stable or a c-equilibrium. One actor's solution is incompatible with those of other actors; the actors cannot realize or satisfy their respective value orientations or goals in the given interaction situation. For instance, rivals or persons of unequal status would be oriented, on the basis of their relationship, to realizing unequal outcomes: they would fail to find a social equilibrium in interaction situations with only equal outcomes, or when none of the unequal outcomes satisfy their value orientations or goals. For this reason, genuine competitors can not find mutually satisfying outcomes in the PD game (or, for that matter, in zero-sum or chicken and other confrontation games).[43] And, similarly, enemies would find pure assurance games — with outcomes benefitting them both — problematic, unless they were to interpret suboptimal outcomes as a "loss" to both.

3. Games without equilibria appropriate for the relationship implies not only that participants will not know what to expect and will be unable to predict likely interaction patterns and outcomes in which they are engaged. They also imply unstable interactions. Under these conditions, they are motivated to restructure these situations — or to avoid the game if

that is at all possible. Consider the cases of rivals and of friends in interactions situations where they find no proper social equilibria. Rivals or genuine competitors, each interested in maximizing the difference between his own outcome and that of the other(s), would find situations lacking proper differentiated outcomes as problematic. There are no compatible or feasible collective solutions in this case. Playing the game as given would imply uncertainty and confusion, also with the possibility of erosion or redefinition of their relationship (of course, they may try to bracket the experience, thus preserving in this way a particular conception of their relationship). Otherwise, if given the opportunity, they would try to restructure game conditions.

Game situations where all the outcomes are unequal would be problematic for nondifferentiated friends. They would find a zero-sum type game incompatible with or inappropriate for their solidary relationship. If "forced" to play the game, they would be likely to redefine their possible goals in the situation — for instance, that of "minimizing differences." Such a goal could, under the specific game circumstances, be interpreted, and normatively defended, as consistent with the friendship orientation. Of course, if given the possibility, they might refuse to play or transform the game into one of mutual gain.

In sum, the concept of c-equilibrium implies that there exists an interaction and outcomes satisfying or realizing the participating actors' values or goals within their respective judgment systems and within the particular social relationship(s) on which their judgment systems are based. A social equilibrium in a game is a set of normatively compatible actions that are meaningful in a particular social structural context.[44] In the absence of such social equilibria, actors are motivated to restructure game conditions and/or their relationship (in some cases, they may refuse to play the game).

Social Roles and Moral Agency

All human action raises issues of their ethical aspects. What is considered to be moral in decisions that affect human conditions, persons or groups? What moral assumptions, often implicit, are involved in judgment processes and actions? What moral dilemmas arise in the particular roles social actors play *vis-à-vis* one another? How do they try to deal with these?

At the core of SGT framework are concepts such as norms, values and judgment processes, enabling one to describe and analyze actors' orientations about right and wrong and good and bad in particular interaction situations. In contrast, rational choice and game theories provide little or no analytical capability to address such matters, in large part because they lack conceptual tools to deal with social values, norms, value predicaments and conflicts. The utilitarian foundation is simply too all too constraining.

Most discussions on ethical issues assume some form of moral agency, but one is all too often not told about the different social contexts — cultural frames, social relationships and roles — which are responsible for the formation and conceptualization of this agency. Thus, roles in market and administrative settings entail differing normative guidelines and directives. In market settings, it is appropriate to make one's own calculations and to pursue one's own interests — within certain limits of course. In an administrative setting, one's role as a subordinate entails the norm to carry out orders, to obey the policies and regulations of an authority. Of course, there are limits to the realization or implementation of roles in such settings. When one follows the logic of the market to an extreme, one becomes a ruthless "exploiter" of others or a "bandit." Or following the logic of a bureaucratic role to an extreme makes one into the "bureaucratic personality," "heartless" and also often ineffective. In both of these cases, the formal or institutionalized morality is constituted in social roles. Of course, in practice, humans as moral agents often take an *active part* in the interpretation and reformulation of their moral positions and moral obligations in the context of market, administrative or other social settings.

The sociological analysis of ethical processes should and can take into account the particularities of the social dimension. Much social action — including the judgment acts underlying specific strategic acts — is role based. In general, social activities are patterned on the basis of the different roles humans play in different social contexts and social systems. Human beings in their various roles are recognized as *social* agents with particular moral orientations or sentiments. Thus, one is led to examine how different roles function as *sources of moral obligation*.

Social actors are often in situations where more than one role applies which give rise to moral dilemmas or conflicts. We can take Sophocles' play *Antigone* as an illustration of the difficulty of dealing with multiple moralities associated with different roles (Burns and Hansson 1992; Machado and Burns 1992). In the play, Antigone chooses to obey her familial duties — to bury her brother's corpse — in opposition to King Creon's law, believing it a sacred duty, superior to all human laws, to bury one's kin. Her brother Polynices had rebelled against the king, but was defeated and therefore treated like an enemy of war: his body was to be left unburied, and therefore his soul would wander through eternity in sorrow and uneasiness. Antigone is condemned to death for her attempt and is buried alive in the vault of the Ladbacidae where she hanged herself. Antigone's conflict was a conflict of moral codes and consequently of duties. Both her role as sister of Polynices and her role as a representative of the Athenian ruling house (she as the daughter of Oedipus and the daughter in law of the ruler, Creon) put her in the dilemma of disobeying either her familial duties or her duties toward the law.

In the play Sophocles pointed at one central issue that can be understood as a dilemma that occupied the mind of many Greek thinkers at that time and still remains a central issue in Western thought and policy: the conflict of public rights versus private (including individual rights). In the play the conflict arises when familial (and also individual morality, that of Antigone), clashes with the system of laws and authority represented by King Creon. Sophocles raised questions about the legality of the law and about the extent to which societal rights can or should prevail over individual rights. And how should the morally responsible individual behave in the face of social institutions that do not support, but rather deny, individual responsibility and that conflict with human nature itself? Such dilemmas and the social conditions and judgment processes that generate them can be specified and analyzed within the SGT social action framework. This is in contrast to the rational choice and classical game theories with their grounding in an utilitarian theory of value and the absence of conceptual tools to deal with ethical matters, value conflicts and moral dilemmas. Burns et al. (1993) examine actors' reasoning processes relating to such conflicts and dilemmas and their attempts at practical resolution, including the transformation of their interaction situations, roles, and role relationships.

CONCLUSION: BEYOND THE RATIONAL CHOICE CONCEPTION OF HUMAN AGENCY

Game theory treats human agents as social atoms, wholly free from social encumbrances, rationally calculating according to a universal formula of pursuing one's own self-interest. Implicitly a particular type of social relationship is assumed, namely one with egoists, who are potentially competitors (but not engaged in a social relationship of competition or rivalry). The theory, in atomizing human agency, largely ignores culture and social structures in which human agents are embedded.

I have introduced an alternative conception of human agency, arguing that it provides a useful point of departure for formulating a social theory of human interaction and games. Among the key dimensions on which SGT and the rational choice approach and game theory differ, I have emphasized: the sociocultural character of human agency, in particular the role basis of human rationality, judgment, and action; the normative and moral aspects of agency; the creative/destructive capability of human agency. More specifically:

Socially Embedded Rationality, Judgment and Interaction

SGT's point of departure is a socialization of game concepts and models by conceptualizing human interaction as socially embedded and subject to the force of human agency. The concept of social embeddedness implies that context-dependent rationality, choice and interaction, including strategic types of action, are defined, constituted and regulated on the basis of social relationships among actors and the cultural and institutional frame in which the interactions take place. Institutional arrangements, organizing principles, cultural forms, social roles, and rules of conduct shape and regulate what actors tend to do, or not to do. The social roles and rules prevailing within neighborhoods or community organizations differ significantly from those within markets or bureaucratic organizations. The specific evaluation and action rules that friends or kinsmen are predisposed to use *vis-à-vis* one another in relevant interaction settings differ significantly from those likely to be used by actors with other types of social relationships, such as competitive or adversary relations.

This "social embeddedness" of games implies then culturally or relationally specific rationalities (specified in value orientations and judgment systems). The rationalities are defined by the roles and role relationship(s) of participating actors. A given role relationship entails certain category and descriptive rules, evaluative, and decision and action rules (including conventions and rituals). For instance, outcomes are evaluated — and preference structures generated — by the actors on the basis of evaluative rules defined *within* their social relationships. A socially contextualized game will have a certain social logic or rationality and context specific equilibria, if these exist. Likely interaction patterns and equilibria are predicted in SGT on the basis of actors' culturally based conceptions of their relationship (with its specific cultural form and history) and their categorization and perception of the interaction situation with particular action possibilities and outcomes.

Stable patterns of judgment and interaction reflect the socially constructed way in which participating actors categorize, evaluate, make judgments and act and, thereby, produce particular interaction patterns. This patterning contributes to the perception of social order and to the stabilization of social structure (see Burns et al. 1992).[45] *Their behavior is then understood as a function of the logic or rationality of social relationships, not individual rationality.*[46] (Of course, in some instances the logic of a social relationship may be one of encouraging individuals to define and pursue their own personal self-interests, that is an individual type of rationality).

Multiple c-Models or Game Theories

The SGT approach points up that there are *many game theories or models* (in this sense it is a generalization of classical game theory). These correspond to different social relationships and the rationalities or action logics based on the relationships. Thus, a social relationship defined for "rational" egoists is only one of several possibilities. Actors may be involved in solidaristic type relationships, relations of superordination/subordination, adversary relationships, among others, each with its own specific category systems, evaluative rules, norms and decision principles. The social interaction logics and patterning of interaction in these relationships — and the specific roles and corresponding judgment systems — differ substantially from that of rational egoists.

The limitations of universalizing the relationship of rational egoists has been stressed here; such a rationality cannot serve as the foundation for a general theory of social action and interaction. Thus, it has been argued here that persons engaged in solidary relationships would not try unconditionally to maximize payoffs for self, but would in general seek to find mutually satisfying outcomes. Actors in a superior/subordinate relationship would be predisposed to authoritarian decision procedures, with the actor of superior status or authority making decisions for the collectivity and for those of inferior status accepting this authority, at least within a range of conditions. They would also expect differential payoffs favoring the superior actor. In general, the actors' social relationships — and the roles and norms involved — implies certain orientations motivating their actions and rules for organizing perceptions, evaluating the situation and making choices. Friends interact according to different rules than rational egoists or rivals, at least in the purest cases. Friends will be more likely than rivals, enemies, or rational egoists to cooperate in prisoners' dilemma or other competitive situations under a range of conditions, and to find the cooperative outcome as a socially natural state or equilibrium. They will also find any zero-sum outcomes as unsatisfactory and would be predisposed to refuse to play the game or to transform it.

The Creative and Unpredictable Aspects of Human Action and Interaction

Actors innovate by producing new options, cultural and institutional forms as well as techniques and technologies. In this way, they change their conditions and patterns of social action and interaction. In other words, they have the capability to actively structure and transform their action conditions, their relationships as well as themselves as social agents.

The Sociology of Rationality and Agency

Classical theory assumes certain *universal rules* as characteristic of "rationality": (1) transitivity of preferences; (2) complete knowledge about action possibilities and outcomes (or probability distributions over them); (3) rational choice or decision procedures.

Such assumptions are not only artificial and limiting for any empirical analyses, but they are morally dubious. They conceal the fact that *the theorist tries to impose on human actors his own conception of a judgment system*, namely that of the universal rational, self-interested actor. In this way, the theorist can claim or judge that a person who does not act according to rational self-interest is irrational, as, for example, "cooperators" in the prisoners' dilemma. The irrational or "deviant" actor simply fails to follow the particular rules or decision principle of the rational choice theorist. Moreover, in constructing a model of the human actor, the theorist adopts coherence as a standard of rational judgment. A rule of transitivity is also imposed, making "greater than" or "lesser than" transitive (taken as axiomatic). The rational choice theorist constructs a judgment system — and makes judgments — in the name of "universal human nature." These constructions differ substantially from those that the actors themselves make or consider appropriate within the frames of their own judgment systems and cultural frames.

What does the SGT framework imply about such core notions as utility maximization or other universal principles so central to rational choice and game theory models (see note 31)? In SGT human actors organize and regulate their activities according to socially defined relationships applying to interaction settings and, in particular, according to the roles they play *vis-à-vis* one another. If the grammars applying to them call for "maximizing," for instance profits, then they are predisposed to do so within their bounded knowledge and action possibilities. The socially constrained profit-maximizing agent may thus seem to adhere to the norms or logic of market capitalism. "Market man" judges all things according to market standards and goals and will be no more loyal, solidary, or self-sacrificing than the market dictates. This is not only legitimate but expected, or even socially required behavior in many instances.

In another social context such as family, friendship or religious settings, social roles and norms may call for specifically normative or ritualistic behavior, giving little or no systematic consideration to outcomes, economic or otherwise, at least in the purest cases. It would be considered socially inappropriate or wrong to behave according to "economic or capitalist" logic in family, friendship or other solidary relations. Other norms and principles guide social action and interaction. In particular, there are norms prescribing sharing as opposed to not sharing and exclusion, or norms against offering or demanding money for many of the services and things people do for one another in family, friendship, religious or other solidary relations. (Of course, the logic of self-interested materialism may penetrate areas of social life such as family, friendship networks, religious settings — and typically in concealed forms — but it is usually subject to social control attempts to eliminate or limit such penetration.)

The SGT generalization of game theory recognizes *a spectrum of judgment systems*. In this perspective the judgment of the rational choice theorist cannot be given *a priori* superiority. The attempts of the rational choice theorist to "universalize" the rational choice judgment system results in paradoxes and contradictions, for instance that "irrational actors" may play the prisoners' dilemma game "better" than "rational actors" in that the former realize the optimal outcome (Luce and Raiffa 1957).

For the perspective of SGT, "rationality" has an obvious and empirically meaningful interpretation, namely, *Actors are judgmentally rational in the sense that they reason, interpret, and act in accordance with their particular judgment systems*. The latter are derived from the social relationship (and more generally the culture in which they find themselves). A judgment system indicates the values they should realize and some of the ways they should do this. It also indicates rules for arriving at "correct" or proper interpretations, inferences and judgments.

This is not to claim that actors never make mistakes in terms of — or deviate from — their judgment systems' forms and guidelines. "Failures" within a judgment system may occur because of, for example: (1) incoherence, ambivalence, ambiguity, predicament; (2) inability to arrive at judgments, or ignorance of ways to bring about realizations of goals or values; (3) judgment processes and their practical realizations leading to "unexpected" or unintended outcomes.

In sum, SGT does not propose a single, universal judgment model, but posits *the universality of judgment systems in human choice and interaction*. Judgment systems are socially constructed and, therefore, *context dependent*. They depend on the social relationships among actors, the particular types of interaction situations in which actors find themselves, and, ultimately, the cultural frame, which is an historical product.

Moreover, SGT does not require full model specification or even decisiveness. Actors often have templates or schemes for decision that must be "filled in" — and they may fill these in in ways depending on their specific action settings, situational analysis, judgments, and interaction processes. Judgment systems and value orientations — social roles and role relationships — are also seen to change over time, as a function of, for example, interaction with others, the acquisition of practical experience, and, in general, social learning.

Notes

1. Among many relevant social science works the following have received considerable attention: Blau (1964), Buchanan and Tullock (1962), Coleman (1992), Elster (1977), Hardin (1982), Harsanyi (1977),

Luce and Raiffa (1957), von Neumann and Morgenstern (1953), Olson (1968), Sugden (1986), as well as a number of others.
2. The same basic structure of rational choice underlies modern decision engineering, operations analysis, management science, decision theory, and the various analytical approaches to improving choices and information systems, more specifically, the blending of aviation fuel, the location of warehouses, the choice of energy alternatives, and the arrangement of bank queues, as well as many other decision problems.
3. It is not my purpose here to offer a systematic presentation or critique of rational choice theory, or game theory in particular. A number of important critical works already exist, among others: Cohen et al. (1972), Collins (1988), Etzioni (1988), Field (1984, 1979), Hogarth and Reder (1987), Hodgson (1986), Hollis (1987), Kahneman et al. (1982), March and Olsen (1976), March and Simon (1958), Mirowski (1986, 1981), Sen (1987, 1982), Simon (1957).
4. This type of reasoning should be familiar to most sociologists, but is foreign to the rational choice tradition and economics. An exception is certainly the work of Coleman (1992), which in its sociological insight and reasoning transcends the inherent limitations of the rational choice approach which he claims his work rests. That is, it transcends the very foundations which it proposes for a theory of human action.
5. Such cultural knowledge — specific organizing principles, rules of conduct, roles and role relationships — enable individuals not only to guide their actions *vis-à-vis* one another, but to anticipate, interpret and understand what others are doing, and, indeed, in combination with situational knowledge, to "simulate" interaction scenarios among participants. Such rule systems also provide a basis for participants to engage in normative discourse, criticism, justification and, in general, the giving of accounts about what is happening or not happening, and why, relating to their ongoing activities (Harré 1979).
6. Another key dimension, which clearly distinguishes the two theories conception of agency, concerns the capacity of self-reflection and self-structuring. In (Burns et al. 1993), this aspect is closely associated with human transformative capabilities and processes.
7. Typically, those applying game theory conflate objective payoffs with social payoffs such as those associated with a given social relationship among participants. "Game payoffs" are *net payoffs*. The SGT approach separates the evaluation process — based on rules derived from actors' social relationships — from the defined outcomes. Evaluative rules within a given relationship, such as one of solidarity or love, are applied to the defined outcomes. Through such evaluative processes, *preference structures appropriate to the relationship are generated*. In other words, preference structures are endogenized; they are generated through the application of evaluative rules characteristic of the given social relationship to defined outcomes.

8. Harsanyi (1977:11) makes this explicit in distinguishing utility and game theories from ethics or ethical theory.
9. The decision or optimality principle which actually guides the choice — for instance, utility maximization, probability-weighted utility maximization, or maximization of minimum utility, among others — depends on whether the actor can associate with each action alternative one particular consequence (the case of decision making under certainty), a distribution of subjective probabilities over a set of alternatives (the case of risk), or just a set of possible consequences (the case of uncertainty) (van Parys 1981:19).
10. The game consists of a sequence of moves, each of which is an occasion for a choice between alternative actions, made by one of the players of the game. A complete sequence of choices (one that the rules define as terminating the game) is said to constitute a play of the game. At each move, an actor is supposed to always know completely what his choices are, but he may not know what choices have been made previously. If at each move every actor knows completely all the choices that have been made thus far in the game, it is said to be a game of perfect information. Otherwise, it is a game of imperfect information. In parlor games, chess and checkers are examples of perfect information games. Bridge and Poker are examples of imperfect information games, since each player usually does not know what hands are held by other players.
11. It is not correct to assume that in a pure game of strategy, each and every actor is necessarily competing with the other actors. In some games (e.g., in the case of parlor games such as bridge), players must form teams and each player should cooperate with those who are on his or her team. In other games such as poker which do not call for such cooperation among designated players, it may be strategically sound or apparently advantageous for two players to form a temporary alliance against another or other players (Jackson 1974:21).
12. Mixed strategy is a central concept within game theory. A mixed strategy is an assignment of real numbers in the interval [0,1] to the action alternatives each actor or player has and, assuming he/she must act, such that the numbers assigned sum to 1. From the SGT perspective, it is a dubious practice to use "strategy" concepts that cannot be incorporated and analyzed within actors' judgment systems and role structures. In other words, the actions of participating actors must be culturally contextualized and their "meanings" specified. In this light, the status of "mixed strategy" is far from unproblematic: such a concept cannot be introduced as an obvious universal — and decontextualized option — for all conceivable games and social situations. Rather, the mixed strategy alternative must be contextualized in actors' socially based judgment system — which is to say the normative and institutional context of the game. Besides such theoretical criticisms,

there are serious mathematical and empirical problems with the notion of mixed strategy (Burns and Griffor 1992).

13. The rational choice approach takes as given one of the major questions which social science should address, namely what are the factors and processes that structure actors' preferences and normative orientations as well as the options available for choice and their outcomes. The "rules of the game" in game theory encompass all factors that impose constraints on — and also define action opportunities for — the agents (Harsanyi 1977:88). However, *this conception of "game rules" conflates social rules and conventions (culture), laws of nature and physical constraint (nature), agency (the skills, knowledge, capabilities, and personal endowments of individuals), and various means of action (technologies, economic resources, military equipment)*. Such conflation might be methodologically defensible whenever the analysis refers to a single play or static game structure. But once we are interested in the possibility that the actors modify the game, e.g., by reinterpreting or altering the social rules and conventions, then a distinction must be made between the "rules" that can be changed, at least over the medium to long run, namely many social rules, and those rules of the game that cannot be changed, such as physical and biological laws — to mention an extreme contrast.

14. In a similar vein Schelling (1963:83) points out: "On the strategy of pure conflict — the zero-sum games — game theory has yielded important insight and advice. But on the strategy of action where conflict is mixed with mutual dependence — the nonzero-sum games involved in wars and threats of war, strikes, negotiations, criminal deterrence, class war, race war, price war and blackmail; maneuvering in a bureaucracy or in a traffic jam; and the coercion of one's own children — traditional game theory has not yielded comparable insight or advice."

    Harsanyi (1977:4–5) writes, "In my opinion game theory — just as individual decision theory of which game theory is a generalization — should be regarded as a purely formal theory lacking empirical content. Both decision theory and game theory state merely what will happen, if all participants have consistent preferences, and actually follow their own interests as defined by their preferences, in a fully consistent and efficient manner. Empirical content is considered only when we make factual assumptions about the nature of these preferences and about other factual matters (e.g., when we assume that people prefer more money to less money, or make specific assumptions about the economic and political resources — and therefore the strategies — available to the participants in a given social situation)."

15. Elsewhere (Burns and Griffor 1991, 1992) it is shown that one can generate mathematical models of what a context consists and how it influences human motivation, judgment, and action. The formalization

makes use of important developments in foundational mathematics (Martin-Lof 1984; Troelstra and van Dalen 1988).

16. The rule systems corresponding to diverse relationships and institutional arrangements can be distinguished from one another in terms of *who* is included and *who* is excluded, *what types of activities are permitted, prescribed or proscribed, who has the right to do what to whom, who has access to or control over appropriate resources in the field(s) of activity* (Burns and Flam 1987). Thus, social rule systems, when implemented, give identity to and pattern in particular ways the interactions in which the actors are engaged, for instance "market behavior" as distinct from "administrative activity," or "democratic political process." When actors implement or realize social rule systems, they not only generate certain interaction patterns and developments — also not always those they intend — but they communicate to one another meanings about what is going on, what it is that they are doing, which social agents are constituted in the situation, how, when, and where. A knowledgeable participant in institutionalized social interactions has acquired grammars of action and interaction, which are also the basis for generating a certain type of rationality or logic of action and interaction.

17. Moreover, the purposes and rules of behavior of any given individual in a particular activity — taking place, for instance, in a bureaucratic or other authority structure — can often be traced to the directives of other agents or of institutions rather than deriving from the immediate agent (Harré 1979). Of course, actors often have their own "private" or personal orientations and motives, fashioned out of individual reflection or in opposition to socially defined purposes and pursuits. Schutz (1962:84) distinguishes between social definition (intersubjective) and private definition of an individual's situation: "One thing is the objective meaning of the social role and the role expectation as defined by the institutionalized pattern (say the office of the Presidency of the United States); another thing is the particular subjective way in which the incumbent of this role defines his situation within it (Roosevelt's, Truman's, Eisenhower's interpretation of their mission)." The SGT treatment of social actors is formulated largely in terms of their positions and role relationships in social structure. Actors' personal characteristics or idiosyncracies are not systematically treated in this work, although these are obviously important factors in many social processes.

18. Of course, each human actor personalizes a role based judgment system as a consequence of her socialization, personal history and practical experience with the role. See note 17.

19. *The social embeddedness of interaction reduces actors' uncertainty* since, in many instances, they know the common social organizing principles and rules that they should, or are likely to, follow in their interactions.

Without such knowledge they would have great difficulty in figuring out what others might or might not do. Their motives, predispositions, creative inclinations, resources and likely strategies, among other elements, would be largely unclear or unknown. This situation arises whenever agents from different cultures encounter one another for the first time, or when situations are seen as very different or new compared to those situations to which established rule systems have applied previously.

Social embeddedness may also generate uncertainty, in that two or more relationships (or distinct rule systems) — each separately providing for a high degree of certainty — might be activated at one and the same time. This can occur because of contradictory features of the two systems, ambiguities in the situation itself, or because the participating actors have opposing interests and advocate different relationships or different interpretations or alterations in rules.

20. A theory such as this seeks to determine what is the *actual judgment system or frame of decision making and action in concrete social settings, how that system arises from the social action context, and how, within that frame, certain types of reason operate* (cf. Simon 1987). Simon argues (1987:39):

    In this kind of complexity, there is no single sovereign principle for deductive prediction. The emerging laws of procedural rationality have much more the complexity of molecular biology than the simplicity of classical mechanics. As a consequence, they call for a very high ratio of empirical observation to theory building. They require painstaking factual study of the decision making process itself.

    The notion of socially embedded rationality, choice, and interaction may be considered a *sociological specification of Simon's procedural rationality* (Simon 1977). Interaction processes have certain procedural rationalities — that is, interaction logics — based on the particular social relationships, roles, and judgment systems applying to interaction.

21. The classical game theory concept of "equilibrium" refers to that game outcome from which no actor has an incentive to move, that is an outcome (or point) beyond which no actor can improve his or situation by unilateral action. In the case of repeated plays there may be incentives for one or more actors to move, but others can sanction forcing the other back to a quasiequilibrium outcome. Nash (1950, 1951) proved that every finite game (allowing mixed strategies) allows at least one equilibrium point. (The equilibrium is strong if each actor's equilibrium strategy is not merely a best reply to the other actor's strategy combination but is in fact the only reply to it (Harsanyi 1977:104).) A theory with no equilibrium or multiple equilibrium is considered underspecified in the rational choice tradition. The modeler has failed to provide a fully and precise prediction for what will happen. One may admit that the theory is incomplete. Another is to recon-

ceptualize the concept of equilibrium, as is done in SGT. The absence of c-equilibria is a meaningful concept. A social equilibrium is not possible in each and every game context defined by actors' social relationship and their description or understanding of the interaction situation. In these cases that is no interaction pattern or outcome that realizes or satisfies each and every actor's value orientation in the situation. Such situations give rise to uncertainty, unpredictability and confusion, bargaining, and usually restructuring of game context parameters. Moreover, in SGT a theorem is proved that if there exists a c-equilibrium point for a game in a given social context (with a defined social relationship and particular action possibilities and outcomes), then there is an algorithm for arriving at the equilibrium (in contrast, the Nash theorem referred to above is only an existence theorem. It offers no basis for finding or identifying equilibria).

22. Social rule systems, including many tacit rules, are not only a more or less common bases on which the participants in any given social relationship, group, organization, or community organize and regulate their social actions and interactions. They also serve as "schemes of interpretation" as well as reference frames in communicating about, and giving accounts of social activities in which participants are engaged (cf Schutz 1962:208). The schemes of interpretation and reference frames for accounting, based on context relevant social rule system(s), establish a certain level of *intersubjectivity*. Along similar lines, Schutz (1962:208, 80–81) observed that the world is not the private world of the single individual but an intersubjective world, common to all of us, in which we have not a theoretical but an eminently practical interest.

23. This proposition holds under conditions where such rules enjoy legitimacy and wide acceptance. Interaction situations, the organizing principles, appropriate resources and strategies,and social behavior becomes highly uncertain whenever actors try to apply incompatible systems of rules, or substantially revise their interpretations and application of the social rules, or try to introduce rule and institutional innovations. For instance, two or more groups may struggle over what organizing principles, rules and procedures will apply to a particular action setting, for instance what principle will govern the distribution of resources, where the issue might concern market versus public solutions. These struggles are often carried out within an institutional framework which constrains the potential innovations and outcomes (Andersen and Burns 1992). In any case, shifts in action logic or social rationality occur whenever one or another of the contending groups gain the upper hand and imposes its rule regime, that is, establishes its social order, although in many cases hybrids and other institutional compromises may be launched.

24. Actors' cultural frames — and categories, beliefs, values and norms — often differ, especially in the modern world with the global movement of peoples and the global communication of ideas (Hannerz 1992). In a certain sense, actors with different cultural and ideological perspectives rarely play the "same game," since the game is conceptualized within each actor's cultural frame. In other words, actors from different cultures, for instance, Muslims, Christians, and Buddhists, are likely to activate or derive judgments systems from their cultural frames that differ substantially. This makes for different knowledge systems, different ways of conceptualizing interaction situations and social relationships (e.g., in the latter case what it means to be kinsmen, friends, rivals, enemies, strangers or unrelated egoists), and structures of perception. Evaluative rules and preference orderings, and normative structures will also differ in ways that must be specified and analyzed utilizing the theory. Ethnic, class and religious misunderstandings and conflicts are common sources of problems in interaction, whether in commerce, politics, diplomacy or military settings. Also, historical developments that reshape cultural forms, beliefs, categories, norms and values generate misunderstandings and conflicts among human groups and communities. For example, the modernization process (generating distinct new cultural perspectives) has entailed, in part, the shaping of overriding or modal judgment systems that are considered "rational." This has resulted, in part, in the emergence of new social relationships such as those occurring in modern capitalism and bureaucracy and the reconceptualization of old relationships such as those of family and community. These changes generated conflicts between "moderns" and "traditionals" as some groups remained committed to, or were unable to change, their cultural perspectives considered traditional.

25. In conceptualizing social activity, one can distinguish between collective/organized action and *aggregate or compositional action*. In the first, actors make decisions and act jointly or as a group or organization. Their decisions and actions are carried out according to certain coordination rules such as voting procedures, a common set of "coordinating norms" or the rule of authority such as that institutionalized in bureaucratic domination (Weber 1968). Social decisions made according to one of these procedures are *binding* on individuals or parts in the group or organization — although, of course, opposition or deviant activities often arise in response to the policies selected. Here one may speak about collective agency, socially constituted agency that makes decisions and acts. For example, the state is a collective actor, or more precisely a complex of actors with a monopoly on the legitimate use of force and the authority to make certain types of rules called laws. It can determine many of the basic rules of the game, property rights and institutions which determine the action opportunities and outcomes of

particular decision processes and games in society (North 1982). In the case of compositional action, individual agents make decisions and take actions within relatively open systems of rules and organizing principles, for example many market arrangements (Burns and Flam 1987; Burns et al. 1993). Actors' responses to a situation are individualistic, entailing individual adjustments, although they may take into account the reactions of others in consideration of their own decisions and actions. The patterning of such action depends very much on the "models" and the information that actors utilize to interpret and analyze the situation and the situational conditions which structure their action possibilities and likely payoffs.

26. Game theory presupposes well-defined rules of the game and objectives for each player without identifying or explaining the social bases of these. Moreover, the rules are assumed to be fully known, unambiguous and consistent. For instance, in game theory a game is either fully cooperative or fully noncooperative; the actors must be able to make firm enforceable agreements or not. Of course, in practice the enforceability or status of rules is often uncertain. Also, actors may try to avoid their force, or to change them. For this reason, SGT conceptualizes and analyzes games with varying degrees of — or changing — well-definedness and coherence of social rule systems (also see Andersen and Burns 1992).

27. For example, powerful human agents engage in making strategic decisions to structure key institutions and cultural forms. However, the ability of even powerful agents and elite groups to shape social structures, cultural formations and patterns of social interaction favorable to their interests is strictly limited. Other structuring forces — including the unintended consequences of actions about which they lack full knowledge or control — alter action capabilities and patterns of interaction, redistribute strategic resources and eventually reshape social structures. As a result of such developments, actors previously in more or less peripheral or disadvantageous positions may gain resources or develop capabilities which enhance their social power or independence relative to those who earlier dominated them. Such developments are often the basis for major social transformations.

28. SGT not only radically departs from traditional game theory in a number of key assumptions and formulations, but extends the theory theoretically, mathematically, and empirically. For instance, Burns et al. (1993) show that n-person and 2-person game theory models can be derived from the SGT general model. These derivations expose in a systematic way the very extraordinary character (from a social science perspective) of many game theory assumptions and formulations.

29. The principal knowledge applied in human interaction is social knowledge belonging to a particular group, organization, or society, namely culture. In the pursuit of their purposes and values, social actors make

use of *common knowledge* — the social stock of knowledge (Berger and Luckmann 1967) — about how to act, with what means, where and when. A core part of this knowledge is the social rule systems for constituting and regulating social action and interaction. This proposition applies generally to human interaction whether the activities concern politics, economic production and exchange, science, art, sports or loving and caring. Particular rule systems apply to specific social contexts. The logic or rationality of social action and interaction in a given setting is generated by the system of social rules applying to actors in the setting. The complex of social rule systems found in any group, community, organization, or nation contribute to making up the culture of that collectivity. On the basis of common knowledge of social rule systems, a group of actors is predisposed to define a particular interaction situation in a given way — that is, within a specific category system. Moreover, they have a common basis to organize, coordinate, regulate and talk about (give accounts of, justify, and criticize) their interactions. Evaluative rules applying to the situation indicate what "goods" should be pursued and what "bads" are to be avoided. Normative rules, including decision procedures, provided a basis for structuring and regulating specific actions and interactions in the situation. A cultural frame, including social relationships defined and conceptualized within a cultural frame, provide common "filters" and "operators" for actors' representation, discrimination, evaluation, choice, social action and interaction. The frame ensures a certain degree of intersubjectivity among actors sharing the frame. Typically, the frame tends to vary among actors, in part because they differ somewhat in conceptualizing, interpreting and applying the frame, due to variation in socialization, personal history and social embeddedness. Indeed, individuals or groups may systematically deviate from the culturally standard frame. In this sense, culture should be viewed as a distributional concept, that is distributed over populations (Hannerz 1992).

30. The SGT approach emphasizes that even in the case that actors have a common cultural frame, with a defined social relationship between them, they often participate in a interaction situation with its own particular or unique features at the same time that the actors have varying conceptions of cultural concepts, social relationships, roles and rules. Thus, judgments can vary in ways that make a significant difference in actors' decisions and interactions and, in particular, their capacity to find compatible solutions and c-equilibria. In general, the actors' mutual awareness, knowledge of the setting, and perceived influence over outcomes in the setting often differ. Variation, inequality and asymmetry are the most common characteristics of human interaction situations, their opposites (the latter an all-too-prevalent premise of RCT).

31. Thus, one may pursue profit as an entrepreneur on a market within the constraints of prevailing laws and norms. Market action is then a rational expression within the constraints of social rules and physical and social ecological settings (cf. Hollis 1987:186). On the other hand, social roles and prevailing social norms in another context such as family, friendship or religious settings may call for norm-following or procedurally oriented behavior, giving little or no systematic consideration to outcomes, economic or otherwise. In general, rationality in different institutionalized settings or domains where particular social rule systems define the situation, actors relationships, roles and judgment systems.

32. Social actors may be individuals or collective agents, in the latter case organized groups, enterprises, government agencies parliamentary bodies, political parties, and nation-states. These engage in information-gathering, evaluation, collective decision making and action, and they mobilize and allocate resources. Collective agents have, of course, internal social structures organizing the formulation and enforcement of rules, the making of collective decisions and the execution of purposeful collective action. Such internal structures are constituted by social rule systems (Burns and Flam 1987).

33. The problem of collective action refers to the failure of memberships of large interest groups — consumers, taxpayers, white-collar workers — to act together to provide themselves with mutually desirable collective goods (Olson 1968:2). These games are characterized by interaction conditions where a certain level of cooperation and self-sacrifice lead to substantial gains but where there are incentives for individual actors to pursue self-interest and defect or "free-ride" rather than cooperate and make some contribution or sacrifice. The rationality of the immediate pursuit of individual self-interest results in suboptimal outcomes and lost opportunities for all.

34. In fact, the PD game played by rational egoists lacks a proper equilibrium. This is in contrast to the results of classical game theory, which indicates the noncooperative outcome as a (nonoptimal) equilibrium. Within the SGT perspective, the stress is on the availability of an outcome that realizes the actors' value orientations and goals in the interaction situation. Rational egoists would find the nonoptimal outcome as a frustration of their values, and would act to assure the optimal outcome. Note that there is nothing *inherent* in the relationship between rational egoists proscribing or inhibiting them from effectively exploiting such opportunities to communicate and reach agreements in the pursuit of mutual gain, provided, of course, that institutional rules allow them. Genuine rivals or enemies, on the other hand, have difficulties inherent in the relationship in using opportunities for communication, making and adhering to agreements, and pursuing opportunities for mutual gain.

35. If the rivals have identical perceptions of the outcomes of the situation ("objectively" defined outcomes, such as those defined for instance by a judge or other external party), then an equilibrium outcome satisfying their contradictory goals will be an impossibility and there will be no equilibrium. They may, of course, have the goal of participating in competition with relative gain outcomes as secondary — that is, an orientation to the competitive activity more than to the outcomes.

36. SGT implies that category and descriptive rules vary as a function of the type of relationship actors have. That is, competitors are likely to organize their perceptions and to describe interaction situations differently than enemies, friends, or rational egoists.

37. The exact nature of the distributive principle characteristic of a domination relationship will depend on the affective quality of the relationship. Relationships characterized by intimacy and mutual loyalty would entail values and distributive principles — and corresponding expectations — to the effect that the interests and needs of subordinates be taken into account (a type of paternalism or patron-client relation). Payoffs or outcomes would still be asymmetric, at the same time that the outcomes for subordinate or lower status would expect to satisfy certain norms of justice or decency. Domination relationships may take an entirely different form, where, for instance, A is indifferent to or dislikes subordinates. If it is within his power, A would assess and choose outcomes advantageous for himself with little or no consideration of the outcomes for the Bs.

38. SGT predicts, other things being equal, a strong correspondence between social relationships and types of decision procedures, evaluative rules, and norms which the participating actors utilize (and, consequently, the actions and interactions they generate). In other words, actors would react to or play, according to SGT, particular games (such as zero-sum and PD situations) differently as a function of their institutionalized relationships and the roles and normative structures in them.

39. "Chicken" and "racing games" belong to a class of games characterized by potential confrontation. Interaction entails high-risk stakes in the case participants pursue competitive or confrontational strategies to gain scarce resources ahead of the other. The game matrix might appear as depicted on the next page.

    The resource might be winning a Formula 1 race, gaining the last space in a parking lot, or achieving dominance over a territory or region (e.g., USA and USSR confrontation in the Cuban missile crisis). In cases where participating actors push their claims to the limit, for example, in an international confrontation the outcome can be very costly to both winner and loser, all-out war. In the case of nuclear confrontation, all-out war may mean mutual extinction.

	Actor B	
	Not confront	Confront
Actor A — Not confront	(0,0)	(10,−10)
Actor A — Confront	(−10,10)	(−5,5)

Obviously, friends — in the purest case — would choose not to confront one another, and the (0,0) outcome would be a social equilibrium for them in a wide range of circumstances. Serious rivals, on the other hand, would be predisposed to confrontation, but would not find this or other interaction patterns as acceptable in such games. Enemies in the purest case would find confrontation a socially natural state or c-equilibrium. (Of course, the costs might be more than they are willing to tolerate, and they would avoid playing games where their enmity runs the risk of self-destruction. Status differentiated actors would find the asymmetric interactions and outcomes as right and proper (at least within some range of conditions).

40. Games of pure or total conflict are those in which what one actor gains, the other loses. In a certain sense, this type of game is a distributional game rather than one of mutual destruction that characterizes the confrontation game. Parlor games have by design the character of "zero-sum" games. In practice, most conflicts have some areas of convergent interests.

41. In assurance or collaborative type games, all participants have the opportunity to make real gains — in money, property, material or human resources. Cooperative activity or collaboration offers the greatest gains in real terms. There are no options such as defection or cheating as in the PD game, offering opportunities for a participant to gain by defecting or cheating behavior. The game matrix can be illustrated as appears on the next page.

Of course, the outcomes would be judged by the actors on the basis of the evaluative rules inherent to the actors' relationships. Rivals would tend to reject the symmetric outcomes, even that providing maximal gain of resources for self; they would instead aim for asymmetric outcomes, which, however, would not provide a stable pattern. Contrast this to rational egoists who would have no difficulty in collaborating in assurance type games. But then they are not *relational competitors* but *situational competitors*, as in the PD game (see note 34).

Persons in a status relationship would find the appropriate asymmetric outcome as right and proper. Enemies would go for interactions

		Actor B	
		Collaborate	Not collaborate
Actor A	Collaborate	10,10	6,3
	Not collaborate	3,6	5,5

and outcomes entailing loss to one another, e.g., the (5,5) outcome (clearly, a loss relative to the potential gain of (10,10) but the latter would call for cooperation which would be incompatible with their relationship and mutual orientations. Even the outcome (5,5) might be problematic for them in that both would prefer seeing the other experience real losses, and, therefore, they might seek to transform the game into a consistently destructive game.

42. Some game setups or interaction situations are much more discriminating than others in eliciting differentiated equilibria for different social relationships. Symmetric assurance games offer possibilities of stable interactions to all relationships examined here except for competitors, since no outcome offers solutions satisfying both their goals at the same time. Of course, competitors having value orientations which make a "tie" acceptable would be satisfied in even assurance type games.

43. This prediction not only differs from that of game theory, but points up the way in which game theory conflates a relationship of rational egoists with one of genuine competitors or rivals. Rational egoists are not true competitors or rivals, only potential or, more precisely, situational competitors. In interaction situations where cooperation provides the best individual outcomes, rational egoists would be predisposed to cooperate in the interest of individual gain. Rivals or genuine competitors would not be disposed to cooperate even in situations offering substantial incentives to cooperate. In the rational choice approach, no theoretical language is provided for conceptualizing or specifying the range of social relationships and structures in which human actors may be embedded and that have a bearing on their orientations and motivations as well as their specific judgment principles and rules of conduct *vis-à-vis* one another.

44. A "mediator" may help actors find a social equilibrium or collective solution within their given relationship and the interaction conditions. This is done by searching for and identifying configurations that realize the actors' respective goals or values inherent in the relationship.

45. Social structure — in the form, for instance, of rules and principles such as those relating to authority or property rights and distributive justice — do not fully determine action opportunity structures and the possible outcomes of societal games. Natural or ecological conditions also play an important role in constraining action possibilities, shaping incentive structures and affecting interaction outcomes.

46. Harsanyi pursues an entirely different strategy in seeking a solution to the problems of classical game theory, in particular, its early failures to generate predictions for many types of game. Instead of a social contextualization such as that of SGT, he chooses to try to find a solution in a better "rational behavior concept," ostensibly by adding additional and more powerful rationality postulates to game theory (1977:4). He states, "Analytically, the main function of these postulates will be to determine other kinds of expectation than a rational actor can consistently entertain about other rational players' behavior. I shall try to show that once we accept these larger and strong set of rationality postulates, we obtain a theory yielding determinate solutions for all classes of classical games described in the game-theoretic literature: for two-person and for n-person games, for zero-sum and non-zero-sum games, for games with and without transferable utility, for cooperative and noncooperative games, and the like."

Bibliography

Andersen, S., and T. R. Burns (1992). *Societal Decision-Making: Democratic Challenges to State Technocracy*. Hampshire, England: Dartmouth.

Berger, P., and T. Luckmann (1967). *The Social Construction of Reality*. Harmondsworth: Penguin.

Blau, P. (1964). *Exchange and Power in Social Life*. New York: Wiley.

Breman, G., and J. Buchanan (1985). *The Reason of Rules: Constitutional Political Economy*. Cambridge: Cambridge University Press.

Buchanan, J., and G. Tullock (1962). *The Calculus of Consent: Logical Foundations of Constitutional Democracy*. Ann Arbor: University of Michigan Press.

Burns, T. (1990). "Models of Social And Market Exchange: Toward a Sociological Theory of Games and Social Behavior." In: *Structures of Power and Constraints*, Papers in Honor of Peter M. Blau, eds. C. Calhoun, M. W. Meyer, and W. Richard Scott. Cambridge: Cambridge University Press.

Burns, T., T. Baumgartner, and P. DeVille (1985). *Man, Decision, Society*. London: Gordon and Breach.

Burns, T., P. DeVille, E. Griffor, and D. Meeker (1992). "The Social Theory of Human Interaction and Games" (manuscript).

Burns, T., and T. Dietz (1992). "Cultural Evolution: Social Rule Systems, Selection, and Human Agency." *International Sociology* 7(3): 250–283.

Burns, T., and H. Flam (1987). *The Shaping of Social Organization Social Rule System Theory with Applications*. London: Sage Publications.

Burns, T., and E. Griffor (1991). "The Social Theory of Human Interaction and Games: An Extension of Classical Game Theory." Paper presented at the International Congress on Logic, Methodology, and History of Science, Uppsala, August.

_____ (1992). "Problems of Social Equilibrium and the General Nash Theorem in an Extended Theory of Games." Paper presented at the World Congress of the International Economic Association, Moscow, August.

Burns, T., E. Griffor, and D. Meeker (1993). *The Social Foundations of Human Rationality, Choice, and Interaction: The von Neumann-Morgenstern Theory of Games Extended*. Uppsala: Institute of Sociology.

Burns, T., and M. Hansson (1992). "Ethical Analysis: Philosophical and Sociological Considerations" (manuscript).

Cohen, N., J. March, and J. P. Olsen (1972). "A Garbage Can Model of Organizational Choice." *Administrative Science Quarterly* 17:1–25.

Coleman, J. S. (1992). *Foundations of Social Theory*. Cambridge: Harvard University Press.

Collins, R. (1988). *Theoretical Sociology*. San Diego: Harcourt Brace Jovanovich.

Czarniavska-Joerges, B. (1988). *Ideological Control in Non-Ideological Organizations*. New York: Praeger.

Elster, J. (1977). *Logic and Society*. New York: Wiley.

_____ (1989). *The Cement of Society*. Cambridge: University of Cambridge Press.

Etzioni, A. (1988). *The Moral Dimension: Toward a New Economics*. New York: Free Press.

Field, A. J. (1979). "On the Explanation of Rules Using Rational Choice Models." *Journal of Economic Issues* 13:49–72

_____ (1984). "Microeconomics, Norms, and Rationality." *Economic Development and Cultural Change* 32:684–711.

Giddens, A. (1984). *The Constitution of Society*. Oxford: Polity Press.

Granovetter, M. (1985). "Economic Action and Social Structure." *American Journal of Sociology* 50:384–510.

Hamburger, H. (1979). *Games as Models of Social Phenomenon*. San Francisco: Freeman.

Hannerz, U. (1992). *Cultural Complexity: Studies in the Social Organization of Meaning*. New York: Columbia University Press.

Hardin, R. (1982). *Collective Action*. Baltimore: John Hopkins University Press.

Harré, R. (1979). *Social Being*. Oxford: Basil Blackwell.

Harsanyi, J. C. (1977). *Rational Behavior and Bargaining Equilibrium in Games and Social Situations*. Cambridge: Cambridge University Press.

Hodgson, G. M. (1986). "Behind Methodological Individualism." *Cambridge Journal of Economics* 10:211–224.

_____ 1989 "Institutional Economic Theory: The Old versus the New." *Review of Political Economy* 1:249–269.

Hogarth, R. and M. Reder (1987). *Rational Choice: The Contrast between Economics and Psychology*. Chicago: University of Chicago Press.

Hollis, M. (1987). *The Cunning of Reason*. Cambridge: Cambridge University Press.

Jackson, P. C. (1974). *Introduction to Artificial Intelligence*. New York: Petrocelli and Charles.

Kahneman, D., P. Slovic, and A. Tversky (Eds.) (1982). *Judgements Under Uncertainty: Heuristics and Biases*. Cambridge: Cambridge University Press.

Karpik, L. (1981). "Organizations, Institutions, and History." In: *Complex Organizations: Critical Perspectives*, eds. M. Zey-Ferrell and M. Aiken. Glenview, IL: Scott, Foresman and Company.

Luce, R. D., and H. Raiffa (1957). *Games and Decisions*. New York: Wiley.

Machado, N., and T. Burns (1992). *The Body in the Law: Some Legal Dimensions of the Medical Handling of Bodies and Body Parts*. Uppsala: Institute of Sociology.

March, J., and J. P. Olsen (1976). *Ambiguity and Choice in Organizations*. Oslo: Universitetsforlag.

March, J., and H. A. Simon (1958). *Organizations*. New York: Wiley.

Martin-Lof, P. (1984). *Intuitionistic Type Theory*. Naples: Bibliopolis.

Mirowski, P. (1981). "Is There a Mathematical Neoinstitutional Economics?" *Journal of Economic Issues* 15:593–613

―――――― (1986). *The Reconstruction of Economic Theory*. Boston/Dordrecht: Kluwer-Nijhoff.

Nash, J. (1950). "Equilibrium Points in *n*-Person Games." *Proceedings of the National Academy of Sciences of the USA* 36:48–49.

―――――― (1951). "Non-Cooperative Games." *Annals of Mathematics* 54:286–295.

North, D. (1982). "A Theory of Economic Exchange: Review of Mancur Olson, *The Rise and Decline of Nations*." *Science* 219:163–164.

Olson, M. (1968). *The Logic of Collective Action*. New York: Schocken Books.

Schelling, T. (1963) *The Strategy of Conflict*. Cambridge: Harvard University Press.

Schutz, A. (1962). *The Problem of Social Reality*. The Hague: Martinus Nijhoff.

Schotter, A. (1981). *The Economic Theory of Social Institutions*. Cambridge: Cambridge University Press.

Sen, A. K. 1982 *Choice, Welfare, and Measurement*. Oxford: Basil Blackwell.

―――――― (1987). "Rational Behavior." In: *The New Palgrave: A Dictionary of Economics*, pp. 68–76. London: MacMillan.

Shubik, M. (1982). *Game Theory in the Social Sciences*. Cambridge: MIT Press.

Simon, H. A. (1957). *Models of Man*. New York: Wiley.

―――――― (1977). *Models of Discovery and Other Topics in the Methods of Science*. Dordrecht: Reidel.

―――――― (1987). In: *Rational Choice: The Contrast between Economics and Psychology*, eds. R. M. Hogarth and M. W. Reder. Chicago: University of Chicago Press.

Sugden, R. (1986). *The Economics of Rights, Cooperation, and Welfare*. Oxford: Basil Blackwell.

Sztompka, P. (1991). *Society in Action: The Theory of Social Becoming*. Chicago: University of Chicago Press.

Troelstra, A. S., and D. van Dalen (1988). *Constructivism in Mathematics*, Vol. 1. Amsterdam: Elsevier Science Publishers.

van Parys, P. (1981). *Evolutionary Explanation in the Social Sciences*. Totowa, NJ: Rowman and Littlefield.

von Neumann, J., and O. Morgenstern (1953). *Theory of Games and Economic Behavior*. Princeton: Princeton University Press.

Weber, M. (1968). *Economy and Society*. New York: Bedminister Press.

Wittrock, B. (1986). "Social Knowledge and Public Policy: Eight Models of Interaction." In: *Social Science and Governmental Institutions*, eds. C. Weiss and H. Wollman. London: Sage.

Zagare, F. (1984). *Game Theory: Concepts and Applications*. Beverly Hills: Sage.

Chapter NINE

Society as Social Becoming: Beyond Individualism and Collectivism

Piotr Sztompka

The developments in sociological theory for the last two decades, which are aptly labelled as "the return of grand theories" (Skinner 1985) or "the new theoretical movement" (Alexander 1988) — provide the intellectual resources for tackling the perennial problem of *social being* in a new way. Two theoretical trends in particular seem to be most significant in this respect: the theories of agency and so-called "historical sociology." Both seem to converge toward a synthetic theoretical standpoint which I elaborate elsewhere as the "theory of social becoming" (Sztompka 1991). And they seem to presuppose the synthetic ontological position which overcomes the old dilemma of agency and structure, individualism and holism. In this paper I turn toward that presuppositional core of the theory of social becoming (TSB), trying to explicate the ontological image assumed there.

FROM POLARITIES TO LINKAGE: THE LEVEL OF COMMON SENSE

It is well known that sociology is strongly influenced by common sense. This invasion of popular beliefs does not omit the philosophical foundations of sociology. Among them, the ontological premises seem particularly vulnerable. There is a sort of natural, spontaneous, ontological bias of popular awareness. People tend to think in terms of substances, to formulate convictions about objects, whereas epistemological or methodological questions are rarely entertained by common sense, some rudimentary ontological claims about what exists and how are universally present.

We shall start our analysis from the reconstruction of commonsense assumptions about social being. The first is the natural, spontaneous inclination toward *ontological realism*: the belief that social objects are real and not imagined, that they reside in the world and not exclusively in thought, that there exists something "out there," even though its image is always molded by perception and reflection. This assumption is recently returning to the foundational base of sociological theories. After various excursions toward solipsism, or — as Robert Merton calls it — "sociological Berkeleyanism" (Merton 1976:175), sociology seems to turn back in the direction of "scientific realism": "the theory that the objects of scientific enquiry exist and act, for the most part, quite independently of scientists and their activity" (Bhaskar 1986:5). Which of course does not preclude the recognition and study of the peculiar reflexivity of social thought: the feedback it has on its subject matter. But the whole idea of a feedback presupposes that the subject matter is there, preconstituted before the act of cognition. Revindication of the reality of society is an example of salutary restrictions of common sense against the excesses of subjectivism. But in more specific ontological issues common sense may be highly misleading, paralyze reflection and petrify biases. We shall have to scrutinize those seemingly self-evident premises carefully and critically. And in due time, go beyond them.

The most dangerous tendency of common sense is the dichotomization of reality; splitting it into neat, separate parts, forms, modes — or even into isolated worlds. There are three pervasive dichotomies of this sort: *individual-society*, *statics-dynamics* and *potentiality-actuality*.

The first dichotomy is most common, and articulated most clearly. It refers to kinds of objects delimited in the field of experience. It conveys the opposition of persons and groups (or other societal wholes). The mutual difference is perceived in all four aspects in which such objects may manifest their being: separatedness, causality, power and process.

Thus, a person has a feeling of individual identity, *separate* from the identity of groups, organizations or institutions. Myself — as opposed to my family, my tribe, my town, my nation, my party, my church. They seem to be external entities, even though I belong to all of them. This feeling is enhanced by the fact that I may migrate from one group to the other, enter or leave them, or even belong to many overlapping groups at the same time, and still remain myself.[1]

People set themselves goals and aims, strive to attain them, and from time to time do achieve what they wanted. They exert *causal influence* on reality, producing tangible effects. The same may be said of groups which have targets and sometimes succeed in reaching them. But both kinds of causal effectiveness are perceived as distinct. My personal goals and efforts seem a different thing from the goals and efforts of my community, ethnic group, nation, profession, government, social movement. My personal strength, effectiveness, is something different from theirs.

Of course the groups to which I belong, even though separate, are not isolated from myself. I have some *power* over them; I may influence their operation or their goals, for example by casting a ballot or becoming a leader. But most often I feel their oppressive grip over myself; they constrain what I do and even what I think and want. The point is that both kinds of power are again seen as separate; my own power *vis-à-vis* the group is different from the group power *vis-à-vis* myself. This feeling is enhanced by the fact that both powers often clash, and usually my chances are worse.

People have biographies, careers — continuous, cumulative stories of actions, efforts and achievements. Similarly, groups (families, nations, states) have histories. But both are perceived as separate *processes*. My personal fate goes its way, and the fate of my community, country, neighborhood — their own ways. I think of them as independent, partly parallel, partly divergent. This feeling is enhanced by the fact that some people live happy and successful lives in periods of social crisis and decay, while others experience personal catastrophes amid social expansion and prosperity.

Thus in all four aspects in which real objects can be grasped — separatedness, causality, power and process — people tend to oppose what is individual, private and personal to what is social, public and collective; they see themselves and societal wholes as separate entities; they construe individuality and totality as distinct worlds.

The second dichotomy, not so clear-cut as the earlier one, refers to the ways in which various objects — individual and social — manifest their being. This may be described as the opposition of statics versus dynamics, dating at least to A. Comte. In human life, as well as in the life of a society, there is obviously some stability, continuity, persistence and order, but also there is fluidity, transformation and change. Common sense tends to perceive them as separate states, distinct phases, different periods of existence. There seem to be usual times of routine, repetition, orderliness, calm and tranquility; and unusual times of disruption, chaos, novelty and change.

Finally, the third dichotomy, perhaps least intuitive, refers to the mode of existence taken by various objects — individuals as well as social wholes. It opposes potentiality and actuality. If we think of ourselves or other people it is common to distinguish capacities, talents and abilities from accomplishments and realizations. We perceive a constant gap between what we could possibly have, and what we have in fact — our inherent endowment and the results of its implementation, aspirations and achievements, our reach and our grasp. The same applies to our perception of groups: nations and states, sport teams and social movements, corporations and cities. The point is that we tend to perceive the potentials and realizations separately. This feeling is enhanced by the fact that some people or groups seemingly devoid of inherent capacities happen to reach a lot, and others, richly endowed with potential, end in failure and misery.

But even though common sense pushes toward sharpening of those three oppositions, already at this rudimentary level of awareness there appear some corrective emphases, hints at the mutual links between separated objects, forms or modes of existence, dim recognition of their *relatedness*, and acknowledgement that they are separate but not entirely so. This is expressed by characteristic phrases: "yes, but," "on the other hand," "from the other side," etc. And it is very symptomatic indeed.

Thus, when still accepting the dichotomy of individual and society, it is recognized that part of individual identity is derived from the membership in groups, and part of group identity is an aggregated effect of the quality of members. Yes, I am a unique self, but part of that uniqueness resolves in my being a Pole, a Cracovian, a professor. Yes, Poland is a distinct country, but part of that specificity derives from the traits and qualities of Poles. The existence of an individual and the group seem to merge.

The same is true of the aspect of causality. Sticking with the distinction of individual efficacy and group efficacy, it is felt that part of what an individual accomplishes derives from the resources, facilities and opportunities provided by the group, and the secret of group's success in attaining its targets lies, at least in part, in members' efforts. Yes, I am an autonomous causal agent, but part of that agential strength is due to the support of groups to which I belong. Yes, this social movement has won miraculous victories and changed society, but it did it because its followers manifested courage, determination and persistence. Again, the causal effectiveness of individuals and groups seem to merge.

Perhaps the strongest experience of two-sidedness, or fusion of individual and social factors, has to do with the aspect of power. It is a common human predicament to feel free and constrained, autonomous and dependent, to be a master and a slave, producer and product, creator and creature at the same time. Yes, I have choice, I take decisions, I depend on myself and yet I feel the constant, oppressive presence of society;[2] I repeatedly collide with the wall of norms, values, expectations, requirements, sanctions for noncompliance. But on the other hand I realize that those societal contexts which surround and bind me, are not God-given but produced by people. True, they control us, but as all human products they can be changed, so I should have at least some say in shaping or controlling them.

This ambivalence is emphasized by several sociologists. Let me just quote some characteristic formulations. The "facticity" of the outside world, "the way in which society is experienced by individuals as a fact-like system, external, given, coercive" clashes with individual capacity of "making and remaking it through their own imagination, communication and action" (Abrams 1982:2). This is a "two-sided world": "a world of which we are both the creators and the creatures, both makers and prisoners; a world which our actions construct and a world that powerfully constrains us" (p. 2). This leads to ambivalent and constantly alternating self-definitions as "puppet-masters" or "marionettes": "It is part and parcel of daily experience to feel both free and enchained, capable of shaping our own future and yet confronted by towering, seemingly impersonal, constraints" (Archer 1988:x).

Finally, keeping to the distinction of biography and history, people become aware of their interplay. Biographies are found to depend not only on personal effort but historical conditions, and history is perceived as some complex effect of individual biographies. True, I am the architect of my own career, the author of my personal fate, yet there are limits to what I can do under given historical circumstances. Sometimes it is easier, sometimes more difficult to get what I want, and it clearly depends on the vicissitudes of historical process. There are good times and bad times, easy times and hard times. On the other hand, history is not running independently of what people do with their lives. Its course is somehow related to individual successes or failures. Thus my biography cross-cuts with history.

In this way the strict dichotomy of individual and society is bridled already by common sense, which perceives not only their *separation*, but various *linkages*.

Similar correctives appear with respect to two other dichotomies. Thus people become aware of the mutual dependence of static and dynamic aspects of social life. They experience the tension between the force of tradition, inertia, routine, tendency to keep things unchanged and the opposite craving for novelty, innovation, difference, change. They feel torn between the encountered, inherited conditions and the projected, or imagined improvements. They stand on the stairs between the past and the future, realizing suddenly that there are no stairs but a moving escalator.

Finally the rigid opposition of potentiality and actuality is alleviated by the universal experiences of dissatisfaction, unfulfillment, discontent, frustration, a sort of permanent gap between aspirations and realizations, ideals and realities — and incessant human efforts to close that gap. People recognize that wherever they seem to achieve something, to grab the vanishing point of their goals, the distance between what now seems possible and what is already achieved renews itself, only at the higher level of fulfillment. Their raised potentialities, are again behind actualizations. Thus they perceive that there is some constant, mutual interplay between the potential and actual modes of their life, their capacities and possibilities and their attainments.

Let us take stock. In this part of the article I have attempted to reconstruct the ontological intuitions underlying the common-sense thinking about society. It was shown that in spite of the typical, natural predilection for producing clear-cut oppositions and dichotomies, this thought-pattern clashes with the more or less common experience of ambivalence, mutual linkages, interpenetration or outright fusion of initially separated objects, aspects or modalities of social life. If my reading of popular consciousness is correct, this fact is highly symptomatic, and must be taken as a crucial heuristic hint for developing the discursive, critical ontology of society. And for constructing the theory of society, which after all is only the more sophisticated common sense.

META-THEORETICAL AND THEORETICAL DILEMMAS

Let us change the key of our analysis now, and move from the level of common sense to the level of meta-theoretical discourse, where some presuppositions about the nature of society have also been articulated since the birth of sociology. We shall discover the gradual elaboration of ontological standpoints strikingly parallel to the intuitions of common sense: the same movement away from the polarized opposition of rigid, simplified, one-sided claims toward the recognition of mutual linkages, interpenetrations and syntheses.

The story starts with the birth of sociology, when the founding fathers took up the attempt to define the subject matter of a new discipline. There were two obvious candidates for the ultimate constituents of society: collectivities (groups, communities, societies, etc.) or persons (individual human beings). Some, like H. Spencer focused on social wholes:

> We consistently regard a society as an entity, because, though formed of discrete units, a certain concreteness in the aggregate of them is implied by the general persistence of the arrangements among them throughout the area occupied. And it is this trait which yields our idea of a society. (Spencer 1893:I/436)

Others, like J. S. Mill, focused on individuals:

> Men in a state of society are still men. Their actions and passions are obedient to the laws of individual human nature. Men are not, when brought together, converted into another kind of substance with different properties, as hydrogen and oxygen are different from water. (Mill 1884:573)

This controversy, with its underlying dichotomy of individuals and social wholes, set the agenda for theoretical disputes till our time. S. Nadel identifies "the focus of sociology and its perpetual problem" as "the relation of the social order and individual being, the relation of the unit and the whole" (Nadel 1957:401). D. Martindale claims that "there are no more basic problems to men attempting to account for themselves and for their social world than the comparative significance to be assigned to the individual and to the collective" (Martindale 1964:461). A. Dawe testifies: "Sociology has been perennially concerned with the problem of the relationship between the individual and society; the problem being that of reconciling their competing claims" (Dawe 1978:363).

At the meta-theoretical level the dispute has been running under various names: individualism versus collectivism (Martindale 1964), atomism versus holism (Sorokin 1966), compositive versus holistic position (Ginsberg 1968), individualism versus holism (Gellner 1969). And more often than not it revolved around epistemological or methodological questions, defining proper modes of sociological cognition, or the valid forms of sociological explanation.[3] But of course it has also an ontological core, involving primary presuppositions about the nature of society. In this paper I am dealing exclusively with this aspect of the debate. D. Martindale is right:

> No orientations to the problems of existence are more fundamental than those which take the individual as primary (individualism) and those which take the collective as primary (collectivism). (Martindale 1964:453)

Inevitably, in this ontological mode the controversy had to touch all four dimensions of being: separatedness, causality, power and process. First, it addressed the issue: what is the ontological status of objects constitutive of society? When social wholes (groups, collectivities, communities) were considered, the answers took the form of *metaphysical holism* (sociological realism), treating them as reality *sui generis*, or *metaphysical individualism* (sociological nominalism), treating them as mere congeries of individuals (or even sheer illusions arising in human imagination). P. Sorokin summarizes the earlier claim: "The organized social groups (social systems) or cultural systems have a reality *sui generis*, and in their structure, properties and behavior display most significant differences from those of a mere sum of their unassembled and unintegrated components" (Sorokin 1966:133). S. Lukes gives the apt formulation of the latter claim: "In the social world only individuals are real. Social phenomena are constructions of the mind and do not exist in reality" (Lukes 1968:122).

When the issue was approached from the other side, and the nature of human individuals was considered, the correlative answers took the form of so-called *sociologism* emphasizing the socially molded nature of a *homo sociologicus* (via mechanisms of internalization, socialization and social control producing individual replicas, embodiments, microcosms of society); or *autonomism*, emphasizing independence, indeterminacy, self-control of *homo creator*. Notice, that all standpoints share one common presupposition. They clearly recognize two kinds of objects as different and separate: persons and groups. This reminds us of that first natural dichotomy, so typical of common sense.

Another phrasing of the dichotomy addresses the issue of how causality operates, or more precisely what are the ultimate causal agents in society. According to J. Agassi: "The major question to which holism gives rise concerns the relation between the distinct interests of the group and those of the individuals belonging to it" (Agassi 1973:190). Thus, for individualists, only persons have aims and goals, can strive to reach them, act purposefully and produce effects. As J. O. Wisdom puts it: "Institutions do not have aims — only individuals have aims, interests, needs, intentions, or make decisions" (Wisdom 1970:272). For holists, groups or institutions have aims and goals of their own, are able to act and influence the world. Again, the intimation of separatedness of two kinds of objects is clearly there.

Sometimes the problem is reduced to the question of relative power of individuals and groups *vis-à-vis* each other. The proponents of *social determinism* locate the power in groups, which are seen as constraining or facilitating, blocking or molding everything that human beings do and think. As J. O. Wisdom puts it: "In the extreme form of what, following Gellner, we may best call holism, societal power overrides individuals who have no share of it" (Wisdom 1970:272). The proponents of opposite standpoint which may be called *voluntaristic constructivism* emphasize the exclusive power of individuals to mold social wholes and control their operation. J. W. N. Watkins gives straightforward statement of this standpoint: "No social tendency is somehow imposed on human beings from above (or from below) — social tendencies are the product (usually undesigned) of human characteristics and activities and situations, of people's ignorance and laziness as well as of their knowledge and ambition" (Watkins 1957:271–272). The either/or logic of the controversy is clearly noticeable.

Finally, the issue relates to the level where the causal process (a temporal sequence of interrelated events) is seen to be running. For some authors, representing what may be called *actionism* (or behaviorism, or interactionism — depending on their more specific theoretical options), the process unfolds exclusively at the individual level embracing the conduct of people. For others, who are sometimes called *developmentalists* (or historicists) there is an independent, specific logic of a process at the macro-level of social wholes. L. Addis provides a technical formulation of this position: "The sociological variables form a closed system, i.e., there is a process among the sociological variables alone ... and psychological variables, e.g., individual choices and items of behavior are irrelevant to the social process. The social process is causally independent of human direction" (Addis 1969:322). The implication that there are two separate or parallel domains where social processes operate is easily drawn.

Descending one step, from the level of meta-theoretical assumptions to the level of sociological theory, the opposition of the individual and society is found to generate two distinct traditions of theorizing. A. Dawe refers to them as two sociologies and describes as

> a basic dualism of sociological thought and analysis on which the entire history of the discipline has turned. Throughout that history, there has been a manifest conflict between two types of social analysis, variously labeled as being between the organismic and mechanistic approaches, methodological collectivism and individualism, holism and atomism, the conservative and emancipatory perspectives and so on... Modern sociology centers on the opposition between a sociology of social system [or as more recent discussions would put it, of social structure, P.S.] and a sociology of social action. (Dawe 1978:366)

Another opposition, between static and dynamic aspect of social life, is of equally long ancestry and equal contemporary relevance. Again, it was born in the works of the founding fathers. A. Comte may be credited with introducing the dichotomy of social statics and social dynamics, and H. Spencer with the distinction of structures and functions. The timeless image of social anatomy, the stable arrangement of components of society, was opposed to the more fluid, moving and time-infused image of social physiology and evolution. Stability was opposed to functioning and historical transformations of societies. At the meta-theoretical level, the *synchronic view* of society began to be treated separately from the *diachronic view*; the substantive focus on social entities, their continuity and persistence was seen as different from the focus on social processes and their incessant modifications and transformations. In sociological theories it has bred a corresponding split into another pair of two sociologies: the sociology of social order was put against the sociology of social change, the so-called "Hobbesian problem" (how stability is possible) against the "Marxian problem" (how changes occur). A theory of change was supposed to look rather different from a theory of systems. Sociological practice, both in research and education reflects this belief quite clearly.[4]

The third dichotomy, of potentiality and actuality, is most visible in those sociological theories which formulate (or implicitly assume) the image of society in some natural state, or the vision of true human nature, and oppose both to the conditions actually obtaining, limiting or destroying human potential. "Views of human nature are essentially views of human capacity and potential" (Dawe 1978:369). As such they may serve as criteria of appraisal of existing social arrangements. Sometimes the comparison works backwards: the society and human beings are seen as departing from some early, original state of harmony, well-being and happiness. Sometimes the comparison works forwards: the prospects of some future return to natural conditions, when human capacities, abilities and drives will find their full, unbridled expression, are grasped by means of more or less utopian visions of possible, good society.

These are pervasive themes of the whole history of sociology, but particularly of those schools which self-consciously assumed critical and emancipatory mission. Already in the 19th century, their most extensive statement appeared in Marxian theory of alienation, with its underlying image of human "species nature," and the triple scheme of pre-alienated (pre-class) societies of the past, alienated, class societies of the present, and alienated (classless) societies of the future.[5] From different philosophical premises, the opposition of the natural will, producing human world of Gemeinschaft, and distorted rational will giving birth to inhuman Gesellschaft — is proposed by F. Tönnies (Tönnies 1955 [1887]). Somewhat similar tones appear in G. Simmel's distinction of autotelic sociability, as natural human drive, and instrumental, profit-oriented, egoistic attitude toward others, typical of modern, industrial societies (Simmel [1910] 1971:128). The same *leitmotifs* appear time and again, up to the present time in all critical accounts of bureaucracy, technology, ideology, totalitarianism and recently the syndrome of modernity as a whole. They are treated as pathological and antihuman developments, which must be replaced by alternative arrangements opening again the opportunities for human self-realization, harmony with nature, community with others, freedom and creativeness. In all such theories, the mismatch between the possible level of human potentials, and their limited actual realizations is strongly intimated.

BRIDGING OPPOSITIONS

So far we have traced the developments in social thought (at the meta-theoretical and theoretical level) which seem to mirror the typical orientation of common sense — to separate and oppose the individual and society, the static and dynamic aspects and potential and actual modes. But sooner or later, again following the pattern of common sense, sociological discourse gets uneasy with those dichotomies, and ambivalent about the one-sided, biased ontological and theoretical options they dictate. There is a noticeable drift away from extreme positions, which become liberalized by additional provisos, and in effect brought closer to their counterparts. Each of two sociologies becomes infused with some insights of the other, and loses its rigid, dogmatic quality.

This trend is most clearly visible if we look again at the first dichotomy, of the individual and society, its corresponding ontological expression in individualism versus holism, and its theoretical implementation in the sociology of action versus the sociology of systems (or structures). The canonical form of individualism, asserting that human individuals are the only real objects present in a society, gets into trouble when sociologists inevitably encounter some properties which cannot be predicated of single human beings. They become aware that there are some global traits, sometimes intangible and hard to define, sometimes metaphorical and anthropomorphic, but impossible to ignore. Such notions as popular enthusiasm, social effervescence, group morale, national character, anomie, social apathy, mobilization, progressivism, popular will, disorganization, social malaise, disaster-culture, traditionalism and many more seem to refer directly to social wholes. The defenders of individualism may still try to evade this implication by claiming that those traits describe only the aggregated effects of the co-presence of multiple individuals. Some seemingly global traits may be treated as characterizing the social bonds — the network of relations binding individuals together (e.g., if they are intimate, friendly or based on mutual loyalty, we speak of high morale). Some other seemingly global traits may be treated as a direct sum of purely individual skills, motivations and attitudes (e.g., if many people are highly educated, we may speak of the high educational level of the country).

But this strategy of defense fails against the phenomenon of emergence — when aggregates of people (groups, communities, societies) manifest some characteristics which can in no way be computed or predicted on the basis of the individual endowment of members, nor the geometry of their interpersonal links, and which run beyond or against the intentions of individual actors. There seem to be some properties clearly perceivable in a society which cannot be explained by aggregation, or by complication, nor by summing of individual intentions. Sociologists use various terms to refer to such properties; most often they speak of "unintended consequences," "unanticipated consequences," "latent effects" or "composite outcomes." Sometimes they also invoke A. Smith's idea of "unseen hand" which produces certain patterns on the macro-level, out of dispersed, egoistically motivated individual choices; or G. W. F. Hegel's concept of the "cunning of reason" — "a neat name for the various ways of summing consequences so as to create patterns and spring surprises" (Hollis 1987:58).

At the level of ontological assumptions, these observations are taken into account in some released, more open versions of individualism. Developing some hints of K. R. Popper, his student J. Agassi defends a position known as *institutional individualism*. It is marked by the allowance of some specifically social objects, namely institutions, to the ontological field of society. Institutions are understood normatively, as "conventional means of coordination between individual actions" (Agassi 1960:208). They attain some emergent, autonomous quality. As I. C. Jarvie puts it: "Institutions are, so to speak, a third force in the society and their existence and importance is the reason sociology is autonomous with respect to psychology" (Jarvie 1970:113). Thus the modified standpoint

> accords with the classical individualistic idea that social phenomena are but the interactions between individuals. Yet it does not accord with the classical individualistic-psychologistic idea that this interaction depends on individuals' aims and material circumstances alone; rather it adds to these factors of interaction the existing interpersonal means of co-ordination.(Agassi 1960:212)

This position implies "the denial of psychologism; the claim that the social sciences are autonomous and not reducible to psychology; that there exist distinct social yet not psychological entities (called institutions, customs, traditions, societies, etc.)" (Agassi 1975:145). The concession made toward a holistic pole is pretty obvious.

Another liberal variant of individualism goes under the name of *situational individualism*. It emphasizes the unavoidable presence of wider, institutional context in any individual action: "an individual is always an individual in a setting of institutions" (Wisdom

1970:277), "among the cardinal realities facing the individual ... are his social surroundings, especially institutions... These are as concrete and as real as his physical surroundings" (Jarvie 1972:xiii). Such context is responsible for the fact that actions produce unforeseen unintended consequences, which were not calculated by the actors. But actions produce also "existential emergents," i.e., phenomena which are of a "different order of eventuality" (p. 292), represent fundamental novelty, and their nature could not have been calculated at all prior to their appearance.

The third variant of individualism which J. O. Wisdom proposes under the label of *transindividualism* allows this kind of consequences, which are finally severed from acting individuals (even though unwittingly produced by them), acquire autonomy with respect of them, and can therefore be considered as specific, extra-individual social wholes. "A social whole — he says — may consist of individuals' purposes, their unintended consequences, and their 'emergent consequences'" (Wisdom 1970:293). Thus all three permissive versions of individualism, sticking to its basic tenets, allowed the social wholes (in the disguise of institutions) through the back door.

The same tendency to release initial rigid formulations may be encountered in those sociological theories which start from individualist premises. The good example is provided by the exchange theory, as it has evolved from the early statements of G. Homans, still clearly informed by psychological reductionism and behaviorism, and allowing no other ontological objects than persons and their conduct. For him "the ultimate units of social behavior are men and their actions" (Homans 1967:62; 1974:12). Everything else is resolvable into human actions and their more or less complex configurations: "Human institutions and human societies often appear so well established and so powerful that they dominate individual men and escape human control altogether... It is not true that these monsters consist of the actions of men and something more. They are the actions of men; they can be analyzed into individual actions with nothing left over" (Homans 1973:551). These are strong claims. But already in the much more liberal variant of P. Blau it is recognized that human actors carry exchanges in preexistent structural context, and the theory tries to account for the emergence, and autonomization of such structures *vis-à-vis* acting individuals. "The study of social life is concerned with the relations among people and thus always with emergent properties in the broadest sense of the term" (Blau 1964:3). Finally, in the modern network analysis, the focus moves to the level of social wholes, unravelling the regularities and patternings of structures per se (Emerson 1972).

Another illustration of such intellectual movement, working in the opposite direction, is to be found in those theories which incorporate the sociological model of personality. This is the case with symbolic interactionism, which locates the reflection of social context in the segment of the self, referred to as "me" and opposed to "I" (Mead 1964 [1934]), or known as "looking-glass self" (Cooley 1964 [1902]). It is also characteristic of the theories of action informed by psychoanalysis, which identify the superego (as opposed to id), as the segment of personality internalizing social expectations (norms, values, institutions) (Parsons 1964). In both examples the reflection of social wholes is located in the minds of acting individuals. Thus concession toward holism is made either by extending the individual action toward its external context, or by including the context in the internal constitution of actors.

The liberalizing trend occurs also in those ontological standpoints and sociological theories which start from holistic premises. Metaphorically speaking, whereas the individualist theories were slowly moving up, toward the recognition of emergent social wholes, the collectivist theories will be found to be moving down, toward the recognition of emergent persons. Even the most committed proponents of super-individual systems cannot but realize that those systems comprise individuals, and that those individuals clearly manifest a certain autonomy: at least some of them, and all of them sometimes exhibit freedom, independence, ability to choose, indeterminacy, flexibility, sovereignty, nonconformity, deviance or creativeness. An individual seems to escape, at least in part, from the social determination, systemic mold, structural constraints. People are always able to insulate themselves, at least in some measure, against societal power. In the apt formulation of D. Wrong they are "social but not entirely socialized" (Wrong 1961), or in the language of A. Giddens "they can always act otherwise" (Giddens 1984:9) — that is, differently than even the strongest systemic requirements would make them act. This partial autonomy of human individuals was already grasped in G. Simmel's suggestive notion of unsociable sociability (Simmel 1971 [1908]), or the concept of "the social solitary" (Bronowski 1977:162). All those intuitions indicate various marks of real existence of human beings, apart from or at least occupying some autonomous niches within the social wholes. Individuals are seen as partly emergent with respect to the wider social context: they have traits and tendencies and exhibit patterns of conduct not fully reducible to the requirements of the system or constraints of structures.

A good example of this intellectual evolution may be found in the holistic theory par excellence, structural-functionalism. If we look at the portrait of an individual as drawn within early functionalism, we shall see people reduced to "cultural dopes," performers of preset roles, marionettes of the system, microcopies of structures. The "oversocialized image of man" criticized later by Wrong (1961) is clearly there. Other commentators notice this bias too: "Given the strong systemic emphasis of the structural-functional school, the very autonomy of the individual — in his orientation to the social situation — has been neglected. He was reduced thereby to a 'socialized' role performer acting according to the presumed needs of the social system" (Eisenstadt and Culeralu 1976:197). The same point is made by W. L. Skidmore: "When Parsons deals at the social system level, he is almost forced by the mode of analysis to abandon concern with the individual (the model of man) in favor of treating 'roles' as the system-constituting units at the social system level" (Skidmore 1975:111).

But such a rigid, one-sided view is soon released. Parsons himself, turning to the analysis of social action acknowledges the presence of "an independent determinate selective factor," the factor of "volition or will," or else "freedom or autonomy" of the will (Parsons 1968:I/45). He points out explicitly that action is "a process in which the concrete human beings play an active, not merely adaptive role" (p. 439). And "the creative, voluntaristic element which we have found to be involved in the factor of ends precludes action ever being completely determined" (Parsons 1934:287). The significance of this shift in the assumptions about an individual does not escape commentators. J. F. Scott points out that "Parsons ... argued that a primordially creative element, independent of the natural world of 'heredity and environment' was active in valuation and the choice of goals" (Scott 1969:246). And Skidmore confirms: "In Parsons's voluntaristic emphasis ... there is considerable room for choice on the part of the individual and self-determination of action. The model of man is definitely constructed in terms of alternatives and modes of choosing between alternatives" (Skidmore 1975:180). The movement toward the emphasis on contingency, voluntarism, possibilism is even more pronounced in modern neofunctionalism (Alexander 1985), which is opening to various insights of individualistic and microsociological approaches.

The upward evolution of individualistic theories, and the downward evolution of holistic theories, significantly narrows the gap between the two. From the individualistic side, the ontological standpoint which may be called *emergent structuralism* bridges the gap toward holistic bank. It still asserts that individuals are the ultimate components, the real substance of society, but concedes the emergence of specific traits and regularities resulting from their plurality and organization; the autonomous mechanisms of structures. Those structures are seen as imposing some constraints and limitations over individual freedom and liberty. In other words, individuals are shown to be partly imprisoned in structures.[6] From the holistic side, the bridge toward individualistic bank is provided by the ontological standpoint which may be called *emergent personalism*. It still asserts the existence of super-individual social wholes *sui generis*, but concedes the partial autonomy of individuals, who exhibit traits and regularities emergent with respect to their social context, the autonomous mechanisms of action. Those actions are seen as partly insulated from structural determination, manifesting human freedom and independence. In other words, the grip of structures over individuals is released.

We may bring together the main points, concerning which most sociologists seem to reach consensus, by reintroducing the fourfold typology of the aspects of existence: separatedness, causality, power and process. How do the individual and social objects fare in these categories, as the result of mutual rapprochement of individualistic and holistic positions? First, individuals and societies are separate but mutually interpenetrated entities. Societies consist of individuals, but they are more than the sum of individuals. Individuals are constituents of society, but not just parts, retaining autonomous being. Second, the causal efficacy of individuals and groups is mutually correlated. Groups are causally effective but only due to coordinated individual efforts of their members. Individual efforts may be truly consequential only in connection with others, in the context of groups. Third, individual and social power are reciprocal. Societies are produced and controlled by individuals but not entirely as intended, and individuals are molded and controlled by society but are never its perfect replica. Fourth, biography and history overlap and intermesh. History consists of the confluence of biographies, superimposed, running parallel or overlapping with each other, but is not reducible to any of them (it exhibits its own track, logic, tendency), and biographies are influenced by history but not entirely, retaining considerable self-determination.

Recently, the traditional opposition of the individuals and social wholes tends to be rephrased in more modern language as the relationship of actions and structures, and the considerable area of consensus as to their reciprocal linkage and mutual dependence seems to appear, too. No structures exist apart from some actions, which produce and support them; they have only "virtual existence" (Giddens 1984:17). But by the same token, no actions exist apart from some structures which facilitate or constrain them; thus actions also have "virtual existence." There are no actionless structures, and no structureless actions. But on the other hand, structures are more than the sum of actions — they are networks of autonomous character, *collective emergents* having some properties and regularities of their own. And similarly, actions are more than direct structural effects — they are *individual emergents* not completely determined by structures and possessing some autonomy.

TOWARD A TRUE SYNTHESIS

Notice how strongly the idea of dualism, two-sidedness of the social world, is reaffirmed after a long detour into one-sided, dogmatic absolutizations. After almost two centuries, the theoretical discourse is returning to its common-sense roots, rediscovering those pervasive intuitions of ambivalence, tension and mutuality between individual and social levels which were always experienced by common people. But of course, the time was not entirely lost. We return much richer in analytical sophistication, conceptual insights and theoretical illuminations provided by meta-theorists and sociologists of both orientations; individualists and holists alike, both in their rigid and more open, permissive conceptions. Yet, we cannot stop here. There is the need for overcoming both fragmentary syntheses: emergent structuralism and emergent personalism, and producing a synthesis of syntheses, acknowledging the mutual emergence (and mutual autonomy), as well as the baffling fact of mutual virtual existence of individual and social spheres. Two convictions strongly rooted in intellectual tradition — that the human being is a social animal, but also that society is a human product — urgently demand reconciliation. This will require not only parting with some seemingly self-evident assumptions of sociological theories, but also going beyond common sense, eradicating some widespread illusions which have acquired the status of obvious truths. Only in this way will sociological theory finally be able to prove its worth as the mode of discourse superior to common sense.

There are two deeper symptoms of this synthetic persuasion gaining ground in modern sociological theory. One is the almost obsessive theme of paradoxes, ironies, dualisms, or dualities — covered also by the idea of dialectics in its neutral, nonideological sense. L. Schneider gives the sweeping overview of this theme. He traces the "dialectical bias" in the entire history of sociological thought, but concedes that "dialectical perspectives continue on into contemporary sociology," "having been involved in some of the most fundamental insights in sociology"(Schneider 1971:668–669). Several more concrete concepts which express the dialectic theme are distinguished: unintended consequences, "heterogony of ends" (displacement of goals), "cunning of reason," sudden reversals of evolutionary trends, circular processes, paradoxical effects, coalescence of opposites, etc. And he ventures a hint that dialectic may well reveal "some very potent 'logic' or 'grammar' of social life" (Schneider 1971:677). If we look at the work of some other modern sociologists we shall find good illustrations of Schneider's points. Let us take just two examples.

R. K. Merton has a penchant for uncovering paradoxes in human life. The most familiar of these is perhaps the one situated in the theory of anomie: "the structure of society and culture, ordinarily thought of as operating to produce patterned behavior in rough accord with social norms could, under designated conditions, operate to produce deviant behavior (both aberrant and nonconforming)" (Merton 1964:231). In another place Merton maintains that "the very elements which conduce toward efficiency in general produce inefficiency in specific instances" (Merton 1968:254). Another paradox is discovered in bureaucratic structures where "activities originally conceived as instrumental are transmuted into self-contained practices, lacking further objectives" (Merton 1968:187–188), or more precisely when "the organizational means become transformed into ends-in-themselves and displace the principal goals of the organization" (Merton 1976:102). In the theory of propaganda we find the famous boomerang effect: "Under certain conditions ... people respond to propaganda in a fashion opposite to that intended by the author" (Merton 1944:1). This list of paradoxes could be extended.[7]

The same *leitmotif* pervades Peter M. Blau's work. He focuses on paradoxes, dilemmas, opposing factors: "There is a dialectic in social life, for it is governed by many contradictory forces" (Blau 1964:336).

The main pattern responsible for the incessant dynamics of society is described as follows: "Although there is a strain toward reciprocity in social relations and a strain toward equilibrium in social structures, the same forces that restore balance or equilibrium in one respect are imbalancing or disequilibrating forces in others, which means that the very processes of adjustment create imbalances requiring further adjustments" (p. 7). Just two examples of innumerable paradoxes or dilemmas that result: "The effective achievement of collective goals requires organizations with committed and loyal members, but attachments to organizations preclude the mobility necessary for individuals to safeguard their investments and receive a fair return in turn" (p. 167), or "The very outstanding qualities that make an individual differentially attractive as an associate also raise fears of dependence that inhibit easy sociability and thus make him unattractive as a sociable companion" (p. 316).

The concern with dialectics in all its forms is the first symptom of the implicit strain toward synthesis, toward a multidimensional view of society which would combine opposites, merge levels, resolve dilemmas and reject one-sided biases. Another symptom is the career of peculiar, mediating concepts, which are multidimensional by their very nature, referring neither to human individuals nor to super-individual wholes, but rather conveying some fusion of both levels. In the history of sociology, this category of concepts may be illustrated by such ideas as *representations collectives* (Durkheim), class consciousness (Marx), hegemony (Gramsci), praxis (Lukacs), etc. In modern sociology one may find such fashionable and influential notions as habitus (Bourdieu), historicity (Touraine), figurations (Elias), mobilization (Etzioni), anomie (Merton), duality of structure (Giddens), agency (Archer), and many others. It is not easy to say what is exactly the referent of these concepts, what kind of objects are described, because clearly they are neither people nor systems. This very difficulty is a signal that the traditional dichotomy of the individual and society is intuitively felt to be insufficient.

In our discussion so far we have traced the slow evolution of the ontological premises of sociological discourse, as expressed both at the meta-theoretical as well as theoretical level. The tendency to depart from initial one-sided and rigid standpoints and approach some middle-of-the-road consensus was clearly visible. It replicated similar movements at the level of common sense, leading toward the recognition of the dualities and ambivalences of human experience. Each of the originally opposite two sociologies was found to come closer to the other pole, mutually borrowing some important insights. And yet the result is not fully satisfactory. It does not account for the pervasive intuitions of "dialectics" — dilemmas, paradoxes, ironies, contradictions — so common in sociological theory. And it does not identify the ontological referent of significant sociological concepts, dealing neither with individuals nor societal wholes. Thus the synthesizing effort cannot stop here; it must move on toward a third sociology, instead of simply combining the two. In this way we shall finally part with constraining premises of common sense.

FOUNDATIONS OF THIRD SOCIOLOGY

The project of a third sociology attempts to draw ultimate, radical implications from the common and unresolved experience of duality and ambivalence, appearing in common sense, sociological theory and meta-theory alike. What kind of reality must be postulated to account for such experiences? What is the underlying essence of human society which would make such experiences understandable? There are limits to heuristic usefulness of common sense for sociological discourse. So far we have exploited all that could be drawn from common sense. Now we have to leave common sense, because together with suggestive insights, sociological theory has inherited some common-sense illusions, transmuting them into more sophisticated theoretical fallacies. Only by getting rid of them can we approach the true nature of social reality.

The first is the *illusion of egocentrism*. We think of ourselves (and by implication, of other people) as self-contained, integral, separate entities, possessing independent existence. But it is only an illusion of our egocentric self-consciousness. If we are separate at all, it is only as things, as skin-bound bags full of flesh (if you pardon the brutality of this depiction). All that is human in us is neither separate, nor independent. C. H. Cooley was making this point already at the beginning of our century:

> The individual is not separable from the human whole, but a living member of it, deriving his life from the whole through social and hereditary transmission as truly as if men were literally one body. He cannot cut himself off; the strands of heredity and education are woven into all his being. (Cooley [1902] 1964:35)

And in another place:

> Self and society are twin born, we know one as immediately as we know the other, and the notion of a separate and independent ego is an illusion. (Cooley 1962 [1909]:5)

Our truly human nature is derived from society, expressed through society, existing only due to the links with society. We cannot live but with other people, for others, aside others, together with others, against others. Even when physically alone or isolated, we still preserve those links in our minds — in our language, education, morality, attitudes, motivations, loyalties, self-identifications, dreams, plans, etc., etc. As R. Fletcher comments on Cooley:

> We cannot define the boundary of an individual self by throwing a kind of sheath about his skin. A human mind is not like that. It is not limited to the boundaries of the body. A person cannot be so defined. The dimensions of his mind are spread along all avenues of his perception and social awareness. (Fletcher 1971:II/485)

There is no escape from society, except for death, which turns us back into non-human, material state. Why not draw ultimate conclusions from this fact? Why maintain that the individual and society are separate and opposed entities? Why not see ourselves as merely parts, components, elements of wider social fabric? Why not admit that we have only *virtual individual existence*?

The second is the *illusion of reification*. We think of states, bureaucracies, economies, political regimes, social systems, etc. — as superindividual, towering, often oppressive edifices standing above ourselves, distant from us, independent from our will and yet controlling our lives. But this is only an illusion of our distorted imagination, the product of our tendency to create hypostases. If social objects are superindividual at all, it is only in their material, physical substratum: barracks and tanks, offices and courtrooms, prisons and hospitals, planes and cars. Their truly social, institutional nature consists entirely of people and their actions. They exist only so long and insofar as some individuals fill the material shell with certain actions. Without them, there are no social wholes, at most dead physical skeletons of societies — like in the sad museum of Pompei or in that terrifying scene from the *Last Shore* when after nuclear war the buildings of a city remain intact but there are no people. G. Homans makes the point with typical clarity:

> The characteristics of social groups and societies are the resultants, no doubt the complicated resultants but still the resultants, of the interaction between individuals over time — and they are no more than that. (Homans 1974:12)

Societies are made of individuals and exist only through individuals. Why not recognize that fact? Why maintain that social wholes are somewhere above us living their own, separate lives? Why not admit that they have only *virtual social existence*?

The transmutation of those illusions at the level of theoretical discourse produces the fallacy of epiphenomenalism, in its two pervasive versions. One is the *fallacy of individualistic epiphenomenalism*, which treats social wholes as emanations of individual minds, imagined concepts rather than tangible objects. Here only individuals are endowed with true existence and societies exist only in human heads. Another is the *fallacy of collectivistic epiphenomenalism*, which treats individuals as emanations of society, as puppets, marionettes, fully diluted in society. Here, only societies are endowed with true existence and people exist only as the raw material of society. Both views are wrong. Why not admit that both societies and individuals are real, only integrated so closely, that there is no way to disentangle that fabric, to separate the threads? Let us quote C. H. Cooley again:

> A separate individual is an abstraction unknown to experience, and so likewise is society when regarded as something apart from individuals... "Society" and "individuals" do not denote separable phenomena... Through both the hereditary and the social factors in his life a man is bound into the whole of which he is a member, and to consider him apart from it is quite as artificial as to consider society apart from individuals. (Cooley 1964 [1902]:36–38)

And in another place: "Self and society go together as phases of a common whole" (p. 5). Why not recognize that neither individuals nor wholes are even conceivable apart from each other? There is no way to think of human individuals outside of some social context, because the very definition of what it means to be an individual must contain reference to some social wholes, be it family, tribe, local community, nation, professional group, etc. Similarly, there is no way to think of social wholes apart from individuals who make them up, because the very definition of any social whole must include some reference to its components: members of groups, incumbents of positions, performers of roles, etc.

This leads us finally to the central claim of this paper: what truly exists in society, in the full ontological sense, is the *unified socio-individual field*, the third level of reality between traditionally conceived levels of totalities and individualities. Social wholes and human individuals have only virtual existence, their separation and mutual opposition is the product of false, distorted imagination: commonsense illusions, and theoretical as well as meta-theoretical fallacies.

The concept of a socio-individual field provides the final solution to the first ontological dichotomy that we distinguished at the outset: overcoming the opposition of the individual versus society. But what about two remaining dichotomies: statics versus dynamics and potentiality and actuality? For some time we have left them aside, concentrating exclusively on the first. Now we have to bring them back into the discussion. It will be shown that the oppositions they convey are equally illusory and fallacious, and the concept of a socio-individual field brings a bonus, allowing to overcome them as well.

Thus the separation of static and dynamic aspects of social reality, of persistence and transformation, stability and movement, order and change, must also be seen as fully artificial. No social entities (whether wholes or individuals) exist in a timeless void; they are always located in the temporal context, as moments, episodes or phases in a continuous, sequential chain of a process. But conversely, no social process exists per se, devoid of some substratum, without something that is changed, transformed, modified. All social objects undergo constant movement, because they are in the process of incessant change — to use somewhat metaphorical language, they are living. But they also retain some identity; they are different and yet the same objects for varied spans of time — in metaphorical terms they have their particular lives. "Life" in this wide, liberal meaning is simply constant self-transformation. If we think of social reality as a unified socio-individual field, we may now extend this notion as a *living socio-individual field*.

The last dichotomy, the opposition and separation of potential and actual modes of social being, is equally artificial. In fact, they are intimately linked by mutual feedback loops. Potentialities (capacities, abilities, skills, facilities, resources, etc.) are manifested in conduct, but they are not given. Rather they are shaped by earlier conduct (experience, training, learning, etc.), themselves produced by actualizations. And in turn, their actualizations reshape potentialities for future conduct enriching tradition, resources and possibilities. There is an incessant back-and-forth oscillation between what is possible and what actually occurs, and it extends in time. This I propose to grasp by the concept of becoming. Thus we arrive at the ultimate characterization of social reality, as a *living socio-individual field in the process of becoming*.

To avoid this long and awkward phrase I propose a simple category of *social becoming* as the comprehensive term covering the peculiar socio-individual constitution, and the peculiar processual mode of existence of social reality. In this idea all six poles of ambivalence so pervasive in the perceptions of society (whether in common sense or theoretical discourse) are merged and fused: persons and groups, order and change, possibilities and realities. Society in the ontological image proposed here exists only as social becoming. In its very essence it is multidimensional, ambivalent, dualistic and dialectical. This is the peculiar, unique mode of social being which provides the specific subject matter for sociological science.

THE ANATOMY OF SOCIAL BECOMING

Let us examine the anatomy of social becoming a little more closely. What is this peculiar reality made of? We have to identify its ultimate components, and then the forms in which they are combined and aggregated. There are numerous candidates for the status of elementary social particles, that have been proposed in sociological theory: persons, actors, actions and behaviors in various brands of individualism; interactions, joint actions, social relations, roles and status-roles in various versions of structuralism; groups, collectivities and communities in theories informed by holism or collectivism; symbols, values, norms, beliefs and interests in subjectivist theories. Perhaps this list is incomplete. But none of the received ideas fits the ontology of social becoming. For this perspective, the ultimate atoms of social reality are *events*.[8] Society is made of social events. Why events? Because they are the only elementary ontological objects bridging all three dualisms or dichotomies, which we have found illusory and fallacious. In their own constitution, social events are fusing individualities and totalities, persistence and change, potentiality and actuality. Events always have this synthetic quality, comprising three dimensions of being; they are located at the crossing of three axes organizing human experiences in society. Whatever event we take, at the micro-scale (e.g., eating breakfast), or at the macro-scale (e.g., waging war), it relates to some person or persons acting in the context of some social whole which is supported or reshaped by the action; it involves some sequential changes but preserves relative continuity of their subject; and it displays some capacities transformed in their realization, turning into new capacities.

The events do not occur in isolation from others. They make up clusters and sequences, routines and procedures, chains and processes; spatio-temporarily connected, involving pluralities of people in diversified social contexts. The totality of *directly* interlinked events, *co-present in a society*, may be covered by the category of *praxis*. This idea represents the functioning, operation of the socio-individual field in any given time. There is a correlative idea which represents the potentiality (capacity) of a socio-individual field for generating robust and consequential praxis. This is grasped by the term *agency*.[9] Agency and praxis are two sides of the incessant social functioning; agency actualizes in praxis, and praxis reshapes agency, which actualizes itself in changed praxis.

The highest level of aggregation and complication appears, when it is recognized that the existence of the socio-individual field does not resolve only in its operation (functioning), but extends itself, spreads temporarily in historical time — in other words, when events are seen not only as directly co-present, but as *linked in mediated way* via their lasting results. Events (praxis) leave effects: material residues, memory traces, structural arrangements, institutional forms, etc., which make up historical tradition. They are intended and unintended, recognized and unrecognized, but together make up real circumstances, conditions, situations for further events (praxis). The network of events extends beyond direct co-presence in praxis, and acquires continuity thanks to the indirect mediation of conditions produced by earlier praxis, as the foundation for later praxis. In terms of our conception, this is precisely what is meant by *history*. History is the continuous chain of praxis mediated by tradition, the latter representing the results of praxis and conditions for praxis at the same time. The crucial property of history is the cumulativeness of tradition, the permanently growing scope of received heritage from earlier praxis, constraining but also facilitating (providing enriched resources) for later praxis.

Let us pull the strings of our argument together, reiterating the central claims:

- Individuals and social wholes are one unified, mutually integrated, interpenetrated, undividable field. Neither exists separately or independently.

- Individuals and social wholes possess causal efficacy only in their fusion; neither is effective alone.

- Individuals have power over social wholes in the same measure in which the wholes have power over them. People produce social wholes and are their products at the same time.
- The social process runs at its own, specific third level, embracing the socio-individual field; neither biographies nor societal fates have independent course.
- Society is made of social events, which are directly aggregated in praxis and indirectly in history.
- Society is in the process of continuous self-transcendence, constantly renewing and enriching its agential potentiality. In other words, society is in the process of the incessant, contingent movement of becoming.

This ontological image underlies what may be called "the third sociology" as opposed to both the sociology of action and sociology of structures, or better as merging both of them in the synthetic, more adequate approach to social reality.

It carries a strong, and two-edged critical message. It is equally opposed to radical, extreme liberalism, atomism, personalism and individualism as it is to radical, extreme historicism, totalitarianism, collectivism, holism. It presents the human world as two-sided, dualistic and "dialectical" finding in this ambivalence the peculiar challenge and unique taste of human fate.

Notes

1. The idea that overlapping role-sets and status-sets are the source of individual autonomy is convincingly argued by R. Laub Coser (Coser 1975:237–264).
2. R. Dahrendorf gives this experience the apt name: "a vexatious fact of society" (Dahrendorf 1968:23).
3. For the review of various epistemological and methodological positions in the dispute, see Sztompka (1979:83–128) and Udehn (1987).
4. For a long time, it was extremely characteristic to find chapters on social change relegated to the very end of sociological textbooks and treated as completely separate from the discussion of groups, organizations, structures, institutions, etc. Similarly in academic curricula the courses on social change are still offered as something different from other topics.

5. This "historiosophical" idea of alienation is picked up and elaborated by contemporary neo-Marxists, e.g., E. Fromm with his notion of a "sane society" (Fromm 1963), or H. Marcuse with his "alternative project" for mankind (Marcuse 1964). It must be distinguished from more down-to-earth "sociological" discussions of alienation as a multidimensional, descriptive concept for grasping certain crucial aspects of modern society (see Seeman 1959; Srole 1965).
6. Until recently I considered "sociological structuralism" as the adequate solution of the dilemma of individuals and social wholes, of individualistic and holistic claims (Sztompka 1979:chap. 7). Now I recognize that it is only half of the solution, producing only partial synthesis.
7. I discuss them more extensively in my intellectual biography of R. K. Merton identifying irony and paradox as basic themes of his sociology (Sztompka 1986a).
8. Of course I have in mind *social events*, as opposed to natural events, occurring within any human intervention, even though sometimes relevant for human populations (rainfalls, hurricanes, earthquakes, floods, volcanic eruptions, climatic changes, etc.).
9. I explicate this notion in detail and discuss the powerful theoretical movement characterized by the evolving focus on agency ("theories of agency") in Sztompka (1991).

Bibliography

Abrams, P. (1982). *Historical Sociology*. Ithaca: Cornell University Press.

Addis, L. (1969). "The Individual and the Marxist Philosophy of History." In: *Readings in the Philosophy of the Social Sciences*, ed. M. Brodbeck, pp. 317–335. New York: Macmillan.

Agassi, J. (1960). "Methodological Individualism." *The British Journal of Sociology* 2:244–270.

_____ (1973). "Methodological Individualism." In: *Modes of Individualism and Collectivism*, ed. J. O'Neill, pp.185–212. London: Heinemann.

_____ (1975). "Institutional Individualism." *The British Journal of Sociology* 26:144–155.

Alexander, J. C. (1982). *Theoretical Logic in Sociology*, Vol. 1: *Positivism, Presuppositions and Current Controversies*. London: Routledge & Kegan Paul.

_____ (Ed.) (1985). *Neo-Functionalism*. London: Sage.

Alexander, J. C. (1988). "The New Theoretical Movement." In: *Handbook of Sociology*, ed. Neil J. Smelser, pp. 77–102. Newbury Park: Sage.

Archer, M. S. (1988). *Culture and Agency*. Cambridge: Cambridge University Press.

Bhaskar, R. (1986). *Scientific Realism and Human Emancipation*. London: Verso.

Blau, P. M. (1964). *Exchange and Power in Social Life*. New York: Wiley.

Bronowski, J. (1977). *A Sense of the Future*. Cambridge: MIT Press.

Cohen, P. S. (1968). *Modern Social Theory*. New York: Basic Books.

Collins, R. (1988). "For a Sociological Philosophy." *Theory and Society* 17:669–702.

Cooley, C. H. (1962). *Social Organization*. New York: Schocken Books.

_____ (1964). *Human Nature and the Social Order*. New York: Schocken Books.

Coser, R. L. (1975). "The Complexity of Roles as a Seedbed of Individual Autonomy." In: *The Idea of Social Structure*, ed. L. A. Coser, pp. 237–264. New York: Harcourt Brace Jovanovich.

Dawe, A. (1978). "Theories of Social Action." In: *A History of Sociological Analysis*, eds. T. B. Bottomore and R. Nisbet, pp. 362–417. New York: Basic Books.

Eisenstadt, S. N., and M. Culeralu (1976). *The Form of Sociology: Paradigms and Crises*. New York: Wiley.

Emerson, R. M. (1972). "Exchange Theory, Part II: Exchange Relations and Network Structures." In: *Sociological Theories in Progress*, eds. J. Berger, M. Zelditch, and B. Anderson, Vol. 2, pp. 58–87. Boston: Houghton Mifflin.

Fletcher, R. (1971). *The Making of Sociology*, Vols. 1–3. New York: Charles Scribner's.

Fromm, Erich (1963) *The Sane Society*. London: Routledge & Kegan Paul.

Gellner, E. (1968). "Holism Versus Individualism." In: *Readings in the Philosophy of the Social Sciences*, ed. M. Brodbeck, pp. 254–268???. New York: Macmillan.

Giddens, A. (1984). *The Constitution of Society*. Cambridge: Polity Press.

Ginsberg, M. (1968). *Essays in Sociology and Social Philosophy*. Baltimore: Penguin Books.

Hollis, M. (1987). *The Cunning of Reason*. Cambridge: Cambridge University Press.

Homans, G. C. (1967). *The Nature of Social Science*. New York: Harcourt Brace & World.

―――――― (1973). "Fundamental Social Processes." In: *Sociology: An Introduction*, ed. Neil J. Smelser, pp. 549–594. New York: Wiley.

―――――― (1974). *Social Behavior: Its Elementary Forms*. New York: Harcourt Brace Jovanovich.

Jarvie, I. C. (1970). "Understanding and Explanation in Sociology and Social Anthropology." In: *Explanation in the Behavioral Sciences*, eds. R. Borger and F. Cioffi, pp. 231–247. Cambridge: Cambridge University Press.

―――――― (1972). *Concepts and Society*. London: Routledge & Kegan Paul.

Lukes, S. (1968). "Methodological Individualism Reconsidered." *The British Journal of Sociology* 19(2):119–129.

Marcuse, Herbert (1964). *One-Dimensional Man*. Boston: Beacon Press.

Martindale, D. (1964). "The Roles of Humanism and Scientism in the Evolution of Sociology." In: *Explorations in Social Change*, eds. G. K. Zollschan and W. Hirsch, pp. 452–490, Boston: Houghton Mifflin.

Mead. G. H. (1964). *On Social Psychology*. Chicago: University of Chicago Press.

Merton, R. K. (1964). "Anomie, Anomia, and Social Interaction: Contexts of Deviant Behavior." In: *Anomie and Deviant Behavior: Discussion and Critique*, ed. M. Clinard, pp. 213–242. New York: Free Press.

―――――― (1968). *Social Theory and Social Structure*. New York: Free Press.

―――――― (1976). "The Unanticipated Consequences of Social Action." In: *Sociological Ambivalence*, by R. K. Merton, pp. 145–155. New York: Free Press.

Merton, R. K., and P. Kendall (1944). "The Boomerang Response." *Channels (BBC)*, 21(7):1–7.

Mill, J. S. (1984). *A System of Logic: Ratiocinative and Inductive*. London: People's Edition.

Nadel, S. F. (1957). *The Theory of Social Structure*. London: Routledge & Kegan Paul.

Parsons, T. (1934). "The Place of Ultimate Values in Sociological Theory." *International Journal of Ethics* 45:282–316.

_____ (1964). *Essays in Sociological Theory*. Glencoe: Free Press.

_____ (1968). *The Structure of Social Action*, Vols. 1 and 2. New York: Free Press.

Ritzer, G. (1989). "Agency-Structure and Micro-Macro Syntheses: Consensus in Contemporary Theorizing?" Uppsala: SCASSS (Swedish Collegium for Advanced Studies in the Social Sciences) (mimeographed).

Schneider, L. (1971). "Dialectic in Sociology." *American Sociological Review* 36:667–678.

Scott, J.F. (1969). "The Changing Foundations of the Parsonian Action Scheme." In: *Sociological Theory*, ed. W. L. Wallace, pp. 246–267. London: Heinemann.

Seeman, Melvin (1959). "On the Meaning of Alienation." *American Sociological Review* 24(6):783–795.

Simmel, G. (1971). *On Individuality and Social Forms*, ed. G. N. Levine. Chicago: University of Chicago Press.

Skidmore, W. L. (1975). *Sociology's Models of Man*. New York: Gordon & Breach.

Skinner, Q. (1985). *The Return of Grand Theory in the Human Sciences*. Cambridge: Cambridge University Press.

Sorokin, P. A. (1966). *Sociological Theories of Today*. New York: Harper & Row.

Spencer, H. (1893). *Principles of Sociology*, Vols. 1–3. London: Willimans and Norgate.

Srole, Leo (1965). "A Comment on Anomie." *American Sociological Review* 30(5):757–762.

Sztompka, P. (1979). *Sociological Dilemmas: Toward a Dialectic Paradigm*. New York: Academic Press.

_____ (1986). *Robert K. Merton. An Intellectual Profile*. Houndmills Basingstole: Macmillan.

_____ (1991). *Society in Action. The Theory of Social Becoming*. Cambridge: Polity Press; Chicago: University of Chicago Press.

Tönnies, F. (1955). *Community and Association*. London: Routledge & Kegan Paul.

Udehn, Lars (1987). *Methodological Individualism: A Critical Reappraisal*. Uppsala: Uppsala Universitet.

Watkins, J. W. N. (1957). "Historical Explanation in the Social Sciences." *The British Journal for the Philosophy of Science* 8:104–117.

Wisdom, J. O. (1970). "Situational Individualism and the Emergent Group-Properties." In: *Explanation in the Behavioral Sciences*, eds. R. Borger and F. Cioffi, pp. 271–296. Cambridge: Cambridge University Press.

Wrong, D. (1961). "The Oversocialized Conception of Man in Modern Sociology." *American Sociological Review*, No. 2, pp. 183–193.

Chapter TEN

Sociology as a Discipline of Disagreements and as a Paradigm of Competing Explanations: Culture, Structure, and the Variability of Actors and Situations

Göran Therborn

This paper is going to argue three theses. Sociology is, or should see itself, as a discipline of disagreements, i.e., as a set of interrelated endeavors with certain common contours within which theoretical, methodological and substantial disagreements are thriving. Second, together with related approaches in political science and anthropology, sociology has a specific paradigm of competing explanations, that is, a characteristic mode of explanation containing a huge set of rival theories. In other words, there is a way in which sociology's claim to be a scholarly discipline, a *wissenschaftliche*, can be linked up with its irreducible diversity. Here, the emphasis will rest on the cornerstones of the discipline rather than on its internal disagreements; on the explanatory paradigm rather than on the rival contenders to this paradigm (this is mainly for reasons of exposition). My aim is a more fruitful collegial debate, not a grand reconciliation or synthesis.

Implied in the first two arguments is a third, which, given the context of publication, should be made explicit here. In sociology as an ongoing endeavor, the social philosophical, or meta-sociological issue of agency and structure is not necessarily a central problem. The reorientation of social theory, which seems to be called for, had at this point better concentrate primarily on the implications and the interrelationships of culture and structure, and on explanatory questions of the variability of actors and the variability of situations.

The value of bringing out such an intradisciplinary linkage seems to be fourfold. The process of thinking it through, of formulating, and of discussing it constitutes moments of constructive self-reflection. Once available to the awareness of sociologists, it should extend the circles of understanding among practicing sociologists, which, other things being equal, presumably should appeal to people professionally committed to the acquisition of knowledge. Third, to the individual sociologist, an active consciousness of the basic angles of the sociological undertaking can serve as a reminder, a compass or a source of inspiration in the thicket of concrete research work. Finally, an awareness of common bearings and a widening of more or less comprehensible communication should promote the accumulation and diffusion of sociological knowledge.

THE ARENA OF DISAGREEMENTS

In spite of its interminable acerbic polemics, baroque soliloquies, and simply dispersed myopic specializations, the overwhelming part of the activities of sociologists (empirical as well as theoretical) may be circumscribed by a few basic variables. We can find most activities by sociologists within an area identifiable by two dimensions. One is the *focus* of the sociologist's investigation or reflection, what he/she looks at, thinks about. On a level of simple generality and abstraction, the sociological focus may be on social actors and their actions, or on social systems and their processes, including the outcomes or consequences of one or the other. Actors may be individuals, groups or organizations. Social systems should be understood here in a broad sense as ensembles of interrelated elements, including institutions, modes of production, forms of life, patterns of distribution, sets

Table 1. The Sociological Arena

	Formation of study objects	
Focus	Cultural actors and action	Structured/ing actors and action
	Cultural systems and processes	Structured/ing systems and processes

of values and beliefs, and theorized systems, from dyads to the world system. Social actors and social systems may be seen as different analytical foci upon the same set of phenomena. But their interrelationship and their relative merit may be objects of heated disagreements.

A second axis of sociological practice is made up of certain basic assumptions of the *formation* or the substantive constitution of the focused objects of study. The poles of this dimension have been referred to in a number of ways, directly or more obliquely. They seem to be best grasped in terms of culture and structure, in the sense culture and social structure are currently distinguished from each other (cf. Alexander 1990; Archer 1988; Haferkamp 1990; Runciman 1989).

Cautiously stated, the argument, then, is that most of what sociologists have done and are doing takes place on the stage above. But to serve its purpose of contributing to self-clarification and self-reflection, the meaning of the concepts of culture and structure will have to be spelled out. This should be done in a nonidiosyncratic, ecumenical way; at the same time I have to make some substantive propositions, as there is no consensus of definitions to draw upon.

As a starting point, we may take Talcott Parsons' ([1937] 1968) "neoclassical synthesis" of sociology as a "voluntaristic theory of action," the original arguments of which even severe critics of Parsonsianism have found "compelling and unexceptionable" (Lockwood 1992:382). Parsons distinguished between normative and conditional elements of action and argued that what characterized and brought together classical sociology was its analytical incorporation of both. The normative and the conditional refer to what is here called culture and structure. In systems focusing on "the problem of social order," there ensued in the wake of Parsons a long debate about how such an order had better be conceived, whether as a consensual or as a coercive one. This is another way of expressing aspects of culture and structure. However, the normative and consensus approach does not adequately convey the rich potential of cultural sociology. Nor do the concept of nonnormative, power and coercion provide a satisfactory illumination of the formative assumptions of structural analysis.

Instead, the concepts may be elaborated along the following lines. *Structure* refers to the distribution of resources/opportunities and constraints/risks within a social system or among a set of actors. Commonly used notions, such as social structure, power structure, class structure, family structure and role structure, are subsumable under that definition, as well as the more specific network conception of structure (e.g., in Wellman and Berkowitz 1988). While not synonymous with Giddens' (1984:25) use of the structure concept, the definition proposed here does include a basic point of his "structuration" theory; namely, that structure "is always both constraining and enabling." A social order, however brought about and maintained, involves a stable patterning of resources and constraints.

The distributions of resources and constraints are usually social constructions. As such, they may be looked at both as structured by social actors and systems and as structuring actors and systems, as locating them in a structure.

The structural distribution involves two major variants. One provides a set of *institutional endowments* (of resources and constraints), inscribed in, defined by a given social system: whether a formal organization, family type, religion, gender system or mode of production. Mainstream sociological tradition would here talk about roles, Marxists would refer to class positions. The other variant we may call provisionally *a-institutional*: *contingent* resources and constraints have a certain stability without being defined by the institutional system under investigation.

While institutional structuring is an important foundation of analytical sociological theory, a good part of empirical sociology developed to deal with the latter. The differentiation of the sociology of religion from theology, law from jurisprudence, work from organization engineering, and economic sociology from economics has involved, above all, an attention to the possible differences between institutional pre/proscriptions and the de facto patterning of religious beliefs, legal systems, work and business actors on markets.

Power and money are certainly central features of resources and constraints, but at this point there appears to be little gain in immediate sight from any classification of resources and constraints. But a couple of points might be added. Although started from Parsons' conceptualization of theories of action, structure in the sense used here is not necessarily nonnormative, nor, for that matter, noncultural. A role structure, for instance, involves normative specifications of resources and constraints to the incumbent. Resources may also be taken to include "cultural capital." The defining aspect of structure here is the patterning of resources and constraints.

Structuring may also crucially involve *time* and *space*. The temporal sequence of, say, sibling actors or industrial economic systems have been found to be important allocations of resources/opportunities. Similarly significant is spatial location, of centrality or peripherality, of distance or proximity.

The *size* of a population or a social system is still another significant aspect of the structuring of resources and constraints, an explanatory track opened up by Georg Simmel ([1908] 1964), pointing to "the significance of numbers in social life." Peter Blau (1977) has followed up on Simmel with a large set of propositions about how social action is affected by group size and by the heterogeneity and the inequality of group members.

Culture may be taken generally as a universe of meaning. To belong to or to make use of a culture means to share, to have learned and to use a universe of meaning. In this perspective, norms and values are only part of shared learning. On the other hand, human actions and human products, while invested with meaning, would not, as in classical cultural anthropology, be regarded as elements of culture. While their structural location provides actors with what they have and with what they face, culture makes them who they are and what they can see.

Without any claim to exhaustiveness, we can discern three crucial components of culture in the sense used here. Culture provides *identity* by a differentiation from the rest of the world. To belong to a culture means to be distinct from the rest of the world. In cultural sociology so far, this aspect of culture seems to have been relatively neglected. But its crucial importance to a sociological understanding of collective action, of alienation, of social order and social order and social conflict will be noncontroversial.

Further, to be part of a culture means to have learned a certain *code of cognition*. Language is, of course, a key element of this component, which may be conceived more broadly as a view of what the world looks like, as a *Weltanschauung* as well as a specific cognitive competence. Third, although no necessary order is being argued, a culture contains a set of values and norms, asserting what is right or wrong, beautiful or ugly, and other evaluative standards.

Cultures should not be seen as primordial or essentially delimited entities. Their range is both an analytical and an empirical question. The same culture concept may be applied to civilizations, politically bound societies, classes, genders, generations and to groups of all sizes. In complex societies, cultures are usually nested, with one culture nested within another in sometimes complicated interrelationships.

Cultural systems would then refer to systems of identities, worldviews and values, and cultural actors would refer to actors distinguished by the culture they belong to. As against a cultural system's emphasis on cultural configurations and thereby socialized actors, a combative cultural actor's approach would focus on interpreting actors. Certain kinds of cultural action seems to be of particular pertinence to distinctive cultural components, ritual, communication and evaluation, respectively.

In some such way, the bulk of sociological activities may be outlined. Inside those four cornerstones of cultural and structured/ing systems and their processes, and cultural and structured/ing actors and their actions, there is also ample room for a cumulative exchange of results from different perspectives, as well as for polemic disagreements.

EXPLANATION IN THE SOCIAL SCIENCES

In contrast to some other conceptions of social science, the sociological, and even less, the kindred anthropological enterprise, is not above everything else geared to explanation. Without going into epistemological controversies, we may say that to explain something means giving a plausible account of why it occurred in a situation in which there was at least one other possibility. To find out and to describe how actors act, systems operate, and what cultures and structures look like count among the pleasures of sociologists. So do the interpretation and the conceptualization of social phenomena. However, as social scientists, sociologists are also called upon to explain. In my humble opinion, sociological theorizing indeed has as a central task to provide explanatory framework and explanatory theories of some generality. Nonetheless, that opinion seems to be a minority view in current general sociological theorizing, which is dominated by interpretative conceptualizations of one variety or another.

Recently, however, classical and neoclassical sociological theories are being increasingly challenged by rational choice models of various sorts, all primarily aiming at explanation (Becker 1976; Coleman 1990; Elster 1986, 1989; Hechter et al. 1990; Lindenberg 1990). This rationalist cause may be embraced, rejected (which seems to be the most popular sociological response so far), or taken as a stimulus for an open-ended reconsideration of a number of theoretical questions. This writer belongs to the latter category.

Against the background of the rationalist arguments, it is possible to see more clearly that the mainstreams of sociology do have a common explanatory framework. If the concept of paradigm has any relevance at all to social disciplines full of contending schools, it seems that it should be at the level of the mode of explanation, hardly at that of school theories. Furthermore, it is also possible to see more clearly the problems as well as the strengths of this type of explanation.

The social sciences try to explain two sets of phenomena: *human social action* and *outcomes of human social action*. To put it that way means to say that social systems and systemic processes can be taken as reducible to social action and its outcomes in the sense of not requiring any specifically systemic mode of explanation. Processes of Marxist modes of production, Parsonsian social systems, economic markets and even Luhmannian systems (Luhmann 1984:chap. 4) can be, and are, explained in terms of social action and its consequences.

Social scientists are concerned with why humans act the ways they do in social relationships. Second, we are interested in a set of phenomena which we might summarize under the rubric of consequences of human social action, thinking primarily of effects upon the persistence, change or disappearance of social actors and social systems. The recent rationalist challenge, as its brand name "rational choice" indicates, has concentrated mainly on the first explanatory issue; in fact, so has most explanatory theory in social science, which may derive from the reasonable consideration that the most important outcomes of action are those which affect future social action. Explaining the outcomes of action is then theoretically secondary to explaining action, as the latter explanans indicates the former explanandum.

Let us then lay out explanations of action. The minimum elements of explanandum are a set of actors, a set of situations and a set of feasible actions, which has at least two options. The academic division of labor has to a large extent divided disciplines and subdisciplines of social study along the types of action studied — economists looking at actions by all kinds of market entrepreneurs, political scientists looking at those of politicians and citizens, educationists looking at those by teachers and pupils and sociologists looking at a bit of everything except the most specifically economic, political, etc., types of action. However, both the neoclassical syntheses of sociology and the current challenge of rational choice models regard pragmatic division according to sets of actions as scientifically irrelevant, or at least secondary. We are then left with two dimensions along which to distinguish explanations of social action, their treatment of the set of actors and their treatment of the set of situations.

There is a crucial distinction in explanatory approaches that treat situations as variable and those that treat them as given, either as predetermined or as randomly variable. The two latter treatments are by no means synonymous, but for the sake of neat simplicity, the table below does not divide the two. According to whether they take the actor or the situation as given (random) or variable, we can distinguish the social disciplines and indeed the so-called behavioral sciences by locating the major explanatory division within psychology, as well as between behaviorism and psychologies of internal dynamics.

With certain exceptions, rational choice models are characterized by their treatment of the actors as given. The latter are assumed to have given preferences and maximizing propensities, and the rest to be randomly different.

The typical game theoretical approach takes both the actors — as rational anybody — and the situation as a predetermined given, the latter by a payoff matrix (Luce and Raiffa 1957; Harsanyi 1982; Axelrod 1984). The explanatory focus is on questions such as: What is the optimal strategy for each player in the given game situation? Does the game have an equilibrium (one or more)? If so, what? Game theory is also being extended to dealing with games in multiple arenas, games nested within others, e.g., institutional or constitutional games (Tsebelis 1990), in which the basic explanatory logic becomes similar to that of economics.

In the characteristic economic mode of explanation, action is explained by variations of the situation, basically by changes in (relative) prices and incomes (Becker 1976; Frey and Pommerehne 1990:171–172; Lindenberg 1990:256 ff.; Elster 1989:97–98). Actors are given, assumed to be utility maximizers, with "stable preferences":

Table 2. Explanations of Social Action

Actors	Situations	
	Given	Variable
Given	Game theory	Economics, Behaviorist psychology
Variable	Sociology, anthropology, traditional political science, dynamic psychology	Composite models

"preferences are assumed not change substantially over time, nor to be very different between wealthy and poor persons, or even between persons in different societies and cultures... The assumption of stable preferences provides a stable foundation for generating predictions about responses to various changes" (Becker 1976:5).

As Przeworski (1986:88) has put it, "the power of neoclassical economics lies in being able to separate the analysis of *action at a particular moment* from everything that created the conditions under which this action occurs" (emphasis added). Situational variability consists of the probable cost/benefit consequences of different options in moments of choice. When (probable) incentives change, actors act differently in a predictable way.

The assumptions of maximizing and of stable preferences do not necessarily require any exclusively egoistic or pecuniary preferences, not even that preferences be universally the same (cf. Hechter et al. 1990:3–4). The "utility function" of a particular set of actors may be specified in different ways, and in ways differing from that of other sets. The crucial point is another one, i.e., that economic explanations and predictions characteristically get going from a baseline of actors with given preferences and decision rules.

The sociological (and anthropological and dynamic psychological) explanatory starting point is typically the opposite of the economic one. Instead of assuming that, for all meaningful scientific purposes, human preferences are stable and that "tastes" do not "differ importantly between people" (Stigler and Becker 1977:76), sociologists and anthropologists start from the viewpoint that actors differ across categories and groups of various sorts and also over historical time. In the sociological-anthropological vision, social action varies because actors vary, belonging to different groups, genders, classes, societies, etc.

On the other hand, the variation of situations, or circumstances of action, tends to be taken as randomly given. Or, in interpretative sociology, the situation is given by the actors' definition(s) of it. The options available to the sociological actor typically vary, not with the immediate action situation, but with the actor's values, norms or interpretation of the situation, and with the actor's location in social structure. The latter may sometimes be referred to as the "situation" of the actor, but that "situation" is a more or less permanent feature of the actor, not to be conflated with the circumstances of a piece of action to be explained. The alternatives are culturally defined or "structurally patterned" (cf. Stinchcombe 1975:14 ff.), in relation to which action situations are not held to "differ very importantly." Stinchcombe, in his brilliant analysis of the arguably most lucid of sociological explainers, Robert Merton, calls the "socially structured alternatives" (Stinchcombe 1975:12) in Merton's theory alternatives "structured" by the actor's cultural belonging and structural location.

Political science, both its behavioral and its constitutional variant, traditionally anchored its explanations in the actors, their different positions, values or interests, while hardly aiming at any general theory of political action. Recently, political science has become increasingly oriented towards adaptations of economic models.

The contrast between the characteristic core of economic and sociological explanations is eloquently expressed by Amitai Etzioni's recent sociological counterblast against neoclassical economics. Etzioni (1988:95) argues "that the majority of choices involve little information processing [about the situation] or none at all, but that they draw largely or exclusively of affective involvements and normative commitments [of the actors]." In other words, according to Etzioni, actors care little about the situations they are in and how the latter have changed, but act upon their actor-specific involvements and commitments. Actors "habit" and "inertia," rather than prices and efforts, govern most choices (p. 161).

On the other hand, not all sociologists are ("neoclassical") "sociologists." James Coleman's (1990:665) social theory is explicitly isomorphic with that of economics, distinctive from the latter primarily through its analyses of exchanges of rights to act and of their implications. The microsociological "expectation states" theory of Joseph Berger et al. (1985) also focuses on how situational conditions shape actors' expectations of others.

It should be added, furthermore, that composite explanatory frameworks exist too. Typically, they combine a "sociological" differentiation of actors with an "economic" attention to situational variation. Examples from economic theory would be theories in which the different actor endowments or "asset specificity" of (sets of) actors are central, such as theories of international trade or of organization (Williamson 1985). Marxist class analysis using microeconomic modelling (Przeworski 1985) constitutes another illustration. Certain kinds of economic sociology (e.g., White 1988) make up a third subvariant. All of them concentrate on variation within actors' resources, in particular stable and systematic variation. However, Coleman (1990:132) underlines the importance of the "constitution" of a social system, i.e., the initial distribution of control over resources among actors; in his theory this is regarded as secondary and derivative of norm- and constitution-generation among any set of rational actors.

On the whole, I suspect that major advances in sociological theory and in sociology-kindred political science will involve coming to terms with how different actors act in different situations.

THE CULTURAL AND THE STRUCTURAL VARIATION OF ACTORS

Actors act the way they do, according to the typical sociological mode of explanation, because of their cultural belonging, their structural location or due to an interaction between those two variables. Sociologists differ and argue about the relative weight of the two master sets of variables, as well as about the relative importance of the major aspects of each. The explanatory variables are usually not held as being individually determinant. Rather, cultural belonging and structural location determine rates or probabilities of action in a population of actors.

The wide span of sociological explanations is an arc with two bridgeheads, identified in the first major neoclassical synthesis of sociology, Talcott Parsons' ([1937] 1968) *The Structure of Social Action*, although formulated as a "frame of reference," rather than as a mode of explanation. The one bridgehead was constituted by the values and norms of the actors, the other one by their conditions of action; in other words, by (an aspect of) cultural belonging and by structural location, respectively. In Robert Merton's work (1957), the second fundament was paid some important attention in mainstream sociology in the form of "opportunity structure" (cf. Sztompka 1986:162–163). It was later given full honors with the attainment of sociological citizenship by Marxist class analyses and of radical readings of Weberian foci on power.

The more full-blown neoclassicism that emerged out of adding a sociologized Marx and a de-idyllicized Weber to Parsons' first formulation has been further enriched by incorporating legacies of Mead, phenomenology and linguistic theories. This synthesis has yet to be been properly codified, and certainly has not attained the status of an explanatory theory. The single authors, who have contributed most to it, Jurgen Habermas (1982) and Anthony Giddens (1984), have not been primarily interested in explanation, and both have used their penetrating classical studies primarily as underpinnings to personal conceptual schemes. But it is this broad river, or perhaps better, delta, of main sociological streams which are carrying the prevailing sociological mode of explanation in terms of the cultural and/or structural variation of actors.

The two sets of actors' determinants, cultural or structural, may be regarded as primary or secondary to each other, as competing or as interacting with each other. Parsonsian sociology or cultural political science (Almond and Verba 1963; Verba et al. 1987; Wildavsky 1987) and Marxism represent the two variants of the primacy positions, the former attributing primacy to the culture, the latter to structural location. A vista of competing bases for creating actors' (in this case, voters') attachment may be found in Adam Przeworski's (1985) conception of political sociology, with different parties/political entrepreneurs in the competition. A neoclassical sociological example of cultural and structural interaction is Robert Merton's explanation of deviance: "It is, indeed, my central hypothesis, that aberrant behavior may be regarded sociologically as a symptom of dissociation between culturally prescribed aspirations and socially structured avenues for reaching these aspirations" (Merton 1968:188).

However, here we shall not go further into textual exegesis of contemporary sociology. It seems to be more in line with the constructive purposes of this article to use the space available for some notes on the power and the limitations of this kind of explanation.

To explain social action by the *location of actors in a structure* of resources/opportunities and of constraints/risks (or dangers) will mean, at least implicitly, to assume a causal mechanism virtually identical to that of rational choice explanations, i.e., actors' (implied) rational calculation and selection of alternatives under given resources and constraints. The main difference is rather the time span of the resources and constraints. Economic explanations tend to regard it as rather short, and therefore as part of the situation of the actors. The relative prices of alternative options is the paradigmatic case. Sociological-type explanations, on the other hand, tend to take the distribution of resources and constraints as stable over the normal time horizon of the investigation, and therefore as characteristic of the location of the actors. From this angle, "interest," such as class, group or gender interest, rather than "choice," comes into the center of the account.

Different empirical concerns as well as different assumptions about the social world may be major reasons for the different kinds of explanations. Where sociologists tend to see classes, strata, genders, communities, ethnicities and networks, economists are typically prone to see individuals. In any case, there appears to be no great obstacles in the way for researchers to use both types of structural explanations according to the concrete issue.

Explanations by the *cultural belonging of actors*, on the other hand, are more directly at odds with rational choice assumptions. But in the background there is also a very different set of intellectual interests. To learn, to understand and to interpret cultural variation are major concerns to many sociologists and social scientists of a sociological-anthropological bent, an interest professionally absent in the typical economist or political economist. An eloquent contrast to the characteristic sociological concern is provided by the militant Chicago economists George Stiger and Gary Becker (1977).

After having argued in an entire article "de gustibus non est disputandum" (here meaning roughly, "tastes need not be bothered with"), accounting for, for example, addiction and advertising effects by changes in (psychologically redefined) process and income, Stigler and Becker (1977:89) add as an aside at the end: "Needless to say, we would welcome explanations of why some people become addicted to alcohol and others to Mozart!" That is the kind of question sociologists begin with.

Cultural explanations correspond to what rationalist theories call "preferences" and "information." As we have pointed out above, the sociological counterpart to preferences is not simply norms or values. It also includes (a sense of) identity/difference. A recent high-flying cultural theory is based on an explicit (and very specific) combination of what we here call identity and norms, the elaboration of Mary Douglas' "group-grid" conceptualization (Thompson et al. 1990). Moreover, knowledge is not primarily treated as situational information, but rather as a cultural code through which the world is cognitively appropriated.

An inherent problem of cultural variation explanations is their tendency to ad hoc-ness and the risk of tautology. A brief, noncomplacent overview might do well looking at explanations by the cultural variability of actors from that angle.

Cultural *values* can have explanatory power to the extent that they mean something more than A acts in favor of x because he/she belongs to a culture that values x. Their elementary power derives from an aspect of culture inherent in all everyday definitions and connotations of the latter. A culture is, among other things, a bundle of learned preferences and norms. Therefore there are much fewer cultures than preferences or tastes. The likelihood of a North American middle-class Jew being an addict of Mozart is, for example, much higher, than that of a Javanese laborer; or the likelihood of a working-class Irishman or Finn to be addicted to distilled alcohol is much higher than that of an Islamic peasant. Sociologists assume these bundles of cultural standards to have a certain persistence. The typical American tourist, for example, is sociologically expected to behave similarly in vastly different situations and locations around the globe.

The *cognitive code* derives its explanatory clout from its amount of stability over time and situations, from the degree to which members of a certain culture perceive, talk about and thereby react to phenomena and events in ways specific to them. In contrast to economists, sociologists regard talk as a form of action, also worthy of explanation. And here, of course, the "choice" model of action is on the verge of breakdown. A speech community may define what may be talked about.

But that should apparently not be taken in the strong sense of early twentieth-century linguistic anthropology. The so-called Whorf hypothesis of linguistic structures constraining cognition has only in minor parts been sustained by the sociology of language (Fishman 1971:340 ff.). On the other hand, cultural codes do govern verbal interaction, attention, perception, capacities to learn and to remember. Put in other terms, the cultural belonging of actors affects the kind and the amount of information they acquire, store and make use of.

An attention to and an understanding of cultural codes will also be necessary to grasp the use of symbols in, say, politics or religion.

A third basic aspect of cultural belonging is having a shared *identity* with some people and a shared differentiation from some other people. As a variable explaining social action, this identity/differentiation is an important determinant of collective action. To identify with other people means in a certain sense not to make any difference between them and me, and therefore a preparedness to sacrifice for the sake of others who are identical with me.

Identity/difference further operate by entailing common, culture-specific stances of trust and mistrust in people. This aspect of cultural belonging has explanatory force to the extent that it is true, that humans in a predictable manner discriminate between people they identify with and others — when controlling for other information — and act towards the former differently than towards the latter.

To sum up, while researchers working at cultural explanations hardly regard as paramountly desirable the skeletal parsimony, bereft of almost all empirical flesh, sought after by rational choice theorists, the risk and the weaknesses of ad hoc-ery should not be left out of attention. On the other hand, cultural explanations are not correctly dismissable as necessarily ad hoc or trivial.

ACCOUNTING FOR SITUATIONAL VARIABILITY

The relative neglect of situation variation is an inborn weakness of, or limitation to, handed down sociological explanations. It has already been hinted at, however, that such a neglect is neither commendable nor necessary. There are indeed some ways at hand for turning sociological explanations in terms of actor variability into composite models of actor and situation variation.

One possibility is to go for cultural definitions of situations. Hereof, there are at least two theoretical variants, one coming from the corner of sociological organization theory and political science (March and Olsen 1989), the other from rational choice and economics-inspired sociology (Lindenberg 1990).

March and Olsen connect a rule-driven *homo sociologicus* with situational variability via a "logic of appropriateness": "Political actors associate specific actions with specific situations by rules of appropriateness ... defined by political and social institutions and transmitted through socialization" (1989:23) They continue pointing out three typical questions and one imperative of what they call "obligatory," as opposed to anticipatory action: (1) What kind of situation is this? (2) Who am I? (3) How appropriate are different actions for me in this situation? (4) Do what is most appropriate.

Lindenberg, for his part, arrives at a similar conclusion of social norms as "situationally prescribed goals of action" (1990:273) from a theory of rational choosers able to concentrate on maximizing only one thing at a time with culturally defined "production functions" for harvesting social approval, physical well-being and minimization of loss.

The power of either variant would seem to depend on the extent to which the life of a given population is organized into normatively defined situations, something which we may suspect to be variable across social systems and historical time.

Another approach would start from a recognition that social actors are both culturally anchored and structurally located, and then focus on the variable situations of the interaction of culture and structure. Any situational changes of the incentives of the structural position may then be assumed to affect, weakly or strongly, directly or laggedly, cultural norms, beliefs and identifications, and thereby actors' actions, either strengthening cultural orientations or eroding them and stimulating cultural evasion and innovation.

The final example to be mentioned here would involve no more than adding a shorter time to the structural analysis of actors. It would mean making room for significant variations in the situations of classes, genders or otherwise structurally located actors. More concretely, it might involve importing some standard economic concepts, like relative price and opportunity cost, into mainstream sociology. The importance of this kind of situational variation would depend on the permeability of culture.

OUTCOMES OF ACTION: TRACING THE CAUSAL LOOPS

The scattered tribe of sociologists is interested in all sorts of consequences of human action. However, as a systematic explanatory enterprise, sociology (anthropology, sociology-related political science and historiography) should be particularly concerned with two sets of action outcomes: with cultural belonging and with structural location. Only thereby could a causal loop accountable for both actions and action outcomes be established.

A major difficulty of sociological-type outcomes analysis is the nondiscovery of any kind of strong equilibrium mechanism (in spite of all concerns with social and cultural order) in cultural and in structural relations. Furthermore, there are few broadly recognized dynamics, either cultural or structural. True, there are sophisticated theories of cultural cycles (Hirschman 1982; Schlesinger 1986), now mainly outside of sociology proper but originally developed within it (Sorokin 1937–41). Marxism entails a set of predictions of structural dynamics, capital centralization, working-class concentration, increasingly social character of the forces of production, etc. (cf. Cohen 1978; Therborn 1989; Wright et al. 1992:pt. 1). From Spencer and Durkheim there developed another conception of structural dynamics, focusing on horizontal differentiation of structural locations (Luhmann 1985; Alexander and Colomy 1990). Justified or not, it remains true, I think, that there is little consensus of cultural and/or structural dynamics.

Why and when do people change identity, e.g., to or from an ethnic identity? Why and when do people become, or cease to be, religious? What makes norms change? Or, more abstractly, why do people adhere to a particular culture? Under what conditions do they leave? On the structural side, under what conditions do institutional patterns of distribution and noninstitutionalized positioning change? When and to what extent are state steering and/or collective action capable of altering the institutional structure, or the location of categories within it? When can institutionalized allocations of resources be subverted (cf. Sztompka 1991)?

Outcomes of action may be distinguished into two major subsets. They may pertain only to what happens to the culture and the structure to which the actor belongs, in which he/she is located. And they may also, or even primarily, affect the relationship to other cultures and structures. The former is often known as the problem of reproduction or as the systemic tendencies of the social system. The latter leads to historical encounters, or *rendezvous manques*, which constitute a particularly important category of situations of action, culturally and structurally defined situations.

Culturally determined actions have a strong inherent tendency to reproduce the culture they have sprung from, its sense of identity, its worldview, its values and norms. True, at least two intrinsic problems of cultural reproduction can be easily singled out, which may be taken as providing the elementary stuff of cultural dynamics. One is the socialization of new members, which is never easy and which may become problematic to the extent that the structural circumstances have changed since the forming moments of the parent generation. The other is the difficulty for any intense cultural commitment to be maintained for very long, even well within the lifespan of one generation.

Insofar as actors act the way they do, because of their location in a structure of resources and constraints, the structural outcome is the result of a game of strategic interaction which may or may not have one or many equilibria. The original distribution may become more equal, more polarized or it may stay put, in spite of all attempts at changing it. The analysis of strategic interaction has been developed in very stylized forms in the study of markets and simple games, but it has been foreshadowed also in historical materialism and in organization theory (in the latter case since Robert Michels' "iron law of oligarchy"). It needs to be taken into the center of the analysis of the rather entangled structures which sociologists are mostly interested in. Consequences of action upon the relationship between cultures or structures may well be analyzed with a view to actual or potential *competition* between cultures and structures. Competition, so far rather little systematically considered by sociologists (but see Runciman 1989), is an approach to cultural-structural analysis with great promise: a change of culture or cultural belonging, or of a distributive structure, means a change to another culture or structure; the persistence of a given culture or structure means the failure of another to get established (cf. Therborn 1980:77 ff.). It should not be put into a necessarily evolutionist straitjacket, leaving room for the possibility of contingent encounters with reversible effects.

Four illustrative types of examples of such variations of cultural and structural interrelations may convey a few ideas of how outcomes of actions feed back upon the cultural/structural variability of actors.

(a) *Isolation*. Other things being equal, it seems that a crucial determinant of the persistence or change of a given culture or structure is its amount of isolation. The more isolated a culture or structure is, the more stable, the more resistant to efforts at change. From the point of view of explaining action, the more isolated a culture or structure is the more likely it is to determine the actions of its members. Actions which have the effect of altering the degree of isolation of a given culture or structure can be expected to affect their impact on social activity by exposing it to the competitive influence of other cultures and structures.

The isolation of a structure should be understood as the degree to which actors within a given setup of resources do not have access to other sets of resources. For instance, the extent to which people without property or organizational command lack resources of collective power, through autonomous mobilization, or access to a dissenting part of the ruling elite.

(b) Nonisolated cultures relate importantly in terms of the relative structural location of their members, extra-culturally defined, most directly in terms of coercive capacity, but also in terms of relative prosperity. Vice versa, nonisolated structures relate to each other also with reference to the relative cultural standing and self-confidence of their privileged and nonprivileged members. The general situational variable here may be termed the *relative cultural-structural coupling*.

Under given conditions of alien cultural exposure, the more relatively powerful/prosperous the members of a given culture, the more stable it should be and the more attractive to members of other cultures. Isolation and relative power should be seen as multiplicative variables. Decreasing isolation and a turn to an increasing prosperity gap made the East European socialist cultures increasingly vulnerable or unattractive in the course of the 1980s, for instance.

The mechanism of cultural-structural coupling can also be seen from the structural side. In Eastern Europe, as in West Germany for that matter, immediately after World War II, a capitalist structure of the economy was widely discredited by its association with underdevelopment, the Depression and the fallen Nazi regime. Extensive socializations had wide support. Later, however (in West Germany sooner), exclusive property rights and wide income differentials came to be viewed as (part of) the necessary underpinnings of freedom and democracy, since the former are now closely associated with the democratic postwar boom of the West.

(c) The degree of *affinity* of two or more cultures and structures that come into contact with each other should also be expected to affect the chances of a given one to be influenced by another. In our Eastern European example, this seems to be illustrated by the fact that the earliest and the strongest penetration of Western liberalism and liberal conservatism coincides with the areas of Western religions, of Catholicism and Protestantism. In the contact between a given culture or structure and others, the elements of the latter most akin with the former are most likely to be accepted by the members of the former culture or structural location.

(d) Where very different cultures come into contact with each other and are kept in contact by strong forces of structuration, we should expect processes of *creolization*, the emergence of new cultural syntheses, through selective combinations and mutations of the constituent cultures. The concept has developed with regard to the colonial and post-colonial worlds (cf. Hannerz 1987), but it might also be used in other contexts, including Eastern Europe and Central

Asia. Along similar lines one might also think of the possibility of the rise of creole structures.

In all of the above types of varying cultural and structural situations, predictions of outcomes may very well be approached in terms of actors' situated choice. Decreasing isolation means a wider range of choice, and, other things being equal, that at least some actors should be expected to choose options which they were previously cut off from. We should expect more people to choose a culture represented by people of power and prosperity than one by incapacity and poverty, or a culture providing more prospects of power and prosperity rather than one coupled with less (cf. Rogowski (1985) on reasons for choosing nationalism). From the structural side, we should have no reasons for surprise if more people came to support a distributional pattern associated with high rather than with low cultural prestige. People should be more ready to choose to embrace or support a culture or structure having an affinity with something positive they are familiar with; or, if belonging to two coexisting ones, they should be expected to adapt them so as to make them more affinitive. Creolization may be seen as a refusal to choose one or the other of two strongly linked but very different cultures or structures and as opting for some creative combination. That option should be attractive to people who are already entrepreneurs in some cultural or structural sense.

In the context above, rational choice appears one fruitful approach to understanding how cultural belonging and structural location are changed or maintained as outcomes of actors' choices and actions. Freed from the assumption of stable universal preferences, the interpretation of human action as a manifestation of rational choice in situations of constraint is a central part of what Max Weber called a *verstehende* sociology. Rational instrumental behavior (*zweckrationales Sichverhalten*) or "rationally interpretable behavior" (*das rational deutbare Sichverhalten*) was according to Weber ([1922] 1988:429) "very often the most appropriate 'ideal type.'"

However, it should not be forgotten, that belonging to a culture is constitutive of human actors, not something actors choose. Although deliberate choice may well be involved in processes of adhering to or abandoning a culture, the most important (because most influential) parts of the latter are hardly possible to choose in a situation of opportunities only, regardless of the actor's prior cultural stamp. Rational choice has a legitimate place within sociology, and confrontation with the developed models of the former could advance the latter. But the recent interdisciplinary debate has also reaffirmed the old sociological conviction that norms, beliefs and identities are irreducible to instrumental rationality. Coping with the tension between those two conclusions is, in my view, the best way ahead.

TO CONCLUDE

The sprawling activities, theoretical as well as empirical, of sociologists need some ecumenical codification as a basis for highlighting achievements and lacunae, and thereby as a foundation to build higher. Such an endeavor should not try to cover up the persistent disagreements which are characteristic of the discipline, nor should it ignore contributions and challenges of adjacent academic departments.

The present effort has ventured to hold up a picture of what sociologists study, as cultural and structured/ing actors and their actions and as cultural and structured/ing systems and their processes. Culture, it has been argued, has at least three principal components: identity/differentiation, a cognitive code, and values and norms. Structures refer to the patterning of resources and constraints, and are of two fundamental sorts: institutional endowments and contingent distributions.

Sociology has further a specific mode of explanation, in terms of the cultural and/or structural variability of actors, a kind of explaining which is used with regard to systems and systemic processes, as well as to actors and their actions. A good part of basic intrasociological disagreements concern the relative importance of this or that actor variable. This typical sociological mode of explanation is the opposite of the economic one, which tends to take actors as given or random, while focusing on the variability of situations. In spite of the archetypical opposition between the two explanatory frameworks, possibilities of linking together and of using both rational choice and situational variability in sociology have been suggested.

Bibliography

Alexander, J. (1990). "On the 'Autonomy' of Culture." In: *Culture and Society: Contemporary Debates*. eds. J. Alexander and S. Seidman. Cambridge: Cambridge University Press.

Alexander, J., and P. Colomy (Eds.) (1990) *Differentiation Theory and Social Change*. New York: Columbia University Press.

Almond, G., and S. Verba (1963). *The Civic Culture: Political Attitudes and Democracy in Five Nations*. Princeton: Princeton University Press.

Archer, M. (1988). *Culture and Agency*. Cambridge: Cambridge University Press.

Axelrod, R. (1984). *The Evolution of Cooperation*. New York: Basic Books.

Becker, G. (1976). *The Economic Approach to Human Behavior*. Chicago: Chicago University Press.

Blau, P. (1977). *Inequality and Heterogeneity*. New York: The Free Press.

Cohen, G. A. (1978). *Karl Marx's Theory of History: A Defence*. Oxford: Oxford University Press.

Coleman, J. (1990). *Foundations of Social Theory*. Cambridge, MA: The Belknap Press.

Collins, R. (1988). *Weberian Sociology*. Cambridge: Cambridge University Press.

Elster, J. (Ed.) (1986). *Rational Choice*. Oxford: Blackwell.

_____ (1969). *The Cement of Society*. Cambridge: Cambridge University Press.

Etzioni, A. (1986). *The Moral Dimension*. New York: The Free Press.

Fishman, J. (1971). "The Sociology of Language: An Interdisciplinary Social Science Approach to Language in Society." In: *Contributions to the Sociology of Language*, ed. J. Fishman. The Hague/Paris: Mouton.

Frey, B., and W. Pommerehne (1990). "A Comparative Institutional Analysis in the Arts: The Theater." In: *Social Institutions*. eds. M. Hechter et al. New York: Aldine de Gruyter.

Giddens, A. (1984). *The Constitution of Society*. Cambridge: Polity Press.

Habermas, J. (1982). *Theorie des kommunikativen Handelns*, 2 vols. Frankfurt: Suhrkamp.

Haferkamp, H. (Ed.) (1990). *Sozialstruktur und Kultur*. Frankfurt: Suhrkamp.

Hannerz, U. (1987). "The World in Creolization." *Africa* 57(4):546–559.

Harsanyi, J. (1982). *Papers in Game Theory*. Dordrecht: D. Reidel.

Hechter, M., K.-D. Opp, and R. Wippler (Eds.) (1990). *Social Institutions*. New York: Aldine and de Gruyter.

Hirschman, A. (1982). *Shifting Involvements*. Oxford: Basil Blackwell.

Lindenberg, S. (1990). "Rationalitat und Kultur. Die verhaltenstheoretische Basis des Einflusses von Kultur auf Transaktionen." In: *Sozialstruktur und Kultur*, ed. H. Haferkamp. Frankfurt: Suhrkamp.

Lockwood, D. (1992). *Solidarity and Schism*. Oxford: Clarendon Press.

Luce, R. D., and H. Raiffa (1957). *Games and Decisions*. New York: Wiley.

Luhmann, N. (1984). *Soziale Systeme*. Frankfurt: Suhrkamp.

─────────── (Ed.) (1985). *Soziale Differenzierung*. Opladen: Westdeutscher Verlag.

March, J., and J. Olsen (1989). *Rediscovering Institutions*. New York: Free Press.

Merton, R. (1957). *Social Theory and Social Structure*. Glencoe: The Free Press.

Parsons, T. [1937] (1968). *The Structure of Social Action*. New York: The Free Press.

Przeworski, A. (1985). *Capitalism and Social Democracy*. Cambridge: Cambridge University Press.

─────────── 1986. "Le defi de la methodologie individualiste a l'analuse marxiste." In: *Sur l'individualisme*, eds. P. Birnbaum and J. Leca, pp. 77–106. Paris: Presses de la Foundation Nationale des Sciences Politiques.

Rogowski, R. (1985). "Cause and Varieties of Nationalism." In: *New Nationalisms of the Developed West*, eds. E. Tiriyakian and R. Rogowski, pp. 87–108. Boston: Allen & Unwin.

Runciman, W. G. (1989). *A Treatise on Social Theory*, Vol. 2. Cambridge: Cambridge University Press.

Schlesinger Jr., A. (1986). *The Cycles of American History*. Boston: Houghton Mifflin.

Simmel, G. [1908] (1964). "Quantitative Aspects of the Group." In: *The Sociology of Georg Simmel*, ed. K. Wolff, pp. 87–177. New York: The Free Press. (Originally in G. Simmel, *Soziologie*, 1908).

Sorokin, P. (1937–41). *Social and Cultural Dynamics*, 4 vols. New York: American Book Company.

Stigler, G., and G. Becker (1977). "De Gustibus Non Est Disputandum." *American Economic Review* 67:76–90.

Stinchcombe, A. (1975). "Merton's Theory of Social Structure." In: *Idea of Social Structure. Papers in Honor of Robert K. Merton*, ed. L. Coser, pp. 11–33. New York: Harcourt Brace Jovanovich.

Sztompka, P. (1986). *Robert K. Merton. An Intellectual Profile*. Houndmills Basingstoke: Macmillan.

―――――― (1991). *Society in Action: The Theory of Social Becoming*. Cambridge, Polity Press.

Therborn, G. (1980). *The Ideology of Power and the Power of Ideology*. London: Verso.

―――――― (1989). "States, Populations, and Productivity." In: *Politics and Social Theory*, ed. P. Lassman, pp. 62–84. London: Routledge.

Thompson, M., R. Ellis, and A. Wildavsky (1990). *Cultural Theory*. Boulder: Westview Press.

Tsebelis, G. (1990). *Nested Games*. Berkeley: University of California Press.

Verba, S. et al. (1987). *Elites and the Idea of Equality*. Cambridge: Harvard University Press.

Weber, M. (1988). *Gesammelte Aufsazte zur Wissenschaftslehre*. Tübingen: Mohr/UTB. (1st ed. 1922)

Wellman, B., and S. D. Berkowitz (Eds.) (1988). *Social Structures: A Network Approach*. Cambridge: Cambridge University Press.

White, H. (1988). "Varieties of Markets." In: *Social Structures: A Network Approach*, eds. B. Wellman and S. D. Berkowitz, pp. 221–260. Cambridge: Cambridge University Press.

Wildavsky, A. (1987). "Choosing Preferences by Constructing Institutions: A Cultural Theory of Preference Formation." *American Political Science Review* 81:3–21.

Williamson, O. (1985). *The Economic Institutions of Capitalism*. New York, The Free Press.

Wright, E. O., A. Levine, and E. Sober (1992). *Reconstructing Marxism*. London: Verso.

Index

A

Abrams, P., 29, 49
action, 11, 125–127, 129, 151
   and language, 129–132
   collective, 37, 51
   in new Marxist theory, 85–87
   in pragmatic theory, 136–139
   nonreductive theory of, 134
   organized vs. aggregate, 238n
active society, theory of, 36
actor
   actor vs. subject, 151
   in Marxist theory, 83–84
   return of, 143, 145–146, 150
agency, 202–204, 216, 270, 276
   agency-structure linkage, 8–10
   history of the idea, 25–28
   main theories of, 35–43
   moral agency, 225
agent, 9, 10, 104, 111
   collective, 27, 185, 241n
   corporate vs. primary, 42
   "Great Mean" as agents, 26
agential coefficient, 43
   see also historical coefficient
ahistorism, 44, 46, 47

Alexander, J., xii, xiii, xiv, 8, 34, 76n, 77n
alienation, historiosophical vs. sociological concepts, 278n
Althusser, L., 145
anti-positivist revolution, x
Archer, M., 29, 41, 42
Aron, R., 78n

B

Baudrillard, J., 157, 174, 176
Bauman, Z., 31, 32, 55
Bhaskar, R., 97, 112, 118n, 252
biography vs. history, 255
Blau, P., 264, 269–270
boomerang effect, 269
   see also unintended consequences
Boudon, R., 146, 146, 148, 149, 150, 159
Bourdieu, P., xiii, 4, 9, 152, 153, 154, 155, 156, 173
Bourricaud, F., 146
Buckley, W., 35
Burns, T., 40

C

Coleman, J., 292
Collins, R., xi, 8
conflict theory, 31
    conflict vs. consensus, 54n, 55n
Cooley, C., 271, 272, 273
creolization, 301
    Crozier, M., 38
culture, 287–288
    cultural frame, 240
    globalization vs. diversity, 238n

D

Dahrendorf, R., 28, 29, 31, 32, 33, 54n
Derrida, J., 128, 177, 178, 179
developmentalism, 259–260
deviance, 54n
dialectics, 269
Dilthey, W., 127
disorganized capitalism, 86
distanciation, 132
Dobry, M., 155
domination, 242n
duality of structure, 39, 122
see also structuration
Dubet, F., 151

Durkheim, E., 64, 64, 66, 67, 68, 70
    "Durkheim Problem," 30
    Durkheim's vision of action and actors, 65–68

E

economicism, 100
educational capital, 153
Eisenstadt, S., xii
Elias, N., 48
Elster, J., 107–109, 118n, 156
emergence, 262
epiphenomenalism, 273
    collectivistic, 273
    individualistic, 273
epistemic fallacy, xi
epistemological bias in theorizing, x–xi
    see also ontological turn in theorizing
equilibrium, 212, 220, 236n
    in various social relationships, 22–24
    social equilibrium, 224
Etzioni, A., 36, 292
event, 50, 134, 275
    great event, 50
    social vs. natural, 278n
    see also socio-individual field
eventuation, 50
experience, 90–91, 132

INDEX

explanation, 288
  multilevel explanation, 15
  sociological explanation, 288–233
  unicausal explanation, 71

F

facticity of society, 28, 38
field of possibilities, 53
figurational sociology, 56n
figurations, 48–49
Foucault, M., 145, 168, 176, 168, 179
free-riding, 241n

G

Gadamer, H, 131, 140
game, 233n
  collaborative, 243n
  game rules, 234n
  game theory, 205
  of conflict, 243n
  of strategy, 206, 233n
Giddens, A., xi, xiii, 30–31, 33–34, 38–39, 40, 54n, 55, 117n, 286
grand theory, ix
"Great Men" doctrine, 26

H

Habermas, J., 18n 131, 172, 185, 190n, 192n
habitus, xiii, 9, 10, 152, 270

Heidegger, M., 128, 130
hermeneutics, 125, 127, 132, 133, 136
historical coefficient, 52–53
  see also agential coefficient
historical sociology, 35
  ascendance of, 48
  main representatives, 48–52
  the origins of, 43–48
historicism, 99, 259
  radical historicism, 99
historicity, 33–34
holism, 259
Homans, G., 26, 31, 264, 272
homo oeconomicus, 64, 75, 69, 70, 71, 72, 74
  see also rationality
homo psychologicus, 63
homo sociologicus, 65, 69, 70, 74, 258
humanistic sociology, x

I

imperialism of the object, 30
indeterminism, 147
individualism vs. holism, 5, 11–13
  see also holism, methodological individualism
innovativeness, 229
institutional individualism, 263
  see also transindividualism

J

Jarvie, I., 263

L

Laclau, E., 92–95
life-chances, 33
Lloyd, C., 51–52
Lyotard, J.-F., 175, 176, 177, 179

M

Marxism, 144
   analytical Marxism, 114n, 116n
   humanist Marxism, 87–92
   neglect of social action, 84
   see also post-Marxism
   structuralist Marxism, 144
Mead, G. H., 136–137
Merton, R., xiv, 27, 269, 293–294
metaphor of growth, 47
meta-power, 26–27
metatheorizing, 6, 16–17
methodological holism, 12–13
methodological individualism, 11, 12, 146, 147, 156
   in recent French sociology, 146–147
   see also situational individualism, transindividualism
methodological relationism, xvi, 5, 13, 14, 16
   forerunners of, 15–17

micro-macro linkage, 6–8
   see also agency-structure linkage
middle-range theory, xiv
Mill, J. S., 257
Mills, C. W., 47
mobilization, 36
modern condition, 55n
   see also post-modern condition
Mongardini, C., 32
morphogenesis, 35–36, 41–42, 55n
   double morphogenesis, 42
   of agency, 42
   see also social becoming, structuration
Mouffe, C., 92–96
multidimensional theory, xiii, 30, 110, 111, 127

N

neofunctionalism, 266
   see also structural-functionalism, dynamic functionalism
Nisbet, R., 34, 47, 77n

O

ontological turn in theorizing, xi–xii
   see also epistemological bias in theorizing
overdetermination, 93, 97

oversocialized image of man, 30, 266

P

paradigm, 289
paradoxes in social life, 28–30, 269
Parsons, T., 266, 285, 293
personalism, emergent, 267
philosophical sociology, 17
Polanyi, K., 72
populist history vs. elitist history, 51
positivism, x
post-industrial society, 37, 171
post-Marxism, xv, 87, 92, 93, 95, 100, 101, 107, 109, 110
   analytical post-Marxism, 100–109
   see also Marxism
   textualist post-Marxism, 92–94
postmodern age, 169, 179–173
postmodern condition, 168–169, 184
postmodernism, 167–168
post-structuralism, 145, 170, 173
   see also structuralism
pragmatism, 136, 137
   its theory of action, 136–139
praxis, 276
prisoners' dilemma, 218–219

processual approach, 50, 52, 274
Przeworski, A., 101–107, 291

R

rational choice, 87, 107, 197, 198, 199, 202, 289, 290, 294, 295
   rational choice theory, 205; critique of, 207–229
rational choice theory vs. social theory of games, 202–204
rationality, 149–150, 229, 230, 231
   context-dependent rationality, 200
   institutionally specific rationality, 200
reductionism, 97
   actionalist, 88, 92, 97, 99, 101, 104, 109
   class, 106
   structuralist, 84, 85, 100, 101, 109, 110, 111
reification, 272
representative activities, 26
reproduction, 152
   see also habitus
Ricoeur, P., 127, 132–133, 134–135, 136, 138
Rorty, R., 136, 170, 189n
rule regimes, 40
rule systems, 40, 211, 213, 235n, 237n

S

scientific realism, 252
Segerstedt, T., 55n
self-guidance
 theory of, 36
 see also active society
self-producing society, 37
Simmel, G., 148, 150, 265, 287
situational individualism, 263
 see also methodological individualism, transindividualism
situational variability, 297
Skockpol, T., 54
sociability, 73
social action, 69, 125, 126, 127
 in Marx's theory, 84–87
social becoming, XIII, XV, 113, 251, 274, 275–277
 see also socio-individual field
social class, 102–103
 as historical agent, 104–105
 class-for-itself vs. class-in-itself, 102, 103, 104
social embeddedness, 227
 generating uncertainty, 236n
 reducing uncertainty, 235n
social movements, 37, 181, 182, 183
 new social movements, 180, 181, 182, 183
 working class movement, 181

social rule, 211, 214
 see also rule regimes, rule systems
social system, 284
socio-individual field, xv, 113, 273, 274, 277
 see also events, social becoming
sociological imagination, 47
sociological philosophy, xi
sociologism, 258
sociologist as historian, 56n
solipsism, 252
Spencer, H., 257, 260
strategic interaction, 300
structural differentiation, 47
structural-functionalism, 31, 46, 54, 266
 dynamic functionalism, 55n
structuralism, 36, 144–145
 constructivist structuralism, 4
 emergent structuralism, 2677
 see also post-structuralism
 structuralist reductionism, 84
structuration, xiii, 39, 286
 see also duality of structure
 structuration theory, 38–39, 55n
structurism, 51–52
synthetic trend in theorizing, xii–xiii, 4–5
systems theory, 10

T

"Third Sociology," 271–275
  see also "Two Sociologies"
Thompson, E. P., 88–92
Tilly, C., 47–48, 50
Tönnies, F., 261
Touraine, A., 37, 150–151
transindividualism, 264
  see also methodological individualism, situational individualism
"Two Sociologies," 260
  see also "Third Sociology"

U

unintended consequences, 27, 52, 100, 215, 239n, 263, 264, 269, 276
  see also boomerang effect

W

Weber, M., 11, 27, 45, 69, 70, 71, 146, 302
  "Weber Problem," 30
  Weber's individualistic approach, 70
  Weber's vision of action and actors, 69–72
Wrong, D., 30